Theories of Choice

Theories of Choice

The Social Science and the Law of Decision Making

Edited by

STEFAN GRUNDMANN

AND

PHILIPP HACKER

OXFORD
UNIVERSITY PRESS

OXFORD
UNIVERSITY PRESS

Great Clarendon Street, Oxford, OX2 6DP,
United Kingdom

Oxford University Press is a department of the University of Oxford. It furthers the University's objective of excellence in research, scholarship, and education by publishing worldwide. Oxford is a registered trade mark of Oxford University Press in the UK and in certain other countries

First Edition published in 2021

Published in the United States of America by Oxford University Press
198 Madison Avenue, New York, NY 10016, United States of America

British Library Cataloguing in Publication Data

Data available

Library of Congress Control Number: 2020942401

ISBN 978–0–19–886317–5

DOI: 10.1093/oso/9780198863175.001.0001

Foreword

Guido Calabresi[*]

What is one to say about this remarkable collection of essays? First and foremost, that each essay is extraordinarily interesting and useful in itself, and that the collection is even better. The contrast of approaches, styles, and—to some extent—disciplines employed, helps the reader to see the strength of each approach, the problems each has, and the possibilities and advantages of using more than one.

But beyond these words of praise, I would like to add a few words about a way in which I have read these essays that I hope the reader will also employ. It reflects two questions that have obsessed me recently and that I discuss in part in my own recent book, *The Future of Law and Economics*.[1] The first is: to what extent do the expounders/proponents of each approach to social choice propose their approaches because they deem them best at getting to the results—the goals—they wish to achieve? And to what extent, instead, do they propose the approach because they like it, because they view the approach as a good in itself, even if it might be a less efficient, more costly, or less effective way of achieving the goals sought? The second question is very similar to the first. To what extent will an approach be accepted by a polity because of its effectiveness in reaching the polity's desired goals, and to what extent, instead, will it be preferred because the members of the polity like it, take pleasure in using, and being a part of that approach?

These questions bear asking with respect to each of the approaches to social choice collected here. In a way there is nothing new about the questions. Ronald Coase in his celebrated article on *The Nature of the Firm*,[2] after positing that firms existed because sometimes command is less costly (more efficient) than markets, added in passing that firms might exist also because some people *like* that form of command. I have noted that one cannot understand Hayek's wholehearted embracing of markets simply on the basis of a belief that markets reach desirable results.[3] One must also realise that he loves free markets *in themselves*. A market-based society brings him joy! And similarly, Trotsky advocates centralised command not only because he believes it to be efficient—which he does—but also because he loves it!

* Sterling Professor Emeritus and Professorial Lecturer, Yale Law School; Senior Judge, U.S. Court of Appeals for the Second Circuit.

1 Guido Calabresi, *The Future of Law and Economics* (Yale University Press 2016).

2 Ronald H. Coase, 'The Nature of the Firm' (1937) 4 Economica 386.

3 Calabresi (n 1) 209 n 38.

Systems, and approaches to social choice, like goods, must be judged both as means of reaching results and as ends in themselves; as ways of getting from here to there, and as things that have their own inherent value, items that are in our utility functions. There is nothing odd, or wrong, with that. It is no more peculiar than the fact that people eat caviar because they like it, even though as a way of feeding oneself it is not very efficient. And since systems—jointly and severally—are also up for adoption by polities, the question also must be asked: how much do members of the relevant polity like the approach, enjoy being guided by it, despite its costs and failures? That is, we must ask not only how much the proponent likes caviar as against codfish but how much people in the relevant society do.

One of the chapters (Reisch, Sunstein, and Kaiser), interestingly, suggests that the relevant approach proposed—nudging—is liked. It is not clear to me, though, whether people like it because they believe it to be efficient, to be an effective way of reaching results, or because they *enjoy* being nudged, or at least enjoy it more than possible alternatives.

Towards the end of *The Future of Law and Economics*, I propose a way of making value choices, of determining what subsidiary values should be furthered because they bring about the highest joint maximisations of certain agreed-upon basic values. I urge this as an effective and useful way to affect legal choices. And I believe that it is. But I must confess that I also like doing things that way, thinking about things that way.

Does that take away from the approach's desirability? Not at all, but it is well to be aware of the extent to which each of us proposes, and a polity accepts, an approach to social choice, because of its inherent qualities—because we or the relevant polity like it—and the extent it is favoured because it is effective at getting to the results we or the polity seeks.

I hope you will read these wonderful essay with these questions in mind and I believe that if you do you will find them—if that is possible—to be both more useful and more enjoyable.

Contents

B. Institutions, Networks, and Courts

List of Contributors

Matthew D. Adler, Richard A. Horvitz Professor of Law and Professor of Economics, Philosophy and Public Policy, Duke University; Founding Director, Duke Center for Law, Economics and Public Policy

Marlies Ahlert, Professor of Microeconomics and Public Economics, Department of Law and Economics, Martin Luther University Halle-Wittenberg

Simon Deakin, Professor of Law, University of Cambridge

Christoph Engel, Director, Max Planck Institute for Research on Collective Goods

Andreas Engert, Professor of Law, Free University of Berlin

Luca Enriques, Professor of Corporate Law, University of Oxford

Stefan Grundmann, Professor of Transnational Private Law, European University Institute, Florence; Professor of German, European and International Private and Business Law, Humboldt University of Berlin

Philipp Hacker, Professor for Law and Ethics of the Digital Society, European New School of Digital Studies, European University Viadrina, Frankfurt (Oder)

Geneviève Helleringer, Professor of Law, ESSEC Business School; Lecturer, Law Faculty, University of Oxford

Adrienne Héritier, Emeritus Professor, European University Institute, Florence

Christopher Brett Jaeger, Acting Assistant Professor of Lawyering, NYU

Micha Kaiser, Assistant Professor, Copenhagen Business School

Lucia A. Reisch, Professor, Copenhagen Business School

Alessandro Romano, Assistant Professor, Bocconi Law School

Anne-Lise Sibony, Professor of Law, UC Louvain

Cass R. Sunstein, Robert Walmsley University Professor, Harvard Law School

Jennifer S. Trueblood, Associate Professor of Psychology, Vanderbilt University

Julian Velasco, Associate Professor of Law, Notre Dame Law School

Theories of Choice and the Law—An Introduction

Stefan Grundmann and Philipp Hacker

Abstract: This introduction highlights the importance of theories of choice for the law, but it also stresses the need to distinguish and decide between different types of choice theories for concrete legal applications. It first discusses the problem of selecting an appropriate theory of choice, from the many varieties that have developed in the past decades, for a specific regulatory problem. Second, it advocates making explicit the sometimes hidden epistemic and normative assumptions behind choice-theoretic models. Third, it argues for a genuinely normative assessment, and a conceptual reconstruction, of theories of choice before their application to specific legal problems. The chapter concludes with an overview of the four Parts of this volume.

Choice is a key concept of our time. It is a foundational mechanism for every legal order in societies that are, politically, constituted as democracies and, economically, built on the market mechanism. In these contexts, choice is, on the one hand, the essence of democratic decision making; this is why political participation and expression are the subject of manifold constitutional protections. On the other hand, decentralised coordination through choice is a key criterion for the success of market economies, as von Hayek forcefully demonstrated already in 1945 in his comparison of market-based and planning-based economic models.[1] Thus, choice can be understood as an atomic structure that grounds both political and economic processes. Simultaneously, however, instances and interpretations of choice, and the questions flowing from its detailed and increasingly contested understanding, are concrete enough to inform and guide

[1] Friedrich von Hayek, 'The Use of Knowledge in Society' (1945) 35 American Economic Review 519; and for the choice between the two main models of and choices between business organisation, firm, and market, Ronald A. Coase, 'The Nature of the Firm' (1937) 4 Economica 386.

Stefan Grundmann and Philipp Hacker, *Theories of Choice and the Law—An Introduction* In: *Theories of Choice.*
Edited by: Stefan Grundmann and Philipp Hacker, Oxford University Press (2021).
DOI: 10.1093/oso/9780198863175.003.0001

discussions that relate to concrete social and legal problems. This is precisely the subject of this book.

I. The Problem of Selecting Appropriate Theories of Choice

Given the importance of choice for liberal societies, it is no surprise that theories of choice abound. While they proliferate in the social sciences, they explicitly and implicitly inform legal arrangements and legal norms in manifold ways, too. Regulators and scholars draw on a wide range of theories—from rational choice theory[2] to behavioural economics,[3] from public choice[4] to deliberative democracy[5]—to explain how individuals, institutions, and societies make legally relevant decisions, enact laws, or adapt to them. The chapters in this volume testify to the growing toolbox interdisciplinary legal and social science scholars have at their disposal when dealing with regulatory problems. Our contributors not only discuss the promises and limitations of more rational or more behavioural approaches to decision making[6] and game theory,[7] but also draw on a range of theories less prominent in the (legal) literature so far to show how they can be operationalized and applied to concrete social problems. These more heterodox

[2] See, e.g., from the extensive literature, Richard A. Posner, *Economic Analysis of Law* (9th edn, Wolters Kluwer 2014) 3–26; Thomas S. Ulen, 'Rational Choice Theory in Law and Economics' in Baudewijn Bouckaert and Gerrit De Geest (eds), *Encyclopedia of Law and Economics* (Edward Elgar 1999) vol 1, 790; Steven Shavell, *Foundations of Economic Analysis of Law* (Harvard University Press 2004) 1–2; Louis Kaplow and Steven Shavell, *Fairness versus Welfare* (Harvard University Press 2006) 7 n. 12; Andrew T. Guzman, *How International Law Works. A Rational Choice Theory* (Oxford University Press 2008).

[3] See, e.g., from the extensive literature, Christine Jolls, Cass R. Sunstein, and Richard Thaler, 'A Behavioral Approach to Law and Economics' (1998) 50 Stanford Law Review 1471; Russell B. Korobkin and Thomas S. Ulen, 'Law and Behavioral Science: Removing the Rationality Assumption from Law and Economics' (2000) 88 California Law Review 1051; Eyal Zamir and Doron Teichman (eds), *The Oxford Handbook of Behavioral Economics and the Law* (Oxford University Press 2014); Eyal Zamir and Doron Teichman (eds), *Behavioral Law and Economics* (Oxford University Press 2018); Cass R. Sunstein and Lucia A. Reisch, *Trusting Nudges: Toward a Bill of Rights for Nudging* (Routledge 2019); Christopher Brett Jaeger and Jennifer S. Trueblood, 'Thinking Quantum: A New Perspective on Decisionmaking in Law' (2019) 46 Florida State University Law Review 733.

[4] See, e.g., from the extensive literature, James Buchanan and Gordon Tullock, *The Calculus of Consent* (University of Michigan Press 1962); Geoffrey Brennan and James Buchanan, *The Reason of Rules: Constitutional Political Economy* (Cambridge University Press 1985); Daniel A. Farber and Philip P. Frickey, *Law and Public Choice: A Critical Introduction* (University of Chicago Press 1991); Dennis C. Mueller, *Public Choice III* (Cambridge University Press 2003); Daniel A. Farber and Anne Joseph O'Connell (eds), *Research Handbook on Public Choice and Public Law* (Edward Elgar 2010).

[5] See, e.g., from the extensive literature, Jürgen Habermas, *Between Facts and Norms. Contributions to a Discourse Theory of Law and Democracy* (William Rehg tr, MIT Press 1996); Christopher F. Zurn, *Deliberative Democracy and the Institutions of Judicial Review* (Cambridge University Press 2007); Richard J. Lazarus, 'Congressional Descent: The Demise of Deliberative Democracy in Environmental Law' (2005) 94 Georgetown Law Journal 619.

[6] See particularly the contributions by Engel, Deakin, and Reisch, Sunstein, and Kaiser in this volume.

[7] See the contribution by Ahlert in this volume.

theories include complexity theory,[8] strategic interaction analysis,[9] social welfare functions,[10] information cascades and herding,[11] network theory,[12] quantum decision-making theory,[13] and analytic philosophy combined with (social) psychology.[14]

These contributions mirror a trend which has significantly grown in recent years. It changes the ways in which interdisciplinary research impacts on the law and guides the framing of concrete legal problems and the quest for legal solutions: while much of the twentieth century was marked by interdisciplinary legal analysis being predominantly informed by *one* neighbouring discipline (often economics, with the predominance of the economic analysis of law),[15] recent years have shown that a *multi-dimensional* interdisciplinarity, drawing simultaneously on several disciplines, can also inform law making and legal analysis in a precise and, at least potentially, more nuanced way. An increasing number of scholars,[16] including ourselves,[17] contributes to this endeavour in the hope that the blind spots and limitations of one specific neighbouring discipline (e.g., the fixation of

[8] See the contribution by Hacker in this volume.
[9] See the contribution by Héritier in this volume.
[10] See the contribution by Adler in this volume.
[11] See the contributions by Engert and Grundmann in this volume.
[12] See the contributions by Enriques/Romano and Grundmann in this volume.
[13] See the contribution by Jaeger and Trueblood in this volume.
[14] See the contribution by Helleringer in this volume.
[15] Guido Calabresi, *The Future of Law and Economics* (Yale University Press 2016) 235–54.
[16] See, e.g., Yuval Feldman and Orly Lobel, 'Behavioural Trade-offs: Beyond the Land of Nudges Spans the World of Law and Psychology' in Alberto Alemanno and Anne-Lise Sibony (eds), *Nudge and the Law. A European Perspective* (Hart 2015) 301 (arguing that behavioural economics needs to be complemented by a more holistic reception of psychology, particularly social psychology); similar approach in Alberto Alemanno and Anne-Lise Sibony, 'Epilogue: The Legitimacy and Practicability of EU Behavioural Policy-Making' in Alberto Alemanno and Anne-Lise Sibony (eds), *Nudge and the Law. A European Perspective* (Hart 2015) 325, 340; Anne-Lise Sibony, 'Can EU Consumer Law Benefit from Behavioural Insights? An Analysis of the Unfair Practices Directive' (2014) 22 European Review of Private Law 901 (drawing on behavioural economics and social psychology); Gunther Teubner, 'Law and Social Theory: Three Problems' (2014) Ancilla Juris 182; German version: Gunther Teubner, 'Rechtswissenschaft und -praxis im Kontext der Sozialtheorie', in Stefan Grundmann and Jan Thiessen (eds), *Recht und Sozialtheorie im Rechtsvergleich: Interdisziplinäres Denken in Rechtswissenschaft und -praxis* [Law in the Context of Disciplines: Interdisciplinary Approaches in Legal Academia and Practice] (Mohr Siebeck 2015) 145; in a similar vein also Calabresi (n 15); for competition law in particular, see Ioannis Lianos, 'The Emergence of Forensic Economics in Competition Law: Foundations for a Sociological Analysis', CLES Working Paper No. 5/2012, <https://ssrn.com/abstract=2197025>, 19 et seq.; Oliver Budzinski, 'Monoculture versus Diversity in Competition Economics' (2008) 32 Cambridge Journal of Economics 295.
[17] See, e.g., Stefan Grundmann, Florian Möslein, and Karl Riesenhuber (eds), *Contract Governance. Dimensions in Law and Interdisciplinary Research* (Oxford University Press 2015); Stefan Grundmann, Hans-W. Micklitz, and Moritz Renner, *Privatrechtstheorie* (Mohr Siebeck 2015); Stefan Grundmann, Hans-W. Micklitz, and Moritz Renner, *New Private Law Theory—A Pluralist Approach* (Cambridge University Press 2020); Philipp Hacker, *Verhaltensökonomik und Normativität. Die Grenzen des Informationsmodells im Privatrecht und seine Alternativen* [Behavioural Economics and Normativity. The Limits of the Disclosure Paradigm in Private Law and Its Alternatives] (Mohr Siebeck 2017)(drawing on behavioural economics and normative political theory); Georgios Dimitropoulos and Philipp Hacker, 'Learning and the Law. Improving Behavioral Regulation from an International and Comparative Perspective' (2017) 25 Journal of Law & Policy 473 (using game theory, social

economic analysis of law on efficiency;[18] the over-indebtedness of (early) behavioural economics to laboratory experiments)[19] can potentially be avoided.

As a result, the beginning of the century has already seen a considerable increase in public visibility of questions of interdisciplinary methodology—to name but a few, bounded rationality is increasingly seen as a new paradigm,[20] informing important parts of after-crisis regulation;[21] the wisdom of the crowd is a concept present in the public sphere;[22] and herding is seen as one of the core causes for the global financial crisis.[23] These are good times, we believe, to think broadly about choice, more precisely: about the interplay between theories of choice and specific legal problems. Venturing beyond the dichotomy of rational versus behavioural approaches and taking stock of the heterogeneity of theories of choice, however,

psychology, and cognitive psychology); Wolfgang Fikentscher, Philipp Hacker, and Rupprecht Podszun, *FairEconomy. Crises, Culture, Competition and the Role of Law* (Springer 2013) (harnessing institutional and behavioural economics as well as economic anthropology); Stefan Grundmann, 'Pluralistische Privatrechtstheorie: Prolegomena zu einer pluralistischen Rechtstheorie als Desiderat aus einer pluralistisch verfassten Wertegrundlage ("normativer Pluralismus")' (2020) RabelsZ 84 (forthcoming); Stefan Grundmann, 'Pluralism and Private Law Theory: How From a Pluralist Legal Value Basis Only a Pluralist Law Theory Can Ensue ("Normative Pluralism")' (2020) 68 American Journal of Comparative Law (forthcoming) (on the heuristic, normative, and ontological foundations of such choice of open and richer interdisciplinary approaches).

[18] From the extensive critical literature, see Jules L. Coleman, 'Efficiency, Utility, and Wealth Maximization' (1980) 8 Hofstra Law Review 509; Ronald M. Dworkin, 'Is Wealth a Value?' (1980) 9 Journal of Legal Studies 191.

[19] See, for the classical critique, Steven D. Levitt and John A. List, 'What Do Laboratory Experiments Measuring Social Preferences Reveal About the Real World?' (2007) 21 Journal of Economic Perspectives 153; Steven D. Levitt and John A. List, 'Homo Economicus Evolves' (2008) 319 Science 909; see also Robert J. Oxoby, 'Experiments and Behavioral Economics' in Morris Altman (ed), *Handbook of Contemporary Behavioral Economics: Foundations and Developments* (M.E. Sharpe 2006) 441, 445 et seq.; Matteo M. Galizzi and Daniel Navarro-Martínez, 'On the External Validity of Social Preference Games: A Systematic Lab-Field Study' (2018) 65 Management Science 976; but see also Judd Kessler and Lise Vesterlund, 'The External Validity of Laboratory Experiments: The Misleading Emphasis on Quantitative Effects' in Guillaume R. Fréchette and Andrew Schotter (eds), *Handbook of Experimental Economic Methodology* (Oxford University Press 2015) 391; James Alm et al., 'On the External Validity of Laboratory Tax Compliance Experiments' (2015) 53 Economic Inquiry 1170.

[20] See references in n 3.

[21] See, e.g., Emilios Avgouleas, 'The Global Financial Crisis, Behavioural Finance and Financial Regulation: In Search of a New Orthodoxy' (2009) 9 Journal of Corporate Law Studies 23; Oliver Blanchard et al. (eds.), *In the Wake of the Crisis: Leading Economists Reassess Economic Policy* (MIT Press 2012); Robert Grosse, 'Bank Regulation, Governance and The Crisis: A Behavioral Finance View' (2012) 20 Journal of Financial Regulation and Compliance 4; Riccardo Viale et al. (eds) *The Behavioural Finance Revolution: A New Approach to Financial Policies and Regulations* (Edward Elgar 2018).

[22] See, e.g., Joshua Becker et al., 'The Wisdom of Partisan Crowds' (2019) 116 Proceedings of the National Academy of Sciences 10717; Zhi Da and Xing Huang, 'Harnessing the Wisdom of Crowds' (2019) 66.5 Management Science 1847–67; James Surowiecki, *The Wisdom of Crowds* (Doubleday 2004); see also the early study by Francis Galton, 'Vox Populi (The Wisdom of Crowds)' (1907) 75 Nature 450; and the contributions by Engert and Grundmann in this volume.

[23] Stavros Stavroyiannis and Vassilios Babalos, 'Time-Varying Herding Behavior within the Eurozone Stock Markets during Crisis Periods' (2019) 12.2 Review of Behavioral Finance 83–96; Viral V. Acharya and Tanju Yorulmazer. 'Information Contagion and Bank Herding' (2008) 40 Journal of Money, Credit and Banking 215; Peter Haiss, 'Bank Herding and Incentive Systems as Catalysts for the Financial Crisis' (2010) 7.1/2 IUP Journal of Behavioral Finance 30.

not only opens possibilities for novel insights and scholarship but also creates a significant problem for the interdisciplinary traveller: a selection problem. What is lacking is a coherent theory, a meta-theory as it were, of choosing a theory of choice for the various legal arenas in which individual, collective and organisational decisions matter. How can the regulator, how can a scholar know which of the manifold theories available to her provides the best fit for the problem at issue? Anne-Lise Sibony takes up this subject explicitly in her contribution to this volume. In the following, we offer some preliminary remarks on this issue.

This selection problem concerns first of all the heuristic approach of the regulator or scholar, that is the direction in and the degree to which she reaches out to other disciplines to find support and materials for solving the problem at hand.[24] As the present volume shows, various theories and sub-theories of choice may be drawn on to found a legal or political argument. In this introduction, we cannot, unfortunately, develop a general meta-theory for selecting a theory of choice. In fact, we believe that the selection problem, in concrete instances, is so deeply intertwined with the specific subject matter it arises from that it may be impossible to formulate a general solution for the selection problem.[25] It is a central tenet of the philosophy of science, at least, that general, rational criteria for positively selecting (as opposed to negatively falsifying) a theory cannot be formulated.[26] However, in the following paragraphs, we would like to discuss three criteria which may be applied as pragmatic guidelines for the solution of the selection problem in specific instances: the proximity of conditions of applicability; the degree of development of the theory; and the ability to generate novel perspectives. This step is (primarily) about the gathering of relevant material, not yet about a ranking of it (on this issue, see below section III)—even though both issues may be closely linked as well.

The first condition refers to context: it seems reasonable to select theories of choice for a particular problem to the extent that the conditions for the applicability of the respective theory match the conditions under which the legal problem is likely to

[24] See Stefan Grundmann, Hans-W. Micklitz, and Moritz Renner, 'Privatrechtstheorie—Eine Einführung' in Stefan Grundmann, Hans-W. Micklitz, and Moritz Renner (eds), *Privatrechtstheorie* (Mohr Siebeck, 2015) 1, 18–20; Hacker (n 17) 4 et seq.

[25] This is particularly obvious for a 'value tracking method' as proposed by Stefan Grundmann, 'Pluralism and Private Law Theory: How From a Pluralist Legal Value Basis Only a Pluralist Law Theory Can Ensue ("Normative Pluralism")' (2020) 68 American Journal of Comparative Law (forthcoming), where it is argued that legal theory as far as it concerns a choice of disciplines beyond law is linked to the value basis in law—for instance constitutional values—in that those disciplines have to be given prioritarian consideration that are particularly focused on the values ranking highest in the legal hierarchy; see also below section III.

[26] Drawing on Thomas S. Kuhn, this thought is developed explicitly by Wolfgang Stegmüller, *Probleme und Resultate der Wissenschaftstheorie und Analytischen Philosophie*, Vol. 2, Subvol. 3 (Springer 1986) 81 et seq., 347 et seq.; following this view, for legal theory, Marietta Auer, 'Privatrechtsdogmatik und Bereicherungsrecht' in Marietta Auer et al. (eds), *Festschrift für Claus-Wilhelm Canaris* (de Gruyter 2017) 509, 525 et seq.; more optimistic concerning the possibility to develop a philosophical meta-epistemology of interdisciplinary legal research Marietta Auer, *Zum Erkenntnisziel der Rechtstheorie* (Nomos 2018) 49 et seq., 52.

arise.[27] For example, in his contribution to this volume, Christoph Engel argues that behavioural theories of choice (behavioural game theory) often rely on the *voluntary* interactions between *strangers*, and that these preconditions are matched in real life in rich institutional settings which favour, and enable, generalised trust. If his analysis is correct, it may make little sense to apply a behavioural theory of choice, in the specific sense in which he discusses the concept (particularly the prisoner's dilemma), when seeking a regulatory solution for a situation marked by pervasive knowledge, among the actors, of the qualities and likely choices of the other actors. Hence, more generally, if the conditions under which the theory applies are sufficiently close to the 'facts of the case', an argument can be made for using the specific theory. More importantly, where these conditions diverge, it seems unlikely that the use of the specific theory will prove fruitful. Thus, the proximity of conditions is itself not a sufficient, but a necessary condition for relying on a certain theory of choice.

A second element to consider when selecting a particular theory of choice is intradisciplinary consensus and, to the extent possible, validation according to the accepted norms of the specific field.[28] Hence, the degree of development of the theory according to those actively contributing to advancing the theory materially, and according to those working in neighbouring theoretical disciplines, should be factored in; speculative or single-study findings should be treated with utmost caution. While there is obviously always a risk that theories may have to be revised or are superseded over time, the risk of basing an analysis on a theory discredited soon after seems particularly high when the theory is not yet thoroughly developed, or, in empirically oriented research, corroborated by sufficient empirical evidence. In a number of disciplines, the degree of development of the theory can be measured, to a certain extent, by the degree of reproducibility, validity, and coherence of its concepts and outcomes.[29] For example, the reproducibility crisis pertaining to empirical psychological research[30] certainly does not rule out referring to that discipline, but it adds a note of caution to legal conclusions unilaterally

[27] See also the chapter by Sibony in this volume.

[28] Stegmüller (n 26) 349–52,

[29] There is, however, no unique measure for any of these desirable properties, and some definitions or desiderata (e.g., internal and external validity) may conflict to a certain extent; cf Edward G. Carmines and Richard A. Zeller, *Reliability and Validity Assessment* (Sage Publications 1979); G. David Garson, *Validity and Reliability* (Statistical Associates Publishing 2013); Christoph Engel, 'Behavioral Law and Economics: Empirical Methods' in Eyal Zamir and Doron Teichman (eds), *The Oxford Handbook of Behavioral Economics and the Law* (Oxford University Press 2014) 125; Arthur Schram, 'Artificiality: The Tension between Internal and External Validity in Economic Experiments' (2005) 12 Journal of Economic Methodology 225; see also Hacker (n 17) 151 et seq.

[30] Open Science Collaboration, 'Estimating the Reproducibility of Psychological Science' (2015) 349.6251 Science 943; Daniel T. Gilbert et al., 'Comment on "Estimating the Reproducibility of Psychological Science"' (2016) 351.6277 Science 1037; Valen E. Johnson et al., 'On the Reproducibility of Psychological Science' (2017) 112.517 Journal of the American Statistical Association 1; Jay J. Van Bavel et al. 'Contextual Sensitivity in Scientific Reproducibility' (2016) 113.23 Proceedings of the National Academy of Sciences 6454.

based on findings affected by the reproducibility problems. While this is not the place to comment on the reproducibility crisis as such, we would nevertheless like to note that a certain maturity of a theory may be conducive to its interdisciplinary leverage. Hence, scholars and regulators should exercise particular care when using very recent theories or, when drawing on empirically oriented sciences, theories with a lack of a broader empirical foundation. In a time in which not only fake news but also fake science has become a major issue,[31] methodological rigour seems all the more desirable.

Third, the choice of a theory of choice may be influenced by the degree to which the theory adds a novel perspective to the problem at hand. This criterion, however, is intertwined and partially in conflict with the second one: the less mature or the more revolutionary a theory, the more it may include novel and original aspects.[32] This is why, clearly, we do not wish to argue for a conservative bias toward more traditional theories; rather, one might make a twofold argument and first say that also young and emergent theories should pass a certain threshold of maturity and methodological rigour that generates sufficient confidence in its results. Second, however, once this threshold is passed, the third criterion favours theories which make new aspects of the regulatory problem relevant or which help to explain new parts of the problem. After all, this is precisely where interdisciplinary research can make a positive impact and where it adds value to the more doctrinal analysis of legal conundrums.

Without doubt, there may be other factors to consider in order to solve the selection problem in interdisciplinary theory. Since reasonable people will tend to disagree on the merits of one theory versus another, we would like to suggest that one final strategy is crucial: transparency concerning the reasons for the choice of a certain theory of choice. Particularly in policy-oriented contexts, this seems indispensable both as a basis for reasoned disagreement and as a guard against selection decisions driven by outcome, not content.[33] Indeed, what should be avoided at all costs is what one may term an 'academic bias',[34] in which a certain theory (e.g., rational choice theory, behavioural game theory) is used primarily because the results of the theory, when applied to the specific legal problem under scrutiny, happen to coincide with the normative predispositions of the person making the selection. As Kathryn Zeiler succinctly warned, 'cherry-picking [from a large body of evidence] to support one's predetermined stance leads to unhelpful and

[31] Dietram A. Scheufele and Nicole M. Krause, 'Science Audiences, Misinformation, and Fake News' (2019) 116.16 Proceedings of the National Academy of Sciences 7662; Selcuk Besir Demir, 'Predatory Journals: Who Publishes in Them and Why?' (2018) 12 Journal of Informetrics 1296.

[32] See generally Thomas S. Kuhn, *The Structure of Scientific Revolutions* (4th edn, University of Chicago Press 2012), particularly ch 6.

[33] Hacker (n 17) 6 et seq.

[34] Hacker (n 17) 4 et seq.

often misleading representations of the science'.[35] Similarly, cherry-picking theories of choice based on their outcome leaves more questions open than are answered. Hence, theoretical diversification ought to be accompanied by transparent justification. Clear disclosure of the reasons speaking for and against the selection of a particular theory of choice facilitates a critical discourse about the scope of application of specific theories, about the foundations and the limits of interdisciplinary scholarship in general, and about an epistemic pluralism in which different theories may, and must, compete for transdisciplinary reception.

II. The Hidden Assumptions of Theories of Choice

In disclosing the reasons for a particular selection decision, the makers of that selection—and the contributors to this volume in their respective chapters—seek to enquire into the hidden assumptions behind the theories of choice and their relevance for legal analysis. More specifically, two kinds of premises are embedded in such theories, premises which are sometimes under-reflected in their application to questions of regulation and law: epistemic rationality assumptions and implicit normative assumptions.

The degree to which full, bounded, or alternative modes of rationality are assumed amongst actors differs widely between the theories.[36] While this is often made explicit, sometimes the indebtedness of a model or an argument to certain shades of rationality is not openly discussed. Again, transparency seems an easy but necessary cure. To the extent that such limitations lead to biased or wrong predictions in certain areas in which actors do not conform to the rationality assumptions—because they are, for example, more or less boundedly rational than the theory (implicitly) postulates—the law is bound to draw inaccurate consequences from the theory. Notably, this does not only concern cases in which actors behave in a boundedly rational manner while the theory predicts rational behaviour; the inverse pattern may also be found, for example, in the behaviour of sophisticated financial actors when confronted with the predictions of behavioural finance. And, to add to that difficulty, boundedly and fully rational actors may make decisions in parallel, particularly but not only in situations of collective choice.[37]

Second, the contributions to this volume seek to unearth the implicit normative foundations of the theories under scrutiny. Whenever the theories are installed as a yardstick or a tool of measurement and prediction, the relevant normative

[35] Kathryn Zeiler, 'Cautions on the Use of Economics Experiments in Law' (2010) 166 Journal of Theoretical and Institutional Economics 178, 179.

[36] See the references in n 2–5.

[37] See, e.g., the discussion of the knowledge problem of behavioural economics in the contribution by Hacker in this volume.

assumptions are imported as well. Rational choice theories tend to gravitate toward efficiency, understood as total welfare maximisation, as the overarching legal goal;[38] however, by framing biases as deviations from a normative model of rational decision making, behavioural theories of choice also are prone to import the rational actor model implicitly as the benchmark of legal analysis.[39] The debate on the desirability of debiasing testifies to this intricacy.[40] Modes of rational action and efficiency considerations are obviously not, by far, the only normative criteria that can be furthered by the application of theories of choice to legal problems.[41] 'Prioritarian' social welfare functions that give greater weight to the impact of policy choices on the poor, as analysed by Matthew Adler in his contribution to this volume, are one important instantiation of such a very differently oriented normative approach and benchmark;[42] the use of nudges to spur behaviour oriented toward fairness and contribution to public goods is another example.[43] Importantly, these normative commitments also need to be made visible and explicit in order to facilitate a robust normative discourse on the—area-specific—desirability of such constructs. When applied to policy analysis, seemingly descriptive characteristics tend to take on a normative dimension, thus eroding the categorical difference postulated between 'positive' and 'normative' analysis.[44] If descriptive models contain a normative thrust, the law should take greater care than has been taken until now to decide which theories to operate with and which to avoid. Do we want to assume rational decision making in situations with mixed constituencies as the one described above (some acting in a boundedly rational way, others in a rational way)? Should we distinguish between different kinds of questions on which the decision is made (e.g., those pertaining to standard consumption decisions versus those relating to existential questions for those affected)?[45] In all these questions, normative reasoning and critique cannot be deflected by pointing to the fact that

[38] See the references in n 2.

[39] See, e.g., Jolls, Sunstein, and Thaler (n 3) 1475, with reservations ibid. 1508 et seq.; Georgios Dimitropoulos, 'From Choosing to Learning: Path Dependencies of Nudging, and How to Overcome Them' in Alexandra Kemmerer et al. (eds), *Choice Architecture in Democracies* (Hart/Nomos 2016) 339.

[40] See Hacker (n 17) 291 et seq.

[41] See again Jolls, Sunstein, and Thaler (n 3) 1508 et seq.

[42] See also Matthew D. Adler, 'A Better Calculus for Regulators: From Cost-Benefit Analysis to the Social Welfare Function' (25 February 2017) Duke Law School Public Law & Legal Theory Series No. 2017-19, https://ssrn.com/abstract=2923829; Matthew D. Adler, *Well-Being and Fair Distribution: Beyond Cost-Benefit Analysis* (Oxford University Press 2011).

[43] Hacker (n 17) particularly §§ 7–8; Philipp Hacker, 'Nudge 2.0—The Future of Behavioural Analysis of Law, in Europe and Beyond' (2016) 24 European Review of Private Law 297, 315–17.

[44] See, on that difference, Francesco Parisi, 'Positive, Normative and Functional Schools in Law and Economics' (2004) 18 European Journal of Law and Economics 259.

[45] For normative arguments in favour of such a distinction and arguing that this is already inherent in current European Court of Justice (ECJ) case law: Stefan Grundmann, ‚Targeted Consumer Protection' in Dorota Leczykiewicz and Stephen Weatherill (eds), *The Images of the 'Consumer' in EU Law—Legislation, Free Movement and Competition Law* (Hart 2016) 223.

certain theories are only 'tools of measurement'—they always imprint their normative undercurrents on the subject matter.

III. A Pluralism of Methods and Legal Theory

One important underlying assumption of the choice of methods, theories, and disciplines that should help to analyse choice and its role in matters of law is that *pluralist* interdisciplinary approaches and research have (important or even decisive) advantages over interdisciplinary approaches referring to only one adjacent discipline. One could call these latter approaches 'monistic' interdisciplinary approaches, especially if only *one* ultimate benchmark is chosen against which to assess results in law (for instance, 'efficiency', 'total welfare', or 'consumer welfare'). Such an approach would moreover be still more problematic if a benchmark was chosen as the only one that clearly does not rank as the highest, but rather at an intermediate level within the classical legal and societal prime value bases. These classical legal and societal prime value bases are to be seen primarily in constitutions and then in other value bases that find their justification in decisions taken in a fully fledged democratic discourse and process—that is, typically laws. Such primacy of constitution and decisions taken in a fully fledged democratic discourse and process does not constitute an accepted hierarchy only from a legal perspective, but from the largely majoritarian political consensus in Western societies today and hence relevant for all social sciences.

Different criteria can be discussed that could support such a claim of completeness or even superiority claim of *pluralist* interdisciplinary approaches. One core argument has already been indicated and could be termed as the 'heuristic strength' of a pluralist interdisciplinary approach—referring to broader openness and readiness to incorporate theories from very different disciplines that would convey insight that might be important for law. A second core aspect could be termed the 'ontological strength' of a pluralist interdisciplinary approach.[46] This refers to the fact that such an approach would convey to legal scholarship (broadly informed in a whole variety of disciplines) the task of accommodating and balancing different approaches. Such a weighing and balancing process—so typical for law since it has been the (first) discipline which analyses society and political choices—would have two aspects in the main. It would need to strive to accommodate, to the best extent possible, the richness of theories from all disciplines with the *existing* constitutional and democratically decided value basis ('*de lege lata*'). Moreover, it would need to strive to further develop this value basis for the *future* in the light of such

[46] More in detail on ontological and heuristic 'superiority' arguments and with a good number of additional examples that elucidate the 'heuristic richness' argument Grundmann (n 25).

societal beliefs and convictions analysed in all the social sciences and even beyond ('*de lege ferenda*').

In a third and perhaps the most important perspective, a pluralist interdisciplinary approach has been argued to be normatively required ('normative superiority'), and this aspect falls largely into two lines.[47] The first line of argument starts from the finding that those prime value bases found in Western democracies characterised by subjecting (public) power to the rule of law and by organising their economies as market economies—that is, constitutional and/or democratically decided upon value bases—are all pluralist by nature. Pluralism of values is thus characteristic of, but also normatively corroborated in, Western democracies under the rule of law and with market economies—from the United States and other American states to (most of) the European and (some) East Asian states.[48] For the European Union in particular, this is even explicitly spelt out, namely for its Charter of Fundamental Rights.[49] While traditionally legal theory and positive law are seen as being largely distinct from each other—and also that they should be kept distinct from each other[50]—in our context, an argument to the contrary would seem more convincing. Given a strong pluralism in the relevant value bases (constitutions and acts democratically decided upon), it would seem rather obvious that the interdisciplinary insight would need to come from a pluralist set of disciplines. In other words, the most fruitful insight—both in terms of intellectual richness, relevance, *and* legitimacy—can be expected and would primarily need to be taken from those disciplines that focus most on a particular value at stake. Thus, economic theory would have more to contribute when efficiency is at stake than

[47] More broadly on these two lines of normative argument, see Grundmann (n 25).

[48] On this (prevalent) understanding of Western societies and their constitutions, for instance in the European Union, the United States, or in Germany, see, for instance: Stephen Tierney, *Constitutional Law and National Pluralism* (Oxford University Press 2005); Neil Walker, 'The Idea of Constitutional Pluralism' (2002) 65 The Modern Law Review 317; Udo Di Fabio, 'Grundrechte als Werteordnung' (2004) Juristenzeitung (JZ) 1; also Michal Ovádek, 'Constitutional Pluralism between Normative Theory and Empirical Fact', VerfBlog, 23 October 2018, https://verfassungsblog.de/constitutional-pluralism-between-normative-theory-and-empirical-fact/; very early already on the repercussion of this (largely accepted) view on legal methodology, see Ernst Fraenkel, *Deutschland und die westlichen Demokratien* (6th edn, Kohlhammer 1974) 197 et seq.; Oliver Lepsius, 'Rechtswissenschaft in der Demokratie' (2013) 52 Der Staat 157.

[49] Art. 2 phrase 2 TEU names pluralism as the key characteristic of societies and jurisdictions in the European Union. For a sociological reading of fundamental rights as guaranteeing such differentiation of the different areas, layers, and beliefs in (Western) societies, see Gert Verschraegen, 'Human Rights and Modern Society: A Sociological Analysis from the Perspective of Systems Theory' (2002) 29 Journal of Law and Society 258; on the repercussions of normative pluralism in the EU Fundamental Rights Charter on—for instance—European Contract Law, see Dan Wielsch, 'The Function of Fundamental Rights in EU Private Law—Perspectives for the Common European Sales Law' (2014) 10 European Review of Contract Law 365, 370–72.

[50] For such distinction—also as fundamental requirement of proper legal theory conceptualisation—see, for instance, Marietta Auer, *Zum Erkenntnisziel der Rechtstheorie—philosophische Grundlagen multidisziplinärer Rechtswissenschaft* (Nomos 2018), esp. 27–38; Herbert L.A. Hart, *The Concept of Law* (3rd edn, Clarendon 2012), 238–76 (Postscript) (stressing the requirement of homogeneity of theory); Thomas Vesting, *Rechtstheorie* (2nd edn, C.H. Beck 2015) paras 10–13 (legal theory as a 'perspective of second order').

when solidarity or human dignity is at stake.[51] If, however, constitutions and acts democratically decided upon declare all three as being relevant, pluralism in disciplines and a pluralist legal theory seem indispensable—as a matter of principle and overall approach in the integration of adjacent disciplines and their theories within the reasoning used in legal scholarship. A second line of arguments is about implementation, and it progresses from the overall idea to application in individual settings. The core question in individual, concrete settings is that of the legitimate mix of disciplines, potentially a hierarchy between insights stemming from different disciplines, potentially also a balancing and weighing of those insights. The overall question is how order can be established between diverging insights from a set of various disciplines. The editors of this volume have proposed (slightly) diverging approaches. They propose either consulting a decision-theoretic meta-theory developed and, in principle, broadly accepted in political philosophy—that of minimum values (material and immaterial) being guaranteed for all members of society (maximin rule)—in order to decide between competing theories of choice in cases of uncertainty;[52] or they propose a value-tracking mechanism via which the relevant core values to be realised have to be searched for in the constitution or relevant Act, and then a particular insight most in line with this value is to be preferred.[53] In particular areas, the outcome may then be that the legal acts are exclusively about efficiency—and then, reverting solely to economic theory, they may also be justified. This, however, is by no means always the case, even in core areas of economic law such as, for instance, financial services law. In other areas, one approach may be prime, even though the residual importance of others cannot be neglected. For instance, as far as human dignity requires, only this value may be paramount, while beyond that, others may be consulted. In yet other areas, different values may be of similar importance and an exercise of weighting each may be mandated.

Thus, while pluralism of disciplinary perspectives and theories would seem to have important advantages in terms of heuristics, ontology, and normative foundations, it remains a challenge open for ample debate in the future to find ways to make the interplay within such a rich fundus legitimate and foreseeable.

[51] This is made explicit also in economic theory itself, namely when it distinguishes issues of efficiency (on which economic theory is focusing) from issues of redistribution that it explicitly leaves out: see, for instance, Louis Kaplow and Steven Shavell, 'Should Legal Rules Favor the Poor? Clarifying the Role of Legal Rules and the Income Tax in Redistributing Income' (2000) 29 Journal of Legal Studies 821; in this sense, albeit from a different angle, already Karl Polanyi, *The Great Transformation* (Farrar & Rinehart 1944); then following this path, for instance: Andrew T.F. Lang, 'The Legal Construction of Economic Rationalities?' (2013) 40 Journal of Law and Society 155.

[52] See the contribution by Hacker in this volume, and Hacker (n 17), 159 et seq., 188 et seq., 352 et seq., for a recourse to theories of justice in the political philosophy, and specifically to the maximin rule (John Rawls).

[53] For such a value tracking method Grundmann (n 25); and in principle already Stefan Grundmann, 'Methodenpluralismus als Aufgabe—zur Legalität von ökonomischen und rechtsethischen Argumenten in Auslegung und Rechtsanwendung' (1997) 66 RabelsZ 423.

IV. The Four Parts of the Book

The chapters of this book investigate these matters in one introductory Part (Foundations), followed by three Parts on individual, collective, and organisational choice. The hypothesis is that, both on the side of theory—in the different disciplines involved—and on the side of reconstruction in legal and regulatory terms, important differences will be found between these three dimensions (individual, collective, and organisational choice), for instance with respect to the areas of the law most fruitfully analysed under each category. While there are certainly overlaps and while these three dimensions clearly do not exhaust the possible perspectives, they nevertheless seem particularly meaningful, both with respect to the theoretical foundations and to a reconstruction in law and regulation. They can serve as points of reference or even as archetypes with respect to the modes of decision making, and with respect to law and regulation reacting to it.

Part I (Foundations) gravitates around a critical discussion of the two outstanding approaches to decision theory proper: rational choice theory and behavioural economics. It introduces key theories of choice discussed in the book and sets the stage for a more detailed analysis in the further chapters. In this, rational choice constitutes a first building block because it was, and remains, dominant as a hypothesis for theory building in (institutional) economics, but also more generally in the social sciences. Today, however, bounded rationality research can be discerned as the most important limitation both from the perspective of theory building and from that of reconstruction in the realm of rule-making. Hence, it constitutes a second building block. The relevance of behavioural economics for legal analysis is still much under debate, and the contributions by Deakin and Engel strive to define the proper scope of application of these theories within legal contexts. With the third building block, one problem of the tripartite division suggested above becomes apparent: individual decision making is possible in 'parametric' situations, that is where decisions are made without other people's choices being of any relevance, but individual decision making is also possible in 'non-parametric' situations of mutual dependence between decision makers. We nevertheless think that game theory, focusing on this situation, can still be construed as a building block of individual decision making. Therefore, the chapter by Ahlert on game theory and the law forms part of our first—more general—Part. It is equally relevant, however, both for collective unorganised decision making and for decision making in organisations, and it analyses both rational and behavioural choice possibilities.

The second Part of the book (Individual Choice and the Law) analyses specific situations and fitting applications of these first three theoretical building blocks (rational choice, behavioural approaches, game theory) in contexts of individual decision making. Since individual choice is given particular leeway where party autonomy is most pronounced, most examples stem from contract law, consumer markets, and the digital economy. This section contains a discussion of data, from a worldwide survey, on the acceptance of one of the leading but contested instantiations of behavioural law and economics: nudging (in the chapter by Reisch, Sunstein, and Kaiser); an application of different theories of choice to different forms of uncertainty arising in regulatory contexts (the chapter by Hacker); and an appraisal of consumer choice in online environments, including a thorough discussion of the selection problem (the chapter by Sibony).

As is well known, individual decisions become a matter of law and regulation not so much in Rousseau's state of nature but by affecting others, that is, in situations of common interest. We think that for theory building, and for law and regulation, two situations of collective choice are particularly distinct: collective choice where the decision making is not organised by a predefined framework (analysed in Part III: Collective Choice and the Law); and those instances where an institutional framework does exist (analysed in Part IV: Organisational Choice and the Law). Again, whether such a framework exists or not cannot be seen as a simple binary code but a continuum in which, however, archetypes of strong organisational framing and those of particularly weak organisational framing can be distinguished.

Part III investigates collective choice in settings in which the interaction of agents is only weakly institutionally mediated. Collective choice, in these settings, points toward the construction of political entities, and to regulatory decisions of primary importance for a polity; hence the future of the European Union (the chapter by Héritier) and risk regulation (the chapter by Adler) are particularly suitable for analysis in these terms. However, the concepts of wisdom of the crowds or herding can also be understood as collective decision making, and they have become even more paradigmatic in the aftermath of the global financial crisis. Markets, for example, prediction of stock markets, aggregate individual choice into collectively relevant outcomes; therefore, they form the last example discussed in this Part (the chapter by Engert).

This paves the way for topics constitutive of organised decision making, discussed in the fourth and final Part of the book. When it then comes to organisational choice, that is collective choice taken in a framework highly organised for collective decision making, the firm and the public hierarchy (agencies) appear as being paradigmatic. The firm merits an entire sub-part, with two contributions, from a general decision-theoretic (the chapter by Velasco) and from a network theory perspective (the chapter by Enriques and Romano). Decision theory has been applied less, however, to those other 'organisations' which are increasingly discussed today: networks as hybrids between firms and markets (the chapter by Grundmann); and institutions in general and conflicts of interest in particular (the chapter by Helleringer). The final chapter then returns to a venerable institution—juror decision making—but offers a fresh perspective on it through the lens of quantum decision-making theory (the chapter by Jaeger and Trueblood). Since quantum decision-making theory aims to synthesise parts of the literature on behavioural biases, the closing chapter directly connects with the discussions of the chapters in Part I of the volume. In this sense, the wheel comes full circle.

In all these contributions, the volume finally aims to strengthen the bridge between scholars in the European Union and the United States, a bridge that, despite all individual encounters and exchanges, is currently perhaps still too weak. We are grateful to the Fritz Thyssen Foundation for having provided support to a conference which brought together theorists of choice from both sides of the Atlantic, and which inspired this book. As the world is facing an increasing number of challenges on a global scale—from pandemics to global warming and international trade, from economic inequality to digital divides—a deeper interconnectedness between these two spheres of knowledge seems indispensable in order to find analytical answers to these pressing questions; or, as it were, to make the right choices in a global environment of growing risk and uncertainty.

PART I
FOUNDATIONS

1

The Proper Scope of Behavioural Law and Economics

Christoph Engel[1]

Abstract: Behavioural law and economics applies the conceptual tools of behavioural economics to the analysis of legal problems and legal intervention. These models, and the experiments to test them, assume an institution-free state of nature. In modern societies, the law's subjects never see this state of nature. However, a rich arrangement of informal and formal institutions creates generalised trust. If individuals are sufficiently confident that nothing too detrimental will happen, they are freed up to interact with strangers as if they were in a state of nature. This willingness dramatically reduces transaction cost and enables division of labour. If generalised trust can be assumed, simple economic models are appropriate, but they must be behavioural, since otherwise individuals would not want to run the risk of interaction.

I. Epistemics and the Law

Jurisprudentia, non juris scientia.[2] Throughout the centuries, legal scholars have cautioned against defining their field as a science.[3] The law has to govern people's lives. Legal decisions have direct consequences for the real world. And alas, reality is rich and unruly. But the law is not exempt from epistemology. All understanding is selective. It homes in on one aspect of a much richer phenomenon. This one aspect can be rigorously defined. Rigorous definition is a precondition for reliable empirical investigation. One is able to formulate a theoretical claim about a causal

[1] Helpful comments by Hanjo Hamann, Majbritt Sterba, and the participants of the 2017 EUI workshop on Theories of Choice, are gratefully acknowledged.

[2] Although this has not always been seen as a conflict. Digestas 1, 1, 10, 2 (Ulpianus): 'Iuris prudentia est divinarum atque humanum rerum notitia, iusti atque iniusti scientia'.

[3] For a particularly powerful voice see Julius von Kirchmann, *Die Wertlosigkeit der Jurisprudenz als Wissenschaft* (Springer 1848). For a review of the book see Christoph Engel, *Julius Hermann von Kirchmann: Die Wertlosigkeit der Jurisprudenz als Wissenschaft, Berlin 1848* (Juristenzeitung 2006) 614.

Christoph Engel, *The Proper Scope of Behavioural Law and Economics* In: *Theories of Choice.*
Edited by: Stefan Grundmann and Philipp Hacker, Oxford University Press (2021).
DOI: 10.1093/oso/9780198863175.003.0002

relationship, and to test for its presence in some well-defined dataset. One may set a precise criterion for provisionally accepting the hypothesis, provided the counter-hypothesis is sufficiently unlikely to be supported by the data.

Legal scholarship that is not content with establishing the internal consistency of a set of normative precepts[4] therefore faces a dilemma. The legal scholar should only be confident of the correspondence[5] between a claim about the world and the evidence if this claim is derived from theory, and tested according to the standards of the social sciences. However, this same legal scholar will loathe being constrained by the architecture of the conceptual framework, and by the conventions of empirical research. How could she neglect an aspect of the underlying conflict of life, just because theory has not focused on it, data are insufficient, or standards of empirical research are excessively rigorous?[6] In the empirical disciplines, this conflict is often also presented as one between the internal validity of a test (the design safely excludes alternative explanations) and its external validity (the price for achieving internal validity is simplification, consequently what one studies is only analogous to what one wants to understand).[7]

Since this is a true dilemma, the gap between scientific research and reality will never be completely closed. But this is not to say that legal scholars should not care. They advise legal decision makers. Whoever makes a decision has to take on responsibility. If the decision maker has serious doubts whether a scientific proposition is adequate for the case at hand, she will rightly put the proposition aside. But legal decision makers, and their scholarly advisers, should not do so lightly. He who wants to see everything will see nothing. Selective attention is a precondition

[4] As for instance the 'Reine Rechtslehre', Hans Kelsen, 'Was ist die reine Rechtslehre?' in *Demokratie und Rechtsstaat Festgabe zum 60 Geburtstag von Zaccaria Giacometti* (Demokratie und Rechtsstaat Festgabe zum 60 Geburtstag von Zaccaria Giacometti, Polygraphischer Verlag 1953) 143–62. On coherence theories of law see Barbara Baum Levenbook, 'The Role of Coherence in Legal Reasoning' (1984) 3 Law and Philosophy 355; Neil MacCormick, 'Coherence in Legal Justification' in Aleksander Peczenik (ed.), *Theory of Legal Science* (Reidel 1984); Aleksander Peczenik, 'Law, Morality, Coherence and Truth' (1994) 7 Ratio Juris 146.

[5] For epistemic background see Marian David, 'The Correspondence Theory of Truth' in *Stanford Encyclopedia of Philosophy* (Center for the Study of Language and Information (CSLI), Stanford University 2010).

[6] More on this conflict from Christoph Engel, 'Empirical Methods for the Law' (2018) 174 Journal of Institutional and Theoretical Economics 5.

[7] There is an extended debate over external validity: see Bobby J. Calder, Lynn W. Phillips and Alice M. Tybout, 'The Concept of External Validity' (1982) 9 Journal of Consumer Research 240; Glenn H. Bracht and Gene V. Glass, 'The External Validity of Experiments' (1968) 5 American Educational Research Journal 437; Craig A. Anderson and Brad J. Bushman, 'External Validity of "Trivial" Experiments. The Case of Laboratory Aggression' (1997) 1 Review of General Psychology 19; John G. Lynch Jr, 'On the External Validity of Experiments in Consumer Research' (1982) 9 Journal of Consumer Research 225; Jeffrey W. Lucas, 'Theory-testing, Generalization, and the Problem of External Validity' (2003) 21 Sociological Theory 236; Arthur Schram, 'Artificiality. The Tension Between Internal and External Validity in Economic Experiments' (2005) 12 Journal of Economic Methodology 225; Gregory Mitchell, 'Revisiting Truth or Triviality. The External Validity of Research in the Psychological Laboratory' (2012) 7 Perspectives on Psychological Science 109.

for seeing sharply. Ignoring scientific insights should be exceptional. Legal scholars should rather focus on the fit of proposed conceptual frameworks and supporting evidence with the conflict of life they are facing. Does the scientific concept zero in on the one aspect of the conflict that seems critical for the normative argument the lawyer wants to make?

Actually, if legal scholars use this research strategy, their attitude is no different from the attitude of social scientists who advise policy makers. These scholars have coined the metaphor of a 'zoo of models'.[8] If the object of your curiosity has a fur and four legs, you should not immediately take it to be a bear. It could also be a mouflon, a wolf, or a weasel. The metaphor suggests that each model, or concept, more generally speaking, has its framework conditions. The model only helps make relevant statements about reality if there is a sufficiently good match between the model and the aspect of reality in which one is interested. To stick with the same example: if one is interested in sexual reproduction, it may suffice to classify all these animals broadly as mammals, but if one wants to understand in which habitat they have a chance to survive, more fine-grained distinctions are in order. Assessing the match between a model and the object of study, or the research question for that matter, is not a mechanical exercise. There is no meta-theory from which the conditions for applying some theory, or some empirical method for that matter, could be logically derived. Whether a given theory has a good fit for the problem at hand is a matter of judgment.

Ultimately, judgment requires intuition. When it comes to selecting theoretical frameworks and empirical methods, this intuition should be professionally trained.[9] The intuitive component should also not be radicalised. It usually will be possible to spell out the key reasons why some framework seems more adequate, and a competing framework seems less adequate. But the choice of framework, or of empirical method, cannot be proven to be right. The scholar must argue for her choice.

This is what the current chapter sets out to do for an increasingly popular import from economics into law. It often is referred to as behavioural law and economics. In the next section I sketch the building blocks of the approach. It essentially is an extension of (neo) classical law and economics. It therefore inherits key concepts from economic (game) theory. Using a classic 2×2 prisoner's dilemma for illustration, in section III I am asking whether this model has a good fit with the legal conflicts it is meant to elucidate. Section IV concludes.

[8] Apparently, the metaphor has originally been coined by Helmut Bester. I owe it to Martin Hellwig. Physicists have even earlier colloquially talked about 'the particule zoo', https://en.wikipedia.org/wiki/Particle_zoo.

[9] Lorraine Daston calls the resulting epistemic ideal 'truth', to be distinguished from 'objectivity', Lorraine Daston and Peter Galison, *Objectivity* (Zone Books 2007).

II. Behavioural Law and Economics

Behavioural law and economics is a sister of (neoclassical) law and economics.[10] Both scholarly fields are interested in explaining the normative problems that the law is meant to address, and legal intervention, with the reactions of individuals who strive for personal utility subject to constraints. In this perspective, a real-life conflict only calls for legal intervention if the socially detrimental action of one individual is not held in check by other individuals who also pursue their personal interests. Hence the approach relies on equilibrium analysis. It makes assumptions about individuals' utility functions and predicts outcomes in the absence of legal rules. It compares these outcomes with the prediction if the legal order intervenes in some well-defined manner. There is a case for legal intervention if the former state of affairs is further away from the social optimum than the latter, taking any pecuniary and non-pecuniary cost of the intervention into account.

The key difference between neoclassical and behavioural law and economics is the set of assumptions the analyst makes about the utility function of a representative member of society.[11] While first-generation law and economics models often have assumed that individuals exclusively maximise personal monetary profit,[12] behavioural models allow for richer definitions of utility,[13] and in particular for social preferences.[14] Other extensions concern the cognitive side of human behaviour. They particularly allow individuals' reactions to changes in the opportunity structure to be imperfect.[15]

Neoclassical and behavioural law and economics have been particularly interested in cooperation problems. Such problems take their definition from welfare economics.[16] This normative branch of economic theory homes in on one normative goal: allocative efficiency. Scarce resources should end up in the hands of those individuals that can use them most productively. This does not exclude trade. Efficiency need not be established right from the start. Actually, one of the most

[10] For introductions see Eyal Zamir and Doron Teichman, *The Oxford Handbook of Behavioral Economics and the Law* (Oxford University Press 2014); Kathryn Zeiler and Joshua C. Teitelbaum, *Research Handbook of Behavioral Law and Economics* (Edward Elgar 2017).

[11] Alternatively, the analyst may allow for heterogeneity, and will then predict outcomes conditional on assumptions about the type space.

[12] See the classic manuals by Richard A. Posner, *Economic Analysis of Law* (6th edn, Aspen Publishers 2014); Robert Cooter and Thomas Ulen, *Law and Economics* (4th edn, Prentice Hall 2012).

[13] For an overview see, e.g., Colin F. Camerer, *Behavioral Game Theory. Experiments in Strategic Interaction* (1st edn, Sage u.a. 2003); Roger Frantz et al., *Routledge Handbook of Behavioral Economics* (Routledge 2016).

[14] For an overview, see Ernst Fehr and Klaus M. Schmidt, 'The Economics of Fairness, Reciprocity and Altruism. Experimental Evidence and New Theories' (2006) 1 Handbook on the Economics of Giving, Reciprocity and Altruism 615.

[15] A good illustration can be found in learning models; see, e.g., Colin F. Camerer and Teck Hua Ho, 'Experience-Weighted Attraction Learning in Normal Form Games' (1999) 67 Econometrica 827.

[16] For background see Allan M. Feldman, *Welfare Economics and Social Choice Theory* (12th edn, Kluwer u.a. 1997).

important insights of this discipline is the Coase Theorem. As long as property rights are well defined, contracts can be enforced, preferences are common knowledge, and transaction cost is zero, the initial allocation of property rights is immaterial. Through trade, resources end up with those individuals who place the highest valuation on them.[17] Of course, in many contexts of life these assumptions are heroic, which then justifies legal intervention.

A classic situation that does not fulfil these assumptions is the prisoner's dilemma.[18] It assumes that two individuals who are in conflict with each other have to decide simultaneously whether to cooperate or to defect. Simultaneous choice rules out trade. Utilities are such that both individuals would collectively be best off if both of them cooperate. But individually each of them gets her highest utility if she defects while the other cooperates, and each of them gets her lowest utility if she cooperates while the other defects. If both defect, both get their second worst outcome. This is why defection is inefficient. The society of these two individuals would have higher welfare if both cooperate, but both of them have an incentive to defect.

Table 1.1 is the standard representation of the game. A row-player R interacts with a column-player C. Each of them has a binary action set. They can either cooperate or defect. Utility is conditional on the choice made by the other player. The first number in each cell stands for R's utility, the second for C's utility. Pay-offs are indicated ordinarily. Hence 4 > 3 > 2 > 1 holds. However, in this version, the model does not specify by how much one utility differs from the other. It does also not assume that utilities are equidistant. These additional assumptions are not necessary because players maximise utility. It is also not assumed that a utility of some level (say 3) is the same for each player. This additional assumption is not necessary since the numbers already reflect the overall individual assessment of the outcome. C may for instance be rivalistic and prefer a large over a small pay-off gap. Such a

Table 1.1 Prisoner's dilemma

		player C	
		cooperate	defect
player R	cooperate	3,3	1,4
	defect	4,1	2,2

[17] Ronald Coase, 'The Problem of Social Cost' (1960) 3 Journal of Law and Economics 1.

[18] Lawyers interested in more background are referred to Douglas G. Baird, Robert H. Gertner, and Randal C. Picker, *Game Theory and the Law* (Harvard University Press 1994); Fritz Wilhelm Scharpf, *Games Real Actors Play. Actor-Centered Institutionalism in Policy Research* (Westview Press 1997).

preference does not change the equilibrium as long as this non-standard utility is not strong enough to change the order of the desirability of outcomes.

If the model correctly captures the conflict, the model makes a clear prediction. The outcome ranked highest (4) is preferred over the outcome ranked second highest (3). This is why the individual defects if she assumes that her counterpart will cooperate. The outcome ranked third highest (2) is preferred over the outcome ranked lowest (1). This is why the individual defects if she assumes that her counterpart will defect as well. In the game theory literature, the former motive is sometimes referred to as 'greed', and the latter motive is sometimes referred to as 'fear'.[19] Both motives support the same choice. Game theorists therefore call cooperation 'dominated'. This makes the prediction very robust. One need not know individuals' beliefs. It also does not matter whether individuals are uncertain about their opponent's choices. Even if the opponent were to randomise between both choices, their best response would not change.

This robustness of the prediction has led policy analysts to talk of the 'tragedy of the commons'.[20] A fairly rich behavioural literature has investigated whether this prediction holds empirically, both in the lab[21] and in the field.[22] We have also contributed to this literature, and have found that, in the lab, the prisoner's dilemma is a game of multiple motives. Gains from cooperation, optimism, inequity aversion, risk aversion, and loss aversion are all needed to explain choices in the prisoner's dilemma.[23]

III. The Prisoner's Dilemma as a Tool for Legal Analysis

Many conflicts of law lend themselves to an analysis in terms of a 2 × 2 prisoner's dilemma.[24] Every citizen is best off individually if others constrain themselves for

[19] K. T. Ahn et al., 'Cooperation in PD Games. Fear, Greed, and History of Play' (2001) 106 Public Choice 137.

[20] Garrett Hardin, 'The Tragedy of the Commons' (1968) 162 Science 1243.

[21] See, e.g., Anatol Rapoport and Albert M. Chammah, *Prisoner's Dilemma. A Study in Conflict and Cooperation* (University of Michigan Press 1965); Andrew M. Colman, 'Cooperation, Psychological Game Theory, and Limitations of Rationality in Social Interaction' (2003) 26 Behavioral and Brain Sciences 139; Ananish Chaudhuri, 'Sustaining Cooperation in Laboratory Public Goods Experiments. A Selective Survey of the Literature' (2011) 14 Experimental Economics 47.

[22] See, e.g., Elinor Ostrom, *Governing the Commons. The Evolution of Institutions for Collective Action* (Cambridge University Press 1990); Elinor Ostrom et al. (eds.), *The Drama of the Commons* (National Academy Press 2002); Joseph Henrich and Robert Boyd, '"Economic Man" in Cross-Cultural Perspective. Behavioral Experiments in 15 Small-Scale Societies' (2005) 28 Behavioral and Brain Sciences 795.

[23] Christoph Engel and Lilia Zhurakhovska, 'When is the Risk of Cooperation Worth Taking? The Prisoner's Dilemma as a Game of Multiple Motives' (2016) 23 Applied Economics Letters 1157.

[24] Game theorists sometimes argue that even a prisoner's dilemma is not institution-free, in that the game is well-defined. I do not want to engage in this debate over semantics. I use the term institution-free as free from interventions with the intention to overcome the social dilemma.

the sake of the environment, while she herself pollutes that environment.[25] Every citizen is best off individually if others obey traffic rules while she drives at her own convenience.[26] Every citizen is best off individually if others are vigilant and stand up against rule violations while she ignores the signs of disorder.[27] Every citizen is best off individually if others respect her property while she appropriates whatever appeals to her.[28] But if no-one protects the environment, no-one follows traffic rules, no-one keeps disorder in check, and no-one respects property, the whole society is worse off. Everyone must find their individual ways to survive in a polluted environment, on chaotic streets, with the threat of violence, and with property at the mercy of thieves. Some may be able to create their own individual safety nets. But this is at best unnecessarily costly, and most likely quite imperfect.

Analysing such conflicts of life in terms of the 2 × 2 prisoner's dilemma provides the law with a justification for sovereign intervention, and with a recipe for the design of legal rules. If the economic model is appropriate, the socially undesirable outcome results from the fact that individual and social well-being fall apart. This invites interventions that change incentives. Threatening heedless citizens with criminal sanctions,[29] and the obligation to compensate victims for damages,[30] are ways of doing this. This is also where behavioural insights become relevant. If the original model is appropriate then behavioural research informs legal policy about the underlying social problem, and helps it design better interventions. If social preferences are sufficiently strong and robust, what looks like a prisoner's dilemma

[25] For background see, e.g., Daniel W Bromley, *Handbook of Environmental Economics* (Blackwell 1995).

[26] On the relationship between individual rationality and rule following see, e.g., Viktor Vanberg, 'Rational Choice, Rule-Following and Institutions' in Uskali Mäki, Bo Gustafsson, and Christian Knudsen (eds.), *Rationality, Institutions and Economic Methodology* (Routledge 1993) 171–200.; John C. Harsanyi, 'Rule Utilitarianism, Rights, Obligations and the Theory of Rational Behavior' in John Harsanyi (ed.), *Papers in Game Theory* (Springer 1982) 235–53.

[27] This result is referred to as the second-order prisoner's dilemma, Toshio Yamagishi, 'The Provision of a Sanctioning System as a Public Good' (1986) 51 Journal of Personality and Social Psychology 110; Douglas D. Heckathorn, 'Collective Action and the Second-Order Free-Rider Problem' (1989) 1 Rationality and Society 78.

[28] For a formal model see Gary Stanley Becker, 'Crime and Punishment. An Economic Approach' (1968) 76 Journal of Political Economy 169.

[29] This is the rationale of the deterrence theory of criminal law, see, e.g., Samuel Cameron, 'The Economics of Crime Deterrence. A Survey of Theory and Evidence' (1988) 41 Kyklos 301; Dieter Dölling et al., 'Is Deterrence Effective? Results of a Meta-Analysis of Punishment' (2009) 15 European Journal on Criminal Policy and Research 201; Steven N. Durlauf and Daniel Nagin, 'The Deterrent Effect of Imprisonment' in Philip J. Cook, Jens Ludwig, and Justin McCrary (eds.), *Controlling Crime: Strategies and Tradeoffs* (Chicago, Chicago University Press 2011) 43–94; Paul H. Robinson and John M. Darley, 'Does Criminal Law Deter? A Behavioural Science Investigation' (2004) 24 Oxford Journal of Legal Studies 173.

[30] This is the rationale for the deterrence theory of torts, see W. Jonathan Cardi, Randall D. Penfield, and Albert H. Yoon, 'Does Tort Law Deter Individuals? A Behavioral Science Study' (2012) 9 Journal of Empirical Legal Studies 567; Theodore Eisenberg, 'Measuring the Deterrent Effect of Punitive Damages' (1998) 87 Georgetown Law Journal 347; Theodore Eisenberg and Christoph Engel, 'Assuring Civil Damages Adequately Deter. A Public Good Experiment' (2014) 11 Journal of Empirical Legal Studies 301.

in pay-off space may not be one in utility space.[31] As long as the dilemma does not become salient, citizens may also not immediately grasp the dilemma structure of the conflict and may maintain a socially beneficial cooperation routine.[32] If a sufficient fraction of the population holds at least weak social preferences, imperfect sanctions may compensate for this weakness, rather than being pointless (which they would for hard-nosed profit maximisers).[33]

But is it appropriate to analyse such conflicts of life in terms of a 2 × 2 prisoner's dilemma? The match seems intuitive. But does it abstract from elements of reality that are critical for the normative assessment and reaction? The model makes a lot of assumptions. Interaction is anonymous. There is no communication. It is not possible to solve the conflict by agreement. There is no room for third-party intervention. Interaction is one-shot only. It is an interaction between two individuals only. Each individual has to make a yes or no decision and cannot make intermediate choices. There are no dynamics.

All these assumptions matter for the dissolution of cooperation problems. Individuals are less selfish if they are identified.[34] Communication increases willingness to take others' legitimate interests into account.[35] If people are able to choose their partners, or are matched to similar partners, they cooperate more.[36] A credible threat with third-party intervention almost perfectly removes the dilemma.[37] If the interaction is repeated (and the end of the relationship is uncertain), theory predicts multiple equilibria, including perfect cooperation.[38] If the

31 For this modelling strategy see, e.g., John Geanakoplos, David W. Pearce, and Ennio Stacchetti, 'Psychological Games and Sequential Rationality' (1989) 1 Games and Economic Behavior 60.

32 On inertia resulting from routines see Tilmann Betsch et al., 'Has the World Changed? My Neighbor Might Know. Effects of Social Context on Routine Deviation' (2014) 28 Journal of Behavioral Decision Making 50.

33 Christoph Engel, 'Social Preferences Can Make Imperfect Sanctions Work. Evidence from a Public Good Experiment' (2014) 108 Journal of Economic Behavior and Organization 343

34 Terence C. Burnham, 'Engineering Altruism. A Theoretical and Experimental Investigation of Anonymity and Gift Giving' (2003) 50 Journal of Economic Behavior and Organization 133; Martin Dufwenberg and Astri Muren, 'Generosity, Anonymity, Gender' (2006) 61 Journal of Economic Behavior and Organization 42; Francisco Alpizar, Fredrik Carlsson and Olof Johansson-Stenman, 'Anonymity, Reciprocity, and Conformity. Evidence from Voluntary Contributions to a National Park in Costa Rica' (2008) 92 Journal of Public Economics 1047.

35 Daniel Balliet, 'Communication and Cooperation in Social Dilemmas: A Meta-analytic Review' (2010) 54 Journal of Conflict Resolution 39; Oliver Bochet, Talbot Page, and Louis Putterman, 'Communication and Punishment in Voluntary Contribution Experiments' (2006) 60 Journal of Economic Behavior and Organization 11; Vincent Crawford, 'A Survey of Experiments on Communication via Cheap Talk' (1998) 78 J Econ Theory 286.

36 Simon Gächter and Christian Thöni, 'Social Learning and Voluntary Cooperation among Like-minded People' (2005) 3 Journal of the European Economic Association 303.

37 Josef Falkinger et al., 'A Simple Mechanism for the Efficient Provision of Public Goods. Experimental Evidence' (2000) 90 American Economic Review 247.

38 Robert J. Aumann, Michael Maschler, and Richard E. Stearns, *Repeated Games with Incomplete Information* (MIT Press 1995). Empirically, results are less simple. If there is no institutional backing, cooperation tends to decrease over time. If there is room for disciplining free-riders, for instance by individuals engaging in costly punishment, it increases over time. Ernst Fehr and Simon Gächter, 'Cooperation and Punishment in Public Goods Experiments' (2000) 90 American Economic Review 980.

individual dilemma is embedded in a social context, social norms matter more.[39] Individuals tend to cooperate imperfectly,[40] and are therefore more likely to co-operate if they are not facing a yes or no decision. Cooperation is a social phenomenon that evolves over historical time.[41]

It seems that all these assumptions are violated if the prisoner's dilemma is used to analyse legal problems. Individuals either know each other in the first place, or they could at least communicate. Before they let a conflict escalate, they could talk to each other. Private law makes it possible to write contracts on almost anything, and certainly on promises that make the world a better place. Such contracts can be enforced in court. Even if individuals do not rely on the legal system, they can exploit the fact that they interact with each other repeatedly. This makes it possible to build reputation. None of the conflicts listed at the beginning of this section is between just two individuals. All of them engage large communities. All conflicts happen in historical time and context so that there is room for socially desirable solutions to evolve. Seemingly, modelling these conflicts of life as 2 × 2 prisoner's dilemma is therefore grossly misplaced. These conflicts of life seemingly are just not the right habitat for the model. The legal analyst should search for another animal in the zoo of models that is better adapted to these living conditions.

Yet I want to claim that this conclusion should not be drawn. Modern societies are characterised by a pronounced degree of generalised trust.[42] Most individuals are willing to engage with strangers, even in the absence of formal institutional safeguards against the risk of being exploited. Generalised trust has multiple sources, including the family,[43] civil society,[44] and the fabric of neighbourhoods.[45] It has been shown to react to personal experience,[46] which is why immigrants tend to adopt the degree of generalised trust in high-trust countries.[47] And, most

39 On conditions for and the effect of guilt aversion see, e.g., Martin Dufwenberg, Simon Gächter, and Heike Hennig-Schmidt, 'The Framing of Games and the Psychology of Play' (2011) 73 Games and Economic Behavior 459.

40 Urs Fischbacher and Simon Gächter, 'Social Preferences, Beliefs, and the Dynamics of Free Riding in Public Good Experiments' (2010) 100 American Economic Review 541.

41 Joseph Henrich and Robert Boyd (eds.), *Foundations of Human Sociality. Economic Experiments and Ethnographic Evidence from Fifteen Small-Scale Societies* (Oxford University Press 2004).

42 For cross-country comparisons see Christian Bjørnskov, 'Determinants of Generalized Trust. A Cross-country Comparison' (2007) 130 Public Choice 1; Pamela Paxton, 'Association Memberships and Generalized Trust. A Multilevel Model Across 31 Countries' (2007) 86 Social Forces 47; Tim Reeskens and Marc Hooghe, 'Cross-cultural Measurement Equivalence of Generalized Trust. Evidence from the European Social Survey (2002 and 2004)' (2008) 85 Social Indicators Research 515.

43 Eric M. Uslaner, 'Where you Stand Depends upon Where your Grandparents Sat. The Inheritability of Generalized Trust' (2008) 72 Public Opinion Quarterly 725.

44 Paxton (n 42).

45 Melissa J. Marschall and Dietlind Stolle, 'Race and the City. Neighborhood Context and the Development of Generalized Trust' (2004) 26 Political Behavior 125.

46 Jennifer L. Glanville and Pamela Paxton, 'How Do We Learn to Trust? A Confirmatory Tetrad Analysis of the Sources of Generalized Trust' (2007) 70 Social Psychology Quarterly 230; Paul A.M. Van Lange, 'Generalized Trust. Four Lessons from Genetics and Culture' (2015) 24 Current Directions in Psychological Science 71.

47 Peter Thisted Dinesen and Marc Hooghe, 'When in Rome, Do as the Romans Do. The Acculturation of Generalized Trust Among Immigrants in Western Europe' (2010) 44 International

importantly for the present context, there is a relationship between formal legal institutions and the level of generalised trust in a country.[48] If a country is characterised by a high degree of generalised trust, typically appropriate formal institutions and perceived trust are complements.[49] They reinforce each other.[50] Important institutional determinants include the perceived honesty of public officials, democratic representation, policies caring for the needs of the less affluent,[51] the reliability of property rights, and labour market institutions.[52]

Through these channels, pervasive institutional intervention ensures that individual citizens are empowered, and often are even forced to decide as if they were engaged in a naked 2 × 2 prisoner's dilemma with every other member of society.[53] I argue that this is both the purpose and the socially most beneficial effect of the institutional fabric of modern societies. Individuals are freed up to interact as if they were in a state of nature with most other citizens most of the time. Despite the fact that it will technically often be possible to create an explicit and formal ad-hoc regime, most of the time most individuals choose not to do so. This willingness to engage with strangers is an important source of wealth that distinguishes modern from more traditional societies. It enables exponentially more complex social relations, and a much more progressive division of labour.

Note that, ironically, it is precisely heavy-handed and multifaceted institutional intervention that makes it possible for individuals to interact as if they were in an institution-free environment. But for the most part, these rich institutional arrangements serve a different purpose. They do not align individual rationality with social rationality in the individual, ad-hoc relationship with a stranger. Rather, they create and sustain a degree of generalised trust that frees individuals up to interact with strangers on the spot, despite the fact that they have no guarantee that these strangers will act cooperatively.

Migration Review 697. Peter Thisted Dinesen, 'Parental Transmission of Trust or Perceptions of Institutional Fairness. Generalized Trust of Non-western Immigrants in a High-trust Society' (2012) 44 Comparative Politics 273

48 Bo Rothstein and Dietlind Stolle, 'The State and Social Capital. An Institutional Theory of Generalized Trust' (2008) 40 Comparative Politics 441; Peter Thisted Dinesen, 'Where You Come from or Where You Live? Examining the Cultural and Institutional Explanation of Generalized Trust Using Migration as a Natural Experiment' (2011) 29 European Sociological Review 114.

49 Blaine G. Robbins, 'Neither Government nor Community Alone. A Test of State-centered Models of Generalized Trust' (2011) 23 Rationality and Society 304.

50 Blaine G. Robbins, 'Institutional Quality and Generalized Trust. A Nonrecursive Causal Model' (2012) 107 Social Indicators Research 235.

51 Markus Freitag and Marc Bühlmann, 'Crafting Trust. The Role of Political Institutions in a Comparative Perspective' (2009) 42 Comparative Political Studies 1537.

52 Blaine G. Robbins, 'A Blessing and a Curse? Political Institutions in the Growth and Decay of Generalized Trust. A Cross-national Panel Analysis, 1980–2009' (2012) 7 PloS One e35120.

53 A related claim has been made by Kim Mannemar Sønderskov, 'Explaining Large-N Cooperation. Generalized Social Trust and the Social Exchange Heuristic' (2011) 23 Rationality and Society 51; Kim Mannemar Sønderskov, 'Different Goods, Different Effects. Exploring the Effects of Generalized Social Trust in Large-N Collective Action' (2009) 140 Public Choice 145.

Let me substantiate this claim for the first assumption, anonymity. In modern societies it is often technically impossible, prohibitively costly, or normatively undesirable to learn the identity of an interaction partner. It is technically impossible if interaction is on the spot, as on the streets. Finding out who has contributed to a degradation of air is not possible because contributions to the social harm are diffuse.[54] In an open society, immigrants benefit from public goods, and it is ex ante not clear who might engage in socially undesirable behaviour at a later point. Finally, many actions of those living today impact on the quality and the quantity of public goods enjoyed by future generations. Since they are not yet born, they also cannot have a say on today's choices.

Even if the identity of an interaction partner could technically be verified, in modern societies this is often prohibitively costly. Take a franchise chain. Bad behaviour by any franchisee can jeopardise the brand-name capital. But if the franchise chain is large, no individual member can afford to monitor the behaviour of all other members. The cost argument is even more compelling on the Internet. The gains from trade for most micro-transactions would be below the cost of verifying identity.

Finally, for competing normative reasons, the legal order not so rarely guarantees anonymity. This, for instance, holds for whistle-blowers, for job applicants if there is a concern about discrimination, for participants in manifestations that shall not be deterred by a chilling effect, or for privacy reasons. The police will, for instance, usually not disclose the name and address registered for the number plate of a car.

For the same list of reasons, communication between members of society is often not feasible before both of them take action. This can again be technically impossible, for instance among those participating in street traffic. It can be prohibitively costly, for instance, among those engaging in micro-transactions over the Internet. And it can be normatively undesirable, for instance, between a potential employer and a job applicant. If there is no communication, there is also no room for an ex ante agreement. In situations that force anonymity, third-party intervention is impractical; it would at minimum require that the defendant is identified. Since individuals do not know with whom they interact, no long-term relationship may be formed. There is no room for the evolution of a relationship-specific regime.

The foregoing considerations show that in modern societies it is not rare that individuals interact with each other in a way that is essentially the same as interaction among two strangers in a state of nature. To the extent that this seems an appropriate model, the legal assessment of the need for intervention, and the design of interventions, can be guided by economic thinking about the

[54] On the importance of diffuse relationships see Mancur Olson, *The Logic of Collective Action. Public Goods and the Theory of Groups* vol. 124, (Harvard University Press 1965)

simultaneous 2 × 2 prisoner's dilemma. If this is the case, behavioural research becomes critical. As I have explained, the model is appropriate since a complex arrangement of formal and informal institutions has created generalised trust. It would be surprising if individuals were widely willing to trust an environment in which they stand a serious risk of being exploited. Now this is what neoclassical theory predicts for a simultaneous 2 × 2 prisoner's dilemma. Generalised trust is only a plausible source of tolerating a quasi state of nature if it comes with sufficiently strong behavioural qualifications that contain the risk of exploitation.[55] Hence my argument makes a case for behavioural law and economics, while it does not do so for neoclassical law and economics.[56]

While there is thus scope for behavioural law and economics (of the simultaneous 2 × 2 prisoner's dilemma), this model is not appropriate for the legal analysis of each and every relationship that can be modelled this way. The model is, for instance, inappropriate if the parties to the interaction are easily identified. One area for which this holds is financial stability. Instability may result from the choices of financial intermediaries fighting against each other for profit. But the number of relevant players is small in these markets. They are relatively easy to identify. To the extent that antitrust does not make this illegal, these players might contain the dilemma by ex ante contractual arrangements. The financial markets are of course institutionally embedded. But arguably these institutions are not meant to create generalised trust among financial intermediaries. On the other hand, the behavioural effects that help reduce the risk of exploitation among individuals are at least not directly applicable to the decisions made on behalf of financial intermediaries as complex legal entities.[57]

But for other conflicts of law, a behavioural law and economics approach that models the interaction as a simultaneous 2 × 2 prisoner's dilemma has a considerably better fit. This holds for problems that are typically addressed by public law, like most problems of environmental law. It holds for problems typically addressed

[55] Sønderskov (n 53) claims that, as a result of generalised trust, individuals rely in large-*N* cooperation problems on a social exchange heuristic.

[56] Behaviour is of course not necessarily socially minded. Individuals have been shown to be rivalistic; see, e.g., Wim B. Liebrand and Charles G. McClintock, 'The Ring Measure of Social Values. A Computerized Procedure for Assessing Individual Differences in Information Processing and Social Value Orientation' (1988) 2 European Journal of Personality 217, or spiteful, see, e.g. Klaus Abbink and Karim Sadrieh, 'The Pleasure of Being Nasty' (2009) 105 Economics Letters 306. Containing such socially disruptive behavioural inclinations is an important task for institutions. But without allowing for socially beneficial behavioural inclinations, the dismal predictions of the prisoner's dilemma would eventuate. If this is what good-natured individuals experience or expect, many of them will shy away from acting in a socially beneficial manner; see in particular Urs Fischbacher, Simon Gächter, and Ernst Fehr, 'Are People Conditionally Cooperative? Evidence from a Public Goods Experiment' (2001) 71 Economics Letters 397.

[57] On the behaviour of such corporate actors see Christoph Engel, 'The Behaviour of Corporate Actors. How Much can we Learn from the Experimental Literature?' (2010) 6 Journal of Institutional Economics 445.

by private law, like the governance structure of a franchise chain. And it holds for problems typically addressed by criminal law, like following rules.

IV. The Proper Scope of Behavioural Law and Economics

Behavioural law and economics is an interdisciplinary venture. It capitalises on the burgeoning field of behavioural and experimental economics. To a considerable degree, the power of behavioural economics originates in its rigour. Most of the experimental evidence has been generated as tests of models that modify economic games. These models either assume utility functions that transcend profit maximisation, or they assume well-defined, non-standard ways of reacting to information. Legal analysts and policy makers potentially have a lot to gain from applying these powerful conceptual tools to their problems, and by relying on the rich body of experimental evidence to predict the effect of legal interventions.

This transfer of tools and findings from economics, however, presupposes that the models that underlie the exercise are appropriate for the analysis of normative legal problems. This fit cannot be taken for granted. In economics, the models, and their experimental tests, have been created in an attempt at uncovering basic building blocks of human behaviour. In the interest of identifying mechanisms and effects cleanly, the models are highly parsimonious. Experimental tests deliberately abstract from almost all features of the conflicts of life that motivate the investigation. They do so because random assignment to treatment only makes it possible to identify causal effects if baseline and treatment differ by no more than a single feature. The typical experiment completely removes context and exposes participants to a very simple, but usually strategic, choice problem. An illustration is the simultaneous 2×2 prisoner's dilemma.

Many simplifications that are made for the sake of precise theorising and rigorous testing seem to be at odds with lawyers' normative research question. Lawyers intend to define the need for institutional intervention, and find the best institutional design, to address a conflict of life. These conflicts materialise in societies that are rich in informal and formal institutions. The citizens of modern countries never see the institution-free state of nature that behavioural economics assumes.

In this chapter I argue that the insights and findings from behavioural economics are nonetheless valuable for many, but not for all legal problems that could be modelled as simple games. These models are appropriate if citizens interact with each other without having any precise knowledge about the personality or individual context of their interaction partners. It is precisely the rich set of informal and formal institutions that makes room for such interaction. It has the effect of creating generalised trust. If individuals are sufficiently confident that nothing too bad will happen, they are freed up to interact with strangers as if they were in a state of nature.

I have spelt out my argument for conflicts of life that can be modelled as a simultaneous 2 × 2 prisoner's dilemma, but the argument equally holds for other simple games, like coordination problems. The critical question is not the definition of the game but the willingness of individuals to take the risk of interaction without ex ante creating a relation-specific set of institutions. The willingness to do so is key for the success of modern societies. It dramatically reduces transaction cost and increases division of labour. Yet since generalised trust is a precondition, these problems are not adequately modelled assuming that individuals care about personal profit exclusively. If that were the case, individuals would shy away from interacting with strangers whom they anticipate will exploit them. For understanding such situations, and for designing appropriate legal safeguards, it is essential to shift from neoclassical to behavioural law and economics.

References

Abbink, Klaus and Karim Sadrieh (2009). 'The Pleasure of Being Nasty' Economics Letters 105(3): 306–08.

Ahn, K.T., Elinor Ostrom, David Schmidt, Robert Shupp, and James Walker (2001). 'Cooperation in PD games. Fear, Greed, and History of Play' Public Choice 106: 137–55.

Alpizar, Francisco, Fredrik Carlsson, and Olof Johansson-Stenman (2008). 'Anonymity, Reciprocity, and Conformity. Evidence from Voluntary Contributions to a National Park in Costa Rica' Journal of Public Economics 92(5): 1047–60.

Anderson, Craig A. and Brad J. Bushman (1997). 'External Validity of "Trivial" Experiments. The Case of Laboratory Aggression' Review of General Psychology 1(1): 19–41.

Aumann, Robert J., Michael Maschler, and Richard E. Stearns (1995). *Repeated Games with Incomplete Information*. Cambridge, MA: MIT Press.

Baird, Douglas G., Robert H. Gertner ,and Randal C. Picker (1994). *Game Theory and the Law*. Cambridge, MA: Harvard University Press.

Balliet, Daniel (2010). 'Communication and Cooperation in Social Dilemmas: A Meta-analytic Review' Journal of Conflict Resolution 54(1): 39–57.

Becker, Gary Stanley (1968). 'Crime and Punishment. An Economic Approach' Journal of Political Economy 76: 169–217.

Betsch, Tilmann, Stefanie Lindow, Christoph Engel, Corina Ulshöfer, and Janet Kleber (2014). 'Has the World Changed? My Neighbor Might Know. Effects of Social Context on Routine Deviation' Journal of Behavioral Decision Making 28: 50–66.

Bjørnskov, Christian (2007). 'Determinants of Generalized Trust. A Cross-country Comparison' Public Choice 130(1): 1–21.

Bochet, Oliver, Talbot Page, and Louis Putterman (2006). 'Communication and Punishment in Voluntary Contribution Experiments' Journal of Economic Behavior & Organization 60: 11–26.

Bracht, Glenn H. glass, and Gene V. Glass (1968). 'The External Validity of Experiments' American Educational Research Journal 5(4): 437–74.

Bromley, Daniel W. (1995). *Handbook of Environmental Economics* Oxford: Blackwell.

Burnham, Terence C. (2003). 'Engineering Altruism. A Theoretical and Experimental Investigation of Anonymity and Gift Giving' Journal of Economic Behavior & Organization 50: 133–44.

Calder, Bobby J, Lynn W. Phillips, and Alice M. Tybout (1982). 'The Concept of External Validity' Journal of Consumer Research 9(3): 240–44.

Camerer, Colin F. (2003). *Behavioral Game Theory. Experiments in Strategic Interaction.* New York, NY: Sage.

Camerer, Colin F. and Teck Hua Ho (1999). 'Experience-Weighted Attraction Learning in Normal Form Games' Econometrica 67(4): 827–74.

Cameron, Samuel (1988). 'The Economics of Crime Deterrence. A Survey of Theory and Evidence' Kyklos 41: 301–23.

Cardi, W. Jonathan, Randall D. Penfield and Albert H. Yoon (2012). 'Does Tort Law Deter Individuals? A Behavioral Science Study' Journal of Empirical Legal Studies 9: 567–603.

Chaudhuri, Ananish (2011). 'Sustaining Cooperation in Laboratory Public Goods Experiments. A Selective Survey of the Literature' Experimental Economics 14(1): 47–83.

Coase, Ronald (1960). 'The Problem of Social Cost.' Journal of Law and Economics 3: 1–44.

Colman, Andrew M. (2003). 'Cooperation, Psychological Game Theory, and Limitations of Rationality in Social Interaction' Behavioral and Brain Sciences 26: 139–98.

Cooter, Robert and Thomas Ulen (2012). Law and Economics. Upper Saddle River, NJ: Prentice Hall.

Crawford, Vincent (1998). 'A Survey of Experiments on Communication via Cheap Talk' Journal of Economic Theory 78(2): 286–98.

Daston, Lorraine and Peter Galison (2007). *Objectivity*. Cambridge, MA: Zone Books.

David, Marian (2010). 'The Correspondence Theory of Truth.' *Stanford Encyclopedia of Philosophy* (Center for the Study of Language and Information (CSLI), Stanford University.

Dinesen, Peter Thisted (2011). 'Where you Come from or Where you Live? Examining the Cultural and Institutional Explanation of Generalized Trust Using Migration as a Natural Experiment' European Sociological Review 29(1): 114–28.

Dinesen, Peter Thisted (2012). 'Parental Transmission of Trust or Perceptions of Institutional Fairness. Generalized Trust of Non-western Immigrants in a High-trust Society' Comparative Politics 44(3): 273–89.

Dinesen, Peter Thisted and Marc Hooghe (2010). 'When in Rome, Do as the Romans Do. The Acculturation of Generalized Trust Among Immigrants in Western Europe' International Migration Review 44(3): 697–727.

Dölling, Dieter, Horst Entorf, Dieter Hermann. and Thomas Rupp (2009). 'Is Deterrence Effective? Results of a Meta-Analysis of Punishment' European Journal on Criminal Policy and Research 15(1): 201–24.

Dufwenberg, Martin, Simon Gächter and Heike Hennig-Schmidt (2011). 'The Framing of Games and the Psychology of Play' Games and Economic Behavior 73: 459–78.

Dufwenberg, Martin and Astri Muren (2006). 'Generosity, Anonymity, Gender' Journal of Economic Behavior & Organization 61: 4249.

Durlauf, Steven N. and Daniel Nagin (2011). 'The Deterrent Effect of Imprisonment' in P. J. Cook, J. Ludwig and J. McCrary (eds), *Controlling Crime: Strategies and Tradeoffs.* (Chicago University Press) 43–94.

Eisenberg, Theodore (1998). 'Measuring the Deterrent Effect of Punitive Damages' Georgetown Law Journal 87: 347–58.

Eisenberg, Theodore and Christoph Engel (2014). 'Assuring Civil Damages Adequately Deter. A Public Good Experiment' Journal of Empirical Legal Studies 11: 301–49.

Engel, Christoph (2006). *Julius Hermann von Kirchmann: Die Wertlosigkeit der Jurisprudenz als Wissenschaft*. Berlin 1848. 61: 614–14.
Engel, Christoph (2010). 'The Behaviour of Corporate Actors. How Much can we Learn from the Experimental Literature?' Journal of Institutional Economics 6: 445–75.
Engel, Christoph (2014). 'Social Preferences Can Make Imperfect Sanctions Work. Evidence from a Public Good Experiment' Journal of Economic Behavior & Organization 108: 343–53.
Engel, Christoph (2018). 'Empirical Methods for the Law' Journal of Institutional and Theoretical Economics 174: 5–23.
Engel, Christoph and Lilia Zhurakhovska (2016). 'When is the Risk of Cooperation Worth Taking? The Prisoner's Dilemma as a Game of Multiple Motives' Applied Economics Letters 23: 1157–61.
Falkinger, Josef, Ernst Fehr, Simon Gächter, and Rudolf Winter-Ebmer (2000). 'A Simple Mechanism for the Efficient Provision of Public Goods. Experimental Evidence' American Economic Review 90: 247–64.
Fehr, Ernst and Simon Gächter (2000). 'Cooperation and Punishment in Public Goods Experiments' American Economic Review 90: 980–94.
Fehr, Ernst and Klaus M. Schmidt (2006). 'The Economics of Fairness, Reciprocity and Altruism. Experimental Evidence and New Theories.' Handbook on the Economics of Giving, Reciprocity and Altruism 1: 615–91.
Feldman, Allan M. (1997). *Welfare Economics and Social Choice Theory*. Boston, MA: Kluwer.
Fischbacher, Urs and Simon Gächter (2010). 'Social Preferences, Beliefs, and the Dynamics of Free Riding in Public Good Experiments' American Economic Review 100: 541–56.
Fischbacher, Urs, Simon Gächter, and Ernst Fehr (2001). 'Are People Conditionally Cooperative? Evidence from a Public Goods Experiment.' Economics Letters 71: 397–404.
Frantz, Roger, Shu-Heng Chen, Kurt Dopfer, Floris Heukelom, and Shabnam Mousavi (2016). *Routledge Handbook of Behavioral Economics*. London: Routledge.
Freitag, Markus and Marc Bühlmann (2009). 'Crafting Trust. The Role of Political Institutions in a Comparative Perspective.' Comparative Political Studies 42(12): 1537–66.
Gächter, Simon and Christian Thöni (2005). 'Social Learning and Voluntary Cooperation among Like-minded People' Journal of the European Economic Association 3(2–3): 303–14.
Geanakoplos, John, David W. Pearce and Ennio Stacchetti (1989). 'Psychological Games and Sequential Rationality' Games and Economic Behavior 1(1): 60–79.
Glanville, Jennifer L. and Pamela Paxton (2007). 'How Do We Learn to Trust? A Confirmatory Tetrad Analysis of the Sources of Generalized Trust' Social Psychology Quarterly 70(3): 230–42.
Hardin, Garrett (1968). 'The Tragedy of the Commons' Science 162: 1243–48.
Harsanyi, John C. (1982). *Rule Utilitarianism, Rights, Obligations and the Theory of Rational Behavior. Papers in Game Theory*. J. Harsanyi, Springer: 235–53.
Heckathorn, Douglas D. (1989). 'Collective Action and the Second-Order Free-Rider Problem' Rationality and Society 1: 78–100.
Henrich, Joseph and Robert Boyd (eds.) (2004). *Foundations of Human Sociality. Economic Experiments and Ethnographic Evidence from Fifteen Small-Scale Societies*. Oxford: Oxford University Press.
Henrich, Joseph and Robert Boyd (2005). '"Economic Man" in Cross-Cultural Perspective. Behavioral Experiments in 15 Small-Scale Societies' Behavioral and Brain Sciences 28: 795–815.

Kelsen, Hans (1953). *Was ist die reine Rechtslehre? Demokratie und Rechtsstaat. Festgabe zum 60. Geburtstag von Zaccaria Giacometti*. Zürich: Polygraphischer Verlag, 143–62.

Levenbook, Barbara Baum (1984). 'The Role of Coherence in Legal Reasoning' Law and Philosophy 3: 355-374.

Liebrand, Wim B. and Charles G. McClintock (1988). 'The Ring Measure of Social Values. A Computerized Procedure for Assessing Individual Differences in Information Processing and Social Value Orientation' European Journal of Personality 2: 217–30.

Lucas, Jeffrey W. (2003). 'Theory-testing, Generalization, and the Problem of External Validity' Sociological Theory 21(3): 236–53.

Lynch Jr, John G. (1982). 'On the External Validity of Experiments in Consumer Research' Journal of Consumer Research 9(3): 225–39.

MacCormick, Neil (1984). 'Coherence in Legal Justification'. *Theory of Legal Science*. (Springer) 235–51.

Marschall, Melissa J. and Dietlind Stolle (2004). 'Race and the City. Neighborhood Context and the Development of Generalized Trust' Political Behavior 26(2): 125–53.

Mitchell, Gregory (2012). 'Revisiting Truth or Triviality. The External Validity of Research in the Psychological Laboratory' Perspectives on Psychological Science 7(2): 109–17.

Olson, Mancur (1965). *The Logic of Collective Action. Public Goods and the Theory of Groups*. Cambridge, MA: Harvard University Press.

Ostrom, Elinor (1990). *Governing the Commons. The Evolution of Institutions for Collective Action*. New York, NY: Cambridge University Press.

Ostrom, Elinor, Thomas Dietz, Nives Dolsak, Paul C. Stern, Susan Stonich, and Elke U. Weber (eds.) (2002). *The Drama of the Commons*. Washington, DC: National Academy Press.

Paxton, Pamela (2007). 'Association Memberships and Generalized Trust. A Multilevel Model Across 31 Countries' Social Forces 86(1): 47–76.

Peczenik, Aleksander (1994). 'Law, Morality, Coherence and Truth' Ratio Juris 7: 146-176.

Posner, Richard A. (2014). *Economic Analysis of Law*. New York, NY: Aspen Publishers.

Rapoport, Anatol and Albert M. Chammah (1965). *Prisoner's Dilemma. A Study in Conflict and Cooperation*. Ann Arbor, MI: University of Michigan Press.

Reeskens, Tim and Marc Hooghe (2008). 'Cross-cultural Measurement Equivalence of Generalized Trust. Evidence from the European Social Survey (2002 and 2004)' Social Indicators Research 85(3): 515–32.

Robbins, Blaine G. (2011). 'Neither Government nor Community Alone. A Test of State-centered Models of Generalized Trust' Rationality and Society 23(3): 304–46.

Robbins, Blaine G. (2012a). 'A Blessing and a Curse? Political Institutions in the Growth and Decay of Generalized Trust. A Cross-national Panel Analysis, 1980–2009' PloS One 7(4): e35120.

Robbins, Blaine G. (2012b). 'Institutional Quality and Generalized Trust. A Nonrecursive Causal Model' Social Indicators Research 107(2): 235–58.

Robinson, Paul H. and John M. Darley (2004). 'Does Criminal Law Deter? A Behavioural Science Investigation' Oxford Journal of Legal Studies 24: 173–205.

Rothstein, Bo and Dietlind Stolle (2008). 'The State and Social Capital. An Institutional Theory of Generalized Trust' Comparative Politics 40(4): 441–59.

Scharpf, Fritz Wilhelm (1997). *Games Real Actors Play. Actor-Centered Institutionalism in Policy Research*. Boulder, CO: Westview Press.

Schram, Arthur (2005). 'Artificiality. The Tension Between Internal and External Validity in Economic Experiments' Journal of Economic Methodology 12(2): 225–37.

Sønderskov, Kim Mannemar (2009). 'Different Goods, Different Effects. Exploring the Effects of Generalized Social Trust in Large-N Collective Action' Public Choice 140(1–2): 145–60.

Sønderskov, Kim Mannemar (2011). 'Explaining Large-N Cooperation. Generalized Social Trust and the Social Exchange Heuristic' Rationality and Society 23: 51–74.

Uslaner, Eric M (2008). 'Where You Stand Depends upon Where Your Grandparents Sat. The Inheritability of Generalized Trust' Public Opinion Quarterly 72(4): 725–40.

Van Lange, Paul A.M. (2015) 'Generalized Trust. Four Lessons from Genetics and Culture' Current Directions in Psychological Science 24(1): 71–6.

Vanberg, Viktor (1993). 'Rational Choice, Rule-Following and Institutions'. in U. Mäki, B. Gustafsson and C. Knudsen (eds), *Rationality, Institutions and Economic Methodology*. (Routledge) 171–200.

von Kirchmann, Julius (1848). *Die Wertlosigkeit der Jurisprudenz als Wissenschaft*. Berlin: Springer.

Yamagishi, Toshio (1986). 'The Provision of a Sanctioning System as a Public Good' Journal of Personality and Social Psychology 51: 110–16.

Zamir, Eyal and Doron Teichman (2014). *The Oxford Handbook of Behavioral Economics and the Law*. New York, NY: Oxford University Press.

Zeiler, Kathryn And Joshua C. Teitelbaum (2017). *Research Handbook of Behavioral Law and Economics*. Cheltenham: Edward Elgar.

2

Rational Choice and its Limits for the Solution of Social and Legal Problems

Three Observations on Behavioural Law and Economics

Simon Deakin

Abstract: This chapter addresses a number of methodological issues arising from the behavioural turn in law and economics and its claim to have established more realistic foundations for both positive and normative analysis. The first is whether models are necessarily better for being more realistic. Friedman's proposal that the less realistic a model, the more useful it is as a basis for the identification of hypotheses, is rejected on the grounds that this is liable to direct research down fruitless or even erroneous paths. However, models such as the rationality axiom remain approximations of reality, not revealed truths. This leads on to a consideration of the second issue which is whether behavioural research should lead us to reject the rationality axiom. The claim that human beings are systematically wrong in their decision making is shown to be theoretically unsound and empirically unproven. Rather, theory and empirics alike suggest that rationality has a basis in social learning and institutional framing. The third issue concerns the normative conclusions to be drawn from behavioural law and economics. It is suggested that empirical research does not justify privileging 'libertarian paternalism' over alternative approaches to law and regulation. In the era of surveillance capitalism and the panoptic state, it is more than timely to reflect on the merits of collective learning and participatory decision making, democratic practices with adaptive qualities neglected by behavioural law and economics.

I. Introduction

The premise of behavioural law and economics ('BLE') is the need to modify the rational actor model to take into account empirical insights from psychology in general, and 'dual process' theory in particular.[1] Over two decades on from the

[1] Daniel Kahneman, *Thinking Fast and Slow* (Penguin 2009).

Simon Deakin, *Rational Choice and its Limits for the Solution of Social and Legal Problems* In: *Theories of Choice*. Edited by: Stefan Grundmann and Philipp Hacker, Oxford University Press (2021).
DOI: 10.1093/oso/9780198863175.003.0003

foundational contribution by Christine Jolls, Cass Sunstein, and Richard Thaler[2] which opened up this field for law and economics research, it is evident that it has had a profound influence on legal scholarship and, via the concept of 'nudging', on public policy. There is now a vast literature applying the insights of dual process theory to law. However, behind the rise of behaviouralism in law and economics lie some methodological issues which are less frequently addressed. This chapter will look at three issues in particular.

The first is: are models necessarily better for being more realistic? It may seem odd to pose the question in this way: shouldn't legal scholars with an interdisciplinary orientation be among the first to incorporate into their work the insights of empirical research? And wasn't it about time for a correction to the rational actor model, which has been at the core of the modern neoclassical synthesis in economics, and hence in the economic analysis of law, since the middle decades of the twentieth century, given its patently unrealistic foundations? On closer inspection, this is too simplistic a view. In order for any field of empirical enquiry to progress, models, which are more or less unrealistic approximations of the world, are needed. Scientific method—and this includes the social and human sciences—proceeds on the basis of theoretical framing (hypothesis identification) first, followed by empirical testing (benchmarking the hypothesis against the data) second. Results should be regarded as provisional and open to error correction, a process which involves the refinement of models in the light of new data. But models remain models, not revealed truths, and there is inevitably a point at which a data-heavy model ceases to be useful in framing empirical enquiry. Viewed from this angle, the question we should be asking of BLE is not whether its account of human behaviour is more 'truthful' than the alternatives, but whether it is more useful. As we shall see, there is indeed a case to be made for its usefulness, but it is a qualified one.

The second question is this: what exactly have we learned from the range of behavioural studies now available? On balance, the answer is: less than is often claimed, bearing in mind that BLE is still an emerging research programme. Yes, there have been literally hundreds of experimental studies demonstrating flaws in the standard, mid-twentieth century account of rationality. And we are certainly learning a lot from them. But we cannot evaluate the worth of a scientific research programme by simply counting the number of published articles advancing a particular claim. To evaluate empirical research, we must unavoidably seek to understand how empirical results are reshaping or adjusting the theories which underlie the disciplinary paradigm in question. Here, there is quite some uncertainty over the contribution of BLE. This is because the findings of the empirical studies do not lend themselves to a single, uniquely correct reinterpretation of the basis of human behaviour. On the contrary, they are consistent with a number of different

[2] Cass R. Sunstein, Christine Jolls, and Richard H. Thaler, 'A Behavioral Approach to Law and Economics' (1998) 50 Stanford Law Review 1471.

theoretical framings of the rationality axiom, and actively inconsistent with certain theories (including evolutionary psychology) which have a significant claim to our attention, at least as significant as those (most notably dual process theory) which tend to be favoured by proponents of BLE. If there is any single message to emerge from what is now a vast body of empirical research, it is that the rationality axiom should be regarded as modified rather than refuted.

The third question is: how should we evaluate claims for the use of BLE in the design of institutions and policies, in particular 'nudge' theory? The answer to this question is linked to our consideration of the other two. The answer is that nudge theory is not entitled to any special or privileged treatment in public policy terms on the basis of its supposedly superior empirical foundation. This is because its empirical foundation remains contested. But even if there were greater consensus in the scientific community on the status of BLE-related research, the process of translating that research into policy through 'nudging' would still be highly contentious. That is because nudge theory prioritises individual decision making over collective agency in a way which owes little or nothing to science or empirics but a great deal to a particular political position which should be articulated, and defended, as such, by those who wish to advance it.

II. Models Should Be Realistic, but They Remain Models

From its earliest uses in classical political economy right through to its apotheosis in the modern neoclassical synthesis of the mid-twentieth century, the rational actor model was intended as an axiom adopted for the purpose of model building of a mostly mathematical nature. This is not to say that it was regarded as having no basis at all in observed behaviour. F.Y. Edgeworth's *Mathematical Psychics*, published in 1881, is one of the first texts to advance what came to be understood as a neoclassical account of rationality. Edgeworth proposed as 'the first principle of economics' that 'every agent is actuated by self-interest'.[3] This is one of a number of 'definitions' which Edgeworth formulates on the basis that they are self-evident. A footnote elliptically notes that they could equally well be regarded as 'descriptions rather, but sufficient for the purpose of these tentative studies'.[4]

Thus self-interest, in this foundational work, is not assumed without some justification; it is a psychological state synonymous with what Edgeworth, following the utilitarian philosophy of his time, called 'pleasure', but might just as well be referred to as subjective well-being. For the purpose of constructing his model, Edgeworth considered it sufficient to offer an approximation or simplification of

[3] F.Y. Edgeworth, *Mathematical Psychics: An Essay on the Application of Mathematics to the Moral Sciences* (Kegan Paul 1881) 16.

[4] Ibid. 16.

what he took to be a more complex psychological (i.e., material) reality. Other 'definitions' offered by Edgeworth in the same portion of the text are more social in nature, such as the proposition that 'there is free communication throughout a *normal* competitive field',[5] and some are institutional, such as the statement that 'any individual is free to *recontract* with another independently of, *without the consent* being required of, any third party'.[6] The existence of 'free communication', he suggests, is an 'ideal supposition' (he adds, 'you might suppose the constituent individuals collected at a point, or connected by telephones'), but one which is 'sufficiently approximate to existence or tendency for the purposes of abstract science'.[7] Edgeworth offers no equivalent comment on the relevance of the legal principle of freedom of contract (let alone the fine-grained jurisprudence of the doctrine of restraint of trade), perhaps because it was too obvious to be worth restating (Edgeworth was a non-practising barrister, and is described as 'barrister-at-law', rather than as a lecturer in logic, which was his main employment at the time, on the title page of *Mathematical Psychics*).

This is all leading up to Edgeworth's celebrated mathematical formulation of the 'contract curve' which describes 'in what directions [parties to an exchange] will consent to move together ... between their respective lines of indifference, in a direction positive as it may be called for both'.[8] Edgeworth understood his analysis to have revealed, through its mathematical representation of market-based exchange, a 'dynamical' principle of 'human action generally', in which the working of a 'gross force' is 'governed, let on and directed by a more delicate pleasure force'; in other words, the competitive market is both a force acting upon the behaviour of individual agents and also the consequence of their actions which are, in turn, the result of their 'self-interest'. In all this it was not without relevance that 'a perfect field of competition professes ... certain properties peculiarly favourable to mathematical calculation; namely, a certain indefinite multiplicity and dividedness, analogous to that infinity and infinitesimality which facilitate so large a portion of Mathematical Psychics (consider the theory of Atoms, and all applications of the Differential Calculus)'.[9]

At the point of its origins, then, the principle of rationality was a summary representation or condensation of an assumed material and social reality, which was used to drive the construction of a formal model which would reveal additional features of that reality. It was not a simple description but nor was it intended to be entirely divorced from the material and social context to which it was being applied. The mode of argumentation in which it was advanced consisted of the abstract mathematical representation of social forces, and one of the principal

5 Ibid. 18.
6 Ibid. 19. All emphases are in the original.
7 Ibid. 18.
8 Ibid. 22.
9 Ibid. 18.

justifications for its use, along with the related concept of perfect competition, was precisely that it facilitated this kind of deductive mathematical reasoning. There is no suggestion that it would be useful for other modes of inquiry or analysis.

Thus, Edgeworth did not claim at any point in *Mathematical Psychics* that the 'definitions' he used were based on empirical research which he or others had conducted. Nor did he draw any normative conclusions from them. As Peter Newman has pointed out,[10] Edgeworth did not intend to present the perfectly competitive market as a uniquely stable equilibrium; nor did he conceive of utility in entirely subjective terms, as is apparent from his discussion of the economics of redistribution, which reads now as distinctly Rawlsian.

Edgeworth certainly had a working method even if he was not very explicit about it. Milton Friedman, writing in 1950 at the high point of the neoclassical synthesis, was much clearer about his. In defending the apparent unreality of the neoclassical model he did not hold back: 'Truly important and significant hypotheses will be found to have "assumptions" that are wildly inaccurate descriptive representations of reality, and, in general, the more significant the theory, the more unrealistic the assumptions in this sense.'[11] The inversion of the supposed relationship between theory and reality is unavoidable because 'a hypothesis is important if it "explains" much by little, that is, if it abstracts the common and crucial elements from the mass of complex and detailed circumstances surrounding the phenomena to be explained and permits valid predictions on the basis of them alone'; it follows that 'to be important, a hypothesis must be descriptively false in its assumptions'.[12]

Can it really be the case that a theory is *more* useful the *less* realistic it is? This much cited but somewhat under-analysed passage needs to be read in the context of Friedman's overall argument. This is to make the case for an explicative or 'positive' social science which can then form the basis for a separate 'normative' science of policy making (he also identifies but does not discuss an 'art' of policy implementation). The method of the positive social sciences is to test theoretical claims using empirical methods. Theories and hypotheses are constructed out of 'categories' which owe more to formal logic than to description. At the same time, only 'factual evidence' can show whether the categories 'have a meaningful empirical counterpart, that is, whether they are useful in analysing a particular class of concrete problems'.[13] However, rather than showing that a theory is 'right' or 'wrong', the factual stage of the inquiry is used to assess whether it is 'tentatively accepted as "valid" or "rejected"'.[14] Following Popper's account of scientific progress

[10] Peter Newman, 'Francis Ysidro Edgeworth (1845–1926)' in Peter Newman (ed.), *F.Y. Edgeworth: Mathematical Psychics and Further Papers on Political Economy* (Oxford University Press 2003).

[11] Milton Friedman, 'The Methodology of Positive Economics' in Milton Friedman (ed.), *Essays in Positive Economics* (first published 1953, University of Chicago Press 1966) 14.

[12] Ibid. 15.

[13] Ibid. 7.

[14] Ibid. 8.

as the falsification of hypotheses,[15] Friedman argues that 'factual evidence can never "prove" a hypothesis, it can only fail to disprove it'.[16]

On this view, the rationality axiom only has to be posited as such to do its work. Its usefulness lies precisely in its simplicity. And as an axiom, its 'truth' is not at issue. The purpose of empirical testing is to benchmark the hypotheses which it generates. These can be invalidated by evidence—for example, there might be convincing evidence to show that employment rises, rather than falls, in response to the enactment of a minimum wage law. If that is the case, the hypothesis that 'minimum wages cause unemployment', which follows from the basic neoclassical axioms of rationality (maximisation and preference consistency, in the terminology used by Gary Becker)[17] and equilibrium, would need adjusting. It could be that a counter-hypothesis, for example, that 'minimum wage laws cause employment to rise in an imperfectly competitive market', might be advanced instead. But this would not require the abandonment of the underlying rationality axiom (which would simply imply, here, that workers and employers act according to their own separate interests when contracting).

It is Friedman's inversion principle which seems to go too far. This implies that there is no point at which the loss of factual veracity undermines the value of the theory. And indeed, elsewhere in the same paper, Friedman suggests that theories need to be revisited in the light of evidence: 'empirical evidence is vital' in 'constructing hypotheses' as well as in testing their validity, while even the more fundamental axioms or 'assumptions' from which hypotheses are generated need to be 'sufficiently good approximations for the purpose in hand'.

So Friedman did not overlook the case for making models more realistic. The relationship between axioms, hypotheses, and data is not, after all, a straightforwardly linear one: hypotheses are constantly being adjusted in the light of new empirical results, and if evidence moves strongly in favour of one set of related claims and against another, even the more foundational axioms may begin to shift. This can be a protracted process as given disciplinary fields or 'paradigms' are slow to change. Nor is it possible, in most fields of empirical enquiry, to stick to the perfectionist agenda of falsification advocated by Popper:[18] verification of claims through the accumulation of data is the way most science (in the broad sense of the term to include both the physical and social sciences) proceeds. But on the whole, we should prefer models which are 'data-driven' rather than wholly 'theory-derived' in their orientation.

[15] Karl Popper, 'Science as Falsification' in Karl Popper, *Conjectures and Refutations* (Basic Books 1963) 33.

[16] Friedman (n 11) 9.

[17] Gary S. Becker, *The Economic Approach to Human Behavior* (University of Chicago Press 1976).

[18] Popper (n 15).

Models which are wholly unrealistic will have the result of skewing research towards the answering of unproductive hypotheses.[19] Thus models should be driven by new data as well as by theory. At some point, new findings should lead to a revision of the assumptions underlying the model. However, even these more realistic models should be regarded as tentative claims, not authoritative truths. Scientific research is inevitably tentative and in need of continuous error correction through the accumulation of new data.

Jolls and colleagues[20] maintain that their approach is 'consistent with the precept originally proposed by Milton Friedman: Economics should be judged not on whether the assumptions are realistic or valid, but rather on the quality of its predictions'. It is the greater predictive power of the behavioural approach, they suggest, which justifies its use in place of the standard model. On this basis, they go on, in their 1998 paper and elsewhere, to make extensive prescriptive recommendations for the design of laws,[21] and offer broader normative suggestions for recasting the way that 'paternalist' or regulatory laws operate.[22] This paper sets the template for the later, more extensive development of the 'nudge' approach to public policy-making.[23]

On closer inspection, however, the method adopted by Jolls and colleagues[24] is far from being conventionally scientific. They take the normal method of law and economics research to be to 'determine the implications of ... rational maximizing behaviour in and out of markets, and its legal implications for markets and other institutions'.[25] They associate the rationality axiom with Becker's triad of maximisation, preference consistency, and equilibrium. From their premise, their programme consists of substituting for Becker's assumptions the new ones they claim to derive from behavioural research: 'a more realistic conception of human behaviour'.[26] It is on this basis that the wide-ranging programme of institutional redesign sketched out in the 1998 paper and expanded in later works is constructed.

Yet the rationality axiom, whatever its content, remains just that: an axiom. Friedman defended the use of unrealistic assumptions to drive the explicative phase of economic inquiry. As Edgeworth did before him, he recognised that the rationality principle could never be anything more than a very loose approximation of social reality. The approach set out by Friedman, while offering a view of the unreality of models which, as we have seen, is unnecessarily dogmatic, at least

[19] Katarina Juselius, 'Time to Reject the Privileging of Economic Theory over Evidence? A Reply to Lawson' (2011) 35.2 Cambridge Journal of Economics 423.
[20] Sunstein, Jolls, and Thaler (n 2) 1484.
[21] Ibid. 1522–41.
[22] Ibid. 1541–45.
[23] Richard Thaler and Cass R. Sunstein, *Nudge: Improving Decisions about Health, Wealth and Happiness* (Penguin 2009).
[24] Sunstein, Jolls, and Thaler (n 2).
[25] Ibid. 1376.
[26] Ibid. 1545.

has the merit of making no direct empirical claim for the validity of the rationality axiom. In such a framework, the results of empirical research can be judged on their own merits. But once the rationality principle is seen as revealing a universal truth of human behaviour, it serves directly for 'a host of novel prescriptions regarding how to make the legal system work better'.[27]

The use of an axiom to drive policy is not of course unique to BLE; it is inherent in much of the wider 'law and economics' literature and is one of the deep methodological problems associated with this field. However, with BLE, the problem becomes more serious because the claims made for the empirical validity of behavioural insights are seen as lending legitimacy to policy prescriptions which could otherwise be understood as turning on dogma. But what exactly are the implications for theory and policy of empirical behavioural research?

III. The Rationality Axiom Should Be Regarded as Modified Rather than Refuted

'Errors are common in human decision making': if this were the core claim of BLE it would hardly be worth noting. The claim, rather, is more specific: that the pervasiveness of error in social life renders the core axioms of economics untenable. Daniel Kahneman,[28] for example, takes aim at a version of the rationality axiom he describes as follows: 'The agent of economic theory is rational, selfish and his tastes do not change'. Possibly this is, or was, the view of some economists. Maybe there are even some economists (although they must be few in number) who believe that 'homo economicus can think like Albert Einstein, store as much memory as IBM's Deep Blue, and exercise the willpower of Mahatma Gandhi'.[29]

This is, not, however, the account given in the foundational texts of neoclassical economics. As we have seen, Edgeworth's account of the axiom states that every agent is 'actuated by self-interest'. Of the three dimensions of the axiom highlighted by Kahneman, 'rationality' is, in the present context, tautologous, while the other two are not implied by Edgeworth's formula, which does not conflate 'self-interest' with the distinct psychological state of 'selfishness', and can perfectly well take on board the case of changing tastes, which would simply give rise to differently shaped contract curves.

Nor has the notion of rationality in economics remained unchanged since Edgeworth's day. The appearance of the axiom of 'bounded rationality' in the mid-1950s long pre-dates not just BLE but modern law and economics in general. When

[27] Ibid. 1546.
[28] Kahneman (n 1) 269.
[29] Thaler and Sunstein (n 23) 7.

introducing the idea he initially called 'approximate' rationality,[30] Herbert Simon defined his goal in the following terms: 'the task is to replace the global rationality of economic man with a kind of rational behaviour that is compatible with the access to information and the computational capacities that are actually possessed by organisms, including man, in the kinds of environments in which such organisms exist'.[31] Simon was specifically interested in how individuals exercised choice in organisational settings, and his use of different versions of the rationality axiom was part of a project to construct computational models simulating corporate decision making: 'the broader aim … in constructing these definitions … is to provide some materials for the construction of a theory of the behaviour of a human individual or of groups of individuals who are making decisions in an organisational context'.[32]

The theory of bounded rationality holds that human decision making is prone to error though a combination of internal (psychological) and external (environmental) factors. The theory directs attention, at the same time, to the mechanisms by which error might be avoided or corrected through learning and adaptation. This can occur through organisational structures which embed and retain useful information (Simon's original focus), and through institutions (including the legal system) which evolve through error correction and adjustment of their operations in response to signals from their environment. As such, the postulate of bounded rationality has informed numerous fields of inquiry across the social sciences (new institutional economics, evolutionary and epistemic game theory), philosophy (the theory of conventions), and data science (machine learning, natural language processing, and related aspects of research into the field which has come to be generically referred to as 'artificial intelligence').

Simon's project did not neglect the possibility that research in psychology could contribute to an improved understanding of the bases of human decision making. The view that rationality is bounded in part as a result of material or biological constraints on the cognitive capacity of human beings is present in his theory from the start, although underplayed somewhat on the grounds that 'the distance is so great between our present psychological knowledge of the learning and choice processes and the kinds of knowledge needed for economic and administrative theory that a marking stone placed halfway between might help travellers from both directions to keep to their courses'.[33] Partly for this reason, Simon's subsequent work was largely directed at an examination of the external sources of constraints on rationality: in other words, to a study of the social contexts in which decision-making

[30] Herbert Simon, 'A Behavioural Model of Rational Choice' (1955) 69.1 Quarterly Journal of Economics 99, 115.
[31] Ibid. 99.
[32] Ibid. 114.
[33] Ibid. 99.

processes were embedded, and to the organisational and institutional responses engendered by environments which were open and uncertain.

Since the advent of Simon's project, there has been an outpouring of research on the psychological dimensions of human decision making, and it can no longer be maintained that we are in a state of deep ignorance on this issue. Most of the foundational contributions in this field are derived from experiments conducted under controlled settings. Experimental methods, standard for decades in psychology, have crossed over into economics. BLE in a broad sense draws on, and is enriched by, this vast and still rapidly growing literature, to the point where concepts such as 'anchoring', 'framing', and 'loss aversion', along with the 'endowment effect' and 'prospect theory', have practically entered mainstream legal discourse. BLE in the narrower sense of the 'nudge' project is, however, only one part of this wider movement, just as Kahneman's dual process theory is only part of the wider behavioural turn in the social sciences.

It is not clear, in the light of this wider literature, that the best conclusion to draw from experimental and related empirical research is that human decision making is systematically irrational. The field is essentially bifurcated into the two strands originally identified by Simon, one internally focused on the material basis of human cognition, the other looking outwards to organisations, institutions, and norms.

The first strand consists of a search for the material bases of biases and heuristics, which essentially means their biological foundations. Kahneman has suggested that 'system 1' or 'automatic' thinking (to be distinguished from 'reflective' or 'system 2' thinking) is an adaptation to an evolutionary need: 'we have inherited the neural mechanisms that evolved to provide ongoing assessments of threat level, and they have not been turned off'.[34] If, however, dual process theory has a genetic basis, it can best be explained in adaptationist terms. This implies that an explanation based on bounded rationality, rather than irrationality, is required. The distinction is important: according to John Tooby and Lena Cosmides,[35] 'the "irrational" risk aversion posited in Kahneman and Tversky's prospect theory can be replaced by an evolutionarily revised prospect theory, in which individuals can be shown to be adaptively risk-seeking or adaptively risk averse depending on their need level and the probability distribution they face'.

Possibly the idea of 'irrationality' is not one to which Kahneman's body of research naturally lends itself. If so, to suggest that 'the emerging science of choice, consisting of careful research by social scientists over the past four decades', has 'raised serious questions about the rationality of many judgments and decisions that people make', or that 'hundreds of studies confirm that human forecasts are

[34] Kahneman (n 1) 90.

[35] John Tooby and Lena Cosmides, 'The Theoretical Foundations of Evolutionary Psychology' in David M. Buss (ed.), *The Handbook of Evolutionary Psychology Volume 1: Foundations* (2nd edn, Wiley 2016) 27.

flawed and biased'[36] might not be an entirely justified extrapolation from the dual process literature.

An alternative interpretation of the empirical results achieved by 'biases and heuristics' research programmes in experimental psychology is that they indicate the existence of routines which human beings have developed to deal with complex and open environments.[37] Observing social cues, respecting fairness norms, and having regard to the well-being of others are not irrational responses to most of the settings which human beings find themselves in as a matter of everyday societal interaction. A genetic foundation for other-regarding behaviour of the kind revealed by experiments based on the 'ultimatum' and 'dictator' games is not inherently implausible: 'research on judgment under uncertainty is now showing that the human mind is equipped with a toolbox of "fast-and-frugal heuristics", each designed to make well-calibrated judgments quickly on the basis of limited information'; these features of human decision making are 'ecologically rational' in the sense of 'providing good solutions when operating in the task environments for which they have evolved'.[38]

Human behaviour must have a genetic substrate of some kind, but how far the shared genetic make-up of human beings directly influences their behaviour in the diverse economic settings of contemporary market societies remains hard to judge in our present state of knowledge. Probably any such connection is indirect at best and will turn out to be influenced by epigenetic (social or institutional) factors of various kinds. In so far as evolutionary psychology has an input to the understanding of contemporary environments as opposed to those assumed to have operated in the distant evolutionary past, it does not confirm the dualism of 'thinking fast and slow', if that is taken to imply that rationality is a later, more advanced evolutionary stage emerging from an earlier, intuitive approach to decision making, but rather the 'modular' and hence context-specific nature of human cognition.[39] If there is any evidence for a direct genetic influence on economic decision making in contemporary environments, it favours the existence of altruism ('other regarding preferences') as a normal aspect of human psychology, and sees complete egoism ('sociopathy') as unusual.[40]

The second strand of the literature exploring the implications of bounded rationality looks outward to the organisational and institutional context of human decision making. This is a vast area characterised by multiple theoretical perspectives drawing on, among other things, the more explicitly institutional variants of

[36] Thaler and Sunstein (n 23) 8.

[37] Gerd Gigerenzer, *Rationality for Mortals: How People Cope with Uncertainty* (Oxford University Press 2008).

[38] Tooby and Cosmides (n 35) 26.

[39] Ibid.

[40] Samuel Bowles and Herbert Gintis, *A Cooperative Species: Human Reciprocity and its Evolution* (Princeton University Press 2011).

transaction costs economics and the mathematical modelling of game theory (adjusted, in its evolutionary and epistemic branches, to take into account learning and cognition), along with a wide range of empirical methodologies, only some of which are experimental in their orientation; agent-based modelling and ethnographic field work have also played a significant role in shaping research on institutions and norms.[41]

Experimental studies are among the most revealing for the light they cast on the rationality axiom. Numerous experiments have sought to simulate a version of a 'market game' in which the players assume the roles of buyer and sellers under conditions of scarcity. Some of the earliest and subsequently most influential of these studies suggested that in competitive markets with large-numbers bargaining, prices can converge on a more or less efficient (in the sense of market clearing) level within a few rounds of repeated play.[42] Subsequent research has confirmed that agents are generally disposed to act egotistically in market settings, but that they do so on the basis of learning; that is, through observation of the positive payoffs derived *by others* from profit-maximising strategies. In a game populated by agents with different preferences for fairness or 'inequity aversion', egotistical bargaining will emerge as a dominant strategy as long as no single player is in a position to enforce an equitable outcome. Competition from other buyers or sellers as the case may be undermines profit sharing: 'each proposer has a strong incentive to outbid his competitors in order to turn part of the inequality to his advantage and to increase his own monetary payoff' while, conversely, 'even very inequity-averse responders try to turn part of the unavoidable inequality into inequality to their advantage by accepting low offers'.[43] So what matters here is that there is 'an important interaction between the distribution of preferences in a given population and the strategic environment'.[44]

Egoism or 'substantive' rationality can therefore be interpreted as a learned response to particular contexts. It is not (or at least not wholly) a natural or inborn trait, but (to some degree) the product of institutional framing. Markets are instituted environments which depend on a certain mix of legal and social norms in order to function. The competitive market is a particular type of social environment, one in which the best strategic response of agents is generally to maximise profits, but maximisation as such is not a universal or natural feature of human behaviour, any more than the market is a universal or natural form of social organisation.

[41] Amy Poteete, Marco Janssen, and Elinor Ostrom, *Working Together: Collective Action, The Commons, and Multiple Methods in Practice* (Princeton University Press 2010).

[42] Vernon Smith, 'An Experimental Study of Competitive Market Behavior' (1962) 70.2 Journal of Political Economy 111.

[43] Ernst Fehr and Klaus Schmidt, 'A Theory of Fairness, Competition, and Cooperation' (1999) 114.3 Quarterly Journal of Economics 817 834.

[44] Ibid. 856.

A particularly fruitful line of experimental studies comprises those which look at the phenomenon of 'strong reciprocation' in the context of 'social dilemmas' and other versions of the 'public goods game'. A social dilemma, for this purpose, is a context in which individual self-interest and collective well-being radically diverge: it is in the interests of individual agents to renege on shared commitments which, if generally observed, would assist the survival of the group, but which have a weak connection to individual payoffs, at least in the short run. Paying taxes, avoiding paying bribes, or simply adhering to norms generated by public bodies can all be viewed in this light. Game theoretical models predict that a practice of 'altruistic punishment', implying a strategy of contributing to a public good even when to do so is costly for the individual concerned, can emerge under particular environmental conditions. The most salient of these is that defectors from the norm of compliance are 'punished', if only through a refusal to deal, by cooperators.[45] Another is that defection is publicly recognised and sanctioned as such, through the legal system.[46]

Strong reciprocation has been the focus of a number of empirical studies. In one of the most noteworthy, Benedikt Herrmann, Christian Thöni, and Simon Gächter conducted field experiments in multiple countries to obtain evidence on attitudes towards corruption. They report increased rates of altruistic punishment in societies with strong and accountable public institutions, which they associate with high values on survey-based indices for measuring the quality of the 'rule of law'. They then tested for correlations between the rule of law, so defined, and altruistic punishment's opposite, 'antisocial punishment', which describes a phenomenon of *defectors* punishing *cooperators*. Societies in which it is normal to punish someone for refusing to pay or accept a bribe are those lacking an effective or accountable state. The authors conclude: 'if the rule of law is strong, people trust the law enforcement institutions, which are perceived as being effective, fair, impartial, and bound by the law', while 'if the rule of law is weak, the opposite holds'.[47]

The finding that 'altruistic punishment' (punishing defectors, where to do so incurs a cost to reciprocators) is prevalent in democratic societies, whereas its opposite, 'anti-social punishment' (punishing reciprocators), is prevalent in authoritarian ones, is revealing since it suggests that norm-following behaviour is driven by social learning rather than by genetic factors (since there is no relevant genetic variation across the populations concerned). It also implies that what is 'rational' varies from one political and institutional context to another.

[45] Herbert Gintis, 'Strong Reciprocity and Human Sociality' (2000) 206.2 Journal of Theoretical Biology 169.

[46] Manuel Eisner et al., 'From the Savannah to the Magistrate's Court: The Roots of Criminal Justice in Evolved Human Psychology' in Ben Jann and Wojtech Przepiorka (eds.), *Social Dilemmas, Institutions, and the Evolution of Cooperation* (De Gruyter 2017) 61.

[47] Benedikt Herrmann, Christian Thöni, and Simon Gächter, 'Anti-social Punishment across Societies' (2008) 319 Science 1362, 1365.

This is to suggest, then, that the rational actor model should be modified rather than abandoned. On the one hand, 'experimental economics has validated the critics of the rational actor model by demonstrating that both beliefs and preferences are functions of social context, preferences take the individual's current state as a parameter, and maximization often entails using decision-making heuristics as a means of conserving information costs', but on the other, experimentalism has only 'strengthened our appreciation for game theory and the rational actor model, because experimental methodology is firmly grounded in these two analytical constructs'.[48] Thus it is not inconsistent with the idea of bounded rationality to suggest that agents may decide between alternatives in a preference-consistent, that is, transitive way, but with reference to the limits on their knowledge and the nature of their environment.[49] Human agents may express other-regarding preferences ('altruism') by trading them off against other subjective wants.[50] In some settings, such as those of competitive markets underpinned by individual property rights, a stronger version of substantive, egotistic rationality may continue to be a good guide to prediction.[51]

IV. Behavioural Research Does Not Privilege 'Libertarian Paternalism' over Alternative Policy Paradigms

BLE has generated a normative programme which is a variant of nudge theory, 'libertarian paternalism'. Libertarian paternalism is a template for policy and institutional design which combines the view that 'in general, people should be free to do what they like—and to opt out of undesirable arrangements if they want to', with the claim that 'it is legitimate for choice architects to try to influence people's behaviour in order to make their lives longer, better and healthier'.[52] A large part of the case for libertarian paternalism is that it has a tight connection to the empirical research undertaken under the broad heading of the behavioural sciences: 'our basic source of information here is the emerging science of choice, consisting of careful research by social scientists over the past four decades'.[53] But is this claim as secure as it seems?

With the emergence of a major new paradigm in the social sciences, or the physical ones for that matter, it is tempting to believe that new truths are being revealed,

48 Herbert Gintis, 'Experimental economics will foster a renaissance of economic theory' (2008) Working Paper 13 <http://people.umass.edu/~gintis/papers_index.html>.
49 Fehr and Schmidt (n 43).
50 Herbert Gintis, *The Bounds of Reason* (Princeton University Press 2009).
51 Smith (n 42).
52 Thaler and Sunstein (n 23) 5.
53 Ibid. 8.

which should inform policy design. Science needs data to proceed and behavioural research is no different in this respect. As we have seen,[54] theories and axioms, which do not themselves have an entirely empirical foundation, will direct the questions which researchers choose to address, and if there is no feedback between data and theories it is likely that research, no matter how well it appears to vindicate a given theory, will end up going in directions that could be pointless or, worse, erroneous. Errors can be avoided if hypotheses are seen as contingent claims awaiting falsification. However, Popper's falsificationist agenda sets too high a bar. In practice, very little research is conducted with the aim of refuting hypotheses. Most of the time, organised knowledge proceeds through the accumulation of data which are intended to uncover phenomena of wider interest.

Viewed in this way, behavioural research can be seen as a gradual advance in knowledge and understanding which is leading us to rethink some core notions of the social sciences, including the rationality axiom. This is different from suggesting that BLE has uncovered a new truth about human nature which can inform policy design across a range of distinct national, social, and institutional contexts.

A serious difficulty for the claim that dual process theory offers a new account of human behaviour with general application to different policy contexts is that there are many possible interpretations of the empirical findings which have been use to popularise 'nudging'. Even if a consensus eventually emerges on the results of experiments testing the limits of the rationality axiom, and they remain contested to a high degree, a clear scientific consensus on what the empirical findings mean has yet to emerge. The most systematic of the various attempts to fit empirical findings from psychology into a materialist account of the origins of human behaviour, evolutionary psychology, does not fit easily with dual process theory.[55] The 'fast and frugal' conception of biases and heuristics, which is a viable alternative to dual process theory, offers a different interpretation of the implications of experimental research for the rationality axiom.[56]

More generally, the wider programme of research which can be labelled 'behavioural' is tenuously linked, at best, to the agenda set out by the proponents of libertarian paternalism. Much of this research tends to show that strong public institutions which penalise free-riding have fitness properties not captured by the individualist orientation of libertarian paternalism. The implication of research on 'strong reciprocation' is that human beings frequently behave in ways which are individually costly where to do so is believed to be consistent with shared notions of the common good. Strong reciprocation goes beyond the practice of

[54] See section II above.
[55] Tooby and Cosmides (n 35).
[56] Gigerenzer (n 37).

'reciprocal altruism' as it does not depend on expectations of a future return from cooperation. In deep evolutionary time, the emergence of such a practice would have had fitness properties for human communities: if the proportion of strong reciprocators in a group is sufficiently high, 'even self-interested agents can be induced to cooperate in such situations, thus lowering the probability of group extinction'.[57]

In contemporary environments, the willingness of individuals to contribute as a matter of course to public and communal goods continues to have fitness properties for both communities and individuals. It is linked, on the one hand, to equality of social status in a given community and, on the other, to a range of indicators of physical and psychological well-being. The high degree of correlation between inequality of status and income, on the one hand, and adverse outcomes on such measures of social well-being as infant mortality, obesity, mental illness, educational performance, teenage motherhood, and homicide, on the other,[58] suggests that a policy of encouraging individuals to opt in or out of collective provision is not compatible with the general good. And it may not be any more compatible with individual returns even for the relatively well off, who may not feel that they benefit directly from collective provision, but who will be affected nonetheless, psychologically and physically, by its absence. The result of epidemiological research, that 'everything else being equal, it is better to live in a more equal society', applies also to 'the richer part of society' because 'people compare themselves to those who are closer to them—and the more unequal the society, the greater distance between people, even among those with the highest incomes'.[59]

It is beneficial, even to the more wealthy, to live in a relatively more egalitarian society, but it is not rational to contribute to the means needed to create such a society, including public goods extending from collective health and education provision to respecting the rule of law itself, if others are not doing the same. The logic of a society in which there is no meaningful public domain, and where, as a result, the state represents nothing more than the concentration of power in the hands of a given private group, is that those inclined to support social norms are themselves 'punished' by the majority of defectors. Anti-social punishment of this kind is strictly 'rational' in the sense of being the dominant strategy in societies which are unequal as well as being, frequently, undemocratic.[60] But such a response is no more 'natural' or inherent in human behaviour in general than its alternative; it is a function of a specific social and institutional setting.

Thus, if there is a consistent message from the wide range of evolutionary and behavioural studies on attitudes towards public goods and the rule of law, it is that

57 Gintis (n 45) 179.
58 Richard Wilkinson and Kate Pickett, *The Spirit Level* (Penguin 2008).
59 Nicholas Baumard, 'Evolutionary Psychology and Public Policy' in Buss (n 35) 1137.
60 Herrmann, Thöni, and Gätcher (n 47).

rationality is both contextual and normative. Rationality is less a natural human condition, and more a combination of behavioural traits which are shaped by context. Rationality is a norm before it is a fact.

Moreover, given the societal benefits associated with egalitarianism and an effective public realm, the problem with 'nudging' is precisely that it is both libertarian and paternalistic at the same time. Its libertarian aspect privileges individual choice over collective agency, while its paternalistic aspect elevates technocratic decision making over democratic participation in the process of policy making. While a case could presumably be made for these positions, it should be advanced and defended in its own right as a political programme involving contestable values, and not on the basis of empirical social science, to which it is tenuously connected.

V. Conclusion

Behavioural research has undoubtedly enriched our understanding of the rationality axiom. We have learned that it is possible, indeed normal, for human agents to act altruistically and rationally at the same time. Having no regard for others—sociopathy—is unusual in human society, and generally attracts an adverse response. In many environments, it would be highly irrational to behave in anything but a pro-social way. Inequality aversion, in addition to being highly likely to have a genetic basis, is a shared norm in societies which have found solutions to the collective action problem associated with the provision of public goods. Indicators of physical and psychological well-being are strongly correlated with equality of social status, with relative differences mattering more than absolute wealth. If these are not exactly the messages which policy makers generally receive from summaries or restatements of behavioural research, then that is perhaps because other messages—those which stress the 'irrationality' of the general populace and elevate technical fixes over democratic deliberation—have been allowed to take centre stage. At a time when the panoptic powers of states and corporations are only increasing, and when social inequalities are on the rise in many part of the world, this may not be surprising, even if it does suggest that the conditions under which empirical research enters the policy-making realm are only incompletely correlated with the scientific value of that research.

The notion of rationality has become more complex, perhaps at a price, but it would be premature to retire it. Perhaps it is time, just over a century after the emergence of neoclassical economics from its origins in the 'moral science' of utilitarianism, to reconsider the balance between the individual and collective aspects of the hedonic calculus. Legal scholarship and practice, in particular, might benefit from understanding rationality in relational terms. For a human agent to be 'rational' is to acquire the capacity to receive information from the environment and to update beliefs and behaviour in the light of that environmental data, and in a human society of any level of complexity beyond the very basic, this implies the ability to understand the beliefs and preferences of others. Reviving the idea that it is the role of the law to promote this kind of 'rationality'[61] would mark a step forward.

[61] On which, see generally Alain Supiot, *Homo Juridicus: On the Anthropological Function of the Law* (Verso 2007).

3

Game Theory and the Law

Incomplete Knowledge about the Knowledge of Other Players

Marlies Ahlert

Abstract: Classical game theory analyses strategic interactions under extreme idealisations. It assumes cognitively unconstrained players with common knowledge concerning game forms, preferences, and rationality. Such ideal theory is highly relevant for human self-understanding as a rational being or what Selten called 'rationology'. Yet, ideal theory is highly irrelevant for real actors who are in Selten's sense boundedly rational. Starting from essential features of real bargaining problems, elements of Selten's 'micro-psychological' and Raiffa's 'telescopic' behavioural bargaining theory are introduced. From this, an outline of a workable rationality approach to bargaining emerges. It suggests relying on telescopic elements from Raiffa's model to provide general *outcome* orientation and on insights from Selten's aspiration adaptation model of individual decision making to develop *process*-sensitive action advice. A bird's eye view of a prominent recent case of 'bargaining in the shadow of the courts' shows a surprisingly good fit of outcomes with the implications of Raiffa's telescopic approach while remaining compatible with a Seltenian process. Though due to a lack of specific information because the micro-foundations for the telescopic theory cannot be provided, it is at least clear how further case studies and experiments might be put to work here.

I. Aims of the Argument

Classical game theory analyses games in terms of 'reasoning about knowledge'.[1] In doing so, it follows the neoclassical economics tradition of ascribing 'integrated preferences' to all players.[2] These preferences are assumed to be robust,

[1] Ronald Fagin et al., *Reasoning about Knowledge* (MIT Press 1995).
[2] cf. Robert Sugden, *The Community of Advantage: A Behavioural Economist's Defence of the Market* (Oxford University Press 2018).

Marlies Ahlert, *Game Theory and the Law* In: *Theories of Choice*. Edited by: Stefan Grundmann and Philipp Hacker, Oxford University Press (2021). © The several contributors. DOI: 10.1093/oso/9780198863175.003.0004

context-independent, and consistent, while their distribution over 'player types' is commonly known among the players. Assuming cognitively and emotionally unconstrained reasoners, such analyses may lead to 'philosophical' insights into the nature of ideal rationality. Yet, unless it is specified under what conditions the constitutive assumptions of the ideal rational choice model are approximated to and to what extent by 'degrees' of real rationality, relying on the model for descriptive as well as prescriptive purposes in real interactions is precarious. The risks of what has been aptly called Model Platonism[3] are lurking in the background: the perception of the facts of a specific interactive choice-making problem will be distorted by a general model of ideal rationality, which is entirely separated from the facts of real behaviour.[4]

As a subfield of ideal game modelling, ideal bargaining theory based on the stylised representation of bargaining problems offered by Nash[5] emerged. In the spirit of neoclassical economics and classical game theory, the preferences are treated as exogenous to the bargaining process. What is deemed mutually advantageous in outcome space—that is, a potential agreement—is judged according to these *exogenously* given integrated preferences. The underlying outcome-related conceptualisation of bargaining is 'telescopic' in its neglect of all the finer details of the process leading to outcomes. As opposed to the telescopic focus of an outcome-oriented approach in a process-oriented theory of bargaining, the preferences can be treated—at least in part—as *endogenous* to the process itself.

Real actors cannot evaluate full strategy profiles (complete contingency plans of all players for all conceivable contexts and constellations that may arise in the sequential bargaining process). Therefore, evaluating full plans (strategies) according to their outcomes in terms of exogenously given preferences is out of the question for the players themselves. Real actors who are participating in bargaining games will gather information and form their specific preferences in the process of play.

The preceding remarks are relevant for all applications of game theoretic modelling in real-world interactive choice-making. Knowledge of ideal models will not be directly applicable to inform about the behaviour of real players. Quite to the contrary, the risks of Model Platonism in fact suggest that we should avoid relying on ideal rational choice models in the theory and practice of interactive choice-making.

If ideal rationality models can be useful at all, it will be very indirectly, akin to visiting a gym before engaging in a specific activity in sports. The general training

[3] Hans Albert, Darrell Arnold, and Frank Maier-Rigaud, 'Model Platonism: Neoclassical Economic Thought in Critical Light' (2012) 8.3 Journal of Institutional Economics 295.

[4] See on the methodological dualism between ideal and real theory that is underlying the radical separation thesis Reinhard Selten, 'Response to Shepsle and Laitin' in James Alt, Margaret Levi, and Elinor Ostrom (eds.), *Competition and Cooperation: Conversations with Nobelists about Economics and Political Science* (Russell Sage Foundation 1999) 303.

[5] John F. Nash, 'The Bargaining Problem' (1950) 18.2 Econometrica 155.

in a gym helps to develop broad capacities but will not help to develop the specific skills necessary for a particular sport. Analogous to this, faced with a bargaining problem in the shadow of a pending lawsuit, reading a treatise on 'game theory and the law'[6] may be a useful exercise for bargainers or the lawyers advising them, but it will be impossible for them to 'apply' models literally based on ideal rationality to the real world of bargaining. For this, it would be necessary to say how closely real behaviour and real capacities of actors approximate ideal types of rationality in a given situation. Only then would it be viable to take into account what somewhat metaphorically are sometimes called 'degrees of rationality' in assessing the likelihood that the model implications will in fact approximate real-world processes and outcomes.

In my subsequent discussion of what may be called 'bargaining in the shadow of the courts', I will not rely on ideal rational choice modelling at all. However, I will not deny—and I intend to illustrate this by referring to some essential characteristics of a legal case—that telescopic models of bargaining have merit. Yet, they do so not because they share the rational choice assumptions of telescopic bargaining models that are routinely made in the tradition of the seminal work of John Nash.[7] They have merit only because they can rely on empirical evidence provided by studies that relate bargaining situations to their outcomes in a 'telescopic' way. If it comes to the bargaining process itself, the telescopic—though now evidence-based—characterisation of potential agreements in the outcome space of a bargaining problem has to be broken down into specific advice for bargainers who engage in the process of bargaining towards outcomes. When this advice is formulated, empirical psychological regularities governing purposeful human behaviour must be invoked in ways that make no reference to ideal rationality at all. In this context, allusions to degrees of rationality are spurious. However, there remains room for workable concepts of rationality and a telescopic evidence-based theory that relates bargaining situations to their results.

In what follows in section II, I will provide some of the classical non-cooperative game theory background against which a workable rationality approach to bargaining should be seen. In section III select concepts of so-called bounded rationality, which seem highly relevant for a workable rationality approach to bargaining in legal contexts are introduced. In section IV, a recent case of legal bargaining that drew quite some attention when the final version of this paper was prepared is used to illustrate the surprising fit of the predictions of, arguably, the most prominent telescopic workable rationality conception of bargaining with results in outcome space. Section V acknowledges that what has been called a surprising fit is indeed beyond the pale of a detailed explanation in causal process terms and concludes

[6] As Douglas G. Baird, Robert H. Gertner, and Randal C. Picker, *Game Theory and the Law* (Harvard University Press 1994).

[7] Nash (n 5).

with the conventional disclaimer that there is still a lot of work to be done before workable rationality can be put to practical use.

II. (Neo-)classical Non-cooperative Game Theory

A. Basic Assumptions Concerning 'Rational' Preferences

In non-cooperative game theory, the strategic interaction of players is modelled and analysed. In view of the problematic status of the assumption of commonly known given preferences, it is useful to distinguish between *games* and *game forms*. In *game forms* 'players', 'moves of players', and 'the information sets of players' (the information structure) are defined, and possible outcomes of interactions are described. In the game form representation of interactive choice-making, no preference ranking by players of results of strategy combinations is assumed to be given. The game in the traditional game theoretic sense emerges after the players' rankings of plays of the game are captured by representable (consistent) preferences, 'all things considered',[8] and certain common knowledge assumptions are made.

In a game as a well-defined object of classical game-theoretic analysis, each player is assumed to act as a fully rational homo (o)economicus ('HO') on the basis of her preferences on outcomes of alternative plays of the game. To be able to model decisions under uncertainty, preferences are assumed to be representable by a cardinal utility function that is 'linear in probabilities' (i.e., probabilities can be used as weights when forming expected values over all possible results that can conceivably arise from taking some action). The player plans and chooses

1. in view of the future causal consequences of each act taken separately (opportunism)
2. evaluating or ranking acts in a consistent manner that can be *represented as if* maximising some real valued function (coherent preferences)
3. as if maximising behaviour is constrained only externally by resource restrictions but is cognitively and normatively unconstrained (corresponding to condition 1).

Without impairing their 'rationality', preferences may in principle be selfish or unselfish, directed towards higher ideals or material gains, or whatever other factor may apply. In practical applications of game theory in the wild, as in the laboratory, it is, however, typically assumed that preferences will trace some natural aspect

[8] cf. Daniel M. Hausman, *Preference, Value, Choice and Welfare* (Cambridge University Press 2012).

like monetary gains/losses as part of more complex descriptions of *outcomes of a game form*.

To describe this strategy slightly malevolently, the game theorist, first, claims that all subjective rankings are compatible with the formal rationality assumptions of the theory. Then, second, she immediately adds that for practical purposes it is as a matter of convenience assumed that the substantive aims of the actors are represented by the objective quantities like monetary outcomes captured in the game form. But then, third, the fact that the latter assumption is made as a matter of convenience is 'conveniently' forgotten when the results of analyses are presented.

B. Basic Assumptions Concerning Theories of Rationality in Equilibrium

When analysing some strategic interaction as a game, classical game theory assumes that all participating players are rational HO who commonly know the rules of the game (move structure, feasible outcomes, and preferences of all players on outcomes). Due to the common knowledge assumption concerning the game—all players know that all players know that all players know the rules of the game including knowledge of preferences— as a consequence, all players are reasoning about the same object of reasoning; that is, 'the game' (and not only the game form) is well defined.

In view of unlimited reasoning capacities of fully rational players, game theory also presupposes that the theory of rational play itself is common knowledge among the players. Every player analyses the game under the assumption that every player selects a strategy that is a best (fully rational) response to the other players' strategies. Only strategy combinations where each player gives a best response to the other players' strategies can fulfil this requirement. An obvious implication for solution theories is that they can suggest only equilibria as rational play; because, if the theory would suggest a non-equilibrium solution, this implies that at least one individual could unilaterally improve her result and thus would have reason not to follow the theory.

Yet, in many types of interactions there are multiple equilibria. The necessary condition that only theories that suggest equilibria could be commonly known and be complied with leaves open the possibility of alternative such theories. This raises the theoretical problem of determining by which criterion rational players can coordinate on one of them.[9] Unless the theory of ideally rational play that provides a definite strategy prescription singling out one equilibrium *is itself common*

[9] John C. Harsanyi and Reinhard Selten, *A General Theory of Equilibrium Selection in Games* (MIT Press 1988).

knowledge, even ideally rational actors may be exposed to strategic uncertainty. (As long as they do not know which theory co-players adopt, they do not know their 'rationality type'.) If players do not select with respect to the same criterion (the same theory), ignorance of the rationality type of the other players may imply that coordination of strategy choices fails in that players do not end up in equilibrium. Forming theories merely under the assumption that an equilibrium prevails and to ask only what kinds of conditions must be fulfilled for it to prevail seems unconvincing to the extent that the equilibrium assumption itself is.

The preceding issues are of great interest in themselves. A less sketchy and less polemical, more balanced view could easily become book length. For the present mundane purposes, it fortunately suffices to note that in ideal theories of interactive rational choice-making, it is common practice to assume that an equilibrium prevails and that the criterion of equilibrium selection is common knowledge among all players. But what may be necessary for ideal theory purposes may limit usefulness for practical applications. An a priori, ideal theory cannot provide answers to issues of real behaviour anyway. To discriminate between more or less plausible theories concerning real interactive choice-making empirical research is necessary.

In view of the preceding and other criticisms of 'ideal theory', I opt for a 'workable rationality' orientation of game modelling. In particular, when it comes to bargaining in real-world legal contexts, this seems to be the only way to respect the behavioural facts. Yet, other than so-called bounded rationality approaches, I believe we should take into account the merits of what I called a telescopic outcome-oriented approach. While acknowledging the principal desirability of a process-oriented theory of bringing about the outcomes, the empirical evidence supporting models that directly focus on outcomes should be taken seriously (in particular, the work of Howard Raiffa and followers).

Relying on some examples from bargaining, I next reconstruct in a process-oriented way some central characteristics of how boundedly rational actors can find their way towards outcomes in complex bargaining situations (section III). Then I turn to an example which shows how 'telescopic behavioural bargaining theory' details may have some use for specific real bargaining contexts and processes (section IV).

III. Bounded Rationality in Non-cooperative Games

Analysing non-cooperative interaction without assuming ideal rationality amounts to giving up the assumption of 'payoff' maximising players and of common knowledge of HO rationality. This has implications for both how an external observer of interactions and how a decision maker who is involved in an interaction should apply theories of interactive choice-making to practical problems.

A. Perspective of the Behavioural Economist

In his role as an external observer, the goal of the behavioural economist is to explain and predict behaviour of players, and which outcomes will be reached in interactive choice-making in general and of bargaining in particular.

Depending on the economic or social environment the following aspects of cognitive and normative boundedness will be of particular importance:[10]

1. bounded rationality (limitations of cognitive capabilities)[11]
2. bounded willpower (limitations in realising decisions by acting)[12]
3. bounded self-interest (e.g., fairness, altruism)[13]

Empirically, observations strongly deviate from ideal accounts of HO behaviour in games. As far as bargaining is concerned, the classical ultimatum bargaining experiment, the Ultimate Game ('UG'), was formulated with the purpose of refuting the assumption of consistent strictly future-directed choice-making of the HO of classical game theory.[14] Stenographically sketched, in the two-player experiment, a so-called proposer can assign shares of a 'pie'; say, a sum of €10 (divisible in integer amounts of 0, 1, 2, …, 10). The proposer can allocate any of the integer amounts to himself while the second player, the responder, is offered the remainder of the pie. If the responder rejects the monetary amount assigned to her, both get nothing; if she accepts the offer, both get what the proposer assigned (which explains why the term 'ultimatum bargaining game' is used).

The UG in its original form is played once and completely anonymously. There are no consequences that reach beyond the experimental situation itself (no future reputation effects, etc., can play a role). If individuals would be interested predominantly in monetary outcomes, then in the UG, the responder should accept any offer of at least €1 and the proposer should—expecting that response—not offer more than €1. In fact, in UG games, the proposers' modal claim is 50% of the amount to be distributed, and on average about 60%, which is almost always accepted by responders.[15] Since experimental subjects overwhelmingly refute offers of less than

[10] cf. Christine Jolls, Cass R. Sunstein, and Richard H. Thaler, 'A Behavioral Approach to Law and Economics' (1998) 50 Stanford Law Review 1471.

[11] Herbert A. Simon, 'Theories of Decision-Making in Economics and Behavioral Science' (1959) 49.3 American Economic Review 253.

[12] James M. Buchanan, 'The Samaritan's Dilemma' in Edmund S. Phelps (ed.), *Altruism, Morality and Economic Theory* (Russell Sage Foundation 1975) 71; Thomas C. Schelling, *Choice and Consequence* (Harvard University Press 1984).

[13] Werner Güth, Rolf Schmittberger, and Bernd Schwarze, 'An Experimental Analysis of Ultimatum Bargaining' (1982) 3.4 Journal of Economic Behavior & Organization 367; Ernst Fehr and Simon Gächter, 'Altruistic Punishment in Humans' (2002) 415 Nature 137.

[14] Güth, Schmittberger, and Schwarze (n 13).

[15] cf. for an early overview Alvin E. Roth, 'Bargaining Experiments' in John H. Kagel and Alvin E. Roth (eds.), *The Handbook of Experimental Economics* (Princeton University Press 1995) 253; and more recently Werner Güth and Martin G. Kocher, 'More than Thirty Years of Ultimatum Bargaining

33% of the pie and offer more than the smallest feasible positive monetary amount, both response behaviour as well as implied expectations of such behaviour violate the assumption of maximising monetary rewards. Bounded self-interest (fairness, inequality aversion) and bounded rationality (no complete backward induction in search of a subgame perfect Nash equilibrium) are regularities in overt behaviour that are used to explain proposer behaviour in UG. The responder behaviour of regularly rejecting positive amounts of monetary rewards—leaving money on the table—cannot be explained by causal consequences on future rounds of play, if the game experiment is a one-off. The results of the one-off UG experiments therefore refute the central assumption of future directedness of rational choice-making (bygones are not bygones for real actors).

The assumption of self-interest is separate to that of choice-making in view of future causal consequences. If the assumption of self-interest is replaced by concepts of bounded self-interest, it is important to specify the kind of constraints. For instance, if fairness is the constraining concern, it is important to specify which type of fairness norm is assumed to prevail in which contexts. If in bargaining experiments, like UG (including more complex variations of it), roles of players are assigned randomly (symmetric environment), the most prominent distributive fairness norms are egalitarian. Depending on the context and framing of the situation, this can mean an equal split of the feasible gain or equal payment. If roles are not assigned randomly but, for instance, with respect to 'productivity' in creating the pie to be distributed subsequently, the focal norm changes away from egalitarianism. For example, if proposers are more productive in creating the pie than responders (asymmetric environment), they can and will claim more than in the random frame and will tend to succeed.[16]

Steps towards finding a feasible agreement in real bargaining processes have been described in the literature. For example, Selten[17] characterised them as a process of 'aspiration adaptation'. Aspiration levels are characterised by grades to which the goals of players are reached. For each player there is a system of aspiration levels: the first proposal, the players' goal ('what she really wants'), the agreement seen as attainable, a level where a player threatens to leave the negotiation, and the lowest ranked acceptable agreement. If one knows the aspiration

Experiments: Motives, Variations, and a Survey of the Recent Literature' (2014) 108 Journal of Economic Behavior & Organization 396.

[16] cf. Marlies Klemisch-Ahlert, *Bargaining in Economic and Ethical Enviroments: An Experimental Study and Normative Solution Concepts* (Springer 1996) for an analysis of distributive norms in 'thick' or context rich bargaining experiments.

[17] Reinhard Selten, 'Aspiration Adaption Theory' (1998) 42.2–3 Journal of Mathematical Psychology 191.

levels of all players, one can construct a negotiation process and a solution area theoretically.[18]

We can compare Selten's concept with a two-player model originally proposed by Raiffa.[19] The negotiation model as presented in the mature version by Raiffa and colleagues[20] is based on the concepts of a zone of possible agreement ('ZOPA') and best alternatives to a negotiated agreement ('BATNA'). The ZOPA contains all feasible alternatives that are of mutual advantage for both players. A player's BATNA is defined by the best outcome in case the negotiation fails, and may depend on the status quo or on outside options available. The concept also takes into account the first proposals by players as further benchmarks. The agreement the theory predicts is the midpoint of the interval between the first proposals—assuming that the midpoint belongs to the ZOPA. This model can be interpreted as a telescopic one-dimensional simplification of the theoretically more general aspiration adaptation process.[21]

Raiffa and co-authors have collected impressive empirical evidence from many complex negotiation processes involving several dimensions and several rounds. The negotiations of the actors involved in these bargaining processes were not confined to anything akin to the telescopic perspective of a negotiation model that abstracts most of the stages of bargaining. In the sense of neglecting steps of bargaining, the model does not represent negotiation processes. Still, the case-based evidence collected by Raiffa and those working in the same paradigm is empirically informative about regularities concerning negotiation results. In this regard, the Raiffa approach is similar to the field work of Elinor Ostrom[22] on governing the commons or the empirical observations of regularities emergent in laboratory markets by Vernon Smith.[23]

Generally speaking, empirical evidence on regularities in aggregate behaviour is of high practical interest. However, it raises questions concerning the micro-foundations of the telescopic observational regularities in aggregate behaviour. In an explanatory approach that focuses on the causal processes that bring about overt behavioural results, it is necessary to include the reasoning of actors within the limits of their real cognitive capacities.

[18] For an axiomatic characterisation of process and solution area under assumptions of bounded rationality see Marlies Ahlert, 'Aspiration Balancing Agreements: A New Axiomatic Approach to Bounded Rationality in Negotiations' (2007) 29 Analyse & Kritik 121.

[19] Howard Raiffa, *The Art and Science of Negotiation* (Harvard University Press 1982).

[20] Howard Raiffa, John Richardson, and David Metcalfe, *Negotiation Analysis: The Science and Art of Collaborative Decision Making* (Harvard University Press 2002).

[21] Marlies Ahlert and Katharina F. Sträter, 'Refining Raiffa – Aspiration Adaptation within the Zone of Possible Agreements' (2016) 17.3 German Economic Review 298.

[22] Elinor Ostrom, *Governing the Commons* (Cambridge University Press 1990).

[23] Vernon L. Smith, *Bargaining and Market Behavior: Essays in Experimental Economics* (Cambridge University Press 2000).

B. Perspective of the Decision Maker

When analysing the decision making of actors from their participant's perspective, we have to state first what they can know or do not know when they reflect on their options and possible decisions. In UG, for example, the proposer may have some general expectation of the distribution of behavioural dispositions in the population at large but may not exactly know the threshold for acceptance of offers by the specific responder. The proposer must wonder what is the fairness norm the responder has in mind for her threshold? Is it equal split, or does the responder expect less than half of the pie? Moreover, if the fairness aspiration of the responder is not met completely, by an offer too small, how much willpower does she have to accept or reject the offer? And so on.

In answering such questions, proposers can use general empirical information, for example, from experiments and everyday experience. Such general answers reduce proposers' uncertainty. However, additional information about the cognitive processes of the specific responder they are facing is still lacking. In more complex bargaining situations that are not one-off, this specific information may result from the interaction itself. For instance, in a sequence of proposals and counter proposals—other than in case of a single ultimatum followed by a single act of acceptance/rejection—information concerning the co-player's type becomes available. In this 'learning process', each party may begin with a different view on the bargaining problem. Moreover, other than the UG's monetary pie—with a one-dimensional, 'more-rather-than-less' ranking representing some 'natural' order of 'better and/or worse'—the object of the negotiation may be characterised by several dimensions. In multi-dimensional situations, players may reveal how important the different dimensions are to them. Though multi-dimensionality may complicate analyses, differences in importance of dimensions between players can also enlarge the space of possible agreements from the point of view of decision makers.

Still, even if the dimensions are well-defined, there may be a variety of distributive norms that could be applied in context-dependent ways. The application of the possibly divergent norms endorsed by players will lead to the emergence of diverse goals that establish claims or aspirations defined on the dimensions of the problem. In consequence, the bargaining problem will appear to the bargainers as a conflict of norms in which an agreement becomes a compromise between competing norms.

Now, even if mutually advantageous compromises that would lead to better outcomes for all participants exist, it is not a foregone conclusion that they can manage to agree on them. In particular, if, from the variety of applicable norms, actors select the norms they endorse in a self-serving manner,[24] agreements may

[24] For example, Klemisch-Ahlert (n 16); Jolls, Sunstein, and Thaler (n 10).

be foreclosed. In this way, self-serving biases in the selection of norms—as seem particularly characteristic for legal disputes—can explain bargaining impasses or negotiation failures.[25]

Many other examples of so-called biases can be found in the empirical literature. Without going into details, a general message that theories of biases in boundedly rational behaviour have in store for boundedly rational and boundedly self-interested bargainers seems clear: they should—on behalf of fulfilling their own aspirations—be aware of the biases and constraints that may impede reaching mutually advantageous agreements. Another message is that where classical ideal rationality conceptions would simply assume that all rational actors command complete knowledge of interactions as well as of the theories concerning such interactions in a bounded rationality conception, there is a systematic role for advisors. To the role of advisors, I turn next.

C. Perspective of the Advisor

Relying on the empirical evidence that concessions are derived from adapting aspirations, an advisor of negotiators will—on the basis of evidence-based theories of negotiation—have to give advice on which concessions should be made and when. The advisor should do so on the basis of the general law-like regularity that in negotiations there is a sequence of aspiration levels structuring the concession-making process of each negotiator (player). Each player has good evidence-based reasons not to give up an aspiration level too 'early' or too 'easily' for an 'insufficient' quid pro quo.[26] This is supported by the well-corroborated general (evidence-based) observation that concessions made in a negotiation will *irrevocably* (causally) influence the aspiration levels of other negotiators who will not treat concessions once they are made as a matter of further negotiation.

The process of *mutual* concession-making has features of exchange in the original Smithian sense of 'give me that which I want and you shall have this which you want'.[27] Exchange presupposes 'stability of possession' which can be changed only in agreement. In a sequence of exchanges of concessions, a concession received needs to be treated as a kind of possession—like a good that has already changed hands. In that sense, the consequences will be akin to endowment effects (like in the well-known example of a person who, initially endowed with a mug, will ask about twice as much for giving away the mug than she is willing to pay for it if she is initially endowed with money rather than the mug). This implies a central

[25] Linda Babcock and George Loewenstein, 'Explaining Bargaining Impasse: The Role of Self-Serving Biases' (1997) 11.1 Journal of Economic Perspectives 109.

[26] cf. Ahlert (n 18).

[27] Adam Smith, *An Inquiry into the Nature and Causes of the Wealth of Nations* (first published in 1776, vol. I edn Liberty Classics, Liberty Press 1978) 2.

evidence-based principle guiding advice: only if the other players make 'adequate' steps in terms of giving up 'equivalent' aspirations should further concessions be made by an advisee.

Of course, this principle requires prudent judgment to adapt it to specific circumstances. For instance, even if aspirations are balanced, in that they would offer the chance for a mutually advantageous 'exchange' of concessions, somebody has to make a first move. To determine who that should be requires 'clinical' rather than 'statistical judgement'.[28] There is a legitimate role for the personal judgment of the expert advisor, but only *after* he has exhausted his knowledge of regularities that can be supported by statistical evidence.

During all steps of the ongoing negotiation process, reasoning and learning about the aspirations of others will take place and, in addition, reasoning about what the other players know or think about the aspirations of opponents. Players may signal their aspiration levels to the other players, which helps to coordinate concession-making. Such circumstantial conditions and evidence cannot be foreseen by general theories. Only some general aspects of the process can be foreseen. For instance, if somebody does not want to give up a certain level, general observations support the view that giving some *reason* may facilitate the concession-making of others.

The provision of reasons is one of the aspects that tend to be neglected if advice for negotiators is based on evidence-based regularities derived from telescopic simplifications that focus on outcome space. Such neglect of details of real negotiation processes is a necessary consequence of telescopic abstractions. Still, abstract regularities can play a central role in advice giving. The simple stylised example of a recent prominent lawsuit between Apple and Qualcomm and the negotiations that took place in its shadow illustrates how. Relying exclusively on publicly accessible information (in media like *The Economist*, *Die Welt*, etc., that can be easily traced by any user of Google), not only will a stylised picture of the frame of the negotiation that finally led to an out-of-court agreement emerge; beyond this, the potential of telescopic evidence-based negotiation theory for practical purposes stands out.

IV. The Apple Qualcomm Dispute

The two players are the firms Apple and Qualcomm. During the past few years, Apple relied on innovative chips delivered by Qualcomm. Holding patents on the design of these chips, Qualcomm charged 5% on retail prices of all smartphone sales of Apple if the products included Qualcomm-designed chips.

[28] cf. Paul E. Meehl, *Clinical Versus Statistical Prediction: A Theoretical Analysis and a Review of the Evidence* (Echo Point Books & Media 2013).

Apple complained about these charges for several reasons. A central argument of Apple's was that the charge on the whole retail price is inappropriate, since the price also depends on other innovations than Qualcomm chips. Apple argued that Qualcomm exploited an illegitimate monopoly position and it sued Qualcomm in California and in China, demanding more than US$1 billion in damages.

Qualcomm reacted by suing Apple for patent infringement. The firm demanded up to US$10 billion from Apple. Qualcomm also tried to obtain an interdiction to sell Apple smartphones in several countries. In addition, they stopped providing the processors.

Apple started switching to processors produced by the competing chip producer, Intel, substituting Qualcomm products for the fourth-generation ('4G') technology. However, eventually Intel could not deliver high-quality processors needed for the new fifth-generation ('5G') technology. For Apple as a market leader, 5G chips are absolutely essential to produce smartphones meeting the newest standards. This means they will have to rely on products by Qualcomm to sustain their market position and future bottom line.

After the court procedure commenced, Apple and Qualcomm negotiated and reached an agreement out of court. It is said that Apple paid slightly less than US$5 billion to Qualcomm which made several concessions in return. Assuming that this information is correct, two observations can be made. First, the financial side of the agreement surprisingly conforms to the outcome predicted by the telescopic Raiffa theory. Second, we have to take notice of the information-generating role of involving the court system as a device for sending credible rather than arbitrary signals concerning the initial demands of the negotiation.

The two observations can be illustrated (though not fully substantiated) by the publicly accessible information concerning the negotiations outside court. For each player, there is the option not to agree to any proposed agreement. This defines the BATNA in terms of the expected outcome of the lawsuits together with possible consequences for future cooperation between both firms. The ZOPA for the negotiation outside court is defined by the BATNAs of both players. For the sake of simplicity of illustration, let us assume the BATNAs to be equal to the respective claims in court. These amounts became known to both players in the course of initiating court procedures, since they had to reveal them when suing in a non-arbitrary, if partly self-serving, manner.

The range of a court decision Apple has to face is defined by what they would get if they win (US$1 billion), or what they maximally have to pay (US$10 billion) if they lose. (In addition, there are, of course, the costs of the lawsuit and other consequences if they lose, which we cannot include here since we do not know the monetary amounts.) The fact that Qualcomm sued and demanded a very high amount, and also took other legal measures to restrict Apple's market position and profit, might show that Qualcomm was very confident of success. It could also indicate that a self-serving bias influenced Qualcomm's actions in suing and the size of their claim.[29] That Qualcomm was trying to 'bluff' entirely was unlikely in view of the involvement of the courts and the possibility that the bluff might be called in court. In any event, other aspects of the interaction were all too real for Apple. Some of the severe negative consequences for Apple resulting from losing the case were related to future profits without being part of the lawsuit. In particular, Apple was expecting to be dependent on the future delivery of Qualcomm's chips for the new 5G technology.

As turned out while the dispute continued, there is de facto no competition among high-quality providers (Intel withdrew in step with the out-of-court agreement). Though this weakened Apple's position outside court, it strengthened the force of Apple's ('in-court') argument concerning the abuse of a monopoly position by Qualcomm. If the argument concerning the abuse of a monopoly position had prevailed, it would have influenced Qualcomm's prospect of future rent extraction from Apple massively.[30]

The information that emerged during the interaction will have exerted an influence on Apple's and Qualcomm's perceptions of consequences of agreement and disagreement, respectively. This is in line with the process view of bargaining and the information-generating function of that process among boundedly rational actors. It may have motivated the search for, and the speedy emergence of, the agreement that took external observers by surprise.

The range of the court decision Qualcomm had to face was inverse to the range faced by Apple. However, Qualcomm might have had a higher perception of the probability of winning than Apple had of losing. Though Qualcomm, on the one hand, may have found corroboration for the strength of its position in the course of the negotiation, on the other, the outside option for Qualcomm if both did not find an outside agreement included forgone future profit opportunities. In the shadow of the common future, the question essentially must have boiled down to what Qualcomm would be able to charge for its patents (which was clearly dependent on the strength of the anti-monopoly case).

To summarise, in the course of the ongoing negotiations in the shadow of court procedures, information substantiating the interest of *both* players to reach an out-of-court agreement and to maintain a promising further business relationship transpired, and in all likelihood became increasingly shared by both actors. After this illustration of the second observation concerning information-creating aspects of the negotiation process, let us turn next to the first observation concerning the 'surprising fit' with Raiffa's telescopic approach.

[29] Linda Babcock et al., 'Biased Judgments of Fairness in Bargaining' (1995) 85.5 The American Economic Review 1337.

[30] cf. Paul Milgrom and John Roberts, *Economics, Organization and Management* (Prentice Hall 1992) on such extraction in business.

Following the structure suggested by Raiffa, we can roughly define a ZOPA for the outside negotiation by the interval consisting of the worst outcome for Qualcomm, that is, having to pay US$1 billion, and the worst outcome for Apple, that is, having to pay about US$10 billion. The interval of the ZOPA has a spread of about US$11 billion. If we apply Raiffa's 'split the difference' rule, we may consider the interval from the perspective of Apple. Either Apple receives US$1 billion (equivalent to a 'payment' of –US$1 billion by Apple) or it has to pay US$10 billion. The payment interval for Apple is [–1, 10] in billion dollars. The difference is US$11 billion. Splitting that difference yields US$5.5 billion and adding it to –US$1 billion or subtracting it from US$10 billion yields a midpoint of US$4.5 billion. A payment of $US4.5 billion by Apple is roughly what was reported in the media, thus vindicating the prediction of Raiffa's model.

Of course, Raiffa's telescopic approach did not initially translate into specific behavioural recommendations for the lawyers and agents representing both firms. At the beginning of their task they could not calculate a ZOPA, since they did not have sufficient information on the aspirations of the other side. In view of gathering missing information, it seems prudent that Apple decided on suing and Qualcomm on counter-suing. That the respective claims would have to be justifiable in court rendered the claims credible.

In my interpretation, the role of a possible court process in such cases as the Apple Qualcomm dispute is to reveal the claims of both sides that could be justified *in court*. Basing a ZOPA on credible information was avoiding or at least mitigating the risk that unjustifiable ('self-serving') initial claims could provoke a failure of negotiations. (Going to court turned out to be a promotor for the negotiations out of court. Additional facilitators of agreement being the trajectory of 5G development and the perspective of high profits in the future.)

Since the sketch of the situation was based solely on media reports, any further speculations concerning the case seem out of place. However, it seems striking how well the abstract model of Raiffa fares. This may be a pure coincidence but I should like to share the impression that there is a more general message to the effect that it is useful to rely on both the orientation by telescopic bargaining conceptions as general heuristics and the very specific piecemeal information from experimental economic and experimental psychology studies.

V. Consequences

The reasoning about knowledge approach that analyses strategic interaction from the internal point of view of players assumes deliberations that no real human being can perform. It does not help in developing useful advice for boundedly rational actors since the latter are neither willing nor able to follow such advice in pursuit of their given goals.

Empirical and experimental research on how people do, in fact, bargain can teach us some lessons about the scope and limits of normative orientations and cognitive abilities in bargaining situations. For instance, we know something about the empirical likelihood that a responder in an ultimatum game may reject offers deemed too low, even though fully rational opportunism would dictate otherwise. From this, a more specific strategic advice for the proposer not to go below certain thresholds may be derived. Or, to give another example, the information that delaying the point in time of the response may empirically enhance the likelihood of opportunistic rather than norm-guided behaviour on the responder side[31] may induce a proposer to think about how to bring about such a delay.

The risk that the result of allowing for such considerations will invite mere casuistry cannot be denied. However, since the heterogeneity of complex human behavioural responses cannot be denied either—whatever homogeneity ideal extreme theories may assume—we should look for empirically founded theories of intermediate range. We need statistically calibrated diagnostic and predictive instruments that can help going beyond mere expert judgment in practical decision making. The way towards this is not infighting about idealisations of rationality but empirical research on workable rationality. And, as the surprising adequacy of the Raiffa approach in the Apple Qualcomm example seems to indicate, there may be a still insufficiently understood role for telescopic—though not ideal—bargaining models.

In practice, compromises are approached stepwise if feasible, while feasibility or unfeasibility will be revealed only during the process of bargaining. Contrary to theories that rely on exogenously given preferences that evaluate full negotiation strategies, the adaptive behaviour in negotiations should not be classified and ranked in terms of degrees of rationality approaching the ideal standard. The 'rational' in boundedly rational behaviour amounts to an intentional type of goal-oriented, forward-looking choice-making, and not to the pursuit of exogenously given integrated preferences. Workable rationality is bounded and local rather than unbounded and global.

A central message from empirical and experimental research on negotiations is that besides certain general proclivities, situational context always matters. In particular, the psychological theory of aspiration formation and aspiration adaptation in bargaining allows for a context-sensitive approach, since aspirations are formed in context-dependent ways. This being said, it deserves to be acknowledged that the evidence-based telescopic conceptions of bargaining of the Raiffa school that take into account only a few aspects of the problem seem to be working sometimes remarkably well. Opting for the middle ground appears to be the workable rational strategy of theory development here.

[31] cf. Veronika Grimm and Friederike Mengel, 'Let Me Sleep on It: Delay Reduces Rejection Rates in Ultimatum Games' (2011) 111.2 Economics Letters 113.

PART II

INDIVIDUAL CHOICE AND THE LAW

4

Most People Like Nudges—and Why that Matters

Lucia A. Reisch, Cass R. Sunstein, and Micha Kaiser[1]

Abstract: This chapter reports the results of nationally representative surveys in fourteen countries, investigating the attitudes of people towards nudges and nudging, with a particular focus on environmental and health nudges. The countries covered are Australia, Brazil, Canada, China, Denmark, France, Germany, Hungary, Italy, Japan, Russia, South Africa, South Korea, and the United Kingdom. There is strong majority support for both health and environmental nudges in all countries, with the exception of Japan, Denmark, and Hungary. China and South Korea stand out with particularly high acceptance rates. Beyond reporting the results of the combined dataset for the first time, the chapter provides an explanation first, of why policy makers might be interested in public approval or disapproval of nudges, and second, how information of public acceptance can inform both uses of and constraints on nudging.

I. Overview

Behavioural public policy, using so-called nudges[2] to steer behaviour in a way that preserves liberty, is gaining ground worldwide.[3] Recently, a new strand of research has begun to investigate whether and when citizens approve of nudges as a policy tool. Initial surveys explored nationally representative samples in the United States and Canada,[4] several European

[1] This study was supported by grants from the Governing Responsible Business ('GRB') Research Environment at the Department of Management, Communication and Society, Copenhagen Business School (Denmark).

[2] Richard Thaler and Cass R. Sunstein, *Nudge: Improving Decisions about Health, Wealth, and Happiness* (Yale University Press 2008).

[3] Cass R. Sunstein, 'The Council of Psychological Advisers' (2016) 67 Annual Review of Psychology 713–37; Joana Sousa Lourenco et al., *Behavioural Insights Applied to Policy*, Report No. EUR 27726 EN (Joint Research Centre 2016); OECD, *Use of Behavioural Insights in Consumer Policy* (2017) OECD Science, Technology and Innovation Policy Papers No. 36.

[4] Gidon Felsen, Noah Castelo, and Peter B. Reiner, 'Decisional Enhancement and Autonomy: Public Attitudes Towards Overt and Covert Nudges' (2013) 8 Judgment and Decision Making 202–13;

Lucia A. Reisch, Cass R. Sunstein, and Micha Kaiser, *Most People Like Nudges—and Why that Matters* In: *Theories of Choice*. Edited by: Stefan Grundmann and Philipp Hacker, Oxford University Press (2021). © The several contributors.
DOI: 10.1093/oso/9780198863175.003.0005

nations,[5] and most recently, a selection of countries worldwide.[6] Our long-term project is to extend this research by enlarging the country dataset, adding more empirical evidence step by step, and ultimately 'mapping' people's attitudes towards environmental and health nudges across the globe. Indeed, the latter appears feasible. We have started to cluster some of the world's nations into discernible categories of similar nations that we provisionally coined 'principled pro-nudge', 'cautiously pro-nudge', and 'massively pro-nudge' nations.[7]

The present chapter has two goals. First, we offer survey results on public approval from fourteen countries: Australia (AU), Brazil (BR), Canada (CA), China (CN), Denmark (DK), France (FR), Germany (DE), Hungary (HU), Italy (IT), Japan (JP), Russia (RU), South Africa (ZA), South Korea (KR), and the United Kingdom (GB). Where appropriate, we also draw on results from similar surveys conducted in the United States[8] and from Ireland.[9] While the results of both the European[10] and the worldwide survey[11] have been published elsewhere, the present chapter provides a condensed overview on the combined dataset in full.[12] As expected, deviations of results from the earlier studies are negligible and even those might be a product of methodological differences rather than of anything real.

Second, we briefly discuss some implications of these findings. We explore why policy makers might be well advised to investigate the public approval or

Janice Y. Jung and Barbara A. Mellers, 'American Attitudes Toward Nudges' (2016) 11 Judgment and Decision Making 62–74; Cass R. Sunstein, *The Ethics of Influence: Government in the Age of Behavioural Science* (Cambridge University Press 2016); David Tannenbaum, Craig R. Fox, and Todd Rogers, 'On the Misplaced Politics of Behavioural Policy Interventions' (2017) 1 Nature Human Behaviour 0130. doi: 10.1038/s41562-017-0130.

5 William Hagman et al., 'Public Views on Policies Involving Nudges' (2015) 6 Review of Philosophy and Psychology 439–53; Astrid F. Junghans, Tracy T. L. Cheung, and Denise T. D. De Ridder, 'Under Consumers' Scrutiny: An Investigation into Consumers' Attitudes and Concerns about Nudging in the Realm of Health Behaviour' (2015) 15 BMC Public Health 336, doi: 10.1186/s12889-015-1691-8; Astrid F. Junghans, David Marchiori, and Denise T. D. De Ridder, *The Who and How of Nudging: Cross-national Perspectives on Consumer Approval in Eating Behaviour* (Unpublished Manuscript, Utrecht University 2016); Dragos C. Petrescu, 'Public Acceptability in the UK and USA of Nudging to Reduce Obesity: The Example of Reducing Sugar-Sweetened Beverages Consumption' (2016) 11 PLoS One, e0155995, doi:10.1371/journal.pone.0155995; Lucia A. Reisch and Cass R. Sunstein, 'Do Europeans Like Nudges?' (2016) 1 Judgment and Decision Making 310–25; Lucia A. Reisch, Cass A. Sunstein, and Wencke Gwozdz, 'Beyond Carrots and Sticks: Europeans Support Health Nudges' Viewpoint article (2016) 69 Food Policy 1–10.

6 Cass R. Sunstein, Lucia A. Reisch, and Julius Rauber, 'A Worldwide Consensus on Nudging? Not Quite, But Almost' (2017) 12 Regulation & Governance 3, doi:10.1111/rego.12161. The present chapter owes much to this article; however, all presented figures as well as Table 4.2 have been prepared specifically for this chapter.

7 Sunstein, Reisch, and Rauber (n 6).

8 Sunstein (n 3).

9 The Irish data have not been published yet.

10 Reisch and Sunstein (n 5); Reisch, Sunstein, and Gwozdz (n 5).

11 Sunstein, Reisch, and Rauber (n 6).

12 For a detailed analysis: Cass R. Sunstein and Lucia A. Reisch, *Trusting Nudges: Toward a Bill of Rights for Nudging* (Routledge 2019).

disapproval of nudges and how information about public attitudes could inform what officials do in the domain of nudging.

The nations of our dataset were chosen in order to obtain a broad sample of countries with diversity along several lines, including countries widely distributed on a scale from liberal democracies with freedom of speech to authoritarian one-party regimes that closely watch their citizens. We cover four of the five BRICS (Brazil, Russia, India, China, South Africa) countries as well as countries with markedly different levels of gross domestic product ('GDP') and welfare. Finally, we chose countries representing different cultural clusters. The combined dataset includes at least one country from eight of the ten cultural clusters used in cultural studies,[13] with 'Middle Eastern' and 'Southern Asia' missing. Moreover, all of these countries are covered in one of the publicly available worldwide social surveys (e.g., Worldwide Value Survey; OECD Trust in Government Survey), and there are (not always recent, however) data on potentially relevant factors such as social trust, trust in government, and level of corruption or values regarding individualism and collectivism, that we generally investigate. From a methodological perspective, the chosen countries show a decent online penetration of their population as well as sufficiently high literacy rates, which are both prerequisites for online representative surveys.

We conducted online surveys that were representative for age, gender, region, and education for fifteen nudges. About 1,000 respondents per country (2,000 in the United Kingdom) were asked the simple question whether they approve or disapprove of fifteen selected nudges. In order to be able to compare and enlarge the overall dataset, we used the same survey instrument and largely the same methodology applied in both the European[14] and the worldwide study.[15] However, we had to adapt a few socio-demographic variables due to limited comparability. We report briefly on the statistical challenges below.

As mentioned earlier,[16] we find that the nations of the world can be provisionally grouped into three categories. The first category is the largest group of mostly liberal democracies (Australia, Brazil, Canada, France, Germany, Italy, Russia, South Africa, the United Kingdom), with similar results that are also consistent with the existing U.S. data. In this category, there is a general majority approval of environmental and health nudges, with informative qualifications. The second category (Denmark, Hungary, and Japan) shows significantly lower

[13] The ten 'culture clusters' suggested by cultural studies (e.g., Robert J. House et al., *Strategic Leadership across Cultures: The GLOBE Study of CEO Leadership Behaviour and Effectiveness in 24 Countries* (Sage 2014) are: South Asia, Anglo, Arab/Middle Eastern, Germanic Europe, Latin Europe, Eastern Europe, Confucian Asia, Latin America, (Sub-Sahara) Africa, and Nordic Europe

[14] Reisch and Sunstein (n 5).

[15] Sunstein, Reisch, and Rauber (n 6).

[16] Ibid.

approval rates; importantly, however, majorities continue to support most of the tested nudges. The third category consists of nations with massively high approval ratings (China and South Korea are the current examples); these ratings call for a close investigation of potential causal factors, such as the fear of limited anonymity of responses.

II. Our Study

Sampling and survey were performed with the support of German-based GFK (Gesellschaft für Konsumforschung)[17] for the European countries, and for the worldwide countries with the help of Qualtrics,[18] a leading international market research company. To ensure the necessary level of scientific rigour and to reach a high level of online representativeness of the sample (with respect to age, gender, educational level, and region), we monitored and commented on each step of the sampling and survey implementation before and during field time. The details of the sampling and survey have been described elsewhere in detail and will not be repeated here.[19]

We applied the same instrument in all fourteen countries. The core is a questionnaire with fifteen items, each describing a nudge-like policy intervention issued by 'government' (see Table 4.1).

The word 'nudge' was deliberately not used in the questionnaire to avoid framing and (probably unknown) technical language, but we described the policy intervention as clearly and unambiguously as possible. For each item, respondents were asked to indicate whether they 'approve' or 'do not approve' (no scale) of this specific 'hypothetical policy'. The items focused on the environment (e.g., green energy, greenhouse gas emissions) as well as on healthy lifestyles (e.g., obesity, salt intake, meat and sugar consumption). They were designed to represent different levels of governmental intrusion—from soft governmental educational campaigns to government encouraging or requiring defaults to governmental mandates—and included System 1 nudges (non-educative) and System 2 nudges (educative) targeting individuals and supermarkets or movie theatres. We also included one item (for convenience denominated 'Nudge 8') that we would not characterise as a nudge: subliminal advertising against overeating and smoking is a form of hidden manipulation, and hence inconsistent with the standard definition of nudges.[20] Similarly, a meat-free day in a cafeteria (for convenience denominated 'Nudge 15')

[17] http://www.gfk.com.
[18] http://www.qualtrics.com.
[19] Reisch and Sunstein (n 5); Sunstein, Reisch, and Rauber (n 6).
[20] Thaler and Sunstein (n 2).

Table 4.1 The fifteen nudges

1. The federal government requires calorie labels at chain restaurants (such as McDonald's and Burger King).
2. The federal government requires a 'traffic lights' system for food, by which healthy foods would be sold with a small green label, unhealthy foods with a small red label, and foods that are neither especially healthy nor especially unhealthy with a small yellow label.
3. The federal government encourages (without requiring) electricity providers to adopt a system in which consumers would be automatically enrolled in a 'green' (environmentally friendly) energy supplier but could opt out if they wished.
4. A state law requiring people to say, when they obtain their drivers' licence, whether they want to be organ donors.
5. A state law requires all large grocery stores to place their most healthy foods in a prominent, visible location.
6. To reduce deaths and injuries associated with distracted driving, the national government adopts a public education campaign, consisting of vivid and sometimes graphic stories and images, designed to discourage people from texting, emailing, or talking on their cell phones while driving.
7. To reduce childhood obesity, the national government adopts a public education campaign, consisting of information that parents can use to make healthier choices for their children.
8. The federal government requires movie theatres to provide subliminal advertisements (i.e., advertisements that go by so quickly that people are not consciously aware of them) designed to discourage people from smoking and overeating.
9. The federal government requires airlines to charge people, with their airline tickets, a specific amount to offset their carbon emissions (about €10 per ticket); under the programme, people can opt out of the payment if they explicitly say that they do not want to pay it.
10. The federal government requires labels on products that have unusually high levels of salt, as in 'This product has been found to contain unusually high levels of salt, which may be harmful to your health'.
11. The federal government assumes, on tax returns, that people want to donate €50 to the Red Cross (or to another good cause) subject to opt out if people explicitly say that they do not want to make that donation.
12. The federal government requires movie theatres to run public education messages designed to discourage people from smoking and overeating.
13. The federal government requires large electricity providers to adopt a system in which consumers would be automatically enrolled in a 'green' (environmentally friendly) energy supplier but could opt out if they wished.
14. To halt the rising obesity problem, the federal government requires large supermarket chains to keep cashier areas free of sweets.
15. For reasons of public health and climate protection, the federal government requires canteens in public institutions (schools, public administrations, and similar) to have one meat-free day per week

(Table 4.1 reproduced with permission from: Journal of Regulation and Governance, https://onlinelibrary.wiley.com/doi/epdf/10.1111/rego.12161; Table 2, p. 7)

does not qualify as a nudge because it imposes a prohibition on the customer, who cannot easily opt out in favour of a meat dish (except by having to choose another restaurant).

The questions were translated into the respective languages and back translated, and pilot tests were run. In the Computer-Assisted Web Interviews ('CAWI') surveys, the questions were presented in a randomised order and a range of validity and robustness checks (i.e., for time and attention) were included. Responses were allowed to enter the final sample only when they met these standards, were provided by respondents aged eighteen years and older who lived in the respective country, and who used its official language. Only fully completed questionnaires were accepted. However, all the limitations that typically apply to online surveys[21] also apply to our work.

Field work in Europe was conducted in the first half of September 2015; in the worldwide countries, the bulk of data was collected between November and December 2016. We also collected information on the core socio-demographic variables as well as on political attitudes.[22] Comparability of socio-demographic variables among the fourteen countries was given for gender (male/female), age (years), and education (university degree). Comparability was less clear-cut for region and income, and these were for the time being excluded from the analysis of the overall sample.[23] The same holds true for political attitudes: even though this variable was measured in two different ways in the worldwide sample, namely, by recent vote ('Who did you vote for at the most recent elections?') and by a self-assessment conservatism/liberalism scale, we excluded this variable in the analysis of the overall sample. Regarding the former, at the global level, there is no categorisation available comparable to the political groups in the European Parliament; as regards the latter, the scale was only used in the worldwide study and therefore could not be applied to the overall dataset.

The country datasets were merged into one dataset. Approval rates were calculated per nudge and per country, and a multilevel analysis was conducted. The same five independent variables as in the earlier studies were constructed; the fifteen nudges were clustered with respect to their level of intrusiveness. Average approval rates for each dependent variable were calculated. Coding and analysis were done mainly in STATA.[24]

[21] See e.g., Valerie M. Sue and Lois A. Ritter, *Conducting Online Surveys* (2nd edn, Sage 2012)

[22] Full data and survey questions are available in Reisch and Sunstein (n 5) and Sunstein, Reisch, and Rauber (n 6); the survey in the different languages is available from the authors on request.

[23] However, for national analysis, these socio-demographic variables are quite useful to test hypothesis on how socio-demographics are linked to approval.

[24] http://www.stata.com.

III. Results

A. Types of Nudges along Level of Intrusion and Country Cluster

In order to be comparable, we grouped the fifteen nudges in categories, corresponding to levels of depth of intervention: governmental information campaigns (Nudges 6, 7, 12) (Figure 4.1); mandatory information imposed by governments (Nudges 1, 2, 10) (Figure 4.2); mandatory default rules imposed by governments (Nudges 3, 4, 5, 9, 11, 13) (Figure 4.3); mandatory subliminal advertising ('Non-nudge' 8) (Figure 4.4); and mandatory choice architecture in supermarkets and public cafeterias (Nudge 14 and 'Non-nudge' 15) (Figure 4.5). Moreover, we tentatively grouped the countries in our three country categories with respect to average approval per nudge (as marked in different shades in Figures 4.1–4.5).[25]

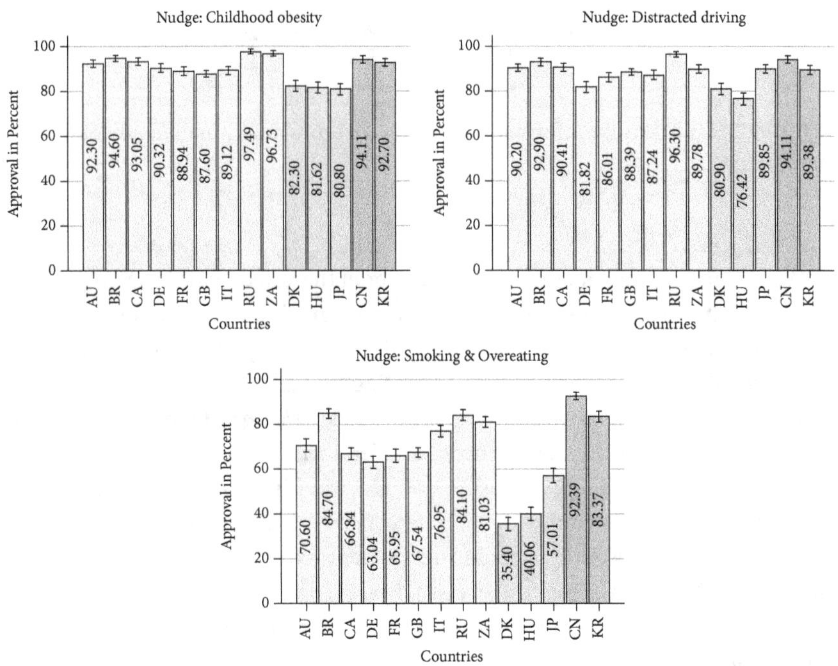

Figure 4.1 Bar charts for information nudges: Government campaigns, total support in %.

[25] Since the analysis is based on the combination of two different data sources into a single dataset, we refrain from including individual sample weights. The following are the results of an unweighted analysis.

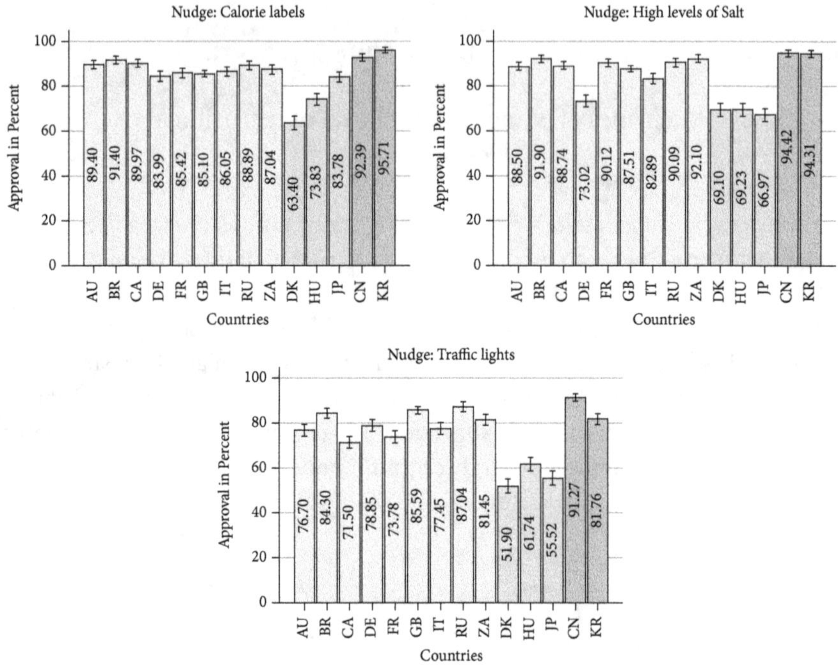

Figure 4.2 Bar charts for information nudges, governmentally mandated; total support in %.

With respect to information campaigns about the risks of childhood obesity and distracted driving, we observe majority support in all fourteen nations. While for childhood obesity and distracted driving, the level of support is overwhelming, it is somewhat lower for smoking and overeating. In particular, Denmark, Hungary, and Japan show comparatively low approval rates. (We do not have an explanation and would require further data in order to offer one.)

Mandatory information disclosure also receives high levels of support and the similarities among the countries are noteworthy. Again, Denmark, Hungary, and Japan are the obvious outliers; majorities do approve of this, but in all cases, these three countries show the highest levels of disapproval.

With respect to default rules, approval levels are lower; in some cases, majorities even disapprove. Consistent with findings in the United States,[26] strong majorities favour not only encouragement of automatic enrolment in green energy but also a mandate to that effect. Moreover, majorities disapprove of a default carbon charge in all countries except for China and South Korea. This pattern remains

[26] Sunstein (n 3).

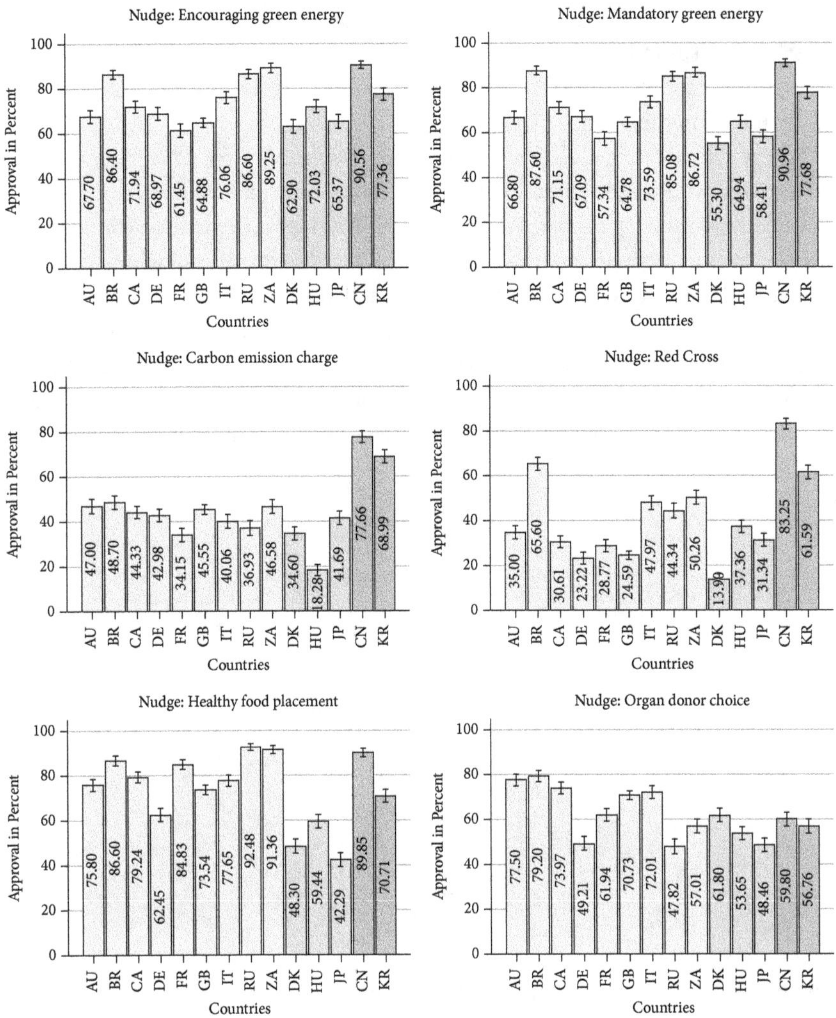

Figure 4.3 Bar charts for default rules, total support in %.

similar in the case of a default charitable donation. The basic principle here seems to have something to do with loss aversion. In general, people do not favour default rules that would take people's money without their explicit consent. Because of their high approval rates, China, South Korea, and (to a lesser extent) Brazil are outliers here.

With respect to healthy food placement and actively opting in to organ donation programmes, the picture is relatively consistent across nations. For healthy food placement, Denmark, Hungary, and Japan are yet again the evident outliers. For organ donation, China and South Korea show what is, for those nations, comparatively low approval ratings. Also, majorities disapprove in Germany and Russia as well as in Japan.

Figure 4.4 shows the markedly lower overall approval of subliminal advertising as compared to the other (real) nudges.

As expected, we see high levels of disapproval of subliminal advertising, even for advertising what might seem to be a good cause. This pattern is roughly followed in Canada, Denmark, France, Germany, Hungary, Japan, the United Kingdom, and Russia. To our surprise, we find massively high approval rates in China and South Korea, and majority support in Australia, Brazil, Italy, and South Africa.

As shown in Figure 4.5, sweet-free cashier zones and meat-free days produced similar patterns of results. The former—a kind of choice architecture designed to promote health—did obtain majority support in all nations except Hungary and Japan, but with a significant spread between the highest rate (in the United

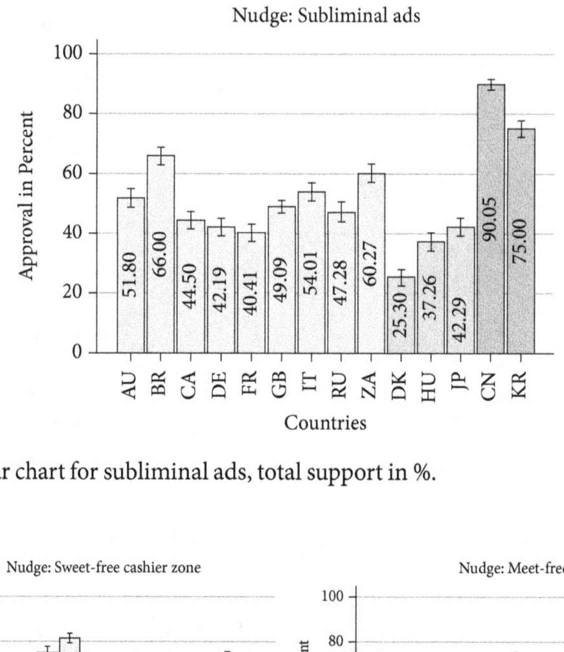

Figure 4.4 Bar chart for subliminal ads, total support in %.

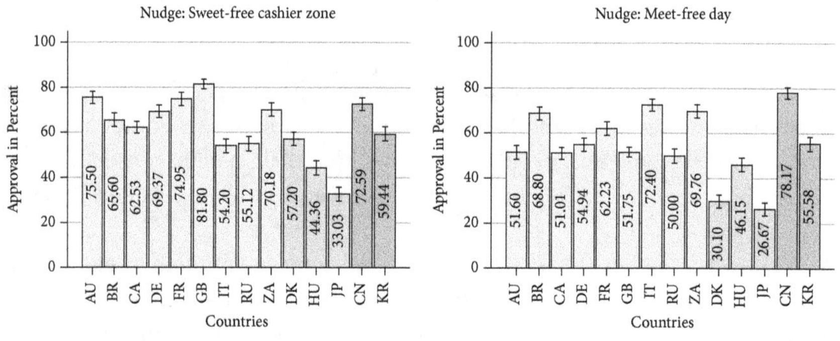

Figure 4.5 Bar charts for other mandates, total support in %.

Table 4.2 Estimates of selected socio-demographics on nudge approval per nudge cluster: results of a multilevel analysis of fourteen countries

	(1)	(2)	(3)	(4)	(5)
Nudge Cluster	**Information: Government campaigns**	**Information: Governmentally mandated nudges**	**Default rules**	**Subliminal advertising**	**Other mandates**
Male	−1.146**	−1.746***	−2.915***	−5.531***	−6.202***
	(0.403)	(0.430)	(0.432)	(0.778)	(0.607)
Age (in years)	0.070***	0.045***	−0.107***	−0.08717***	0.118***
	(0.013)	(0.014)	(0.014)	(0.025)	(0.020)
University degree	0.0953	0.006	−1.122	−2.293	1.736
	(0.630)	(0.674)	(0.677)	(1.220)	(0.951)
Obs.	14,975	14,975	14,975	14,975	14,975
ICC (intercept = country)	0.037	0.142	0.124	0.099	0.096
	(0.014)	(0.047)	0.041	(0.034)	(0.033)

Notes: Estimates of a two-level random intercept model. Dependent variables are the average nudge groups by intrusiveness (Min: 0; Max: 100). The intraclass correlation coefficient ('ICC') is the proportion of total variance that is attributed to the cluster 'country'. Standard errors in parentheses. * $p \leq 0.05$, ** $p \leq 0.01$, *** $p \leq 0.001$.

Kingdom) and the lowest (in Italy). Meat-free days also obtained majority support in all nations with, again, the exception of Denmark, Hungary, and Japan. For this intervention, China was the most supportive and Russia the least.

B. Multilevel Regression

The results of the multilevel regression using the fourteen-country dataset are presented in Table 4.2. We estimated the multilevel regression for each of the five levels of depth of intervention with the approval rates of the fifteen nudges (dependent variables) and calculated mean approval in percentages by level of intervention. We used a selected set of socio-demographic variables (gender, age, and educational level by university degree) as independent variables on individual level and country on the country level. The following model was employed:

$$y_{ij} = \beta_0 + \beta_1 x_{ij} + u_j + e_{ij} \qquad e_{ij} \sim N(0, \sigma_e^2)$$
$$u_j \sim N(0, \sigma_u^2)$$

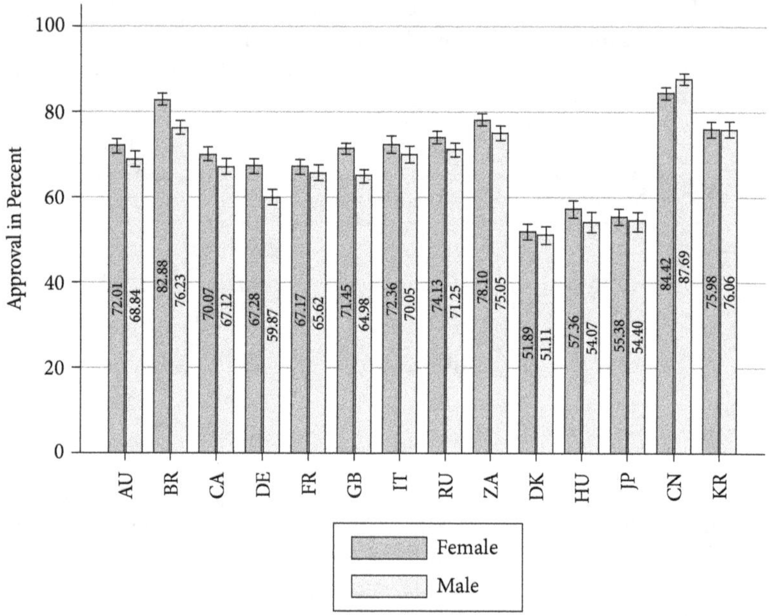

Figure 4.6 Gender differences about all nudges per country, total support in %.

With y_{ij} equal to the average nudge groups by intrusiveness of individual i in country j, x_{ij} is a 1×3 vector of socio-demographic variables, while u_j and e_{ij} are the random components of i and j, respectively.

Strengthening the results of the European and worldwide studies, gender has an effect on the approval rates: women approve of the tested nudges significantly more than men. This holds true for most of the nudges in almost all of the countries (Figures 4.6 and 4.7). This effect is particularly strong for the nudge clusters (4) and (5). We have speculated elsewhere why this might be the case.[27] We also find the same small but significant age effect as in the worldwide study: younger subjects seem to approve greater intrusive interventions slightly more than older subjects. Results for the influence of education are not significant, and political influence has been excluded in light of the impossibility of comparing the relevant datasets.

[27] Sunstein, Reisch, and Rauber (n 6).

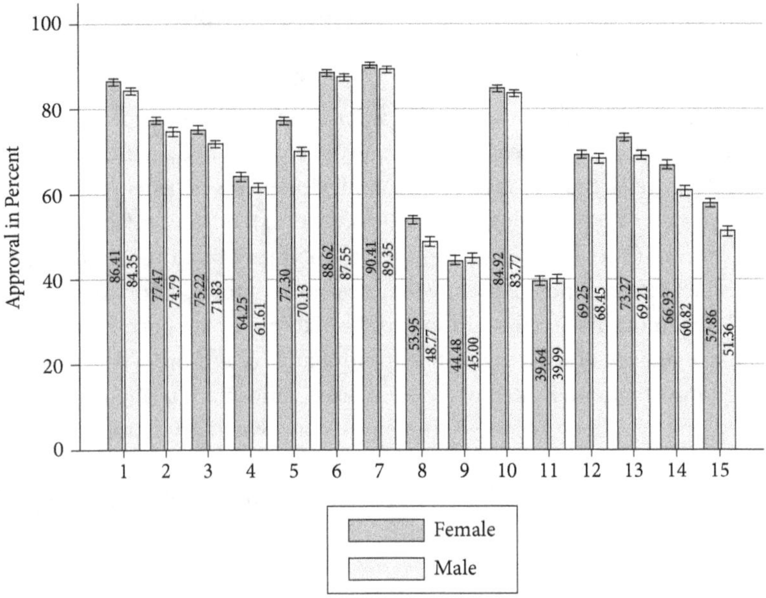

Figure 4.7 Gender differences all countries per nudge, total support in %.

IV. Implications

Overall, we find strong majority support for the tested nudges, with spectacularly high approval rates in China and South Korea, and with qualified exceptions of Denmark, Hungary, and Japan (which also show majority support, at least in general). We also see many similarities among the surveyed countries with respect to the approval of different nudges. The same holds true when we compare the results with the United States.[28] As suggested earlier,[29] it makes sense to group the countries in three clusters: (i) a sizeable group of nations, mostly liberal democracies, where strong majorities approve of health and safety nudges; (ii) a small group of nations where overwhelming majorities approve of nearly all nudges; and (iii) another small group of nations where majorities generally support nudges, but where the level of support is markedly lower than in nations that fall in the first category.

Our principal goal has been descriptive, but in our view, the results have implications for the official use of nudges. The first implication is intensely practical. In democratic nations, and to some extent in non-democratic ones, officials care whether the public approves or disapproves of potential initiatives. A green light

[28] Ibid.

[29] Sunstein, Reisch, and Rauber (n 6).

from the public is a relevant data point, and so is a red light. We have identified an assortment of green lights, and some red ones as well.

We do not mean to suggest that when the public approves, officials will necessarily proceed, nor is it safe to say that when the public disapproves, officials will necessarily decline to proceed. If an initiative promises to do a great deal of good on standard welfare grounds (if, for example, it delivers benefits well in excess of costs, and raises no deontological or other concerns), officials might proceed with it in the face of (initial) public disapproval, and if it promises to be harmful (also on standard welfare grounds, assuming there are no deontological or other concerns), officials will most likely refrain in spite of (initial) public support. But for any government, evidence of what majorities approve and disapprove will provide highly relevant information. In democracies at least, information about what people think might tell public officials something about what is right, or about what is likely to work.

The second implication, which we venture more tentatively, is normative. One need not be a strong believer in the wisdom of crowds to insist that officials should proceed with humility, and that if the public seems committed to a view that some nudges are justified while others are not, that view deserves respectful attention. We have not attempted, in this discussion, to specify the principles that separate approved nudges from disapproved ones,[30] but if the evidence is taken as a whole, it seems clear that strong majorities in most nations will support nudges that seem consistent with the interests and the values of those at whom they are aimed—and that they will reject nudges that do not satisfy that test. As we have suggested, there is also evidence that loss aversion matters, in the sense that many citizens will be sceptical of nudges that take people's resources without their explicit consent.[31]

An investigation of the data here, combined with other such data,[32] begins to suggest the broad outlines of ethical intuitions about the appropriate uses and bounds of nudges. The resulting principles, elicited in mere surveys, certainly should not be taken as authoritative; they may themselves depend on heuristics and biases, as well as incomplete information and inadequate reflection. But such principles, we suggest, deserve careful consideration, at least if one believes in the possibility that on issues of this kind, the ethical intuitions of large populations may not be so far off the mark.

[30] For discussion, see Jung and Mellers (n 4).

[31] Sunstein (n 3).

[32] Hagman et al. (n 5); Jung and Mellers (n 4).

5

Regulating under Uncertainty about Rationality

From Decision Theory to Machine Learning and Complexity Theory

Philipp Hacker

Abstract: Theories of choice, and their legal consequences, dramatically differ based on whether they are premised on rational or boundedly rational actors. This chapter describes the interactions between, and regulatory implications of, three types of uncertainties that the selection of an adequate theory of choice requires. First, it suggests that Knightian uncertainty concerning the distribution of degrees of rationality between regulatees obtains in many regulatory areas. More recently, this has been described as a 'knowledge problem' of behavioural law and economics. This chapter argues that the best regulatory response to the knowledge problem is to frame regulation as a problem of decision making under uncertainty. Second, with the rise of machine learning, it is arguably becoming ever more possible to estimate the level of bias, or even entire rationality quotients, of individual regulatees. This opens the potential for, but also the pitfalls of, personalised law. Third, even Big Data analytics generally only offers a snapshot of a distribution of rationality at one moment in time. Recent economic analyses have suggested behavioural heterogeneity can evolve over time in unpredicted ways that may lead to unforeseen consequences, leading to economic complexity. This calls for a greater role of standards, as opposed to rules, in regulating environments with dynamic behavioural heterogeneity. The chapter focuses on the normative implications of different types of uncertainty. In the end, theories of choice can aid more transparent normative trade-offs but they cannot replace the value judgments, and normative discourses, that balance the involved interests.

Philipp Hacker, *Regulating under Uncertainty about Rationality* In: *Theories of Choice.*
Edited by: Stefan Grundmann and Philipp Hacker, Oxford University Press (2021).
DOI: 10.1093/oso/9780198863175.003.0006

I. Uncertainty and Regulation: The Case of Bounded Rationality

This chapter provides a fresh look at how different types of uncertainty necessitate different theories of choice, and how these are attached to different regulatory implementations. Uncertainty is, of course, a well-known problem in risk regulation more generally.[1] Particularly in the field of new and emerging technologies, be they nuclear energy,[2] genome editing,[3] or artificial intelligence,[4] the evolution of future states of the world is always fraught with uncertainty concerning the path that the technology will take and the risks associated with it. The following sections, however, are dedicated to a specific, underexplored type of uncertainty: the one concerning degrees of rationality of regulation's addressees. Depending on this, the effects of market regulation may differ drastically. For example, if most agents act rather rationally, salient disclosure may effectively remedy information asymmetries; if most agents, however, behave in boundedly rational ways, most forms of disclosure will likely to fail to guide consumers to informed decisions.[5]

However, data and information about the true degrees of rationality exhibited by addressees of regulation are often difficult to come by. This chapter therefore uncovers a cycle of uncertainty. It starts with the lack of information concerning rationality distributions, advances through a possible reduction of this uncertainty via Big Data analytics, and finishes on a cautionary note by reintroducing dynamic uncertainty under conditions of economic complexity. It shows how different regulatory tools, from decision theory and machine learning applications all the way to standards and governance mechanisms, need to be harnessed to confront these different types of uncertainty. Examples ranging from price discrimination to usurious lending and blockchain environments highlight the potential of these techniques in important fields of our contemporary, digital economy.

[1] Millett Granger Morgan et al., *Uncertainty: A Guide to Dealing with Uncertainty in Quantitative Risk and Policy Analysis* (Cambridge University Press 1992); Michael Power, *Organized Uncertainty: Designing a World of Risk Management* (Oxford University Press 2007); Ortwin Renn et al., 'Coping with Complexity, Uncertainty and Ambiguity in Risk Governance: A Synthesis' (2011) 40 AMBIO: A Journal of the Human Environment 231.

[2] See, e.g., OECD, *Improving Nuclear Regulatory Effectiveness* (OECD Nuclear Energy Agency 2001).

[3] See, e.g., Huw D. Jones, 'Regulatory Uncertainty over Genome Editing' (2015) 1 Nature Plants 1; Ulla Bonas et al., 'Ethical and Legal Assessment of Genome Editing in Research on Human Cells' Leopoldina Discussion Paper No. 10 (March 2017).

[4] Executive Office of the US President, 'Preparing for the Future of Artificial Intelligence' (October 2016).

[5] See, e.g., Philipp Hacker, *Verhaltensökonomik und Normativität. Die Grenzen des Informationsmodells im Privatrecht und seine Alternativen* (Mohr Siebeck 2017); Omri Ben-Shahar and Carl E. Schneider, *More Than You Wanted to Know. The Failure of Mandated Disclosure* (Princeton University Press 2014).

II. Knightean Uncertainty: Decision Theory

The rise of behavioural economics in the past decades has spurred a more realistic picture of how economic actors make decisions. A host of empirical studies, both from the laboratory and the field, tell us that people are subject to a number of biases and heuristics that influence decision making.[6] However, the results of behavioural economics do not imply that actors always behave in boundedly rational ways to the same extent; rather, closer scrutiny reveals significant individual heterogeneity with respect to the degrees of rationality exhibited.[7] While some actors more closely align with the rational decision-making paradigm, others show moderate levels of bias, while substantial bias is present in yet other actors.[8] To make things worse, a single person may, of course, act more rationally in one situation and less so in another.

This behavioural heterogeneity gives rise to a true regulatory conundrum: significant uncertainty about the degree of rationality that regulatees exhibit. If legislators and regulators would like legal norms to be informed by empirical insights, this conundrum amounts to what has been termed 'the knowledge problem' of behavioural law and economics.[9]

A. The Source of Uncertainty: Lack of Studies; Limited Internal and External Validity

The reason for this empirical uncertainty is twofold. On the one hand, while many studies have been produced over the years on specific decision situations, informative empirical studies are often still lacking for concrete regulatory questions.[10] For example, no-one has, to my knowledge, tested whether consumers are actually over- or under-optimistic concerning the risks presented by lawnmowers when they make purchase decisions; this would, however, be quite relevant for risk regulation and tort liability.[11]

[6] See, e.g., Colin F. Camerer et al. (eds.), *Advances in Behavioral Economics* (Princeton University Press 2011); Stefano DellaVigna, 'Psychology and Economics: Evidence from the Field' (2009) 47 Journal of Economic Literature 315.

[7] See, e.g., Keith E. Stanovich and Richard F. West, 'Individual Differences in Reasoning: Implications for the Rationality Debate?' (2000) 23 Behavioral and Brain Sciences 645.

[8] Keith E. Stanovich et al., *The Rationality Quotient: Toward a Test of Rational Thinking* (MIT Press 2016).

[9] Alan Schwartz, 'Regulating for Rationality' (2015) 67 Stanford Law Review 1373; Mario Rizzo and Douglas Whitman, 'The Knowledge Problem of New Paternalism' (2009) Brigham Young University Law Review 905.

[10] Christoph Engel, 'Verhaltenswissenschaftliche Analyse: Eine Gebrauchsanleitung für Juristen' in Christoph Engel et al. (eds.), *Recht und Verhalten. Beiträge zu Behavioral Law and Economics* (Mohr Siebeck 2007) 363, 374; Christoph Engel, 'Empirical Methods for the Law' (2018) 174 Journal of Institutional and Theoretical Economics 5.

[11] See Howard Latin, 'Good Warnings, Bad Products, and Cognitive Limitations' (1993) 41 UCLA Law Review 1193.

On the other hand, there are studies investigating over-optimism in other settings.[12] However, the limits of internal and particularly external validity[13] caution against making direct inferences from studies on, for example, over-optimism concerning the consequences of alcohol abuse for decision-making situations involving the regulation of lawnmowers.[14]

B. Regulatory Implications: Decision Making under Uncertainty

As far as concrete regulatory situations are concerned, the dearth of empirical studies and the limits of their validity therefore entail significant uncertainty about regulatees' degrees of rationality. Often, one will only be able to say that some actors are likely to act quite rationally, while others will exhibit significant bounded rationality (with the whole spectrum of actors in between). However, it is unclear how likely it is that most people, in the concrete regulatory situation, behave in one way or another, or what the distribution of rational and boundedly rational actors looks like.

Technically speaking, the probability distributions of the different states of the world—significant rationality, significant bounded rationality—are unknown in many situations for the above-mentioned reasons. This is precisely the situation Frank Knight described as 'uncertainty', in decision theoretic terms, as opposed to a situation of 'risk', in which the probability distributions are known.[15] Scholars have concluded that, in the face of such behavioural uncertainty, behavioural economics should not underpin legal decision making; rather, they advocate a return to the rational actor model and more traditional law and economics.[16] This, however, seems as implausible as uncritically assuming that most people act in boundedly rational ways. Rather, as this chapter suggests, law making in these situations must be conceived of as a case of decision making under uncertainty.[17] Such a perspective not only takes empirical uncertainty both concerning full and bounded rationality seriously, it also opens an entirely new toolbox—the instruments of formal theories of choice—to deal with behavioural uncertainty.

Very simply put, legal decision making can then be imagined as a choice between two possible rules: one tailored to a world of rather full and one to a world of rather bounded rationality.[18] For each alternative, at least two states of the world

[12] See, e.g., David M. DeJoy, 'The Optimism Bias and Traffic Accident Risk Perception' (1989) 21 Accident Analysis & Prevention 333; Neil D. Weinstein, 'Unrealistic Optimism about Future Life Events' (1980) 39 Journal of Personality and Social Psychology 806.

[13] See Robert M. Lawless et al., *Empirical Methods in Law* (Aspen 2010) 36–40.

[14] See the contribution by Christoph Engel in this volume; see also Morgan (n 1) 56–67.

[15] Frank Hyneman Knight, *Risk, Uncertainty and Profit* (Houghton Mifflin Company 1921) 19–20.

[16] Schwarz (n 9); Rizzo and Whitman (n 9).

[17] See also Hacker (n 5) § 5 for a more detailed exposition of the decision theoretic framework applicable under conditions of uncertainty.

[18] This framework can be expanded to cover intermediate rules, see ibid. 181–83.

must be considered: one under which most people act rationally and one under which most people act in boundedly rational ways. We may then start to compare the outcomes of the two rules under the different possible states of the world. The key normative question resides in the choice of the decision-making rule, that is, in the criteria used to rank the different outcomes.[19] Here, a number of different decision-making rules, from aggregate utility maximisation to Rawlsian maximin, may be used. The choice between them necessitates specific normative arguments that cannot be derived from empirical data; this is precisely where the law reaffirms its role as a moderator of value judgments.

C. Example: Price Discrimination

To make things more concrete, we will now apply such a decision-making framework to a hotly debated example of digitally mediated commerce: price discrimination.[20] Generally, price discrimination involves the sale of the same good at two or more different prices or, more precisely, 'the sale of two or more similar goods at prices that are in different ratios to marginal cost'.[21] There are different ways in which sellers differentiate between customers in their pricing strategies. Third-degree price discrimination consists in differential pricing for various groups, for example, student discounts for movie theatres.[22] First-degree price discrimination is more granular; it occurs when the seller has (nearly) perfect information about the reservation price of customers. In first-degree (also called perfect) price discrimination, the seller thus aims to approximate the maximum willingness to pay for each customer.[23]

[19] Anatol Rapoport, *Decision Theory and Decision Behavior* (2nd edn, Palgrave Macmillan 1998) 50–52.

[20] For the general debate around the legality of price discrimination, see, e.g., Frederik Zuiderveen Borgesius, 'Algorithmic Decision-Making, Price Discrimination, and European Non-discrimination Law' European Business Law Review (forthcoming), https://ssrn.com/abstract=3413556; Ariel Ezrachi and Maurice E. Stucke, *Virtual Competition* (Harvard University Press 2016) 85–130; Ariel Ezrachi and Maurice E. Stucke, 'The Rise of Behavioural Discrimination' (2016) 37 European Competition Law Review 485; Christopher Townley et al., 'Big Data and Personalized Price Discrimination in EU Competition Law' (2017) 36 Yearbook of European Law 683; Oren Bar-Gill, 'Algorithmic Price Discrimination When Demand Is a Function of Both Preferences and (Mis)perceptions' (2019) 86 University of Chicago Law Review 217; Omri Ben-Shahar and Ariel Porat, 'Personalizing Mandatory Rules in Contract Law' (2019) 86 University of Chicago Law Review 255; Gerhard Wagner and Horst Eidenmüller, 'Down by Algorithms: Siphoning Rents, Exploiting Biases, and Shaping Preferences: Regulating the Dark Side of Personalized Transactions' (2019) 86 University of Chicago Law Review 581 (585 et seq.); and references in n 29.

[21] George Stigler, *The Theory of Price* (4th edn, Palgrave Macmillan 1987) 210; see also Hal Varian, 'Price Discrimination' in Richard Schmalensee and Robert D. Willig (eds.), *Handbook of Industrial Organization*, Vol. I (Elsevier 1989) 597, 598; Lars A. Stole, 'Price Discrimination and Competition' in Mark Armstrong and Robert Porter (eds.), *Handbook of Industrial Organization, Volume III* (Elsevier 2007) 2221, 2224–25.

[22] Varian (n 21) 600; second-degree price discrimination concerns quantity-dependent non-linear pricing, for example, discounts on large orders, and is not covered here.

[23] Ibid..

Generally, first-degree price discrimination is difficult to study empirically as most companies do not share data on their pricing strategies.[24] However, there is growing evidence that, in data-driven markets, companies inch ever closer from third-degree to perfect price discrimination.[25] The crucial regulatory question is whether to allow or ban such (almost) first-degree price discrimination. There are, of course, different lines of argument that can be advanced in this context. For example, one might argue that individually differential pricing violates basic fairness norms that would dictate that everybody who receives the same good at the same price (or rather, the same ratio to marginal cost).[26] One might counter this argument by pointing to existing pricing differences that are considered legitimate, such as group discounts under third-degree price discrimination. Besides these concerns about fairness, however, the economic consequences of first-degree price discrimination are probably the decisive criterion, particularly for competition law.[27] Importantly, however, these consequences differ vastly, based on whether one assumes rational or boundedly rational buyers.[28] While this renders the treatment of first-degree price discrimination under EU competition law quite unclear and context-dependent,[29] it presents a fitting test case for our decision-making framework.

1. Effects of price discrimination given rational actors

If all demand-side actors are rational, economic analysis suggests that price discrimination[30] is beneficial overall. While there is much nuance in the details, there are five advantages of prices approximating willingness (and ability) to pay. First, it leads to an efficient allocation of goods by preventing cross-subsidisation between actors with different levels of willingness and ability to pay. Therefore, the

[24] Joel Waldfogel, 'First Degree Price Discrimination Goes to School' (2015) 63 Journal of Industrial Economics 569, 569–70; but see Aniko Hannak et al., 'Measuring Price Discrimination and Steering on E-Commerce Web Sites' (2014) Proceedings of the 2014 Conference on Internet Measurement Conference 305.

[25] For empirical evidence on price discrimination in the digital economy, see ibid. 309–10; Jakub Mikians et al., 'Crowd-assisted Search for Price Discrimination in E-Commerce: First Results' (2013) Proceedings of the Ninth ACM Conference on Emerging Networking Experiments and Technologies 1; for an overview, see Christoph Michael Hindermann, 'Price Discrimination in Online Retail', Working Paper (2018); https://www.econstor.eu/handle/10419/181294; see also Dana Mattioli, 'On Orbitz, Mac users steered to pricier hotels' *Wall Street Journal* (New York, 23 August 2012), https://www.wsj.com/articles/SB10001424052702304458604577488822667325882.

[26] See the discussion in Townley et al. (n 20) 703–10.

[27] cf. ibid. 686.

[28] See also the discussion in Bar-Gill (n 20).

[29] See, e.g., Townley et al. (n 20); Francisco Costa-Cabral and Orla Lynskey, 'Family Ties: The Intersection Between Data Protection and Competition in EU Law' (2017) 54 Common Market Law Review 11, 31 n. 100; Inge Graef, 'Algorithms and Fairness: What Role for Competition Law in Targeting Price Discrimination Towards End Consumers?' (2017) 24 Columbia Journal of European Law 541.

[30] For the sake of brevity, price discrimination henceforth will mean price discrimination practised in the digital economy that approaches first-degree price discrimination, even if it does not yet fully reach it.

outcome is Pareto-efficient.[31] Second, in digital markets with high initial fixed costs and low reproduction costs, price discrimination allows the recouping of initial (fixed) production costs, which would not be recoverable if price equals marginal cost.[32] Thus, the possibility of price discrimination arguably spurs market entry and innovation. Third, it incrementally contributes to social and economic equality: more affluent buyers are charged more as they have a higher willingness and ability to pay (Macbook effect).[33]

Fourth, welfare effects are ambiguous, but often positive. The main economic argument against price discrimination is the appropriation of the entire trade surplus by the seller, lowering consumer welfare. However, this claim must be modified for conditions of free entry (monopolistic competition[34] or imperfect competition). In this case, profits are driven (close) to zero,[35] and welfare effects are more ambiguous.[36] Importantly, the social surplus is maximised under price discrimination, both for monopolies and oligopolies,[37] that is, under conditions that are typical of the digital economy, if the seller increases output by serving new markets.[38] The effects on consumer welfare, by contrast, depend heavily on whether consumers with high willingness to pay vary between firms (so-called best-response asymmetry) or not (so-called best-response symmetry).[39] Heterogenous brand preference is an example of best-response asymmetry; high search costs are typically associated with best-response symmetry as they do not vary across firms for individual consumers. Under best-response asymmetry, if competition is sufficiently intense, *all*

[31] Varian (n 21) 602 et seq. (for a monopolistic market) and 643 (more nuanced, for a monopolistically competitive market); see also Dirk Bergemann et al., 'The Limits of Price Discrimination' (2015) 105 American Economic Review 921; Hal Varian, *Intermediate Microeconomics: A Modern Approach* (9th edn, WW Norton & Company 2014) 481–82.

[32] Thierry Rayna et al., 'Pricing Music Using Personal Data: Mutually Advantageous First-Degree Price Discrimination' (2015) 25 Electronic Markets 139, 141.

[33] Benjamin Reed Shiller, 'First degree price discrimination using big data', Working Paper (8 April 2014), http://benjaminshiller. com/images/First_Degree_PD_Using_ Big_Data_Apr_8, _2014. pdf, at 2; Philipp Hacker and Bilyana Petkova, 'Reining in the Big Promise of Big Data: Transparency, Inequality, and New Regulatory Frontiers' (2017) 15 Northwestern Journal of Technology and Intellectual Property 1, 13.

[34] Monopolistic competition characterises markets on which many producers sell products that are differentiated to an extent that they are not perfect substitutes, cf. Varian (n 21) 641.

[35] V. Bhaskar and Ted To, 'Is Perfect Price Discrimination Really Efficient? An Analysis of Free Entry' (2004) 35 RAND Journal of Economics 762; Mark Armstrong and John Vickers, 'Competitive Price Discrimination' (2001) 32 RAND Journal of Economics 579, 594; see also Paul Heidhues and Botond Kőszegi, 'Naïveté-based Discrimination' (2017) 132 Quarterly Journal of Economics 1019, 1020; Varian (n 31) 497.

[36] Stole (n 21) 2230; Kenneth S. Corts, 'Third-degree Price Discrimination in Oligopoly: All-Out Competition and Strategic Commitment' (1998) 29 RAND Journal of Economics 306; Yongmin Chen, 'Paying Customers to Switch' (1997) 6 Journal of Economics & Management Strategy 877, 894.

[37] Stole (n 21) 2229.

[38] cf. Richard Schmalensee, 'Output and Welfare Implications of Monopolistic Third-Degree Price Discrimination' (1981) 71 American Economic Review 242, 243 on output increase as a necessary precondition for efficient third-degree discrimination in a monopoly; same result, but more generally, Hal Varian, 'Price Discrimination and Social Welfare' (1985) 75 American Economic Review 870. Eventually, this depends on the shape of demand functions.

[39] Corts (n 36) 307.

consumers will be offered a low price by *some* firm, and consumer welfare increases overall;[40] conversely, under best-response symmetry, price discrimination is likely to reduce consumer welfare.[41] Thus, consumer surplus may even be increased by price discrimination in imperfectly competitive (but not monopolistic) markets if personalised price reductions outweigh rent capture.[42] A recent paper shows that this is a realistic assumption in digital markets in which firms *asymmetrically* acquire customer information via cookies.[43] Finally, if consumers are appropriately rewarded for disclosing personal information on which first-degree price discrimination can be based, the strategy can even be mutually advantageous for both consumers and sellers.[44]

Effects on consumer surplus are therefore ambiguous, depending on market structure and the basis of price discrimination. If the pro-competitive effect of offering lower prices to some consumers (compared to uniform pricing) dominates the rent-extracting effect, consumer surplus rises; otherwise, it decreases.[45] Under the assumption of rational demand-side actors, price discrimination in the digital economy is therefore likely to be beneficial from a social welfare perspective and at least potentially beneficial from a consumer welfare perspective (e.g., in cases of asymmetric cookie information), although the shifting of the surplus adds a note of caution. Therefore, economic analysis strongly suggests at least to allow price discrimination in scenarios in which consumer surplus is increased (best-response asymmetry) because pro-competitive effects outweigh rent-seeking effects.

2. Effects of price discrimination given boundedly rational actors

The analysis is strikingly different, however, if one assumes that most buyers are boundedly rational. Under this assumption, price discrimination not only approximates willingness to pay but also exhibits another dimension: the exploitation of behavioural biases. Ezrachi and Stucke have aptly called this behavioural discrimination.[46]

Behavioural discrimination works in various ways. First, it is well-known that shrouded price components can lead biased actors to purchase products whose real price exceeds their maximum willingness to pay.[47] Price discrimination allows

[40] Ibid.

[41] Armstrong and Vickers (n 35) 597.

[42] Jacques-Francois Thisse and Xavier Vives, 'On the Strategic Choice of Spatial Price Policy' (1988) 78 American Economic Review 122, 134.

[43] Chongwoo Choe et al., 'Pricing with Cookies: Behavior-Based Price Discrimination and Spatial Competition' (2017) Management Science (2017) 1 13.

[44] Rayna (n 32) 142–43: the idea is to establish the price absent price discrimination as an upper bound, thus only allowing to lower prices by way of price discrimination. While intriguing, and potentially marketable, one must note that this bound is difficult to enforce in markets with multi-dimensional pricing.

[45] cf. Townley et al. (n 20) 693–97.

[46] Ariel Ezrachi and Maurice E. Stucke, *Virtual Competition* (Harvard University Press 2016) ch. 11.

[47] Botond Kőszegi, 'Behavioral Contract Theory' (2014) 52 Journal of Economic Literature 1075.

personalisation of the shrouded component: it can be high for those unlikely to discover or act on them, but low for those likely to discover and act on them.[48] Importantly, such strategies not only exploit naïve consumers but also lower total welfare.[49] Second, inattentive, status-quo biased or otherwise boundedly rational consumers have higher search costs,[50] enabling sellers to extract higher prices from them, lowering consumer surplus (best-response symmetry).[51] Third, also in cases of best-response asymmetry, personalised pricing may shift the demand curve 'to the right',[52] leading to overconsumption[53] by the encouragement of impulse purchases. This is particularly detrimental for low-income consumers, who are left with fewer resources to cover their basic needs. There are a number of different mechanisms that trigger a shift of the demand curve.[54] For example, decoys may be used to make other offers seem comparatively more advantageous. In an empirical study, MIT students were shown to be successfully steered to higher priced magazine subscriptions if a decoy choice was inserted into the subscription options that made the more expensive option seem more attractive.[55] Decoys can therefore be deployed in a personalised fashion to increase users' willingness to pay. Similarly, price steering, that is, the ordering of products to highlight specific products,[56] may be used to raise the attractiveness of certain items artificially. Furthermore, increasing the complexity of product features and pricing dimensions may be used to personalise prices, but also to provoke information overload and to make comparisons with outside options costlier. As noted, higher search costs generally lower consumer surplus in price discrimination settings.[57] Finally, companies may employ personalised savings coupons that serve a dual purpose: they prevent frustration and perceptions of unfairness triggered by differing listing prices,[58] and they exploit loss aversion and reference dependence by framing the purchase as a gain.[59] As one data mining handbook notes, customer-specific incentives 'provided specifically to retain existing customers can be expensive, and successful

[48] Heidhues and Kőszegi (n 35).

[49] Ibid. 1026.

[50] This is modelled in the literature on best-response symmetry, see, e.g., Armstrong and Vickers (n 35); Corts (n 36).

[51] Townley et al. (n 20) 693.

[52] Ariel Ezrachi and Maurice Stucke, 'The Rise of Behavioural Discrimination' (2016) 37 European Competition Law Review 485, 486.

[53] Ezrachi and Stucke (n 46) 105–07, 119–20.

[54] Ezrachi and Stucke (n 52) 486–88.

[55] Dan Ariely, *Predictably Irrational: The Hidden Forces that Shape Our Decisions* (Harper Collins 2008) 4–6.

[56] Hannak et al. (n 24) 306.

[57] See also Townley et al. (n 20) 701 et seq.

[58] cf. Daniel Kahneman et al., 'Fairness as a Constraint on Profit Seeking: Entitlements in the Market' (1986) 76 American Economic Review 728, 732.

[59] Amos Tversky and Daniel Kahneman, 'Rational Choice and the Framing of Decisions' (1986) 59 Journal of Business S251, S261 et seq.

data mining allows them to be precisely targeted to those customers who are likely to yield maximum benefit'.[60]

All in all, if buyers are boundedly rational, price discrimination may have detrimental social welfare effects, and the egalitarian intuition (the Macbook effect) is reversed if price-sensitive consumers are also less experienced and more prone to be exploited by strategies targeting behavioural biases.[61] In this scenario, the *perceived* price approximates maximum willingness to pay, but the real price may be significantly higher than the perceived one, and willingness to pay may be artificially inflated.[62] Price discrimination, then, is not only detrimental from a consumer welfare perspective but also raises additional, and highly significant, fairness concerns as differential pricing enables targeted exploitation of behavioural biases.[63]

3. Deciding on price discrimination law under uncertainty

Economic analysis therefore differs strikingly, depending on whether actors are assumed to be (rather) fully or (rather) boundedly rational with respect to their responses to price discrimination. At the moment, this is an unanswered empirical question. In the face of empirical uncertainty, we should turn to decision theory to compare the different regulatory alternatives. In a simple model, the rational alternative would allow price discrimination, the boundedly rational alternative would ban it. Based on the preceding discussion, the possible outcomes of the implementation of these alternatives can be captured in a 2×2 box.

What is needed, therefore, is a decision rule that ranks the different outcomes. For decision making under uncertainty, three groups of decision rules are discussed in the literature: maximax, maximin, and intermediate rules.[64] Under maximax, one selects the alternative that leads to the overall best outcome (maximise the maximum). From an economic perspective, this is likely to be the rational alternative since, in conjunction with rational actors, it leads to a Pareto-efficient outcome that maximises social surplus. The problem with maximax, however, is that it resembles a high-risk bet: it is uncertain, of course, whether the maximum outcome is really reached. Therefore, decision theorist Anatol Rapoport highlights: 'It is difficult to justify the maximax principle as a rational principle of decision, reflecting, as it does, wishful thinking.'[65]

[60] Ian Witten et al., *Data Mining: Practical Machine Learning Tools and Techniques* (4th edn, Morgan Kaufmann 2016) 26.

[61] Executive Office of the [US] President, 'Big Data and Differential Pricing' (2015) 6.

[62] cf. also Ezrachi and Stucke (n 46) 85–130 118, 120.

[63] See, in detail, Philipp Hacker, 'Personal Data, Exploitative Contracts, and Algorithmic Fairness: Autonomous Vehicles Meet the Internet of Things' (2017) 7 International Data Privacy Law 266, 279 et seq.

[64] Rapoport (n 19) 50–52.

[65] Ibid. 51.

Table 5.1 The economic effects of different legal strategies concerning price discrimination

	mostly rational actors	**mostly boundedly rational actors**
rational alternative: allow price discrimination	efficiency: probable total welfare maximisation; potentially consumer welfare maximisation	exploitation of behavioural biases through pricing
boundedly rational alternative: disallow price discrimination	cross-subsidisation; less efficient resource allocation	protection from exploitation

Conversely, maximin seeks to implement the alternative that offers the 'best worst result' (maximise the minimum).[66] First, therefore, one has to identify the worst outcomes under each alternative, and then decide which of these two is more benign. Clearly, under the rational alternative (allowing price discrimination), the existence of significant bounded rationality leads to the worst outcome: here, price discrimination is likely to exploit behavioural biases. Similarly, under the boundedly rational alternative (banning price discrimination), a rational world engenders the worst outcome: it prevents the efficiency gains of price discrimination from being realised.

A full-blown comparison between these outcomes, and further outcomes generated by intermediate regulatory alternatives such as increased price transparency or price caps,[67] transcends the scope of this chapter. Within the framework contemplated here, two important reasons may be advanced, however, to argue that the worst outcome under allowed price discrimination is even less desirable than the worst outcome under banned price discrimination. First, as noted, overspending of boundedly rational consumers drains resources for basic necessities, which in turn hits the poorest hardest.[68] If this exploitation effect is greater than the Macbook effect, boundedly rational consumers suffer more from price discrimination than from its absence. Since they are, precisely due to their boundedly rational nature, already often disadvantaged in socio-economic ways, this presents a strong argument against price discrimination. Preventing price discrimination, under these conditions, maximises the position of the worst-off group, and therefore aligns with the demands of the Rawlsian difference principle.[69] Second, price discrimination in a boundedly rational world enables the profiting from foreseeable mistakes of the counterparty. From a normative perspective that values minimum standards

[66] Ibid. 51.
[67] See Townley et al. (n 20) 721.
[68] Ezrachi and Stucke (n 46) 120.
[69] John Rawls, *A Theory of Justice* (rev. edn, Harvard University Press 1999) 65–68.

of fairness in market exchange,[70] this should be considered more detrimental than the efficiency loss incurred under the other worst result.

This brief comparison shows that decision theory, in fact, uncovers and renders transparent deep normative questions about the best allocation of resources in society. While maximin implements a Rawlsian difference principle, maximax places a bet on achieving maximum aggregate welfare. The former represents inclusiveness and (Rawlsian) fairness, the latter rewards rational actors. Importantly, intermediate decision-making rules may be harnessed to continuously interpolate between these extreme cases. For example, the rule using Hurwicz' α weights the worst outcome of each alternative by α and the best outcome by $(1 - \alpha)$.[71] For $\alpha = 0$ and $\alpha = 1$, it reproduces the maximax and the maximin rule, respectively. However, by choosing an intermediate value of α, one may continuously vary between the two and hence adapt decision-making frameworks to situations in which more or less risk seeking is desired.

Decision theory therefore offers the tools to embrace and deal with behavioural heterogeneity actively. In closing, it should be noted that the results of their application do not preclude other, less formal concentrations from informing legal decision making. Rather, under a framework of weak consequentialism,[72] decision theory only offers indications for the final regulatory decision, but it is not considered conclusive; other, rights-based assessments can enter, and overturn, the decision theoretic analysis.[73] However, that analysis does offer a transparent way of bringing the key normative trade-offs to the fore. In the price discrimination example, a maximin analysis, which seems attractive for a number of reasons outlined by Rawls himself,[74] suggests banning rather than allowing price discrimination.

III. Approximating Degrees of Rationality: Big Data Analytics

Uncertainty concerning degrees of rationality was key to the preceding decision theoretic analysis. The next two sections of this chapter will explore two different routes in which this uncertainty may evolve, and the regulatory implications these developments beget. On the one hand, digital technology fuelled by machine learning may help to reduce uncertainty and provide regulators with a better understanding of the degrees of rationality prevalent in the marketplace. On the

70 See, e.g., Wolfgang Fikentscher et al., *Fair Economy* (Springer 2013).

71 Rapoport (n 19) 52.

72 See Matthew Adler, *Well-Being and Fair Distribution: Beyond Cost-Benefit Analysis* (Oxford University Press 2012) 24–29.

73 See also Hacker (n 5) § 14 A.

74 Rawls (n 69) 79, 87 et seq. and 134.

other hand, dynamic processes may reintroduce unforeseeability, and uncertainty, over a longer time horizon (see section IV).

A. The Source of Approximation: Big Data and Machine Learning

First, we shall turn to the potential of harnessing digital technology in an attempt to reduce uncertainty about regulatees' degrees of rationality. Even with conventional methods, one may exercise judgment in an attempt to determine to what extent existing empirical research fits the regulatory situation, as Christoph Engel shows in his contribution to this volume. The aim would be to convert the setting of decision making under uncertainty into one of decision making under risk,[75] in which the distributions of rationality are approximately known.[76] In such a setting, a regulator would know with considerable certainty that, for example, 30% of market participants are acting quite economically rationally; 50% moderately boundedly rationally; and 20% heavily boundedly rationally.

Digital technology, and more particularly models that learn from example (machine learning)[77] may be harnessed for this endeavour. In recent years, machine learning technology has increasingly been used to predict personality traits of actors that leave digital footprints online. In several studies, algorithmic models were trained that predicted personality types, degrees of intelligence, and other cognitive parameters reasonably well, based on distributions of Facebook likes,[78] or smart phone usage behaviour.[79] The idea is to elicit independently the target variable from study participants by means of a psychometric test, and to use supervised machine learning to find correlations between digital footprints and the target variable.[80] Only quite recently, a comprehensive psychometric test (CART)[81] has been developed that measures the overall degree of rationality (the Rationality Quotient), as well as degrees of specific bias in various subtests.[82] The results of this test could be used to train machine learning models, analogously to the ones

[75] Knight (n 15).

[76] More precisely, risk would imply a situation in which probability distributions over different states of the world corresponding with different distributions of rationality can be defined.

[77] See on machine learning, e.g., Shai Shalev-Shwartz and Shai Ben-David, *Understanding Machine Learning. From Theory to Algorithms* (Cambridge University Press 2014); Witten et al. (n 60).

[78] Michal Kosinski et al., 'Private Traits and Attributes are Predictable from Digital Records of Human Behavior' (2013) 110 Proceedings of the National Academy of Sciences 5802; Wu Youyou et al., 'Computer-based Personality Judgments Are More Accurate Than Those Made by Humans' (2015) 112 Proceedings of the National Academy of Sciences 1036.

[79] Gokul Chittaranjan et al., 'Mining Large-scale Smartphone Data for Personality Traits' (2013) 17 Personal and Ubiquitous Computing 433.

[80] Michal Kosinski et al., 'Mining Big Data to Extract Patterns and Predict Real-Life Outcomes' (2016) 21 Psychological Methods 493.

[81] This stands for Comprehensive Assessment of Rational Thinking.

[82] Stanovich et al. (n 8).

employed to predict personality traits or intelligence. For example, in the domain of bounded willpower, the CART measures of discount rates show significant heterogeneity.[83] The data could be broken up to identify the percentage of people with high, medium, and low bounded willpower. Machine learning could then correlate these categories with real-world digital footprints. These models may then be used to make predictions about the degrees of rationality of market participants for whom the CART information is lacking. It should be noted that, as model approximation errors remain,[84] such techniques reduce uncertainty (to risk), but do not (of course) provide full certainty about degrees of rationality.

B. Regulatory Implications

Harnessing the power of machine learning enables the application of two different regulatory tools. At an aggregate level, more precise analyses of the advantages and disadvantages of regulatory interventions can be undertaken; at an individual level, legal norms could even be tailored to individual cognitive traits through personalised law.

1. Aggregate level: cost-benefit analysis and social welfare functions

As noted, machine learning may convert a number of regulatory situations from uncertainty into risk by providing more granular information about market participants. Risk arises from an imperfect but workable approximation of the distribution of degrees of rationality, or willpower, across the population. From her extensive research on optimism bias, Tali Sharot, for example, concludes that 80% of the population are over-optimistic;[85] however, given limits of external validity, it seems prudent to qualify this measure with a probability that denotes the likelihood that this distribution (80% over-optimistic, 20% well-calibrated or under-optimistic) is correct. Machine learning could offer similar estimations on different traits.

Wherever this is the case, instead of models for decision making under uncertainty (as in section II), risk-based theories of collective choice can be applied. From the literature, two approaches stand out. First, a cost-benefit analysis ('CBA') can be conducted that weights the respective costs and benefits by the likelihood of their realisation (similar to an expected utility framework).[86] If, for example, we knew the distribution of boundedly versus fully rational actors in settings of price

[83] Ibid. 236–37; 241.

[84] cf. Cars Hommes, *Behavioral Rationality and Heterogeneous Expectations in Complex Economic Systems* (Cambridge University Press 2013) 35.

[85] Tali Sharot, 'The Optimism Bias' (2011) 21 Current Biology R941, R942.

[86] See, e.g., Anthony E. Boardman et al., *Cost-Benefit Analysis. Concepts and Practice* (5th edn, Prentice Hall 2018).

discrimination, we could calculate more precisely the welfare effects of different legal interventions in a more refined economic analysis. Second, as Matthew Adler shows in his contribution to this volume, a social welfare function ('SWF') can be used to evaluate differential consequences for different actors from a collective, regulatory point of view.[87] Such an SWF has at least two advantages over traditional CBA from a behavioural and a normative perspective. First, in behavioural terms, an SWF measures advantages and disadvantages not in dollar amounts but in a measure of well-being that may take into account, for example, behavioural effects such as reference dependence and diminishing marginal utility of money.[88] Second, it highlights the fact that normative choices have to be made to weight the effects of regulation on different groups (e.g., high income versus low income; high net worth versus low net worth; rational versus boundedly rational individuals), and renders such weighting procedures transparent and formally feasible (e.g., through what Adler calls 'preferential SWFs').[89]

In either case, more granular information provided by machine learning predictions enables regulators to balance the advantages and disadvantages of regulatory interventions with greater precision.

2. Individual level: personalised law

If the machine learning model provides information at the individual level, enabling sufficiently reliable predictions of individual degrees of rationality, legal norms could be tailored to these individual characteristics through a controversial technique called personalised law.[90] Essentially, personalised law consists of three steps. First, market participants are scored, through machine learning models, according to some relevant metric that measures, for example, specific biases or rationality quotients. Second, different legal consequences are attached to different scores; for example, if a particular vulnerability is detected, this could trigger specific legal protection aimed at countering the vulnerability. Third, the predicted parameters are stored, and regularly updated, in a database. Quite obviously, if a regulatory agency itself conducts the scoring and storing of the relevant information, this potentially gives the government access to highly sensitive information. Therefore, questions of privacy and abuse of personal data are key concerns that

[87] See also Adler (n 72).

[88] Matthew D. Adler, 'A better calculus for regulators: from cost-benefit analysis to the social welfare function' (25 February 2017) Duke Law School Public Law & Legal Theory Series No. 2017-19. Available at SSRN: https://ssrn.com/abstract=2923829, at 2.

[89] Ibid. 2–4; cost-benefit analysis can also be conducted with distributive weights, see, e.g., Hacker (n 5) 919–26; ibid. 4.

[90] Ariel Porat and Lior Strahilevitz, 'Personalizing Default Rules and Disclosure with Big Data' (2014) 112 Michigan Law Review 1417; Omri Ben-Shahar and Ariel Porat, 'Personalizing Negligence Law' (2016) 91 NYU Law Review 627; Philipp Hacker, 'Personalizing EU Private Law. From Disclosures to Nudges and Mandates' (2017) 25 European Review of Private Law 651; see also the contributions to the symposium issue (2019) 86(2) University of Chicago Law Review, for example, Ben-Shahar and Porat (n 20).

must be addressed in government-based personalisation.[91] There is, however, a second type of personalisation that is company-based.[92] In this variety, companies are placed under specific legal duties vis-à-vis their customers if, and only if, they legally conduct customer scoring. For example, if a company detects that a customer is prone, as a consequence of significant bounded willpower, to be economically harmed by teaser rate tariffs,[93] it could be barred from concluding such contracts with the customer. Under this scenario, the legislator only defines, in the abstract, differential legal consequences for different levels of scores; it does not have access to the scores but rather requires companies to use scoring exercises not only for their own but also for their customers' benefit. This type of personalised law therefore engenders significantly less concern with respect to privacy and data abuse; in fact, it does not go beyond the problems already raised by current legally compliant methods of scoring. While the limitations of personalised law, both in its normative dimension (privacy, data abuse, legal certainty) and its factual components (validity of machine learning predictions, possibility of 'gaming the system'), should not be underestimated, it nevertheless represents, particularly in its company-based form, a promising strategy to harness the power of machine learning not only for idiosyncratic benefit but also for social good.

C. Example: Usurious Lending

An example for the application of the mentioned tools, both at an aggregate and an individual level, is usurious lending. As is well-known, lending can be either exploitative or mutually beneficial, depending on whether the gains of trade are shared between both partners, or the borrower derives negative expected value from the transaction.[94]

To prevent exploitation, many legal orders use a rough proxy: the prohibition of usury. The difficulty, of course, lies in determining the threshold at which legally permissible interest rates end and prohibited usury starts. Under German law, for example, there is a strong indication for usury if the charged rate of interest is twice the market rate of interest or 12 percentage points above the market rate of interest.[95] This, however, obviously neglects vast heterogeneity in repayment

[91] See, e.g., Philipp Hacker, 'The Ambivalence of Algorithms. Gauging the Legitimacy of Personalized Law' in Mor Bakhoum et al. (eds.), *Personal Data in Competition, Consumer Protection and IP Law—Towards a Holistic Approach?* (Springer 2018) 85, 96–98.

[92] Hacker (n 90) 655 et seq.

[93] See, e.g., the analysis in Haiyan Shui and Lawrence M. Ausubel, 'Time inconsistency in the credit card market', 14th Annual Utah Winter Finance Conference (2004), https://ssrn.com/abstract=586622.

[94] Kőszegi (n 47) 1104–10; Michael Grubb, 'Overconfident Consumers in the Marketplace' (2015) 29 Journal of Economic Perspectives 9; John Hawkins, 'Using Advertisements to Diagnose Behavioral Market Failure in Payday Lending Markets' (2016) 51 Wake Forest Law Review 57.

[95] Bundesgerichtshof 13 March 1990, XI ZR 252/89.

probabilities of high interest loans that depend, inter alia, on the degree of bounded willpower.

High temporal discount rates,[96] that is, high degrees of bounded willpower, have been shown to correlate significantly with lower creditworthiness[97] and with high impulsivity, both in financial and non-financial real-world contexts.[98] The correlations concerning financial behaviour, for example, hold up even when one controls for income, education, age, gender, race, or total borrowing.[99] Measures of bounded willpower therefore seem to have real predictive value in forecasting the ability to repay loans on time and to behave generally in a prudent manner financially.

If the machine learning models provide sufficiently precise predictions of degrees of bounded willpower, or even more directly of repayment probabilities, one could, at an aggregate level, define the usury threshold so that it takes real levels of willpower into account. If, among the pool of regulatees in a certain country, the degree of bounded willpower is particularly high, the threshold could be lowered; moreover, it could be dynamically adapted as new data become available. In the alternative, at an individual level, one could provide individual actors with individual user thresholds that are algorithmically tailored to their level of willpower.[100] In this way, more rational borrowers would have greater access to legal credit, while more vulnerable borrowers would be better protected. These individual levels could be established either under a government- or company-based personalisation regime.

IV. Unpredictable States of the World: Complexity Theory

Even Big Data analytics, however, only offers a snapshot of the present, and a prediction of the future derived from past and present data; hence, uncertainty may

[96] Discount rates are measures of time preference; a high discount rate means that an individual strongly prefers immediate over deferred gratification, see Shane Frederick et al., 'Time Discounting and Time Preference: A Critical Review' (2002) 40 Journal of Economic Literature 351, 355 and 358; in the experiments cited below, specifically, delay discounting is used to compute a discount function that plots different discount rates over time.

[97] Stepan Meier and Charles D. Sprenger, 'Time Discounting Predicts Creditworthiness' (2012) 23 Psychological Science 56. Interestingly, the correlation was driven not by the present bias measured by the β factor, but rather by the long-run temporal discount factor δ: participants with low δ exhibited lower credit scores.

[98] Stian Reimers et al., 'Associations Between a One-Shot Delay Discounting Measure and Age, Income, Education and Real-World Impulsive Behavior' (2009) 47 Personality and Individual Differences 973; Harriet de Wit, 'IQ and Nonplanning Impulsivity are Independently Associated with Delay Discounting in Middle-Aged Adults' (2007) 42 Personality and Individual Differences 111; see also Charles Chabris et al., 'Individual Laboratory-Measured Discount Rates Predict Field Behavior' (2008) 37 Journal of Risk and Uncertainty 237, 256 on payment of credit card bills.

[99] Meier and Sprenger (n 97) 57.

[100] See also Hacker (n 90) 673 et seq.

return in a dynamic perspective. This is precisely what complexity theory describes.[101] It reintroduces uncertainty for future states of a system and takes that uncertainty one final step further. In a complexity setting, uncertainty not only concerns the rationality of market actors in different states of the world but even the very evolution of a range of different parameters of these states of the world *as a consequence of* heterogeneous rationality.[102] Such nonlinear, often unforeseeable developments pose a particular challenge to regulation and law making.

A. The Source of Unpredictability: Complexity

Heterogeneous rationality and heterogeneous expectations are modelled in sophisticated, agent-based models.[103] If these agents interact in unconstrained ways using different heuristics, adapting them as they learn over time (e.g., learning by doing and reinforcement learning), complex behavioural patterns arise.[104] Complexity, in the context of economic complexity theory, has a number of characteristic properties that do not arise in simply ordered systems. First, while recurring patterns exist, over time the system evolves in ways that are a priori unpredictable.[105] Second, feedback effects can be described under which local interactions engender global effects, which in turn may have repercussions on local interactions.[106] The 'butterfly effect' in the nonlinear evolution of weather systems is one example of complexity,[107] but financial systems and social systems have equally been described as highly sensitive to initial conditions.[108] Importantly, behavioural heterogeneity can trigger *dynamic* complexity: as the fractions of market actors using different heuristics change over time, this behavioural change leads to nonlinear developments.[109]

[101] See, e.g., Michael Strevens, *Bigger Than Chaos. Understanding Complexity through Probability* (Harvard University Press 2003).

[102] Hommes (n 84) 8–10; ibid. 10–11.

[103] Leigh Tesfatsion, 'Agent-Based Computational Economics: A Constructive Approach to Economic Theory' in Leigh Tesfatsion and Kenneth L. Judd (eds.), *Handbook of Computational Economics*, Vol. 2 (North-Holland 2006) 831.

[104] See, e.g., Hommes (n 84) 8–10.

[105] Tim Blackman, 'Complexity Theory' in Gary Browning et al. (eds.), *Understanding Contemporary Society: Theories of the Present* (SAGE 2000) 139, 140.

[106] Ibid. 142.

[107] William Baumol and Jess Benhabib, 'Chaos: Significance, Mechanism, and Economic Applications' (1989) 3 Journal of Economic Perspectives 77, 92

[108] David A Hsieh, 'Chaos and Nonlinear Dynamics: Application to Financial Markets' (1991) 46 Journal of Finance 1839; Edgar E. Peters, *Fractal Market Analysis. Applying Chaos Theory to Investment and Economics* (Wiley 1994); David Byrne, *Complexity Theory and the Social Sciences* (Routledge 1998); RA Thiétart and B Forgues, 'Chaos Theory and Organization' (1995) 6 Organization Science 19.

[109] Hommes (n 84) 10.

B. Regulatory Implications: Accommodating and Reducing Uncertainty

A number of economists, including the Chief Economist of the Bank of England, have suggested that complexity theory may be used for the predictive modelling of behaviour and outcomes on financial markets, and for financial regulation.[110] Their basic idea is that agent-based models simulating complexity may be better suited to predict tipping points at which systems drift from stable to unstable states. The difficulty of confronting such developments in a legal framework, however, stems from the unpredictability of the future states of the world. Classical decision theory, with its comparison of outcomes arising under clearly defined states of the world, is very difficult to square with complex evolutions.

Therefore, this chapter suggests that two different strategies may be pursued to deal with complexity arising from behavioural heterogeneity. As a first strategy, regulators and law makers may try to *accommodate uncertainty* by crafting a legal framework that flexibly adapts to different states of the world. This suggests that standards, capturing a wide range of situations, rather than rules, should be used to regulate systems prone to complex behaviour, such as financial markets.[111] Rules are precise, their content is known ex ante; standards are vaguer, their content is primarily determined ex post through application and enforcement.[112] For regulating complexity, principles and broad standards seem to provide the more promising option: they can capture the evolving world of uncertainty because they are more openly textured.[113] By virtue of their flexibility,[114] they can accommodate a greater variety of states of the world than the highly technical, precise rules which have come to dominate in today's law of capital markets and finance, and which are built on a precise empirical trigger.[115] Simultaneously, by describing the legal response to the trigger in vaguer terms,[116] standards offer greater discretion to the addressees of regulation, thereby granting leeway for experimentation—a key

[110] Stefano Battiston et al., 'Complexity Theory and Financial Regulation. Economic Policy Needs Interdisciplinary Network Analysis and Behavioral Modeling' (2016) 351 Science 818.

[111] On rules versus standards, see generally Herbert L. A. Hart, *The Concept of Law* (2nd edn, Oxford University Press 1994) 126–33; Ronald M. Dworkin, 'The Model of Rules' (1967) 35 University of Chicago Law Review 14, 22–29; Pierre Schlag, 'Rules and Standards' (1985) 33 UCLA Law Review 379; Louis Kaplow, 'Rules Versus Standards: An Economic Analysis' (1992) 42 Duke Law Journal 557; Francesco Parisi, 'Rules Versus Standards' in Charles K. Rowley and Friedrich Schneider (eds.), *The Encyclopedia of Public Choice* (Springer 2004) 835.

[112] cf. ibid. 382–83; Kaplow (n 111) 560; Hart (n 111) has famously pointed to the vagueness even of precise rules, given the indeterminacy of natural language; however, what is important here is that standards are *even vaguer* than rules because the indeterminacy of natural language affords degrees, cf. ibid. 133.

[113] cf. Hart (n 111) 128–31.

[114] See Schlag (n 111) 400, 424–25; Kaplow (n 111) 590–91.

[115] Ibid. 382.

[116] Ibid. 383.

prerequisite for innovation.[117] That would imply a veritable change of course in EU financial regulation that has, so far, been often marked by specific rules tailored to very precise events and situations. Such an approach stands in tension with attempts of personalisation that tends to be rule-based. However, one could personalise standards by adapting them to certain behavioural traits, but leaving *other* parameters and triggers more vaguely defined.[118]

Such a shift toward a more principle-based approach to the regulation of finance is in line with regulatory reform projects at the EU level. In September 2015, the European Commission launched a public consultation in the form of a call for evidence for a new EU regulatory framework for financial services.[119] The Commission noted the large number of pieces of regulation in the area of finance, the burden imposed by frequent updating, and excessive complexity of the web of rules created in the last years in the financial sector.[120] Specifically, the Commission conceded that a number of rules may be outdated due to technological change.[121] These concerns were reinforced by the response of the British Financial Conduct Authority, which particularly stressed the changes triggered by digitalisation and concomitant challenges for existing legal rules.[122] It noted that 'there will be an increasing need for all measures to be considered in the light of technological developments, to ensure that legislation is appropriately "future proof" and "technology neutral". By this, we mean that legislation should be drafted, to the extent possible, in such a way as to retain applicability in the light of technological developments and innovations.'[123] The Commission included similar concerns in its summary statement on the conclusion of the call for evidence.[124] Building highly adaptable broad standards and principles into the regulatory framework contributes precisely to the 'future-proofing' of legislation. In a similar vein, the European Central Bank has recently called for principle-based regulation of blockchain technology.[125]

[117] cf. Wolfgang Kerber, 'Competition, Innovation, and Competition Law: Dissecting the Interplay' in Damien Gerard et al. (eds.), *Dynamic Markets, Dynamic Competition and Dynamic Enforcement* (Bruylant 2018) 33.

[118] cf. Anthony J. Casey and Anthony Niblett, 'The Death of Rules and Standards' (2016) 92 Indiana Law Journal 1401.

[119] Commission, Call for Evidence: EU regulatory framework for financial services (20 September 2015), available at http://ec.europa.eu/finance/consultations/2015/financial-regulatory-framework-review/index_en.htm.

[120] Ibid. at 3–4, and 6.

[121] Ibid. at 7.

[122] Financial Conduct Authority, The Financial Conduct Authority's Response to the European Commission's Call for Evidence on the EU Regulatory Framework for Financial Services, available at https://www.fca.org.uk/your-fca/documents/eu-regulatory-framework-call-for-evidence, at 5–6.

[123] Ibid. 4.

[124] European Commission, 'Call for Evidence—EU regulatory framework for financial services' COM(2016) 855 final, 12.

[125] European Central Bank, 'ECB Contribution to the European Commission's Consultation on Capital Markets Union Mid-term Review 2017' (2017) 11, https://www.ecb.europa.eu/pub/pdf/other/ECB_contribution_to_EC_consultation_on_CMU_mid-term_review_201705.en.pdf.

The key drawback of standards vis-à-vis clear-cut rules, as is well-known, is ex ante *legal* uncertainty: it is costlier to determine the content of the law prior to action.[126] This, in turn, may dampen addressees' incentives to experiment with,[127] and hence slow down, innovation. Standards, however, simultaneously offer greater leeway to agents, which in turn facilitates innovation. Safe harbour provisions can mitigate legal uncertainty,[128] and over time, precedence partially converts standards into rules.[129] Therefore, overall, standards seem to fit innovative technologies better than rules under conditions of complexity.

As a second strategy, one may attempt to *reduce uncertainty* by rules tackling the sources of complexity: unconstrained interaction between heterogeneous actors. This points to the potentially stabilising influence of governance and coordination mechanisms that seek to order and channel local interactions. It is this second route that is pursued in the final example of this chapter concerning smart contracts and the governance of blockchains.

C. Example: Smart Contracts and the Governance of Blockchains

A blockchain is essentially a distributed database which is regularly updated by participants and in which consensus on the authentic content of the database is reached through decentralised consensus algorithms.[130] Therefore, no central authority authenticates the transactions recorded on a blockchain; rather, it combines an open structure with cryptographically secured verification. Every full participant in the (permissionless) blockchain stores the entire chain on its computer, which publicly records transactions whose parties are identified by pseudonymous public keys.[131] This not only enables direct payments in cryptocurrencies, such as bitcoin, from peer to peer, but also the execution of smart contracts that run on top of open blockchains and that automatically execute transactions once certain pre-coded conditions are reached.[132]

[126] Kaplow (n 111) 564.

[127] cf. Schlag (n 111) 385.

[128] See, e.g., Financial Conduct Authority, Regulatory Sandbox (November 2015), http://www.ifashops.com/wp-content/uploads/2015/11/regulatory-sandbox.pdf.

[129] Kaplow (n 111) 577.

[130] Arvind Narayanan et al., *Bitcoin and Cryptocurrency Technologies. A Comprehensive Introduction* (Princeton University Press 2016); Andreas Antonopoulos, *Mastering Bitcoin: Programming the Open Blockchain* (2nd edn, O'Reilly 2017); for a very short overview, see Jan Witte, 'The blockchain: a gentle introduction', Working Paper (2016), <https://ssrn.com/abstract=2887567.

[131] Ibid. 55 et seq.

[132] For a good introduction, see Narayanan et al. (n 130) ch 10.7; see also Roger Brownsword, 'Smart Contracts: Coding the Transaction, Decoding the Legal Debates' in Philipp Hacker et al. (eds.), *Regulating Blockchain* (Oxford University Press 2019) 311; Jeremy M. Sklaroff, 'Smart Contracts and the Cost of Inflexibility' (2017) 166 University of Pennsylvania Law Review 263; Primavera De Filippi and Aaron Wright, *Blockchain and the Law: The Rule of Code* (Harvard University Press 2018) 72 et seq.;

Transactions on a blockchain, and smart contracts implemented on it, are among the most transparent and predictable events in market interactions. Thus, at first glance, they seem to be far removed from the world of complexity described above. However, upon closer scrutiny, one cannot fail to note that they are implemented on blockchain-based platforms such as Bitcoin or Ethereum, and these platforms patently lack transparent governance structures.[133] While they operate according to an exactly specified protocol that allows for perfectly predictable transactions, the *updating* of, and thus changes to, this protocol are not subject to similarly transparent rules. This leads to unpredictable developments, not at the transaction but at the platform level; these developments, however, impact transactions deeply as well.[134] As I argue in related work,[135] the unpredictability of the evolution of the rules of the game that govern the platforms themselves is caused by a lack of governance mechanisms; in fact, blockchain-based architectures can therefore be fruitfully analysed as complex systems.[136]

This affects the future of smart contracts significantly. Building on an earlier definition by Richard Gendal Brown,[137] a newly minted law in the state of Arizona, passed on 29 March 2017, provides the first legal definition of a smart contract: ' "Smart contract" means an event-driven program, with state, that runs on a distributed, decentralized, shared and replicated ledger and that can take custody over and instruct transfer of assets on that ledger.'[138] Smart contracts, then,

Stefan Grundmann and Philipp Hacker, 'Digital Technology as a Challenge to European Contract Law' (2017) 13 European Review of Contract Law 255, 280 et seq.

[133] Arthur Gervais et al., 'Is Bitcoin a Decentralized Currency?' (2014) 12.3 IEEE Security & Privacy 54; Primavera De Filippi and Benjamin Loveluck, 'The Invisible Politics of Bitcoin: Governance Crisis of a Decentralised Infrastructure' (2016) 5.3 Internet Policy Review 1; Philipp Hacker, 'Corporate Governance for Complex Cryptocurrencies?' in Philipp Hacker et al. (eds.), *Regulating Blockchain* (Oxford University Press 2019) 140.

[134] cf. Houman Shadab, 'What are smart contracts, and what can we do with them?' *Coincenter* (15 December 2014), https://coincenter.org/entry/what-are-smart-contracts-and-what-can-we-do-with-them,section 'Which Chain? What Coin?'; Cheng Lim et al., 'Smart contracts: bridging the gap between expectation and reality' *Oxford Business Law Blog* (Oxford, 11 July 2016), https://www.law.ox.ac.uk/business-law-blog/blog/2016/07/smart-contracts-bridging-gap-between-expectation-and-reality, section 'Particular challenges with public blockchain smart contracts'

[135] Hacker (n 133).

[136] This particularly applies to public, non-permissioned blockchains. Private, permissioned blockchains arguably exhibit these features to a lesser extent, thanks to central steering mechanisms. It will therefore be intriguing to observe the behaviour of Facebook's Libra cryptocurrency, which opts for a rather permissioned format, in the longer run.

[137] Richard Gendal Brown, 'A simple model for smart contracts' (10 February 2015), https://gendal.me/2015/02/10/a-simple-model-for-smart-contracts/; cf. also Vitalik Buterin, 'DAOs, DACs, DAs and more: an incomplete terminology guide' *Ethereum Blog* (6 May 2014), https://blog.ethereum.org/2014/05/06/daos-dacs-das-and-more-an-incomplete-terminology-guide/: 'a smart contract is a mechanism involving digital assets and two or more parties, where some or all of the parties put assets in and assets are automatically redistributed among those parties according to a formula based on certain data that is not known at the time the contract is initiated'; Lim (n 134): 'A smart contact is, at its heart, a computer programme—encoded logic that receives certain inputs and executes a set of instructions to reach one of many pre-defined outcomes.'

[138] Arizona House Bill 2417, passed 29 March 2017, Chapter 97, § 2 Article 5 E.2., https://legiscan.com/AZ/text/HB2417/id/1588180/Arizona-2017-HB2417-Chaptered.html.

are programs that can receive assets and information, and send out assets and information, according to conditions agreed upon by the parties at the moment the program is written.[139] Once these conditions are met, the output is automatically generated, in other words the contract is automatically executed. To send out assets, the program may use the ledger, which guarantees prompt performance.[140] Since the ledger is distributed, the execution, and in fact the entire smart contract, are difficult to manipulate.[141]

However, the program is only as good as its code; it is not impossible that a hacker exploits bugs in the contract code. This is precisely what happened on 18 June 2016, when 'The DAO' was hacked.[142] In this case, a network of smart contracts was formed that created an investment vehicle, a decentralised organisation called 'The DAO',[143] on the Ethereum blockchain.[144] Everyone owning ether could invest (i.e., send ether to the DAO contract); the investors would then decide, by a voting mechanism, how these funds would be spent on the capital markets. 'The DAO' thus collected, within weeks, ether worth roughly US$150 million at the time. However, exploiting a bug in the code, a hacker siphoned off ether worth roughly US$70 million. After a heated debate on the appropriate, technical reaction, the core developers of Ethereum pushed, and implemented, a hard fork that effectively reversed the transaction history of the Ethereum blockchain by undoing the DAO hack.[145] In this, they sacrificed one of the core principles of blockchain technology: its irreversibility. The smart contracts securing the DAO, which were thought to be immutable, were effectively revoked. This move by the core developers laid bare the patent lack of governance mechanisms on the updating level; similar difficulties plague the Bitcoin blockchain in its attempt to enable the scaling to a larger volume of transactions.[146] Structural change at the platform level will, however, inevitably affect smart contracts running on these platforms.

[139] cf. Brown (n 137).

[140] cf. Tim Swanson, 'Consensus-as-a-Service: A Brief Report on the Emergence of Permissioned, Distributed Ledger Systems' (2015) 18, https://www.the-blockchain.com/wp-content/uploads/2016/04/Permissioned-distributed-ledgers.pdf.

[141] Ibid. 15.

[142] For a more detailed account of the hack, see, e.g., Hacker (n 133).

[143] A decentralised organisation is made up of smart contracts and creates an entity, similar to a company or a fund, that manages its own internal capital; see Vitalik Buterin, 'Ethereum White Paper' (2014); Vitalik Buterin, 'DAOs, DACs, DAs and more: an incomplete terminology guide' *Ethereum Blog* (6 May 2014), https://blog.ethereum.org/2014/05/06/daos-dacs-das-and-more-an-incomplete-terminology-guide/; Aaron Wright and Primavera De Filippi, 'Decentralized blockchain technology and the rise of Lex Cryptographia', Working Paper (2016), https://papers.ssrn.com/abstract_id=2580664, 15. Note that, despite its name, 'The DAO' did not constitute a fully decentralised *autonomous* organisation as its post-launch operation was determined not entirely by code but also by human intervention (cf. ibid. 17).

[144] David Siegel, 'Understanding the DAO attack' *Coindesk* (25 June 2016), http://www.coindesk.com/understanding-dao-hack-journalists/.

[145] Alyssa Hertig, 'What is a DAO?' *Coindesk* (no date) http://www.coindesk.com/information/what-is-a-dao-ethereum/; ibid. '[The DAO hard fork] has the effect of rewriting the rules by which the blockchain executes, which is supposed to be impossible.'

[146] Hacker (n 133) 14–16.

The lack of governance mechanisms spurs unpredictability of the evolution of the blockchain protocols. Arguably, it arises out of the unconstrained interaction between highly heterogeneous actors that come to the blockchain ecosystem with varying degrees of rationality, technical savviness, and underlying aims. Therefore, one may aptly analyse cryptocurrencies as complex systems, as a number of empirical studies have successfully started doing.[147] Notably, the high volatility of the value of cryptocurrencies also testifies to their complex nature.[148]

From a regulatory perspective, one promising strategy therefore lies in implementing governance mechanisms. In this, corporate governance may provide a helpful template that could be used and adapted to the blockchain ecosystem.[149] Two features of the corporate governance framework stand out that make it particularly suitable for an application to blockchains. First, corporate governance stresses transparency and a clear and fair distribution of power between highly heterogeneous stakeholders, such as management, shareholders, and other involved parties.[150] This could pave the way for a similar distribution of rights and duties between the body of core developers, regular users, and specific stakeholders of the blockchain ecosystem such as miners and wallet providers. Second, and perhaps even more importantly, corporate governance generally operates with a comply-or-explain framework, under which companies are free either to abide with good governance practices or to disclose the reasons why they choose not to.[151] Similarly, a comply-or-explain approach to blockchain governance would enable each specific blockchain, from large incumbents such as Bitcoin or Ethereum to smaller spinoffs, to pick the governance mechanisms it deems most suitable. Simultaneously, however, it would have to inform existing and potential users about the choices it made, and the reasons for this, so that users and technical analysts can more easily compare the governance structures of different blockchains. The same approach could apply to blockchain-based organisations created on top of existing blockchains through initial coin offerings,[152] such as The DAO and its more recent successors. Corporate governance therefore combines the necessary

[147] Eng-Tuck Cheah and John Fry, 'Speculative Bubbles in Bitcoin Markets? An Empirical Investigation into the Fundamental Value of Bitcoin' (2015) 130 Economics Letters 32; John Fry and Eng-Tuck Cheah, 'Negative Bubbles and Shocks in Cryptocurrency Markets' (2016) 47 International Review of Financial Analysis 343; David Garcia et al., 'The Digital Traces of Bubbles: Feedback Cycles between Socio-Economic Signals in the Bitcoin Economy' (2014) 11 Journal of the Royal Society Interface 20140623.

[148] Ibid. 35; Battiston et al. (n 110) 819.

[149] Hacker (n 133).

[150] See Bob Tricker, *Corporate Governance* (2nd edn, Oxford University Press 2012) 86–88.

[151] Klaus Hopt, 'Comparative Corporate Governance: The State of the Art and International Regulation' (2011) 59 American Journal of Comparative Law 1, 10–11; ibid. 45–46.

[152] On initial coin offerings, see Philipp Hacker and Chris Thomale, 'Crypto-Securities Regulation: ICOs, Token Sales and Cryptocurrencies under EU Financial Law' (2018) 15 European Company and Financial Law Review 645; Jonathan Rohr and Aaron Wright, 'Blockchain-based Token Sales, Initial Coin Offerings, and the Democratization of Public Capital Markets' (2018) 70 Hastings Law Journal 463.

flexibility with an attempt to tackle the sources of unpredictability and complexity in blockchain environments. In doing so, it fulfils the criteria voiced by, inter alia, the European Parliament that call for proportionate, 'smart regulation' tailored to cryptocurrencies without stifling innovation.[153]

V. The Normative Core of Uncertainty Approaches to the Law

The preceding sections have discussed a number of regulatory approaches to uncertainty, ranging from decision theory to the use of Big Data analytics and the tackling of complex behaviour via strengthened governance frameworks. In closing, it seems important to stress that all these techniques, even if they partially rely on rather formal or technical modes of decision making, share the necessity to make deeply normative judgments. Therefore, they should not be understood as a call for techno-regulation;[154] very much to the contrary, these tools may help us to improve our understanding and lay bare the normative core of regulatory decisions affecting heterogeneous actors.

The employment of theories of choice, such as decision making under uncertainty, can arguably make trade-offs more transparent, but it cannot free us from the necessity of deciding between different decision-making rules. These rules are the centre of the analysis as they encapsulate specific weightings of different interests, and, therefore, decide which ones are given primacy. This is embodied, for example, in the stark contrast between a maximax, tailored to maximise social welfare, and a maximin principle that follows the Rawlsian version of fairness. As we have seen, intermediate rules allow us to navigate the space between the two extremes, but they also point to the necessity of determining how to strike this balance with precision.

Similarly, in situations of risk engendered by more granular information driven, for example, by machine learning, the weighting of the interests of different individuals and groups is key at the aggregate level (both for CBA and SWFs). At the individual level, under a more personalised legal regime, questions of privacy and abuse of data highlight the normative implications of government-based personalisation.

Finally, under a complexity framework, normative questions are unavoidable in the determination of the standards apt to govern potentially complex situations. Similarly, the reduction of complexity by means of governance schemes always implies an allocation of specific rights and duties to groups of stakeholders, which is already a contentious exercise under company law and can be expected

153 European Parliament, 'Virtual currencies. European Parliament resolution of 26 May 2016 on virtual currencies' 2016/2007(INI), Arts 4, 14, and 18.

154 See, for a critical discussion, Jürgen Habermas, *The Lure of Technocracy* (Polity Press 2015).

to be even more contested in decentralised blockchain settings. Here, approaches favouring a strong management will be pitted against user empowerment strategies,[155] again necessitating normative judgment calls. All in all, this points to the desideratum of broad public discussions of the core features of the respective regulatory approaches, and to the necessity of a genuinely normative reconstructing of decision theories, implicating the values of the respective legal order in which the regulation is set.[156]

VI. Conclusion: Cycles of Uncertainty and the Law

This chapter has uncovered a dynamic cycle of uncertainty. First of all, a lack of empirical studies, or limits of internal and external validity, engender uncertainty vis-à-vis the degree of rationality of regulation's addressees. This is important in contexts in which the outcomes of regulatory interventions crucially depend on a preponderance of rational or boundedly rational actors in the field. This will typically be the case in market regulation, be it through disclosure, default, or substantial mandatory law, as the reactions of market participants typically differ based on their degree of rationality. To deal with uncertainty arising from lack of empirical information, law makers and regulators should turn to the time-tested tools of decision theory. More precisely, conceiving of the regulatory challenge as a situation of decision making under uncertainty helps to make transparent the relevant trade-offs that the decision maker is facing. Most importantly, it points to the centrality of the choice of decision-making rules that rank outcomes of different regulatory alternatives under more rational or more boundedly rational conditions. The example of price discrimination has shown that the choice of legal alternatives can indeed benefit from a decision theoretic framework; a maximin rule, for example, suggests banning rather than allowing personalised price discrimination based on the tracking of consumer behaviour in digital contexts.

In a second step, regulators can attempt to reduce empirical uncertainty by employing, for example, machine learning models to predict individual behaviour. In this way, uncertainty may be converted into risk, in other words into a situation in which the probability distributions over the respective degrees of rationality are approximately known. At an aggregate level, this means that instead of decision making under uncertainty, CBA, or SWFs can be applied to weigh the advantages and disadvantages of regulatory interventions. At an individual level, the technique of personalised law may be employed to tailor legal consequences precisely

[155] See the proposals to reinforce user voice in Bitcoin Core, De Filippi and Loveluck (n 133) 9; see also Pete Rizzo, 'Bitcoin unlimited: mining power should determine hard Fork' *CoinDesk* (29 March 2017), http://www.coindesk.com/bitcoin-unlimited-mining-power-should-determine-hard-fork-outcome.

[156] See now, in a similar vein, Stefan Grundmann, 'Pluralism and Private Law Theory'(2020) 68 American Journal of Comparative Law (forthcoming); and Hacker (n 5) Part II.

to individual behavioural traits. The example of usurious lending showed how the usury threshold could vary with predicted degrees of bounded willpower; however, it also showed that important challenges, such as the protection of privacy and the prevention of the abuse of personal data by ill-intentioned government officials, must be overcome. Company-based personalisation, which ties specific legal obligations to degrees of knowledge a company has on its customers, offers a potential way out of this impasse.

Such a reduction of uncertainty to more granular levels of knowledge, however, is only possible in relatively stable states of a system. In a dynamic perspective, behavioural heterogeneity may spark unforeseeable developments, as complexity theory shows. Under these conditions, systems drift from stable into unstable states, and the parameters of future states of the world become increasingly difficult to predict. Complexity theory has been successfully applied to the study of financial markets and, more recently, to blockchain environments such as cryptocurrencies. It reintroduces uncertainty even in areas where quite reliable information can be gathered about actors at a certain moment in time. Here, legislators and regulators should, on the one hand, attempt to accommodate uncertainty by turning to standards, rather than rules. Such standards can still be tailored to specific degrees of rationality of market participants; they should, however, be openly textured so as to apply to a large range of other factual circumstances. On the other hand, one may try to reduce uncertainty by providing governance mechanisms that channel and coordinate the unconstrained interaction of heterogeneous agents that triggers complexity in the first place. The example of smart contracting and the governance of blockchains has shown how a corporate governance framework could be applied to mitigate complexity inherent in blockchain applications. Once complexity has settled, through these or other ways, into a somewhat stable state, one may then return to decision making under uncertainty again—and the wheel has come full circle. This implies that regulation itself is best understood as an iterative process, in which learning from previous cycles takes centre stage.[157]

For legislators and regulators, it is therefore crucial to know what scenario they are in. Being conscious of the epistemic conditions for regulation thus becomes paramount. There are two ways in which regulators may proceed to evaluate degrees of uncertainty. First, as Christopher Engel describes in detail in his contribution to this volume, they may look at the assumptions made in the relevant experiments (if any) and determine whether they match closely the situation at hand. Second, they might look for machine learning applications; if the performance of the model is good enough, these models may provide granular predictions. Classical experiments and digital technology may therefore convert uncertainty into risk. However, in contexts in which dynamic unforeseeability has been

[157] Georgios Dimitropoulos and Philipp Hacker, 'Learning and the Law: Improving Behavioral Regulation from an International and Comparative Perspective' (2017) 25 Journal of Law & Policy 473.

experienced (such as financial markets or blockchain environments), one should be cautious to project the state of the present linearly into the future.

The evaluation of alternatives, and the tools available for it, therefore depend on how reliable the empirical information is that guides regulatory choice. Even formal tools of decision making, however, do not render normative judgments and debates obsolete; very much to the contrary, if appropriately used, they may show precisely where normative fault lines lie, and how a conscious balancing of interests is a necessary ingredient of any regulatory intervention. Decision theory does not provide for easy answers, yet it does provide a facilitating template for dealing with hard cases through the law.

6

Did You Say 'Theories of Choice'?

On the Limited and Variable Appetite for Theories in Consumer Law

Anne-Lise Sibony

Abstract: This chapter takes up two difficult questions: 'does the law contain one or more theories of choice?' and, if it does, 'is there a meta-theory to tell us which theory of choice to use in which cases?' Even if one retains a loose definition of what counts as a 'theory of choice', there are reasons to be sceptical about the enterprise of mapping out theories of choice underpinning the law. This is because the supply of such theories is both abundant and incomplete while the demand is generally weak. Consumer protection, which purports to protect 'consumer choice', would seem to be a designated area of law to look for theories of (consumer) choice. However, an enquiry into legislative work on consumer protection reveals paradoxical efforts to confirm the theory that consumers do well with information rather than investigate alternative theories. It also appears that consumer law embeds several different conflicting theories of consumer choice without any sign of a meta-theory indicating which theory applies to which cases. In addition, where there is a theory of consumer harm justifying legislative intervention, it seems to matter little that we do not have a theory for how consumer choice is distorted. In short, the legislative appetite for theories of choice seems limited. Legal scholarship offers a different picture. A space has emerged in which to discuss theories of choice within legal analysis, which is still in the process of being shaped. Tentatively, it is suggested that the legal literature offers a contrast between deep and narrow discussions of theories of choice, and wide and shallow ones.

I. Introduction: Reasons to Lower Ambitions

The ambitious project of this volume is to map out, in a rational and reasoned manner, which theory or theories of choice lawyers and policy makers should use in which situations. This is a commendable enterprise and both the legal scholarship and law making would greatly benefit from having at one's disposal a meta-theory for choosing an adequate theory of choice. We would certainly be better

Anne-Lise Sibony, *Did You Say 'Theories of Choice'?* In: *Theories of Choice.* Edited by: Stefan Grundmann and Philipp Hacker, Oxford University Press (2021). © The several contributors. DOI: 10.1093/oso/9780198863175.003.0007

off if, for example, we could confidently say: 'this issue relates to regulation of business-to-business transactions, and therefore we can safely base regulation on an assumption of perfect rationality as understood in neoclassical price theory', or 'this issue relates to choices many people make after consulting with family or friends, and therefore we need a theory of choice that factors in such social interactions'. It would be splendid to have a well-ordered catalogue of well-defined theories of choice, complete with an index (or an algorithm) allowing legal scholars and policy makers to identify the best-suited theory of choice for their legal project (while speaking of an ideal world, we might as well envisage there would be only one best-suited theory in each case). However, such an orderly correspondence between legal needs and what social sciences have in store by way of theories of choice is elusive.

The first series of reasons why this is the case is to do with what one might call the 'supply side', namely the scholarly disciplines providing theories of choice. The difficulty is not only what they do or do not offer but also how (little) they interact. To the best of this author's knowledge, there is no agreed-upon catalogue of all available theories of choice, and probably not even an agreed-upon definition of what constitutes a theory of choice. In other words, not even the litmus test to be listed in the catalogue is readily available at this point. The very phrase 'theory of choice' is not used in all social sciences. Economists speak about the theory of rational choice and of game theory; philosophers add social choice theory but do not have an overarching category which would encompass all three.

In this chapter, 'theory of choice' has a broad and non-technical sense. It covers any analytical framework applicable to how humans make choices. Rational choice theory is, in this sense, a theory of choice, one that assumes thick rationality. Behavioural insights call the validity of this theory into question on many different grounds but they do not offer an alternative 'theory' in the strong sense of the word because these insights do not form a unified, simple framework.[1] This is so not only because of their possible underdevelopment but also because the level of granularity and realism to which psychologists and other behavioural scientists aspire almost certainly precludes it. Nonetheless, behavioural insights, in their richness and diversity, provide (partial) 'theories of choice' within the broad meaning used here. Indeed, the literature on bounded rationality and bounded ethicality provides analytical frameworks to think about (certain types of) choice situations.[2] Sometimes an accumulation of studies establishing one single behavioural phenomenon is

[1] As Korobkin and Ulen write: 'The end point of this broad research agenda will likely not be a single unified theory designed to explain or predict the full realm of human decision-making behaviour. Rather, it is more likely to be a pragmatic collection of situation-specific insights that can assist policy-makers dealing with relevant problems.' Russell B. Korobkin and Thomas Ulen, 'Law and Behavioral Science: Removing the Rationality Assumption from Law and Economics' (2000) 88.4 California Law Review 1051, 1060, 1075.

[2] For a comprehensive summary of partial theories in the bounded rationality family, see Eyal Zamir and Doron Teichman, *Behavioural Law and Economics* (Oxford University Press 2018), ch. 2. For a

apt to inspire the legislator (without any apparent need for a more comprehensive theory). The ban on inertia selling in European Union ('EU') law is a case in point:[3] the EU Behavioural Insights Team relied on a survey of the literature to recommend adopting this provision. It considered that the extant studies sufficiently established the existence and robustness of the inertia bias to warrant a provision banning firms from exploiting this bias by pre-ticking boxes (e.g., to add insurance when a consumer purchases an air ticket).[4]

To a certain extent, the behavioural literature also contains—albeit diffusely—some elements of a meta-choice between theories of choice. The first one is obvious: this literature as a whole suggests that rational choice theory is never, or only extremely rarely, correct because it would only apply in contexts where no bias exists, which seems very difficult to imagine. In addition, within this body of behavioural scholarship, each behavioural phenomenon has its boundary conditions.[5] The anchoring effect will only obtain in contexts where some piece of information functions as an anchor;[6] a framing effect pertaining to risky choices can only be relevant where the parameters defining alternative options relate to some kind of gain and some kind of loss;[7] blind spots occur in situations where a conflict of interests is present.[8] In other words, because each strand of behavioural research defines its object, it is possible—as well as highly desirable—to pay careful attention to how this object is defined and to use behavioural insights only in their domain of validity. Boundary conditions, however, only constitute building blocks of a meta-theory of choice—a theory that would allow us to choose the fitting theory of choice for a particular type of choice situation. This is due to the fact that, in the real world, behavioural phenomena may co-occur (boundary conditions for each may overlap), and interactions between behavioural phenomena, which should be of concern to legal scholars and policy makers, are as yet still under-researched.[9] In other words, behavioural sciences offer some but not all of the building blocks that would be necessary for a complete meta-theory of choice.

comprehensive summary of partial theories in the bounded ethicality family, see Yuval Feldman, *The Law of Good People* (Cambridge University Press 2018) 19.

[3] Directive 2011/83/EU on consumer rights, [2011] OJ L 304/64, article 22.

[4] Joint Research Center, *Behavioural Insights Applied to Policy* (Joint Research Center 2016) 8.

[5] On the importance of boundary conditions for legal analysis, see Avishalom Tor, 'The Methodology of the Behavioral Analysis of Law' (2008) 4 Haifa Law Review 237, 294 (I use here 'boundary conditions' in the second sense defined by Tor, i.e., 'specific boundary conditions').

[6] The effect has been documented in relation to factual questions (e.g., number on countries in the United Nations) but also willingness to pay and assessment of physical stimuli. Zamir and Teichman (n 2) 80.

[7] But on unclear boundary conditions and magnitude of (this and other) framing effects, see Zamir and Teichman (n 2) 80.

[8] Yuval Feldman, *The Law of Good People* (Oxford University Press 2018) 190.

[9] Yuval Feldman and Orly Lobel, 'Behavioural Trade-Offs: Beyond the Land of Nudges Spans the World of Law and Psychology' in Alberto Alemanno and Anne-Lise Sibony (eds.), *Nudge and the Law: A European Perspective* (Hart 2015) 301.

The second series of reasons why it might be challenging to provide lawyers and policy makers with a fully functional meta-theory of choice to guide them when they need to understand how people make specific choices has to do with the 'demand' side, namely legal scholars and policy makers themselves. The difficulty here is that the demand for a meta-theory of choice is hard to discern, irrespective of the fact that it might be difficult to satisfy if it were readily identifiable. Behaviourally minded scholars in legal academia and behaviourally minded policy advisors and policy makers have certainly increased in number in recent years.[10] In this sense, there is a growing demand for guidance on how to use behavioural insights in government in general.[11] However, if one turns to such guidance documents, it is striking that they envisage nothing like a meta-theory of choice. Instead, they emphasise the need to construct and test ad-hoc theories. A 2017 comprehensive survey of behavioural policy making across developed countries offers a characteristic example. In this report, the Organisation for Economic Co-operation and Development ('OECD') notes that

> [a]pplying behavioural insights is first and foremost an approach to policy making that embeds experimentation into the development of policy and regulation. It starts with the recognition that individuals do not behave as the theories of rational choice may suggest, and that increasingly public bodies endeavour to create evidence-based policies and interventions with a more realistic, and proven, understanding of human behaviour.[12]

The new consensus rejects rational choice theory, but neither replaces it with a single substitute theory (which is not available) nor with a kit comprising a collection of partial theories topped with a meta-theory (which would be akin to an

[10] In this regard, the dissemination work undertaken by the UK Behavioural Insights Team, the OECD, and the World Bank—as well as several active think tanks and the EU Behavioural Insights and Foresights Unit within the Joint Research Center—should be underscored. On the academic front, several books have contributed to bridging the gap between technical psychology articles (a challenging read for lawyers) and popular science books (easy to read but not always sufficiently precise). Among them Rhys Jones, Jessica Pykett, and Mark Whitehead, *Changing Behaviours—On the Rise of the Psychological State* (Edward Elgar 2013); Adam Oliver, *Behavioural Public Policy* (Cambridge University Press 2013); Alemanno and Sibony (n 9); Zamir and Teichman (n 2); Feldman (n 2); Peter John, *How Far to Nudge? Assessing Behavioural Public Policy* (Edward Elgar 2018).

[11] Government, international organisations, and think tanks have produced a number of reports and policy documents to cater for this demand. The UK Behavioural Insights Team was the first to produce several reports: *MINDSPACE* (2010); *Test, Learn, and Adapt* (2013); *EAST Framework* (2014). The OECD and the World Bank followed suit: World Bank, World Development Report *Mind, Society, and Behavior* (2015); OECD, *Behavioural Insights and Public Policies: Lessons from around the world* (2017); *Tools and Ethics for Applied Behavioural Insights: The BASIC Toolkit* (2019). Specialised government departments have also produced sector-specific guidance, for example the US Internal Revenue Service's (IRS) *Behavioral Insights Toolkit* (2017). Several specialised think tanks also contribute to the literature: Ideas42, *Define, Diagnose, Design, Test* (2017); Feng Bing et al., *How Should Organizations Best Embed and Harness Behavioural Insights? A Playbook* (2018), available at http://www.rotman.utoronto.ca/bear.

[12] OECD (n 11).

instruction manual on when to use which theory). Instead, the message to policy makers is: come up with a theory, test it, and, if it does fit the situation, use it to design intervention. Admittedly, the custom-built theory will not emerge from thin air and whoever is in charge of coming up with a candidate theory—possibly a government behavioural insights team—will draw on existing research. It is precisely the role of a specialised unit to know its way around accumulated behavioural knowledge and select insights which could be relevant to a situation in which the government would like to intervene.

Importantly, the moment when the question 'what theories of choice could be useful?' arises is in the earliest stages of policy making. Indeed, this question helps to identify the intervention logic rather than fine-tune the intervention. Asking what will influence choice in a given situation involves scanning the science for relevant insights. For example, concerning the policy issue of how to increase tax compliance, one policy option may be to raise penalties for late payers. This strategy appeals to the rational behaviour of taxpayers by raising the cost of delaying payment. A behavioural insight unit investigating the same policy issue will come up with different theories of what governs the choice to pay now or later, thereby opening the way to different policy options. In relation with this question, the UK nudge unit famously came up with the theory that, apart from liquidity constraints, a late payment could be due to procrastination. Procrastination itself could be targeted by appealing to a social norm ('others have paid already') or by reminding taxpayers that tax money is used to provide public goods. It is only after candidate theories have been identified (here social norm and salience of public good purpose) that different variants of each theory and combinations of both can be tested empirically. This is usually where randomised control trials ('RCTs') come in.[13] For example, they help determine which of several variants of a reminder letter to late taxpayers—all appealing to the social norm and some to other behavioural mechanisms as well—will work best.[14] In other words, systematicity is invited at the fine-tuning stage, after the direction of travel (the theory of choice) has been chosen.

[13] See Michael Hallsworth et al., 'The Behavioralist as Tax Collector: Using Natural Field Experiments to Enhance Tax Compliance' (2017) 148 Journal of Public Economics, 14 (finding that both appealing to social norm and highlighting the public good had a positive effect, but framing had no effect).

[14] Interestingly, it is not the same variants that worked best in the United Kingdom in 2013 and in Belgium in 2018. Teaming up with researchers, the Belgian Tax Office conducted a large-scale experiment similar to the 2013 UK BIT experiment. However, because of the much larger sample, it was possible to test more variants in a statistically robust way. In addition to the effect of simplification, appealing to the social norm and making public good salient, the authors also tested deterrence (highlighting the amount of the fine incurred by late payers). As in the UK experiment, the authors found that simplifying the reminder letter had a positive effect. They also found that deterrence worked better than positive motivation—which seems at odds with the UK results though the experiments are not exactly comparable in this respect. Tax morale treatments (highlighting the public good impact of taxes) did not raise compliance in Belgium and even backfired for most taxpayers, unlike in the United Kingdom. Jan-Emmanuel De Neve et al., How to Improve Tax Compliance? Evidence from Population-wide Experiments in Belgium (2019), CEP Discussion Paper No. 1621.

At the orientation stage, a meta-theory of choice could serve as a compass. Short of a compass (let alone a global positioning system ('GPS')), we should be prepared to recognise that policy actors orient themselves on the map of theories of choice based on their prior knowledge and intuition. Since their knowledge may—understandably—be partial, this could lead to sticking to the familiar areas of the map (say, the most studied behavioural phenomena). Inroads into less familiar areas (say, behavioural ethics) could be dependent on the availability of expert advice, thus creating randomness in the selection of theories of choice for policy purposes. To address this risk, emphasis should be on bringing to the table people who know different theories of choice (whether or not they are so named in their discipline of origin). Such diversity of expertise would ensure that explorations are not limited to the best-known section of the map of theories, the one plotting findings on bounded rationality, but they also venture into other potentially relevant territories, such as those of behavioural ethics or peers' influence on choice. In lieu of a meta-theory of choice, we can create procedures which will foster the representation of diverse theories of choice—rather than a subset of them—at the relevant stage of initiating policy-relevant research.[15]

This author is no exception to the partial knowledge problem, and the present chapter limits itself to offering a few elements for discussing how policy makers and legal scholars approach choosing between theories of choice. It does so with a focus on consumer choice and offers two entries considering different contexts in which such a (meta-) choice is 'theorised' (in a weak sense)—or not—by law makers or scholars. The first entry (section II) focuses on a law-making context. It discusses what theory of consumer choice, if any, is embedded in existing EU legislation and, more broadly, whether a theory of consumer choice is always necessary to legislate on consumer protection. The second entry (section III) turns to an academic context and looks at how a space for discussing theories of choice has emerged in legal scholarship and can take different shapes. Some concluding remarks are offered (section IV).

II. Legislation: Is There a Theory of Choice? The Example of EU Consumer Protection

This section considers theories of choice in the legislative context from two different perspectives. Taking a descriptive perspective, the attention first turns to EU consumer protection which, historically, rests on an information paradigm largely consonant with rational choice theory. Looking at recent pre-legislative practice, subsection A analyses whether the European Commission's commitment

[15] This approach is advocated (in slightly different language) in BIT, Behavioural Government (HMSO 2018).

to a behavioural orientation of EU consumer protection translates as a departure from this theory of choice and concludes that it does not, at least not significantly. Theories of choice, when embedded in legislation, seem to be sticky. From a theoretical perspective, subsection B focuses on the example of drip pricing to show that, in the face of evidence of consumer harm, a theory of choice is not always indispensable to justify consumer protection.

A. EU Consumer Policy: Information-based Theory of Choice can be Sticky

Protecting informed choice has been the mantra of EU consumer protection since its inception. Tellingly, the first political document mentioning consumer protection at the European level was entitled the 'preliminary programme of the European Economic Community for a consumer protection and *information* policy'.[16] Empowering consumers through information has remained at the heart of EU consumer law ever since.[17] The faith in the power of information is such that transparency remains the preferred tool even in complex environments where consumers' attention and understanding are, arguably, limited. A case in point concerns online personalisation practices. A 2018 study conducted for the European Commission found that while surveyed consumers valued information about personalisation to some extent, they were not always proficient in using it.[18] When given transparent information about personalisation practices, consumers identified personalised ranking of offers with reasonable accuracy, but this was not the case for the two other personalisation practices studied, namely targeted advertising and personalised prices.[19] These findings reflect lab conditions, where attention to information is probably more focused than in real shopping contexts, leaving one to suppose that information about personalisation may not be effective in empowering consumers to make smart choices.

It is noteworthy in a policy perspective that surveyed consumers held mixed views about personalisation practices: most consumers believed that personalisation practices had either both advantages and disadvantages or mostly

[16] Council Resolution of 14 April 1975 on a preliminary programme of the European Economic Community for a consumer protection and information policy, OJEU C 92, 25.4.1975, p. 1.

[17] By way of a typical example, the Commission, outlining in 2007 the development of consumer policy in the years ahead wrote that '[e]mpowered consumers need real choices, *accurate information*, market transparency and the confidence that comes from effective protection and solid rights'. European Commission, EU Consumer Policy strategy 2007–2013: Empowering consumers, enhancing their welfare, effectively protecting them, COM(2007) 99 final (my emphasis).

[18] Ipsos-London Economics-Deloitte, Data Consumer market study on online market segmentation through personalised pricing/offers in the European Union 2018, (for the European Commission, https://ec.europa.eu/info/publications/consumer-market-study-online-market-segmentation-through-personalised-pricing-offers-european-union_en) [https://perma.cc/ZAD5-5UN3] (hereafter, 'Ipsos, Personalisation study').

[19] Ipsos, Personalisation study (n 18) 105.

disadvantages.[20] Opinions about personalised pricing were notably more negative than about targeted advertising or personalised ranking of offers.[21] When asked what could change their views about personalisation, and given a choice between various options, receiving information came last.[22] In other words, consumers seemed to be aware that information is not what they need most to protect them from practices they considered at least somewhat problematic.

That information may not be effective in protecting consumers, and that it is also perceived as ineffective did not prevent the EU legislator from regulating personalisation only through information requirements in the 'Modernisation directive' adopted in 2019 to reform EU consumer law.[23] The information paradigm, already mobilised on the topic of personalisation in a 2016 communication,[24] was deemed sufficient, although the recent study commissioned to inform the legislative process cast some doubt about the wisdom of this legislative strategy.[25] The new rules validate all personalisation practices (including price personalisation),[26] subject only to disclosure that prices are being personalised. There is no requirement for this information to be salient or relatable.[27] Despite a general commitment to a behavioural orientation of EU consumer protection and

[20] Ipsos, Personalisation study (n 18) 144–46. On the negative perception of price personalisation, see also OECD, *Personalised Pricing in the Digital Era*, DAF/COMP(2018)13, 23–26.

[21] Ibid.

[22] Ipsos, Personalisation study (n 18) 148 et seq. The other options besides being informed when targeted adverts or personalised pricing/offers are being shown were: having an easy way to 'opt-out' of personalised practices; receiving an explanation about what personal data is collected; being given the opportunity to see/change one's personal data used for personalisation practices; receiving an explanation about the purpose of data collection; receiving an explanation about which third parties access personal data; being informed why a particular advert or a particular search result/price is being shown.

[23] Directive (EU) 2019/2161 amending Directives 93/13/EEC, 98/6/EC, 2005/29/EC, and 2011/83/EU as regards the better enforcement and modernisation of Union consumer protection rules [2019] OJ L 328/7 ('Modernisation directive').

[24] 'Greater transparency is also needed for users to understand how the information presented to them is filtered, shaped, or personalised, especially when this information forms the basis of purchasing decisions or influences their participation in civic or democratic life. If consumers are properly informed of the nature of the products that they view or consume online, this assists the efficient functioning of markets and consumer welfare.' European Commission, Online Platforms and the Digital Single Market Opportunities and Challenges for Europe, COM(2016) 288 final, 10.

[25] The doubts are not highlighted or even expressly formulated in the Ipsos Personalisation study (n 18). This is our own reading.

[26] No attempt is made to distinguish between different types of personalisation. For such an attempt, see Oren Bar-Gill, 'Algorithmic Price Discrimination When Demand Is a Function of Both Preferences and (Mis)perceptions' (April 2019) 86.2 University of Chicago Law Review 217 (distinguishing between algorithmic price discrimination which targets preferences, and price discrimination which targets misperceptions, and arguing that the latter type calls for legal intervention).

[27] New Art. 6, § 1[er] e[a] of Directive 2011/83/EU on Consumer Rights (introduced by the Modernisation directive) mandates disclosing 'where applicable, that the price was personalised on the basis of automated decision-making'. Recital 45 explains that '[c]onsumers should . . . be clearly informed when the price presented to them is personalised based on automated decision-making *so that they can take into account the potential risks in their purchasing decision*' (my emphasis). New item Point 11a added (by the

evidence-based policy making,[28] the new rules seem to be premised on a theory of choice according to which consumers can choose for themselves only if they have all the relevant information. Indeed, the very choice to allow all types of price discrimination suggests that the legislator is assuming that consumers are '(rather) fully rational'.[29]

What is more, the European Commission behavioural studies which seem designed to confirm the soundness of the information paradigm. This is the case of studies undertaken as part of the regulatory fitness and performance programme ('REFIT') of EU consumer law—a retrospective evaluation deemed to assess whether the existing legal framework is still fit for purpose.[30] The report drawn up on this occasion contains four empirical studies on various choice situations regulated by consumer law directives.[31] One study considers how consumers react to price per unit ('PPU') indications (which are mandated by a directive). As the authors of the study point out, such indications are especially useful to consumers when they carry the information that, contrary to expectations, a *small* container of washing liquid is *cheaper* per unit than a large container. The study shows that, in such situations, consumers used PPU indications wisely to de-bias themselves and realise that the heuristic 'big is cheap' does not work: they choose the cheaper product per unit (the one packaged in a small container). In addition, a majority reported doing the maths themselves when PPU indications were not available.[32] This study clearly illustrates how well consumers do with information—and, if one trusts the accuracy of self-reports, even without—explicit information. Another study in the same lot finds that, to a large extent, consumers read, understand, and act upon the information contained in terms and conditions ('T&Cs'). In the experiment, consumers were given the task to choose either an Internet provider or an offer for a consumer credit, and, in either case, were given a choice between one

Modernisation directive) to Annex 1 of Directive 2005/29/EC on unfair commercial practices prohibits as misleading omission the practice of '[p]roviding search results in response to a consumer's online search query without clearly disclosing any paid advertisement or payment specifically for achieving higher ranking of products within the search results'.

[28] This commitment is evidenced by the number of behavioural studies commissioned to inform EU policy, particularly in the field of consumer protection. The studies (seventeen to date) are available at: https://ec.europa.eu/info/policies/consumers/consumer-protection/evidence-based-consumer-policy/behavioural-research_en.

[29] See the contribution by Philippe Hacker in this volume, section II.3.c.

[30] The Regulatory Fitness and Performance (REFIT) programme was established in 2012 by a Communication from the Commission, EU Regulatory Fitness, COM(2012) 746 final.

[31] GfK Belgium, Consumer Market Study to support the Fitness Check of EU consumer and marketing law, 29 (May 2017), hereafter 'Lot 3 study', available at https://ec.europa.eu/newsroom/just/item-detail.cfm?item_id=59332. The report contains four studies: Effects of indicating the price per unit on consumers' behaviour (price indication directive), Consumers' responses towards fair/unfair contract terms (unfair contract terms directive), Effects of durability and reparability information on consumers' behaviour, Consumers' understanding and use of pre-contractual information.

[32] Ibid 379.

provider offering fair contract terms and another offering unfair contract terms.[33] They were exposed to standard (long) T&Cs and simplified T&Cs. The findings were in line with what one might expect from relatively diligent and attentive consumers: when T&Cs were unfair, fewer consumers chose the product (27.7%, compared to 41% when T&Cs were fair), and the difference was larger when T&Cs were simplified (the proportion of consumers choosing the unfair option fell to 22%).[34] Results of the other two studies were also broadly in line with the image of a rational and competent consumer.

While carefully designed and statistically robust, these studies seem to have poor ecological validity because subjects in the study were made to pay attention to information when, in real life, so many stimuli compete for consumers' attention. In this sense, the findings illustrate the demand from the Commission at least as much as how consumers handle information in real life. One important message from behavioural science is receiving attention, namely that simplifying information can help.[35] However, the demand from the Commission also seems to illustrate a continuous and sustained focus on information and a desire to confirm the soundness of the information paradigm on which existing law is built. Behavioural studies seem to be conducted to reinforce and adapt the information paradigm on which EU consumer protection rests, rather than to question it. The underlying theory of choice, though not expressly formulated, seems to remain broadly in line with the rational choice model, at least the version expressed in the average consumer standard.[36] The behavioural turn in which the Commission has engaged in the area of consumer protection clearly embraces smart disclosure.[37] Nevertheless, the focus largely remains on disclosure. The underlying theory of consumer choice is being enriched with the notion that consumers pay limited attention and have limited information processing capacity. However, there seems to be a presumption that this level of attention and this processing capacity are quite high. To date, empirical studies designed to inform the legislative process do not

[33] This was a between-subject experiment so that each participant only had to choose one service provider (of either Internet or credit).

[34] Lot 3 study (n 31) 400. The authors also report differences across products, the effect of simplification being much larger for Internet subscriptions than for consumer credit.

[35] See already Maartje Elshout et al., Study on consumers' attitudes towards Terms and Conditions (T&Cs) 2016 (study for the European Commission, Contract No. 2014 85 12, implementing Framework Contract—EAHC/2011/CP/OI/ECORYS).

[36] In the words of the Court of Justice, the average consumer is 'reasonably well-informed and reasonably observant and circumspect', Case C-210/96, *Gut Springerheide*, EU:C:1998:369, para. 31.

[37] This is apparent in the area of energy labelling. Communication from the Commission, A Framework Strategy for a Resilient Energy Union with a Forward-Looking Climate Change Policy, COM(2015)080 final; 'Commission welcomes agreement on clearer energy efficiency labelling rules to empower consumers', Press release IP/17/691; and most recently, announcing the use of QR codes: 'Clearer and simple energy labels will help consumers save money and contribute to the Energy Union's objectives', https://ec.europa.eu/info/news/clearer-and-simple-energy-labels-will-help-consumers-save-money-and-contribute-energy-unions-objectives-2019-mar-11_en [https://perma.cc/ZK4A-9VWB].

focus on submitting these assumptions to a reality check but seem instead to seek to illustrate that they hold.

This discussion suggests that when a framework for thinking about choice is embedded in existing legislation, such as the information paradigm in EU consumer law, it is sticky. The legislator investigates alternative (behavioural) approaches but with caution, as if careful not to call the primary paradigm into question. Innovations, such as simplification of mandatory information, are welcome as long as they are not too radical.

B. Does the Legislator Need a Theory of Choice?

While it is apparent from the previous section that the legislator might want to preserve some degree of coherence across consumer policy and would, therefore, cling to the information paradigm, does this entail a commitment to a particular theory of choice? A cursory look at legislation and case law suffices to suggest that this is not the case. As applied in EU law, the information paradigm seems compatible with more than one theory of decision making. It fits very well with strong rationality assumptions and an image of rational and attentive consumers who need nothing but accurate information to make good decisions. However, it is also compatible with bounded rationality hypotheses. To date, this versatility of the dominant paradigm permits the coexistence within EU consumer law of very different assumptions about how consumers deal with information. To contrast only a few elements: consumers are, as discussed above, supposed to be able to make an informed choice about whether or not they want to shop on a website that personalises prices based on non-salient information,[38] while, in another piece of legislation (the unfair commercial practices directive), it is acknowledged that information, even if entirely accurate, can be misleading because of how it is presented.[39] In relation to yet another piece of consumer legislation (the unfair contract terms directive), the Court of Justice interprets 'plain intelligible language' in the context of information that is difficult to understand (financial information) as meaning that the consumer must not only be able to understand the text of the contract term from a grammatical point of view but must also be able to appreciate the economic consequences of the term for him.[40] In other words, within existing EU consumer law, one finds more than one view on how consumers deal with information when they choose to engage in a transaction. The reason may be that the legislator is content with a weak degree of coherence so long as incoherence is not too conspicuous. In

[38] Note 26 above.

[39] Art. 6.1 Directive 2005/29/EC concerning unfair business-to-consumer commercial practices in the internal market Official Journal L 149, 11/06/2005, 22–39 (hereafter 'UCPD').

[40] Case C-26/13 Kásler, EU:C:2014:282, para. 75.

this regard, the fact that no theory of choice underpinning consumer law is being made explicit serves the status quo: incoherence is not exposed.

Another reason to think that the law does not always need to elect a theory of choice is that it is sometimes possible to 'jump' from evidence of consumer harm to policy conclusion even without a theory of choice. The example of policy work on 'drip pricing' illustrates this point. It shows that it is possible to reach policy conclusions in the field of consumer protection regarding a practice that is deemed harmful because of its effect on consumer choice, even though the finding of harm is not univocally rationalized under one particular theory of choice. Drip pricing is a practice whereby information about price is given sequentially ('dripped'). Typically, a headline price is advertised at the beginning of the purchase process (e.g., the price for a flight that appears on a flight comparator). Then, additional fees, which may be unavoidable (e.g., credit card surcharge), are incrementally disclosed after the consumer has engaged in the purchasing process. It is consensual that drip pricing is a misleading practice. However, many legal systems do not ban it *per se*, as is, for example, the case in the European Union.[41] This explains why several consumer protection authorities, as well as the OECD, have considered this topic in various policy reports.[42]

In one OECD report, the practice is described as 'a price advertising technique that might trigger behavioural biases such as anchoring and endowment effect to prevent consumers from making optimal choices'.[43] It is noteworthy that existing studies have not reached a definitive conclusion as to which bias or combination of biases is at work. A study commissioned by the UK Office of Fair Trading ('OFT') has shown that drip pricing was more detrimental to consumers than other pricing practices such as dynamic pricing. However, it only provides hypotheses as to the underlying decision-making mechanisms.[44] Three theories of how drip pricing affects decision making were put forward: such pricing (i) increases search costs because of the increased cognitive effort of calculating and comparing prices; (ii) increases the likelihood of errors because consumers may miss the extra part of

[41] Drip pricing is not mentioned in Annex I of UCPD (also not after the reform introduced by the Modernisation directive).

[42] OFT (Office of Fair Trading) (UK) (2013), Partitioned Pricing Research: A behavioural experiment, August 2013, http://londoneconomics.co.uk/blog/publication/partitioned-pricing-research-behavioural-experiment/ [https://perma.cc/Z9BA-FP7P], hereafter 'OFT (2013)'; ACCC (Australia) (2014), ACCC investigation leads to clearer ticket pricing, October 2014, www.accc.gov.au/media-release/accc-investigation-leads-to-clearer-ticket-pricing [https://perma.cc/J9A8-ZM7A]; OECD, 'Use of Behavioural Insights in Consumer Policy', OECD Science, Technology and Innovation Policy Papers, January 2017 No. 36, hereafter 'OECD (2017)', at 25 et seq.; see also OECD, 'Consumer Policy Guidance on Mobile and Online Payments' (2014) DSTI/CP(2011)24/FINAL, www.oecd.org/officialdocuments/ publicdisplaydocumentpdf/?cote=dsti/cp(2011)24/final&doclanguage=en [https://perma.cc/AZU5-4VT5].

[43] OECD (2017), 25.

[44] OFT (n 42), The study considered six price frames: Drip Pricing, Reference Pricing, Time Limited Offers, Volume Discounts, Complex Pricing/Tariffs and Bait Pricing.

the price; and (iii) results in consumers putting more weight on the base price than on the extra part when making decisions ('anchoring').[45] Anchoring-and-adjusting is a behavioural phenomenon whereby we tend to accord importance to an irrelevant number with which we have been primed. Immediately after being primed, we tend to decide (whatever we are asked to decide), taking the anchor as a starting point (as if it were relevant) and adjusting too little upwards or downwards.[46] Other studies on drip pricing have envisaged and tested other behavioural explanations for the effect of such pricing, namely the endowment effect and commitment.[47] The endowment effect captures our tendency to value something more when we possess it than when a different person holds the same thing.[48] According to the endowment 'theory', feeling endowed with something triggers loss aversion so that we do not want to part with that item. To the extent that shoppers feel already endowed with an air ticket that they are in the process of purchasing, loss aversion could explain why they would rather pay the hidden fee than let go of that ticket. Finally, commitment—another psychological phenomenon—could explain the behaviour of consumers with regards to drip pricing.[49] If consumers feel they have already decided to purchase, they have psychologically committed to it even though they have not yet entered a contract.[50] The time and effort they have already spent on the search and purchase before being hit with extra charges will trigger the desire to be consistent with their previous actions and finalise the purchase already underway.

There is no certainty as to which decision theory—in the sense of a partial theory corresponding to one behavioural phenomenon or a particular combination of such phenomena—best explains the effect of drip pricing, which is to lead consumers to sub-optimal choices. Notwithstanding this incomplete understanding of the exact mechanisms at work, the evidence of harm as well as negative

[45] OFT (n 42) 11.

[46] Amos Tversky and Daniel Kahneman, 'Advances in Prospect Theory: Cumulative Representation of Uncertainty' (1992) 5.4 Journal of Risk and Uncertainty 297–323, doi:10.1007/BF00122574. For a review of subsequent work on the anchoring effect: Adrian Furnham and Hua Chu Boo A Literature Review of the Anchoring Effect, (2011) 40.1 Journal of Socio-Economics 35–42, doi: 10.1016/j.socec.2010.10.008.

[47] OFT (UK) (2010), The impact of price frames on consumer decision making, May 2010, https://londoneconomics.co.uk/blog/publication/the-impact-of-price-frames-on-consumer-decision-making-2/ , 80.

[48] In their seminal experiment, Kahneman, Knetch, and Thaler used mugs and chocolate bars from the university student shop. Both were sold for the same price at the shop but the mugs where held to be more expensive by the subjects that were endowed with them than the chocolate bar (and vice-versa), so that subjects were unwilling to part with 'their' good and trade. Daniel Kahneman, Jack Knetsch, and Richard Thaler, 'Anomalies: The Endowment Effect, Loss Aversion, and Status Quo Bias' (1991) 5.1 Journal of Economic Perspectives 193–206, doi:10.1257/jep.5.1.193.

[49] Amelia Fletcher, Drip Pricing: The UK Experience, OFT 2012, https://www.ftc.gov/sites/default/files/documents/public_events/economics-drip-pricing/afletcher.pdf.

[50] Commitment and the desire for consistency across our actions is one of the six influencing mechanisms identified by Robert Cialdini in *Influence: The Psychology of Persuasion* (Harper 2006)ch. 3.

perception[51] justify the recommendation to ban the practice.[52] In this context, a theory of how, exactly, consumers decide to choose the offer that seems cheaper at the outset but might prove costlier in the end seems superfluous. A similar argument can be made more generally about misleading practices: rather than requiring one single established theory of how a practice is misleading, courts will usually be satisfied with any plausible account that the practice is misleading. Such an account can be much less than a 'theory', even a partial one such as a behavioural explanation. Indeed, courts enforced rules on unfair commercial practices long before behavioural explanations were on offer and have not felt the need to theorise deception.

This brief incursion into the territory of misleading practices suggests that the law does not always need a theory of (influence on) choice. Evidence of influence can be enough to trigger a prohibition. Certainly, having a theory of influence may help convince a court that a commercial practice is misleading. It will also help make a policy case for a ban, as in the case of drip pricing, but there is no pressing need to choose between theories of choice.

The picture of theories of choice in the context of legislative work on consumer protection emerging from this section is highly contrasted: something about it seems sticky. The Commission—which is in charge of proposing legislation—chooses not to call the information paradigm into question even when conducting behavioural studies. While constructing empirical studies to validate the information paradigm might seem paradoxical, it also speaks to the openness of this paradigm to more than one theory of choice. Indeed, the EU consumer law, despite being home to the exceptionally rational 'average consumer', is also inhabited by several different figures of consumers, illustrating facets of bounded rationality and responding to distinct theories of choice. It appears, therefore, that the legislator, in the field of EU consumer law, not only does not ground legislation in one single theory of choice but also does not have a meta-theory explaining when which (partial) theory of choice might apply. Consistency apart, one may further doubt whether legislation needs a theory of choice to justify intervention regarding commercial practices that influence consumer choice. As illustrated by the example of drip pricing, it seems possible to justify a ban based on a showing of consumer harm even if it is not backed by a (single) theory of choice explaining exactly how consumer choice is being affected. To sum up, legislative work appears

[51] Shelle Santana, Steven Dallas, and Vicky G. Morwitz, Consumer Reactions to Drip Pricing (2017), http://faculty.tuck.dartmouth.edu/images/uploads/faculty/nemc/Santana_Dallas_Morwitz_Drip_Pricing.pdf [https://perma.cc/5C23-9S2Y.

[52] OECD Recommendation Consumer Protection in E-commerce (2016), Recommendation 16 'Businesses should ensure that advertised prices do not misrepresent or hide the total cost of a good or a service.' See also OECD, *Consumer Policy Guidance on Mobile and Online Payments* (2014), http://www.oecd-ilibrary.org/science-and-technology/consumer-policy- guidance-on-mobile-and-online-payments_5jz432cl1ns7-en.

inconsistent and is mostly silent on theories of consumer choice. This stands in contrast to legal scholarship.

III. Legal Scholarship: The Space for Theories of Choice

Traditionally, legal scholars have not felt any need for theories of choice, let alone meta-theories. 'Lawyers ... go on thinking that their legal instinct and their common sense supplies them with all that is needed and somewhat more.'[53] With these words, in 1908 Hugo Münsberg—then director of the Harvard Psychology Laboratory—expressed his perception of how lawyers, judges, and jury members uncritically approached decision making. To an extent, this quotation also aptly describes the long-standing attitude of mainstream doctrinal legal scholars. While legal scholarship has evolved and become more complex, it is worth pausing briefly on what might be considered an initial state of play, one of separation between legal scholarship and enquiries about how people make choices. So long as legal scholars do not consider decision making as an object of enquiry, there is simply no room within legal scholarship for debating theories of choice, let alone meta-theories. This space has now emerged; it has been carved out and is still in the process of being shaped. While the initial change that led to opening room for this discussion can be traced to the economic analysis of law (subsection A), the specific size and shape it takes varies across legal cultures and strands of scholarship. Schematically, it is possible to distinguish a deep and narrow space and one that is shallow and wide (subsection B).

A. Opening the Space for Theories of Choice

It was the law and economics movement that first introduced a formal theory of choice to legal discourse. Defined broadly as the application of economic theory to the formation, structure, processes, and economic impact on the law and legal institutions,[54] law and economics first and foremost brought new questions to legal scholarship. In mainstream economic analysis of law (the Chicago School), the new object of analysis par excellence was the efficiency of rules and institutions. How people make choices was not an object of study. Rather, a theory of choice was brought in as part of the new analytical kit. Rational choice theory, depicting legal actors and addressees of the laws as rational maximisers, was part of the innovative

[53] Cited by Christoph Engel and Gerd Gigerenzer, 'Law and Heuristics: An Interdisciplinary Venture' in Gerd Gigerenzer and Christoph Engel (eds.), *Heuristics and The Law* (MIT Press 2006) 1–16, 1.

[54] Nicolas Mercuro and Stephen G. Medema, *Economics and the Law: From Posner to Post Modernism* (Princeton University Press 1997) ix.

enterprise, but it was not the focus of discussions. It was used, among other tools, to produce innovative legal scholarship. In this sense, neoclassical law and economics created a space for theories of choice in legal scholarship but also immediately filled that space with a particular theory of choice. The interesting discussion was deemed to lie elsewhere: it was about how this theory applied to existing rules, and what it implied; it was about efficiency and the incentive effects of rules. Any discussion about whether rational choice theory was fitting, such as the work of Herbert Simon,[55] belonged to a separate school (the institutionalist school), which did not gain as much traction in legal scholarship. It could thus be said that the law and economics movement rather indirectly and inadvertently opened up room for theories of choice in legal scholarship. That space lay between different schools of law and economics which had received unequal attention from legal scholars.

It was when behavioural analysis emerged and empirically called into question the rationality hypotheses on which the dominant paradigm of neoclassical economics rested that, by implication, a space for discussing theories of choice was truly open within legal scholarship.[56] The rational choice theory, which had been treated as a reliable tool for legal analysis in the dominant (Chicago) school of economic analysis of law, was being undermined. That created a void[57] and called for revisiting the classics of economic analysis of law, such as the Coase Theorem.[58] For this reason, it is mostly in the behavioural-legal literature that one finds discussions on theories of choice. Behavioural analysis of law consists in applying empirical behavioural evidence to the analysis of law.[59] By nature, it involves discussing how people make certain choices—for example how consumers choose the food, service contracts, or financial products that they purchase—and confronting empirical evidence either with (implicit) behavioural hypotheses embedded in the law (e.g., consumers read, understand, and act upon nutritional information) or with received wisdom about the law (dominant doctrinal opinion).[60] In this strand of literature, behavioural findings are used as reality

[55] Herbert Simon, 'A Behavioral Model of Rational Choice' (1955) 69 Quarterly Journal of Economics 99.

[56] On the history of behavioural law and economics, see Eyal Zamir and Doron Teichman, *Behavioural Law and Economics* (Oxford University Press 2018) 141.

[57] Russell B. Korobkin and Thomas Ulen, 'Law and Behavioural Science: Removing the Rationality Assumption from Law and Economics' (2000) 88 California Law Review 1051.

[58] Russell B. Korobkin, 'The Endowment Effect and Legal Analysis' (2003) 97 Northwestern University Law Review 1227; Russell B. Korobkin, 'Wrestling with the Endowment Effect, or How to Do Law and Economics Without the Coase Theorem' in Eyal Zamir and Doron Teichman (eds.), *The Oxford Handbook of Behavioral Economics and the Law* (Oxford University Press 2014) 300.

[59] Tor (n 5).

[60] For a comprehensive review of food labelling policies, Shmuel I. Becher et al., 'Hungry for Change: The Law and Policy of Food Health Labelling' (2019) 54.5 Wake Forest Law Review', 1305 (confronting policies with extant empirical evidence); on reading/no reading of terms and conditions, see the contrasting findings of Yannis Bakos, Florencia Marotta-Wurgler, and David R. Trossen, 'Does Anyone Read the Fine Print? Consumer Attention to Standard-Form Contracts' (2014) 43.1 Journal of Legal Studies 1 (confronting behavioural assumptions embedded in legal rules with observational

checks.[61] They serve to expose misconceptions in the behavioural priors of law makers—instances where legal instincts and common sense do not serve the law well. Behavioural evidence may also unveil shortcomings in the justifications for specific policies, such as those based on economic analysis—instances where rational choice theory does not serve the law maker well. A comprehensive literature review, which far exceeds the scope and ambition of this chapter, would be necessary to ascertain the exact contours of discussions of theories of choice in behavioural-legal scholarship. The next subsection confines itself to offering some organising thoughts to be tested and refined.

B. Shaping the Discussion of Theories of Choice: Deep and Narrow or Wide and Shallow?

It seems possible to identify two contours which the space for discussing theories of choice in the legal literature can take. One is deep and narrow and the other wide and shallow. Rather than exact descriptors which could capture all available works, these labels aim to name polar opposites, in full recognition that individual behavioural-legal research projects could be plotted in intermediate points on the wide-narrow axis and the deep-shallow axis.[62]

The deep and narrow version of the discussion on theories of choice is one that combines a genuine discussion of competing theories with a set pattern of discussion. Bar-Gill's *Seduction by Contract*[63] offers a relatively pure example of this type. Economic analysis of contract constitutes the starting point. This allows the research question which structures the book to be clearly and explicitly about alternative theories of choice. In the beginning is a theory of choice (rational choice theory) and the enquiry reveals that it does not explain all market developments which can be observed in relation to consumer contracts. Therefore, goes the argument, we need a better theory. This is where behavioural insights come in, to help improve the theory of consumer choice and explain facts better (contractual practices and how consumers respond to them). Then, based on this improved

data) and Maartje Elshout et al., 'Study on consumers' attitudes towards Terms and Conditions (T&Cs)', https://ec.europa.eu/info/sites/info/files/terms_and_conditions_final_ report_en.pdf, [https://perma.cc/FZ7K-LJ57] (tackling questions regarding possible law reform with empirical data from lab studies).

[61] This is one possible use of empirical data in legal discourse. For a typology of such uses see Anne-Lise Sibony, 'Data and Arguments: Empirical Research in Consumer Law' in Hans Micklitz, Anne-Lise Sibony, and Fabrizio Esposito (eds.), *Research Methods in Consumer Law: A Handbook* (Edward Elgar 2018) 165.

[62] For a different use of the notions of 'breadth' and 'depth' in relation to behavioural scholarship in general (rather than specifically in relation to 'theories of choice', which constitute the focus here, see Avishalom Tor, 'The Next Generation of Behavioural Law and Economics' in Klaus Mathis (ed.), *European Perspectives on Behavioural Law and Economics* (Springer 2015) 17.

[63] Oren Bar-Gill, *Seduction by Contract* (Oxford University Press 2012).

understanding of market reality, policy options can be discussed. This is also, by and large, the approach followed by Zamir and Teichman in their textbook, *Behavioural Law and Economics*.[64]

Such discussions of alternative theories of choice may be called deep because they contrast two theories of consumer choice rather than one theory and legal intuition or folk psychology. Both theories are discussed in relation to facts to be explained, rather than representations of facts embedded in the law. They are compared from the perspective of their explanatory power. The relationship between alternative theories of consumer choice is very clear: rational choice theory is treated as the incumbent theory; it is only when rational choice explanations for the observed contracts and prices fail that behavioural economics theory enters.[65] The discussion of alternative theories of choice is deep in that it is about falsification (in the Popperian sense of the word).[66]

At the same time, a discussion of theories of choice such as that offered by Bar-Gill may be called narrow in that the logic of economic analysis entirely shapes it.[67] Not only is rational choice theory the point of reference but the dominance of the economic paradigm is also felt in other ways. Behavioural arguments are used to describe 'market failures' which remained invisible from the vantage point of economic analysis and which are, for this reason, called 'behavioural market failures'. In this analytical framework, it is essential to characterise the effects of behavioural phenomena as 'market failures' because only such failures justify public intervention because of their impact on consumer welfare, total welfare, or both. In other words, economic analysis structures the narrative in which the behavioural arguments are inserted. This feature accounts for exceptional clarity of the argument and also creates limits to what behavioural evidence could find its way into legal analysis of this type. For example, the analysis refers to consumer welfare, and the notion of consumer welfare refers to consumer surplus, consumer surplus is, in turn, defined as the difference between the maximum price a consumer is willing to pay and the actual price she pays. Therefore, recourse to the notion of consumer welfare presupposes that consumers have well-defined preferences over well-defined sets of goods and exhibit decreasing utility functions. Behavioural evidence might call these assumptions into question but inviting such evidence into the discussion would be akin to opening Pandora's box and risk jeopardising the neat structure of the argument.

64 Cited n 55. Most chapters start with the standard law and economics account of key issues in the area of law discussed (unless none is available) and then go on to question and refine the analysis based on behavioural studies.

65 Bar-Gill (n 63) 2.

66 Popper distinguished two meanings of the expressions falsifiable and falsifiability: falsifiable in principle and demonstrably falsifiable. Karl Popper, *Realism and the Aim of Science: From the Postscript to The Logic of Scientific Discovery* (Routledge 1983, reprinted 2000) XXII. Reference is made here to the second meaning.

67 This remark does not apply to Zamir and Teichman's book, which also contains other types of discussions, including honest recognitions that the policy implications of the analyses presented are inconclusive.

By contrast, it is possible to think of wide and shallow discussions of theories of choice. These are more likely to be found in European legal scholarship, where economic analysis does not constitute a natural starting point in the same way as it does in the United States. That economic analysis of law remained a niche activity in Europe has been explained by lesser academic pressure to innovate bearing on European than on American scholars.[68] Thus, partly shielded from competition, European legal scholars could afford the luxury of scepticism vis-à-vis rational choice theory. This state of affairs has a direct bearing on the depth of discussions regarding the theories of choice. Where rational choice theory is not considered the default, behavioural findings will naturally be discussed in relation to what does constitute the default, namely legal intuition and common sense as well as implicit or explicit statements about consumer behaviour found in legislation or court judgments. Rather than asking which competing theories of consumer choice best fit legally relevant facts, scholars will occupy themselves with asking whether courts or the legislator got their facts right. They will confront statements of facts in legislative documents (or pre-legislative work) and court judgments with relevant behavioural insights as well as discuss the relevance of extant empirical findings to the specific legal context at hand.[69] Compared to a test of one theory of choice against an alternative theory of choice, such discussions contrasting behavioural (partial) theories of choice and folk psychology can be called shallow. This is not to say that more in-depth discussions on theories of choice find no place, they do but typically outside the legal literature or on its fringes. This is largely the case of the discussion on the heuristics and biases theory and the fast and frugal heuristics theory (and whether they really constitute alternatives).[70]

However, not encapsulating behavioural arguments in a policy discussion preformatted by economic analysis also implies that there is room for a broader range of behavioural arguments (evidently, such an opening of the frame of discussion has nothing specifically European about it). Besides establishing the existence of behavioural market failures and discussing the merits of policy options,[71] empirical findings from psychology can also be used to discuss the interpretation of

[68] Nuno Garoupa and Thomas S. Ulen, 'The Market for Legal Innovation: Law and Economics in Europe and the United States' in Theodore Eisenberg and Giovanni B. Ramello (eds.), *Comparative Law and Economics* (Edward Elgar 2016) 78.

[69] In relation to court's findings, and for a rare example of a discussion of case law in light of an ad-hoc behavioural experiment, see Kai Purnhagen and Erica van Herpen, 'Can Bonus Packs Mislead Consumers? An Empirical Assessment of The ECJ's Mars Judgment and its Potential Impact on The "Average Consumer" in Internal Market Law' (2017) 40.2 Journal of Consumer Policy 217, doi: 10.1007/s10603-017-9345-0.

[70] Christoph Engel and Gerd Gigerenzer (eds.), *Heuristics and The Law* (MIT Press 2006) (fringes); Alejandro Hortal, 'Nudging and Educating: Bounded Axiological Rationality in Behavioral Insights' (2019) Behavioural Public Policy 1–24. doi:10.1017/bpp.2019.2 (outside).

[71] Yesim M. Atamer, 'Why Judicial Control of Price Terms in Consumer Contracts Might Not Always Be the Right Answer—Insights from Behavioural Law and Economics' (2017) 80.4 Modern Law Review 624 (offering an interesting example of a discussion of EU law structured by a law and economics approach).

the law[72] or methodological issues.[73] The discussion of theories of choice (whether consumer choice, citizen's choice, or choices of firms) may also be wider in a different sense, namely that they incorporate psychological insights other than those that specifically falsify rational choice theory.[74] This includes behavioural ethics, whose perspective is also profoundly disruptive of the rational choice paradigm in that it highlights the limited importance of choice in accounting for certain (dishonest) behaviours.[75] It would also include the as-yet underdeveloped approaches integrating behavioural and sociological findings.

In contrast to legislative work, where there seems to be little interest in formulating theories of choice or choosing between several candidate theories of choice, there is room in legal scholarship for discussing such theories. In the behavioural analysis of law, such discussions are very explicit. They can be deep and narrow or shallow and wide. There is in principle no reason that scholarship cannot spread into other boxes of this 2 × 2, though deep and wide seems particularly challenging while shallow and narrow may seem unattractive. What seems puzzling is that there appears to be a little connection between positive theories of choice, that seek to explain how people make choices in different contexts, and normative reflexion on what exactly deserves protection when it comes to consumer choice. The consumer law mantra that we protect 'informed consumer choice' woefully underdetermined.

IV. Conclusion

This chapter started by naming reasons to lower ambitions regarding theories of choice in legal contexts. First, regarding the 'supply side', there is no complete catalogue of available theories of choice which could be mobilised in either legislative work or legal scholarship. A ready-to-use meta-theory of choice that would instruct lawyers when to use which theory of choice seems even more elusive. Second, the demand side, emanating from policy makers, seems to be characterised by a moderate appetite for theories. Indeed, a look at recent policy discussions in the field of consumer protection confirms that, while there is a strong commitment to protecting consumer choice, there is no attempt at grounding legislation on a robust theory of choice. Paradoxically, the empirical studies commissioned by the European Union seem to be designed to confirm and fortify the information

[72] Anne-Lise Sibony, 'Can EU Consumer Law Benefit From Behavioural Insights?' (2014) 22.6 European Review of Private Law 903.

[73] For example, contribution by Philipp Hacker in this volume and references cited; Tor (n 5).

[74] On this widening, see Orly Lobel and Yuval Feldman, 'Behavioural Trade-Offs: Beyond the Land of Nudges Spans the World of Law and Psychology' in Alemanno and Sibony (n 9) 301.

[75] Yuval Feldman, 'Behavioral Ethics Meets Behavioral Law and Economics' in Zamir and Teichman (n 58) 213.

paradigm that has come under such strong attack from the behavioural literature, rather than falsify it. This is not entirely surprising since falsifying those theories on which the law rests is not, after all, incumbent upon the legislator. It is also noteworthy that European consumer law seems characterised by theoretical eclecticism when it comes to determining how well consumers deal with information. The theories of choice underpinning the law may not be explicit, but it is nonetheless clear that they are very diverse. Despite the plurality of choice theories, no meta-theory of how each might apply in different contexts, in relation to terms and conditions or financial information, for example, seems to be in sight. Equally, when several different theories appear apt to explain that a given practice such as drip pricing can harm consumers, there seems to be no need to choose between them. For policy purposes, theories of harm trump theories of choice.

In contrast to what can be observed in the context of legislative work, legal scholarship has evolved to make room for explicit discussions on theories of choice. The space for such discussions was not always there and it is still in the process of being shaped. While it is still relatively early days, it seems possible to contrast deep discussions of competing theories of choice, which characterise behavioural law and economics, with more shallow discussions of behavioural priors embedded in the law in light of behavioural insights, which can be found in what might be called behavioural doctrinal work. Discussions of theories of choice in the legal literature may also vary as to their scope. They can be narrow, when behavioural findings are used exclusively to document the existence and the magnitude of 'behavioural market failures'. They can be wide, when insights from psychology are brought to bear at any stage in legal reasoning or methodological enquiry. Whatever its shape, a line of research worthy of attention would bring together what has been loosely termed 'theories of choice' in this chapter and the normative question of what deserves protection when the law says it protects choice.

PART III
COLLECTIVE CHOICE AND THE LAW

7

Itinera Europea

Four Scenarios and Their Plausibility

Adrienne Héritier[1]

Abstract: Based on strategic interaction analysis, the chapter assesses the plausibility of the future paths of development of the European Union: a federal state, a differentiated and flexible union, covert integration, or disintegration. Systematically varying either the preferences of the main actors or the macro decision-making rules and external shocks/crises, the analysis comes to the conclusion that a differentiated and flexible union and covert integration are the most likely paths of development. The chapter discusses implications of specific scenarios, such as a possible popular backlash against 'covert integration' and elaborates on the desirability of practical proposals of a change in the European institutional architecture.

I. Introduction

In recent years, the European Union ('EU') has been faced with critical developments, such as the Eurozone crisis, the migration crisis, Brexit, and increasing sovereign popular movements, as well as geopolitical shifts in the international environment. All these developments pose a challenge to EU actors to reconsider the EU's institutional architecture in order to deal with such incisive developments in a better way. Being a 'halfway house' between a supranational and an intergovernmental polity with complex interlinked decision-making processes means that the European Union has been relatively slow in reacting to sudden changes in its external environment and indeed changes also stemming from within the Union. Therefore, the calls for a reconsideration of the given institutional architecture have become more frequent and more urgent.

This chapter, therefore, raises the question of whether the European Union will follow the path of (i) an ever-closer union or a United States of Europe; of (ii) a

[1] This chapter is an extensively revised version of the article, 'Quo Vadis, Europa? Four Paths and their Plausibility' published by International Trade and Policy Development (2019-1). My thanks to the Emerald publishing company and the editorial board of ITPD for the permission of the republishing of a part of the ITPD article.

Adrienne Héritier, Itinera Europea In: *Theories of Choice*. Edited by: Stefan Grundmann and Philipp Hacker, Oxford University Press (2021). © The several contributors. DOI: 10.1093/oso/9780198863175.003.0008

two-tier or more differentiated union with elements of flexibility; (iii) continuing to muddle through with incremental changes on a path of 'covert integration; or (ïv) engaging on a path of disintegration or dissolution? In the following, I will ask which of the four possible scenarios in the immediate and mid-term future of the European Union are most likely to unfold.

Analytically, in order to answer this question, I will use strategic interaction analysis, as developed by Lake and Powell.[2] Strategic interaction analysis departs from the assumption that in order to go beyond the description of political decision making and its outcomes and to seek to explain outcomes, micro and macro aspects of political decision making need to be distinguished. Of course, in reality, actor aspects and environment aspects are closely linked when decisions are taken. But in order to come to systematic explanations and not merely describe decision-making situations, the two aspects need to be distinguished and systematically varied.

On the actor/micro side, strategic choice analysis distinguishes between two attributes of actors. First, actors are assumed to have preferences, defined simply as how they rank the possible outcomes defined by the environment.[3] Actors' basic preferences are desires that remain the same across a wide variety of situations. Actors' situational preferences, by contrast,[4] consist of the ranking of preferred outcomes in specific interaction or negotiation situations which in turn is defined by the particular problem at issue and the constellation of the other actors and their preferences over outcomes with which they negotiate. The second attribute of an actor is his or her prior beliefs about the preferences of other actors with which he or she negotiates. In particular, when actors are uncertain, these beliefs are crucial for the decision about which strategy to choose, and, as a consequence, for the outcome of interaction.[5]

The strategic environment, the macro side, is composed, first, of the actions which are available for the actors. They are summarised according to what could be the outcome of interactions of actors, or the outcome of how decisions and events can unfold.[6] In the context of the question posed here concerning the plausibility of a specific path that the European polity may follow in its further development, the outcomes are (i) a European state; (ii) a differentiated and flexible European Union; (iii) covert integration; and (iv) disintegration and/or dissolution. Second, the environment is composed of an information structure that defines what the actors can know for certain and what they have to infer from the behaviour of the

[2] David A. Lake and Robert Powell, *Strategic Choice and International Relations* (Princeton University Press 1999).

[3] Ibid. 9.

[4] Jeffry Frieden, 'Actors and Preferences in International Relations' in ibid. 3–38.

[5] Ibid. 11.

[6] Ibid. 8, 9.

other interaction partners. Here institutional rules play an eminent role. Keohane[7] argued that one way in which institutions, or institutional rules regulating behaviour, facilitate cooperation among states is by providing more information to state actors of how the other actors are likely to behave, and by providing better possibilities of monitoring each other's behaviour.[8]

As mentioned above, the analytic distinction of actors' attributes and the attributes of the environment implies the possibility of two broad kinds of 'conceptual experiments'.[9] The first conceptual experiment varies the properties of the actors, that is their preferences and beliefs (micro side), while it holds the environment in which they interact (macro side) constant, and derives conclusions or hypotheses about the likely outcome of the interaction. The second conceptual experiment varies attributes of the environment while the actors' attributes are held constant, and derives conclusions or hypotheses about the likely outcome of the interaction. Using this analytic scheme, I will ask: how plausible is it that the four different developments—a European state, differentiated/flexible integration, covert integration, disintegration/dissolution—will be empirically observed?

The four developments constitute different features of the explanandum. I will argue that the plausibility of the respective scenarios happening depends on the micro side (i) who are the most important actors, that is member states and European institutions, and their preferences over a specific path of development; and on the macro side (ii) important factors of the environment, that is the financial and economic crisis; the migration crisis; and (iii) the decision-making rules applied when deciding over the future shape of the polity, that is unanimity, qualified majority voting ('QMV'), simple majority, the use of referenda in member states and the recourse to court rulings.

Using this analytic scheme, I will first ask: what is the plausibility that a federal state or United States of Europe will materialise in the short to mid-term period?

II. Scenario One: A European Federal State

A political union defined as a federal state is characterised by a concentration of decision-making competences for all policies and budgetary issues with institutions at the supranational level. The competence to allocate competences, the 'Kompetenz-Kompetenz', rests with supranational institutions. Member states would be left with implementing powers of the legislative decisions taken at the central level. A European federal state would have a federal parliament which with

[7] Robert O. Keohane, *After Hegemony: Cooperation and Discord in the World Political Economy* (Princeton University Press 1984).

[8] Lake and Powell (n 2) 9.

[9] Ibid..

a majority of members elects a government accountable to the parliament. In a two-chamber form, the second chamber consisting of representatives of member states would also engage in legislation at the supranational level. A central court is responsible for controlling the constitutionality of the laws adopted by the government and the observation of individual rights of the citizens.

Using the analytic scheme described above, in view of actors' preferences over outcomes and given specific macro conditions, as well as in view of the specific institutional rules relevant for the decision-making process, is it plausible that a European state will come about in the near future?

Which are the main actors' preferences regarding a political union or a European state? The main actors shaping the European polity are assumed to be the large member states and the three institutions: the European Council, the European Parliament ('EP'), and the Commission. As to the large member states' preferences, it is only France under President Macron which favours taking some steps to a deepening integration, such as a fiscal union with a European budget and appointing a European finance minister. However, in the outline of its view, the powers of a finance minister (of raising a European tax and appointing such a minister at which level for a European budget) remains unspecified. None of the other large member states of Germany, Italy, Spain, and Poland have proposed such a plan nor have they supported Macron's plan. The German Government's response to Macron's proposal was hesitant and offered limited support for a very restricted form of fiscal union.[10]

More recently, groupings of smaller and larger member states formed joint positions and expressed their preferences as to a possible political union. The Visegrad countries, Poland, Hungary, the Czech Republic, and Slovakia, and the so-called New Hanse League, the Netherlands, Denmark, Finland, and Sweden, and the Baltic states, also stated preferences against the formation of a European state and at best for a weak form of fiscal union, and, what is more, asked for a repatriation of competences or at least strengthening the subsidiarity principle.

In all member states, in view of the increasing influence of right- and left-wing anti-European and anti-immigration parties, the mainstream parties see themselves as under pressure from populist parties using voters' discontent and anti-elite sentiments to build their strength to adjust their agendas against an ever closer union (if ever they favoured one).[11] Thus, except for a few small member states

[10] Macron originally proposed a budget of about 3% Eurozone gross domestic product ('GDP') leading step by step to common fiscal and economic policies with part of the resources coming from a European tax on large tech companies or the financial sector (Jim Brunsden and Mehreen Kahn, 'Macron's lofty Eurozone budget gets downgraded' *Financial Times* (London, 28 March 2019) <https://www.ft.com/content/f0cda4c0-5104-11e9-9c76-bf4a0ce37d49>).

[11] In Finland, the right-wing populists are part of the governing coalition. In Denmark they supported the governing coalition for ten years, as was the case in the Netherlands, although over a shorter period; in Poland and Hungary, they dominate the governments (Swen Hutter, Edgar Grande, and Hanspeter Kriesi, *Politicising Europe: Integration and Mass Politics* (Cambridge University Press 2016)).

such as Belgium and Luxembourg which tend to favour a closer union, there is very little support for a political union from most national governments.

In contrast, judging from the Four and Five Presidents Reports of 2012 and 2015, as well as the White Paper on the Future of Europe of 2017 and the Juncker proposal of 2017 for a transformation of the European Stability Mechanism into a European Monetary Fund ('EMF') under the Commission's direction, the supranational institutions, the Commission and the EP, point to preferences for a political union, at least for the Eurozone countries. The Commission drew up plans for a Eurozone budget in which governments would be offered financial incentives to implement economic reforms agreed with the Commission. Each member state would be set a maximum budget, to be decided in the budget negotiations in 2019, which would be paid out once agreed-upon steps and targets of a reform or investment commitment would need to have been implemented.[12] The EP in its majority supports the plans of the Commission which would constitute steps in the direction of a parliamentary democracy in which the EP elects the (Commission) government. The European Council, by contrast, reflecting the member states' positions, is assumed predominantly to oppose a political union. In sum, actors' preferences as to the scenario of a single European state are very diverse.

The multiple actors' preferences are linked to given macro conditions, important factors in the EU environment, and the relevant decision-making rules in order to explain the outcome of the decision-making process. These macro conditions are the consequences of the handling of the Eurozone crisis and its economic repercussions in member states, and the migration crisis, both ongoing processes. Both conflicts imply redistribution issues. In the course of these crises, the unwillingness to redistribute financial capacity and migrants across the members of the Union emerged very quickly. Thus, the interventions to solve the Euro and the sovereign debt and banking crises led to a cleavage between creditor and debtor states. Both crises have not reinforced solidarity among member states. Quite the opposite; they led to a North–South divide in economic and financial governance as well as to a West–East divide as regards the willingness to accept migrants. These issues weakened the political will of member states to support a deeper political union. In the light of populist sovereign anti-European public opinion in an increasing number of member states, the popular support for such a treaty change appears unlikely.

If we add the macro factor of the relevant decision-making rule—the fact that a reform of the treaties is subject to unanimity rule—it follows that an ambitious reform of the treaty is implausible since the majority of actors is disinclined to form

In Sweden, the Sweden Democrats have gained considerable ground in the election of 2018; in Italy, they are in government.

[12] Brunsden and Kahn (n 10).

a European state. In short, a comprehensive treaty change in favour of a deepening union is implausible.

Moreover, assuming that member states held the same preferences with regard to a political union, there are additional institutional rules which come to bear at the lower, national level in the event of a treaty reform that introduce an element of uncertainty. National parliaments have to confirm a treaty change. Some national constitutional courts, such as the German Constitutional Court, request that the national parliament must confirm an uploading of national competences to the European level. In some member states, national referenda need to be held before a treaty reform can enter into force.

In conclusion, given actors' diverse preferences over the desired outcomes, the negative influence of the various redistribution crises hanging over Europe with their divisive impact, and the requirement to adopt a treaty change by unanimity and submit it national parliaments for confirmation and/or to national referenda in some member states, render a single European federal state improbable.

III. Scenario Two: A Differentiated, Flexible Union

A differentiated or two-speed/two-tier Europe is defined by the feature (i) of individual member states participating in joint policy making in specific areas, while others do not participate in joint policy making in this area (opt-outs); a second feature (ii) is the designed cooperation of a (core) number of member states in joint policy making and joint institutions across *various* policy areas beyond trade integration, while others locate themselves around this core, participating only in a free trade area, or a common market area with specific freedoms.[13]

As assumed under the first scenario, *actors' preferences* about how to shape the institutional architecture of the European polity diverge, ranging from a few small member states favouring a political union, a sizable number of large and small member states favouring a more differentiated, two-tier scenario, and very few opting for disintegration/dissolution. By contrast, the Commission and the EP are assumed to favour a deepening of political union and to be sceptical vis-a-vis a differentiated Union. For the EP, a differentiated Union where its competences would vary, depending on whether the Community method or intergovernmental methods are used,[14] is not attractive. The European Council, given diverse

[13] Bellamy and Kroeger make an interesting distinction between 'substantive differentiation' as regards policy contents, and 'sovereignty' differentiation referring to varying competences' of the involved actors in decision making (Presentation Sandra Kroeger on Differentiated Integration, Robert Schuman Center, 27 March 2019).

[14] As in the case of some measures under the Eurozone governance, e.g., the European Stability Mechanism, or under the Banking Union's Single Resolution Fund, where the form of an international agreement outside the treaties was chosen in order not to include the European Parliament in the decision process (Magnus G. Schoeller and Adrienne Héritier, 'Driving Informal Institutional Change: The

preferences of member governments, are assumed to favour a differentiated or flexible integration course.

The *macro conditions*, as under the first scenario, are assumed to be ongoing effects of the financial/Eurozone crisis and a resulting economic recession in a few member states and the continuing refugee/migration crisis. Both, given the diverse preferences economic policies and dealing with migration, tend to deepen the conflicts among member states and increase the difficulties of finding common solutions to redistributive problems. Since—as under the first scenario—unanimity is required to adopt any kind of treaty reform and such reforms would need to be corroborated by national parliaments or in national referenda, in the light of diverse preferences over outcomes, only incremental changes or a decision-making deadlock can be expected. Even as regards policy measures in which co-decision and QMV are required, nonetheless consensual decision making is still very frequent. Given these institutional macro conditions, differentiated integration offers a way out of the decision-making impasse into which the unanimity rule and consensual decision making may lead. However, it also implies political costs, as we will see later.

In short, pressure to accommodate diverse interests more than ever lead to incremental changes and compromises in the form of opt outs, two-speed integration, and increased voluntary cooperation. Thus, in reaction to the Eurozone crisis, we did not experience a big leap towards a political union. Rather the Six Pack and Two Pack measures to strengthen the European Stability and Growth Pact, the Fiscal Compact, the European Stability Mechanism, Banking Union, and Open Monetary Transactions all reflect a mixed picture of deepening cooperation or centralisation at the supranational level under the auspices of the European Central Bank and the Commission on the one hand, and a strengthening of intergovernmental governance by member states on the other. While the Eurozone group strengthened its own power of crisis management, Germany and other Northern creditor states resisted further centralisation in the form of common bond issuance or other measures to mutualise sovereign debt.[15] By contrast, when Germany, and more recently, Italy, tried to lead a redistributive solution to the refugee crisis, they failed. What emerged was the notion of 'flexible solidarity', where a solution of a redistributive problem offers different options in which nations can contribute. Instead of taking in refugees, some member states may contribute to border control capacity or provide financial resources to the refugee problem.

European Parliament and the Reform of the Economic and Monetary Union' (2019) 41.3 Journal of European Integration 277).

[15] Schoeller and Héritier 2019 (n 14); Lionel Barber, 'Britain after Brexit: Lionel Barber's lecture in Tokyo' *Financial Times* (London, 15 October 2016) <https://www.ft.com/content/e1f4c680-8722-11e6-a75a-0c4dce033ade>.

In conclusion, given actors' diverse preferences over the desirability of the four scenarios, the influence of redistributive crises with their divisive impact, and the need to adopt a treaty change by unanimity and submit it to national parliaments' consent and to referenda in some member states makes it more likely that incremental compromises are found. These small steps result in differentiated integration, such as opt-out clauses, member states' agreements outside the treaties, voluntary cooperation in some areas; in short, a more flexible union with diverse degrees of association which are not irreversible,[16] resulting in an ever more complex and fragmented institutional overall structure.

IV. Scenario Three: Covert Integration

Covert integration is defined as a deepening of integration in terms of uploading of policy-making competences and a definition of more stringent common policy solutions which take place *outside* the main formal democratic political decision-making arenas, Council of Ministers, the European Council, and the EP.

As under scenarios one and two, *actors' preferences* as regards the future design of the European institutional architecture, a political union, or European state, a differentiated integration or a disintegration of the European Union, are assumed to diverge.

Similarly, *the macro conditions*, pressure of the financial crisis, and the resulting economic recession in some member states, as well ongoing migration pressures, are assumed to persist. Given the diverse preferences over outcomes, these conditions tend to deepen the conflicts and increase the difficulties of finding common solutions to redistributive problems. However, as opposed to scenario two, under which differentiated solutions of integration are chosen in a process of designed and negotiated treaty revisions and policy changes in the central political arenas, under scenario three, these macro conditions are expected to lead to a process of covert integration, that is, incremental policy and informal institutional[17] changes *invisible* to the wider public.

This hidden process of deepening integration is a consequence of the existing formal decision-making rules, that is, unanimity or consensus rules under conditions of divergence of interests. Decision making under these conditions increases the likelihood of vague formulations. Even under QMV, given diverse preferences and the prevalent consensus practice, decision outcomes often are compromises containing vague formulations. This in turn allows for a renegotiation of the

[16] Thomas Schmid, *Europa ist tot, es lebe Europa! Eine Weltmacht muss sich neu erfinden* (Random House 2016).

[17] Informal institutional changes are defined as mostly unwritten rules of behaviour which are not subject to formal third party dispute resolution (court decisions).

specifics of a policy or an institutional rule in the course of their application outside the public attention of the open arenas.[18] If actors in favour of deepening integration prevail in these renegotiations, this may inadvertently lead to more ambitious integration in individual policy areas, when specified by executive or judicial actors. Further patterns of covert integration are the delegation of policy making to independent regulatory authorities formulating policy changes in highly technical details, or cutting big, salient controversial issues into small, technical, low-salience issues which are not in the public eye. Similarly, the introduction of parallel options of regulation, European and national, may lead to a crowding out of national regulation because private actors comply with European regulations to save transaction costs. The use of soft modes of integration based on voluntary activities and/or including private actors in public policy making is yet another option, using soft power like benchmarking, with naming and shaming as a means of deepening policy integration. A delegation of decisions to independent regulatory authorities acting outside the political arena[19] is another important mode of deepening integration beyond the political arenas. A further mode of invisible integration of EU policies happens through transversal policies, such as competition policy. State aid, for instance, under the control of the Commission, has been a powerful instrument for making an inroad into national policy shaping competences. By conditioning the acceptance of state aid on soft Commission policy criteria, member states see themselves induced to follow these criteria and have to make plausible why policy measures other than state aid would not be likely to solve the problem at hand. This offers the Commission the possibility of assessing all types of national policy measures even though they do not fall under European competences.[20] In her work on monetarist solidarity, Schelkle shows another mechanism of building upon existing institutions and using their latent capacities 'to bear, diversify and absorb risks' of the Eurozone.[21] She shows how TARGET,[22] by lending to banks with liquidity deficits and borrowing from banks in countries with excess reserves,

[18] Adrienne Héritier, 'Covert Integration of Core State Powers: Renegotiating Incomplete Contracts' in Philipp Genschel and Markus Jachtenfuchs (eds.), *Beyond the Regulatory Polity? The European Integration of Core State Powers* (Oxford University Press 2014); Adrienne Héritier, *Policy Making and Diversity in Europe: Escape from Deadlock* (Cambridge University Press 1999).

[19] Or what Bickerton and colleagues under their notion of New Intergovernmentalism call '*de novo* bodies' (Christopher J. Bickerton, Dermot Hodson, and Uwe Puetter, 'The New Intergovernmentalism: European Integration in the Post-Maastricht Era' (2015) 54.3 Journal of Common Market Studies 703).

[20] Michael Blauberger, 'Of "Good" and "Bad" Subsidies: European State Aid Control Through Soft and Hard Law' (2009) 32 West European Politics 719.

[21] Waltraud Schelkle, 'The Political Economy of Monetary Solidarity: Revisiting the Euro Experiment' (2018) 44.3 Wirtschaft und Gesellschaft 371, 399.

[22] 'TARGET is a platform for registered users with access to central bank reserves, typically wholesale and retail commercial banks, to make payments to each other ... instead of each bank having to entertain an account with every other bank in order process payments' (ibid. 387) they have an account with TARGET.

inadvertently became 'the interbank market maker of last resort',[23] despite this not being its original intention.

Over the past decades, a considerable part of deepening European policy integration evolved through these multiple, hidden paths. Covert integration 'through the back door' raises obvious problems of democratic legitimation of European policy making once citizens realise that the extent of integration has progressed without their being aware of it.

In conclusion, given actors' diversity of preferences of outcomes with regard to the future shape of the Union, and given demanding decision-making rules of unanimity or consensus, covert integration is a likely path to be chosen and in fact has been used very frequently recently. The status quo of policy making is changed invisibly and without explicit democratic confirmation in the central political arenas, a circumstance which may trigger an anti-European backlash.[24]

V. Scenario Four: Disintegration/Dissolution

Features of disintegration are defined first, as a repatriation of specific policy-making competences to the national level or the opting out of member states of specific joint policy areas; second, it may take the shape of the exit of individual member states of the Monetary Union or/and the European Union entirely, such as was decided in the Brexit vote of June 2016. Dissolution of the entire European Union is a planned step of designed institutional change of abolishing the Union altogether.

Actors' preferences are assumed not to favour a planned dissolution of the union, the third option. This holds for all member states and for the Commission and the EP. Preferences for the second option, referenda over an exit of the European Union, as in the United Kingdom, are unlikely to be launched in other member states. Nor have explicit governmental positions of member states been put forward calling for a referendum over an exit from the monetary union. With increasing pressure from anti-European nationalist parties, however, and their possible electoral victories, the possibility of such referenda being held cannot be excluded. The exit decision of the United Kingdom in 2016 did not trigger other exit referenda in other member states. But through the interconnectedness of European politics, it appears to have reinforced nationalist forces in other member states[25] where pro- and anti-Europe divides have emerged, such as in Germany, France, Italy, Spain,

[23] Ibid. 388.

[24] Sara B. Hobolt and James Tilley, *Blaming Europe? Responsibility Without Accountability in the European Union* (Oxford University Press 2014).

[25] Sergio Fabbrini, *Europe's Future: Decoupling and Reforming* (Cambridge University Press 2019).

and Poland, and nationalist populist governments are in power in Italy, Hungary, and Poland, and are part of the governing coalition in Austria.[26]

The preferences of member states as regards the first option, that is, repatriation of competences, are diverse. With the strengthening of the Visegrad formation of Poland, Hungary, the Czech Republic, and Slovakia, as well the New Hanse League formation of the Netherlands and the Baltic and Scandinavian states, such preferences have become more pronounced with respect to migration policy (Visegrad) and fiscal policy (Hanse 2.0).

The macro conditions, as under scenarios one, two, and three, are assumed to be a legacy of the financial/Eurozone crisis and resulting economic recession in some member states and the ongoing refugee/migration crisis. Both, given the diverse preferences the policy measures to take, tend to deepen the conflicts and increase the difficulties of finding common solutions to redistributive problems.

The *decision-making rule* to bring about a treaty change with the intention of abolishing of the Union requires member states' unanimous decision. Given diverse preferences, and the lack of unanimity, this is unlikely to materialise. Individual national referenda over an exit from the Union as individual steps of disintegration are more easily organised. Incentives to resort to such referenda would depend on the relative gain a country would draw economically from an exit, on geopolitical factors, on the handling of distributional economic and migration issues, and the contentedness with the own national policies and institutions,[27] but also the specific exit conditions and with the legacy of Brexit. This experience, in particular due to the implosion of British domestic politics, has not been such as to invite other member states to follow the British example.

VI. Conclusion: '*Fluctuat nec mergitur*'

From the analysis of the political dynamics resulting from actors preferences, macro conditions, and given institutional rules, our conclusion is that, of the four possible scenarios, scenario two of differentiated integration and a multi-tier Europe, and scenario three, of a continuing covert incremental integration, rather than the scenario one of a political union or scenario four disintegration/dissolution, are the most plausible paths to be chosen. This leads to the expectation that the European Union will continue 'to be tossed, but will not sink' ('*fluctuat nec mergitur*') and will continue to be a 'half-way house between intergovernmental

[26] Gideon Rachman, 'Brexit is part of a wider European struggle' *Financial Times* (London, 25 March 2019) <https://www.ft.com/content/c074e980-4ee0-11e9-b401-8d9ef1626294>.

[27] Catherine de Vries, 'Should I Stay or Should I Go? A Reference Point Theory of Public Opinion Towards European Integration' (September 2016) unpublished manuscript, Bergen Stein Rokkat Workshop.

cooperation and supranational powers'.[28] Yet floating along and reacting incrementally in the face of important changes in the economic and social environment may not be enough, and in the case of scenario three, may be risky, since covert integration 'through the back door' raises obvious problems of democratic legitimation of European policy making. When citizens at one point realise that integration has deepened dramatically via hidden channels, without their being aware of it, this may trigger a backlash, manifesting itself, for instance, in the negative outcome of national referenda on European issues or in increasing nationalism. Piecemeal interventions as a reaction to multiple crises tend to reinforce executive and non-majoritarian actors and administrative centralisation[29] because they incur less coordination costs compared to legislative action and treaty revisions.

Scenario two of differentiated and flexible integration is linked with political costs as well. The political costs consist in an even more fragmented and complex institutional decision-making structure which makes it difficult to understand the overall working of the European Union. It also implies that there is no central arena in which *all* relevant issues are brought to the table, considered, and discussed in their entirety by all relevant actors in order to conclude compromises and package deals with the view of reciprocity over time for all concerned and the aim of avoiding that structural minorities always losing out.

Both scenarios also mean that overall considerations of 'reinventing the European Union' are not tackled. Notwithstanding, more recently, proposals for institutional reforms have been put forward from various quarters. Some relate to the overall structure of the European Union, others to specific institutional elements of the Eurozone governance. The most far-reaching plan was proposed by Martin Schulz, the then leader of the Social Democratic Party, for a 'United States of Europe end of 2017'. It was met with deafening silence.[30] The outcome of this advance reflects the analysis made under scenario one: the failure of a plan to establish a federal state.

As regards Eurozone governance, far-reaching proposals were introduced by the French President, Emmanuel Macron, as well as the President of the Commission, Jean-Claude Juncker. While Macron aims at a reform of the Eurozone architecture, proposing a Eurozone budget, a Eurozone finance minister and a Eurozone parliament, the Commission's proposals in particular aim at bringing the intergovernmental elements of economic governance created during the financial crisis, in particular the European Stability Mechanism ('ESM'), an intergovernmental

[28] Barber (n 15).

[29] Federico Fabbrini, *Economic Governance in Europe: Comparative Paradoxes and Constitutional Challenges* (Oxford University Press 2016) 15.

[30] Wolfgang Muenchau, 'Lack of eurozone reform outranks Brexit as the EU's biggest threat' *Financial Times* (London, 17 December 2017) <https://www.ft.com/content/47c734d8-e1af-11e7-8f9f-de1c2175f5ce>.

agreement, into the institutional framework of the European Union.[31] It also provides for the introduction of a Single Minister of Finance, a Eurozone budget, and supports the proposal of transforming the ESM into an EMF,[32] as originally proposed by Germany in December 2017. Supported by the EP, the Commission moreover proposes that the EMF, which would develop new financial capacity, be subject to the normal legislative procedure. It would be able to build up a fund to give short-term loans to countries in economic difficulties and serve as a backstop for the funds that the EU's banking resolution authority uses in rescuing banks. According to the Commission, the EMF would be accountable to the EP. The latter would be able to hold hearings with the agency's head and would receive full yearly reports from the EMF on its activities.[33]

By contrast, the Council is seeking to set up the EMF without resorting to the legislative process, but wishes to maintain intergovernmental control over the EMF, as is presently the case under the ESM. For this purpose, it has set up an informal task force reporting to the Economic and Financial Committee.[34] During the height of the financial crisis, it established the 'task force on coordinated action'[35] to facilitate cooperation among finance ministers. Subsequently it prepared work for the ESM, which is run by Eurozone finance ministers. It is the Economic and Financial Committee's task force that the Council has now charged to deal with the Commission's EMF proposal to transform the ESM into an EMF. It is unlikely that it will follow the recommendation to subject the EMF to be accountable to the EP.[36] Eurozone heads of state will decide in March 2018 on the EMF initiative.[37] This attempt of the Council to circumvent the Commission proposal by using existing, largely unknown, bodies to bring about an important change of economic governance, reflects the scenario three of covert integration.

Closely linked to these plans of how to reform financial and economic governance institutions in the Eurozone is another ongoing important debate revolving around whether to go for a full fiscal union or, more modestly, to complete the Banking Union by adding a Eurozone-wide deposit insurance scheme to the Single Supervision Mechanism and to the Single Resolution Mechanism. It appears that in the face of a stiff opposition, primarily from Northern member states, the plan of a fiscal union is unlikely to materialise and the steps are at present directed towards a completion of the Banking Union. However, this process has run into a

31 Ibid.

32 The German proposal provides for restructuring requests to countries receiving funds from the EMF; Mehreen Khan, 'Expectations over euro summit reform push downgraded' *Financial Times* (London, 15 December 2017) <https://www.ft.com/content/478fc732-e173-11e7-a8a4-0a1e63a52f9c>.

33 Bjarke Smith-Meyer, 'Capitals' power grab for Eurozone enforcer' *Politico* (13 February 2018) <https://www.politico.eu/article/council-plays-for-total-control-of-european-monetary-fund/>.

34 Created in 1999 to review the economic and financial situation of member states.

35 Smith-Meyer (n 33).

36 Ibid..

37 Muenchau (n 30).

deadlock over the question of whether banks should first engage in risk reduction (Northern member states) before going for a risk-sharing mechanism, as favoured by a French-led coalition of Southern member states.[38] Both fiscal union and the deposit insurance fund under Banking Union are redistributive questions, albeit on a different scale. It is, therefore, unsurprising that a decision about a fiscal union has not been tackled in view of diverse member states interests and the need to decide by unanimity. The deposit insurance fund raises redistributive questions, as well, but—given that the two first important components SSM and SRM already exist—it may be introduced in a differentiated[39] and incremental way, or might allow for some differentiation and flexibility. This would reflect scenario two.

Finally, an option of a transformed EU architecture has to be mentioned, where the overall objective is to rebuild the European Union in the sense of *both* selective deeper integration and, at the same time, devolution or repatriation of competences. According to this view, where there is an urgent need of joint action, such as in foreign and security policy as well as migration and asylum policy, competences should be pooled. By contrast, other tasks with no transborder effects, such as some areas in environmental law, health, consumer policy, as well as labour law could be repatriated.[40] The principle of an ever closer union would be reversed to a need for a compelling legitimisation of further union. Such a recomposition of the EU with a simultaneous partial devolution of competences and partial additional closer union would allow consensus building based on a compensation mechanism.

Such ideas are to some extent captured in a comprehensive proposal for a renewal of the institutional architecture of the European Union aiming for a 'decoupling and reforming' of the European Union[41] by forming two separate, but linked, organisations. They would consist of a political federal union on the one hand and an economic community on the other, allowing the European Union to overcome the impasse between 'statists' in favour of scenario one, and nationalists in favour of partial disintegration or repatriation of competences of scenario four.

[38] Jim Brunsden, Mehreen Khan, and Guy Chazan, 'Battle for banking union hangs over the eurozone' *Financial Times* (London, 14 December 2017) < https://www.ft.com/content/d38945d6-e030-11e7-a8a4-0a1e63a52f9c>.

[39] Such as by allowing for access to a deposit insurance fund under differentiated economic conditions.

[40] Such options were discussed at the Bratislava Summit emphasising that policy delivery was the order of the day, focusing on the economy/employment, security, i.e., fighting terrorism; protecting outside borders, digitalisation (David M. Herszenhorn, 'After Brexit... more solidarity, against Euroskeptic barrage' *Politico* (Virginia, 16 September 2016); Hans-Jürgen Papier, 'Zerfällt Europa? (17): Europa zwischen Nationalstaatlichkeit und Einheit' *Frankfurter Allgemeine Zeitung* (Frankfurt am Main, 21 October 2016) <https://www.faz.net/aktuell/politik/zerfaellt-europa/zerfaellt-europa-17-europa-zwischen-nationalstaatlichkeit-und-einheit-14484032.html>.

[41] Fabbrini (n 29) 15.

Similar to the argument developed in this chapter, Schelkle advocates in general terms that reforms

> 'that avoid the need for grand state-building are … not only the more realistic alternative … but the more desirable alternative.[42] Incremental reform … will remain the order of the day. It is the modus operandi or legitimate decision making in a diverse union of democracies: political majorities and their representatives in different member states disagree on such consequential, hard to revise decisions. "Unity in diversity" is a more worthwhile goal for the time being than an "ever closer union"'.[43]

[42] Schelkle (n 21).
[43] Ibid. 399.

8

The Social Welfare Function

A New Tool for Regulatory Policy Analysis

Matthew D. Adler

Abstract: The social welfare function ('SWF') framework is a methodology for assessing governmental policies that originates in theoretical welfare economics and is now widely used in various economic literatures. The framework translates the possible outcomes of policy choice into patterns of well-being among the population of interest, represented by interpersonally comparable well-being numbers. Policies are then ranked in light of some rule for ordering these well-being patterns (such as a utilitarian or prioritarian rule), taking account of the probability that a given policy will lead to a given outcome. This chapter presents the SWF framework, illustrates how it can be used for regulatory policy analysis, and compares the methodology to cost-benefit analysis ('CBA'), currently the dominant policy-analytic tool in governmental practice. CBA eschews interpersonal comparisons and, instead, translates policy impacts on each person into a monetary equivalent relative to the status quo; these monetary equivalents are then added up. While CBA and the SWF framework are broadly similar in being consequentialist and welfarist, and in adopting a preference view of well-being, they employ distinct analytic structures for integrating information about preferences and possible outcomes to arrive at an assessment of the various policies that government might adopt. As the chapter demonstrates, the structural differences between the SWF framework and CBA can yield significant divergence at the level of policy recommendation.

The 'social welfare function' ('SWF') is a powerful framework for evaluating governmental policies, one that has been developed in great detail by academic economists. It originates in theoretical welfare economics and plays a key role in various economic literatures, including optimal tax theory, climate economics, and the measurement of inequality. However, this framework is rarely if ever used by governmental bodies. Instead, cost-benefit analysis ('CBA') is the dominant policy-analysis tool within government.

This chapter describes how the SWF framework can be used for *regulatory policy analysis*—as a methodology for assessing governmental regulation. Section I of the chapter describes the framework. Section II discusses its application to regulation.

Matthew D. Adler, *The Social Welfare Function* In: *Theories of Choice*. Edited by: Stefan Grundmann and Philipp Hacker, Oxford University Press (2021). © The several contributors. DOI: 10.1093/oso/9780198863175.003.0009

Section III contrasts the SWF approach with CBA and challenges some of the standard defences of CBA. Section IV presents the results of a simulation model, with different types of SWFs as well as CBA used to evaluate a hypothetical governmental policy that reduces individuals' fatality risks, at some financial cost. This final section serves as a concrete demonstration of the SWF approach and illustrates how it differs from CBA.

This chapter is intended as a brief and relatively informal introduction to topics that I have written about at much greater length elsewhere. Adler (2012)[1] is a book-length elaboration and defence of the SWF framework. Adler (2016)[2] further drills down on the topic of well-being measurement. Adler (2019)[3] is an introductory text. Adler (2017)[4] provides a much fuller and more technical discussion of the use of SWFs for regulatory policy analysis, as well as a comparison with CBA.[5] The current chapter cuts back on the use of mathematical notation—although that is, in fact, essential to the rigorous elaboration and application of the SWF framework. The reader who wishes a deeper treatment is advised to consult the sources just cited.

A note about the Covid-19 pandemic is worth inserting here. This chapter was drafted prior to the outbreak of the pandemic in 2020, and I have not changed the text below in light of that terrible event. But the pandemic certainly does bear upon the chapter's content. First, it underscores the importance of risk regulation as a domain of governmental policy making. The social distancing measures that governments implemented in response to the pandemic are prime examples of fatality risk reduction policies, as described in the chapter and simulated in section IV. Second, it confirms a central theme of the chapter—namely, the divergence between the SWF framework and CBA. See Adler (2020), contrasting the recommendations of the two approaches with respect to social-distancing policy.[6]

[1] Matthew D. Adler, *Well-Being and Fair Distribution: Beyond Cost-Benefit Analysis* (Oxford University Press 2012).

[2] Matthew D. Adler, 'Extended Preferences' in Matthew D. Adler and Marc Fleurbaey (eds.), *The Oxford Handbook of Well-Being and Public Policy* (Oxford University Press 2016) 476.

[3] Matthew D. Adler, *Measuring Social Welfare: An Introduction* (Oxford University Press 2019).

[4] Matthew D. Adler, 'A better calculus for regulators: from cost-benefit analysis to the social welfare function' (2017) Duke Law School Public Law & Legal Theory Series Working Paper No. 2017-19. <https://papers.ssrn.com/sol3/papers.cfm?abstract_id=2923829>.

[5] On the theory of SWFs, see also Charles Blackorby, Walter Bossert, and David Donaldson, *Population Issues in Social Choice Theory, Welfare Economics and Ethics* (Cambridge University Press 2005); Robin Boadway and Neil Bruce, *Welfare Economics* (Basil Blackwell 1984); Walter Bossert and John A. Weymark, 'Utility in Social Choice' in Salvador Barberà, Peter J. Hammond, and Christian Seidl (eds.), *Handbook of Utility Theory*, vol 2 (Kluwer Academic 2004) 1099; John A. Weymark, 'Social Welfare Functions' in Adler and Fleurbaey 2016 (n 2) 126.

[6] Matthew D. Adler, 'What Should We Spend to Save Lives in a Pandemic? A Critique of the Value of Statistical Life' (30 June 2020) 33 Covid Economics 1, https://cepr.org/sites/default/files/CovidEconomics33.pdf.

I. The SWF Framework

The SWF framework is a *normative* framework. It gives guidance about which policy *ought* to be chosen. More precisely, it is an ethical framework, giving guidance about which policy ought to be chosen as an ethical matter.

This framework works within an established tradition of ethical thought, namely *welfare consequentialism*. In this tradition, ethical 'oughts' are reducible to the goodness of outcomes. An 'outcome' is a possible history of the world: a description of what might have occurred in the past, might be occurring now, and might occur in the future. (Of course, actual policy analysts don't think in terms of full possible world histories but rather they use cognitively tractable models thereof, highlighting the main possibilities of ethical interest.) What a decision maker ought to do, given the choices available to her, depends upon the ethical goodness of the outcomes of those choices.

Welfare consequentialism is the particular (and historically dominant) species of consequentialism which analyses outcome goodness in terms of well-being. I will use symbols such as 'x', 'y', etc., to denote outcomes. Welfare consequentialism says: whether x is better than y depends upon the pattern of individual well-being in x and in y. There is a population of individuals whose well-being is of ethical concern, and it is the sum total and distribution of well-being among these individuals that determines how the outcomes compare ethically.

'Individuals' might include non-human animals, but for simplicity I consider a population limited to human beings. The widest human population of ethical concern is everyone who existed in the past, exists at present, or might exist in the future. However, a governmental decision maker may well adopt a narrower understanding of the population of concern, for example, current citizens of her country.

I will use numbers as unique identifiers for individuals. Individual 1 is a specific person, individual 2 someone else, etc. For simplicity, I assume that the very same N individuals exist in all outcomes.

The SWF framework has three key components: a well-being measure $w(\cdot)$, a rule for ranking well-being vectors, and an uncertainty module. These components together provide a formal and well-structured methodology for implementing welfare consequentialism. I will briefly discuss each component in turn.

The well-being measure $w(\cdot)$ converts each outcome into a list ('vector') of well-being numbers, one for each person in the population. For example, if $N = 4$, a given outcome x might be translated into the vector (15, 19, 50, 20); 15 is the well-being number of individual 1 in x, 19 the number of individual 2 in x, and so forth. A different outcome y might be translated into the vector (17, 21, 43, 80); 17 is the well-being number of individual 1 in y, 21 the well-being number of individual 2, and so forth. More abstractly, a given outcome x becomes the well-being vector $(w_1(x), w_2(x), \dots w_i(x), \dots, w_N(x))$. $w_1(x)$ is the well-being number of individual

1 in x, $w_2(x)$ the well-being number of individual 2 in x, ..., $w_i(x)$ the well-being number of individual i in x.

The $w(\cdot)$ numbers assigned to a given outcome are a numerical *representation* of the well-being facts in that outcome. They *summarise* those facts. More specifically, the SWF framework presupposes that individuals' well-being levels and differences are both intrapersonally and interpersonally comparable, and that the $w(\cdot)$ numbers are such as to represent intra- and interpersonal comparisons of well-being levels and differences. $w_i(x) \geq w_i(y)$ indicates that individual i in outcome x is at least as well off as individual i in outcome y. (This is an intrapersonal comparison of well-being levels.) $w_i(x) \geq w_j(y)$ indicates that individual i in outcome x is at least as well off as individual j in outcome y. (This is an *interpersonal* comparison of well-being levels.) Difference comparisons are similarly represented.

Constructing a $w(\cdot)$ measure requires ethical judgment. How do the multiple aspects of a person's life interact to determine her well-being? For our purposes here, this is an *ethical* question: we are interested in 'well-being' understood as that feature of individuals' lives that undergirds the ethical goodness of outcomes. Different accounts of well-being are proposed by the philosophical literature—hedonic accounts, preference account, objective good accounts—and the construction of $w(\cdot)$ requires a choice between these accounts.[7]

Typically, the SWF framework is married with a *preference* account of well-being—the dominant view of well-being within normative economics more generally. According to the preference account, a given person (Frida) is better off in one outcome as compared to a second if, and only if, Frida prefers the first outcome to the second; and she is equally well off in the two if, and only if, she is indifferent between them. This can be tweaked in various ways; in particular, it seems plausible that Frida's well-being depends upon her *well-informed*, *rational*, and *self-regarding* preferences.

Having opted for a particular account of well-being (be it a hedonic account, a preference account, or an objective good account), we must now make sense of intra- and interpersonal comparisons of well-being levels and differences, and we must construct a $w(\cdot)$ to mirror this information. In my scholarship on the SWF approach, I have laboured to show how this can be done for the preference view of well-being, using so-called von Neumann–Morgenstern ('vNM') utility functions.[8]

I will use the term 'attribute bundle' to mean the various characteristics that drive individuals' preferences, such as income, health, longevity, employment, social life, etc. Frida prefers x to y because she prefers her attribute bundle in x to her attribute bundle in y. A vNM utility function, for a given individual, is such as to represent her preferences with respect to attribute bundles and lotteries over attribute bundles.

[7] Adler (n 1) 155–84.
[8] Adler (n 2); Adler (n 3).

Assume, first, that individuals have common preferences with respect to attribute bundles and bundle lotteries. These are represented by a common vNM utility function, $u(\cdot)$. And the measure of well-being can be constructed as follows: an individual's well-being number in a given outcome is just the utility number (according to the vNM utility function representing the common preferences) of his attribute bundle there. That is: $w_i(x) = u(a_i(x))$, with $a_i(x)$ denoting the attribute bundle of individual i in outcome x.

In reality, of course, individuals may well have heterogeneous preferences over attribute bundles and bundle lotteries. I have demonstrated how the vNM approach for measuring well-being can be generalised to this case.

Let us turn, now, to the second component of the SWF framework: the rule for ranking well-being vectors. This rule is the SWF. (The SWF *framework* is the SWF itself *plus* the well-being measure and uncertainty module.) The well-being measure $w(\cdot)$ and the SWF, put together, serve to generate an ethical ranking of outcomes, using the following master formula:

> Outcome x is at least as good as outcome y if, and only if, $(w_1(x), w_2(x), \ldots, w_N(x))$ is ranked by the SWF at least as good as $(w_1(y), w_2(y), \ldots, w_N(y))$.

The space of possible SWFs is vast. This space can be narrowed down *axiomatically* by positing principles (axioms) that the ranking of well-being vectors should satisfy. The choice of axioms is, once more, an ethical matter. Plausible axioms include the following.[9]

Strong Pareto: if two well-being vectors **w*** and **w** are such that some people are better off with **w***, and no one is worse off, then **w*** is a better vector.

Anonymity: if **w** and **w*** embody the very same pattern of well-being numbers, differing only in the identities of the individuals at the various well-being levels, then the two vectors are equally good.

Separability: the ranking of **w** versus **w*** depends only on the well-being levels of *affected* individuals, those who are not equally well off in both.

Continuity: if **w*** is better than/worse than **w**, then this also holds true for all vectors sufficiently close to **w***.

The combination of these four plausible axioms is extremely powerful. The only SWFs that satisfy all four are so-called generalised utilitarian SWFs. These SWFs are *additive*. The generalised utilitarian class of SWFs includes the *utilitarian* SWF, which ranks vectors according to the simple sum of well-being numbers. It also includes the *prioritarian* family of SWFs, which ranks vectors according to the sum of well-being

[9] In stating these axioms, I use bold lower-case letters as compact symbols for well-being vectors. **w** indicates a particular well-being vector $(w_1(x), \ldots, w_N(x))$, and **w*** another such vector.

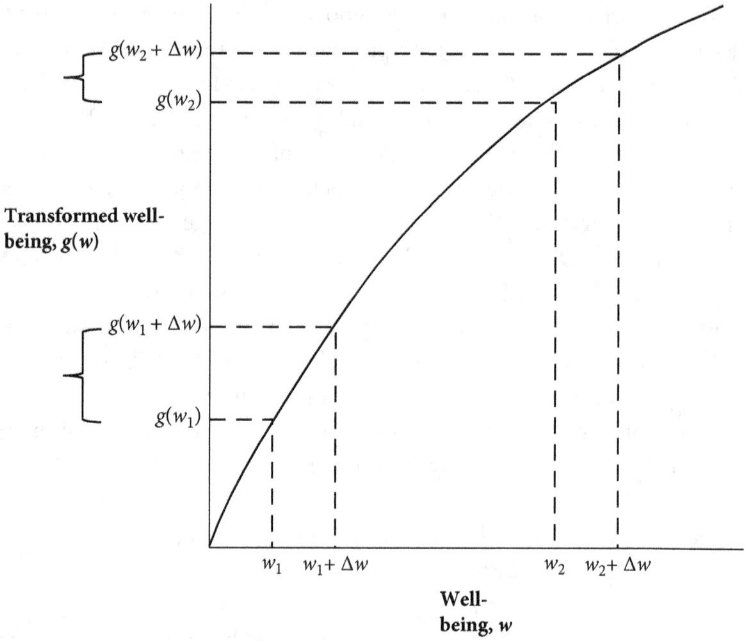

Figure 8.1 An illustration of a prioritarian transformation function, $g(\cdot)$. w_1 is a lower level of well-being than w_2. An increase in well-being by Δw produces a larger increase in transformed well-being if that increase benefits someone at well-being level w_1 rather than w_2.

numbers 'plugged into' a concave transformation function, as illustrated in Figure 8.1.[10] The remainder of this chapter will focus on the utilitarian SWF and prioritarian SWFs. Although other types of generalised utilitarian SWFs exist, these are less attractive ethically, and indeed have been generally ignored by the literature on SWFs.

The utilitarian SWF is the formal expression of *utilitarianism*: the ethical view, dating back hundreds of years to Jeremy Bentham, which enjoins the maximisation of overall well-being.[11] The prioritarian family of SWFs maps onto a more recent proposal in the history of ethics: prioritarianism, introduced by the philosophers Derek Parfit and Larry Temkin in the 1990s, and now much discussed by philosophers.[12] Prioritarianism, unlike utilitarianism, gives greater weight ('priority') to

[10] More precisely, the transformation function is strictly increasing and strictly concave, as is indeed what is shown in Figure 8.1.

[11] Ben Eggleston and Dale E. Miller (eds.), *The Cambridge Companion to Utilitarianism* (Cambridge University Press 2014).

[12] See Derek Parfit, 'Equality or Priority?' (delivered as the Lindley Lecture at the University of Kansas in 1991) in Matthew Clayton and Andrew Williams (eds.), *The Ideal of Equality* (Palgrave Macmillan 2000) 81; Larry Temkin, *Inequality* (Oxford University Press 1993), ch. 9; see generally Nils Holtug, 'Prioritarianism' in William R. Thompson (ed.) *Oxford Research Encyclopedia of Politics* (Oxford University Press 2017), <https://oxfordre.com/politics/view/10.1093/acrefore/

well-being changes affecting worse-off individuals. If Abe is at a lower level of well-being than Bea, then (according to prioritarianism) a given change in Abe's well-being has greater ethical weight than the very same change in Bea's. This is precisely what is achieved by 'plugging' well-being numbers into the concave transformation function, as can be seen in Figure 8.1.

Prioritarianism is a *family* of SWFs, because there are many (indeed, an infinite number of) different concave transformation functions. Picking one such function and summing individuals' well-being numbers transformed by *that* function yields a specific SWF within the prioritarian family. The more concave the transformation function, the greater the degree of priority for those at lower levels of well-being.

The final component of the SWF framework is the uncertainty module. A policy-maker, if omniscient, would know with certainty which outcome would result from each of the various policy options available to her. Real-world decision makers aren't omniscient. The advice that the SWF framework gives them is to think of each policy option as a probability distribution across outcomes. If policy P were chosen, there is some probability that x would result, some probability that y would, etc. If, instead, policy P^* were chosen, there is some probability that x would result (not necessarily the same as the probability of x given policy P), some probability that y would result, and so forth.

It turns out that any given SWF (in particular the utilitarian SWF or an SWF within the prioritarian family) can be associated with a variety of different uncertainty modules. This is a complicated matter.[13] Suffice it to say that the most plausible uncertainty module for the utilitarian SWF is the following: policies are ranked according to the *expected sum of individual well-being*. And a very plausible module for a prioritarian SWF is the following: policies are ranked according to the *expected sum of individual transformed well-being*. In what follows, I assume that the utilitarian and prioritarian SWFs are applied to rank policies (probability distributions over outcomes) in accordance with these respective approaches.

II. The SWF as a Tool for Regulatory Policy Analysis

The SWF framework is applicable to *any* type of governmental policy choice: taxation, infrastructure, benefits programmes, regulation, education, etc. *Any* application of the framework, regardless of policy domain, involves two steps: first, a *predictive* step, namely predicting which outcomes would result from a given

9780190228637.001.0001/acrefore-9780190228637-e-232>; Matthew D. Adler and Nils Holtug, 'Prioritarianism: A Response to Critics' (2019) 18.2 Politics, Philosophy & Economics 101.

[13] Adler (n 1) ch. 7; Adler (n 3); Philippe Mongin and Marcus Pivato, 'Social Evaluation under Risk and Uncertainty' in Adler and Fleurbaey (n 2) 711.

policy, and with which probabilities—in other words, 'translating' each policy into a probability distribution across outcomes; and, second, an *assessment* step, namely applying the $w(\cdot)$ measure, the SWF, and the uncertainty module to rank the various policies on offer thus translated. Variation in the framework's application across policy domains has to do with the details of the first step (e.g., translating *tax* policies into probability distributions across outcomes will require forecasting tools specific to the *tax* domain), and with the modelling of outcomes.

Here, I focus on governmental regulation—more specifically, *risk regulation*, designed to reduce individuals' fatality risks and improve their health. This includes anti-pollution laws, workplace safety measures, design requirements for motor vehicles, pharmaceutical licensure, food inspection and labelling provisions, consumer product safety mandates, etc. Risk regulation is a policy domain where, currently, CBA operates as a major governmental assessment tool—inside the U.S. government, at least, risk regulation is probably the most significant application of CBA—and so it is instructive to see how the SWF framework could also give guidance within this domain.[14] Showing how the SWF framework applies to risk regulation also underscores that the methodology *is* generic. While academic economists frequently use this methodology to assess tax policy, in the literature on optimal taxation[15]—probably its most widespread academic use—the SWF framework transcends tax policy, and a risk regulation example underscores that point.

I have already noted that outcomes are not complete descriptions of possible worlds but rather are cognitively tractable *models* of worlds. In particular, individuals' possible attributes cannot be described in full detail. Rather, the attributes included within the outcome description should, presumably, be both *welfare-relevant* (income, for example, not eye colour) and *causally influenced* by the type of policies being assessed.

Risk regulation measures, if well designed, will reduce fatality risks and/or improve health outcomes, but these benefits are not reaped without a cost. The main downside of risk regulation is a reduction in individuals' income and, thus, consumption (monetary expenditure on marketed goods and services). Risk reduction is achieved by changes in the factors of production (e.g., barring or reducing certain toxic inputs), alteration in production processes ('scrubbers' to reduce air pollution), enhanced inspections, or changes in the design or labelling of final goods. These interventions reduce firms' profits, increase the prices for final goods, and/or reduce workers' wages—all of which are costs ultimately borne by individuals, in the form of reduced income.

[14] See generally Adler (n 4); see also Matthew D. Adler, James Hammitt, and Nicolas Treich, 'The Social Value of Mortality Risk Reduction: VSL versus the Social Welfare Function Approach' (2014) 35 Journal of Health Economics 82; Adler (n 3) ch. 5.

[15] See, e.g., Louis Kaplow, *The Theory of Taxation and Public Economics* (Princeton University Press 2008); Matti Tuomala, *Optimal Redistributive Taxation* (Oxford University Press 2016).

Thus the outcomes employed by the SWF analyst to evaluate risk-regulation policies should, at least, describe individuals' lifespans, health states, and incomes. ('Risk regulation' policies reduce fatality risks and thereby have the benefit of lengthening the lives of *some* individuals. The term 'risk' is used as a label for these policies because this life-extension benefit is stochastic; the policy maker doesn't know *which* individuals' lifespans will be lengthened.)

I will use the acronym 'LHI' history (lifespan–health–income history) to mean an attribute bundle consisting of an individual's lifespan, her health state during each year she is alive, and her income during each year she is alive. An outcome, for purposes of assessing risk-regulation policies, is a possible combination of LHI histories: one such attribute bundle for each person in the population of interest.

This may seem a very complicated setup for modelling policy choices, but three simplifying devices can now be used. First, rather than conceptualising a given policy P as a probability distribution over whole outcomes (combinations of LHI histories for each person in the population), the SWF analyst can instead see P as a combination of *lotteries* over LHI histories, one such lottery for each person. Think of it this way. In the baseline (status quo), if government adopts no new policy, each individual faces a baseline lottery over LHI histories. A given policy P *changes* each person's LHI-history lottery—by changing her risk of dying, health if alive, and/or income if alive. So a given policy P is a *perturbation* to each individual's baseline lottery over LHI histories.

This reconceptualisation of a policy—as a series of lotteries over attribute bundles (here, LHI histories), one such lottery for each person in the population—is possible because of the specifics of the uncertainty module we are using for the utilitarian SWF (expected sum of individual well-being) and for prioritarian SWFs (expected sum of individual transformed well-being). The *expected sum of individual well-being* is mathematically equivalent to the *sum of individual expected well-being*. If we know each person's lottery over bundles, we have sufficient information to determine each person's expected well-being and, thus, the sum of individual expected well-being. Similarly, the *expected sum of individual transformed well-being* is mathematically equivalent to the *sum of individual expected transformed well-being*. If we know each person's lottery over bundles, we have sufficient information to determine each person's expected transformed well-being and, thus, the sum of individual expected transformed well-being. (This may be difficult to grasp without mathematics; see the footnote for a formal explanation.)[16]

[16] Assume N individuals, numbered 1, 2, . . . , N. Let $\pi_p(x)$ denote the probability of outcome x with policy P. Let $W^U(P)$ denote the utilitarian value of a policy as per the uncertainty module we're using for utilitarianism, namely the expected sum of individual well-being; and $W^{PR}(P)$ denote the prioritarian value as per the module we're using for prioritarianism, namely the expected sum of individual transformed well-being. $W^U(P) = \sum_x \pi_P(x) \sum_{i=1}^N w_i(x)$, and $W^{PR}(P) = \sum_x \pi_P(x) \sum_{i=1}^N g(w_i(x))$. But, rearranging

Second, although the theoretical setup for the SWF framework refers to each individual by unique identifier (a number 1, 2, . . . , N), the SWF analyst doesn't actually need to think separately about each individual, picked out by proper name, government identification number, or other unique identifier. Instead, individuals can be modelled as belonging to homogeneous cohorts. A cohort is a group of individuals modelled as facing the same lottery over attribute bundles (here, LHI histories), in the baseline and for every policy under consideration, and as having the same preferences. How to differentiate cohorts is a modelling question (balancing accuracy and tractability). In the case of risk regulation, a cohort might, for example, be identified as all individuals of the same age, whose current income lies in a particular range, and who have certain demographic characteristics useful in predicting preferences, health, and future income.

The analytic setup becomes this. There are M cohorts: $C_1, \ldots, C_M$. In the baseline, all members of a given cohort face a lottery over LHI histories (and thus a particular level of expected well-being/expected transformed well-being). A given policy perturbs this lottery (so that all members of a given cohort now have a different level of expected well-being/expected transformed well-being.)

Third, if the $w(\cdot)$ measure is constructed from vNM utility functions (the method described above), the assignment of well-being numbers to LHI histories can be simplified via standard devices in economics. The members of each cohort are such as to have common preferences and, thus, a common vNM utility function. This is a *lifetime* utility function: it assigns a utility number to each LHI history, namely an entire lifetime described by its longevity, income, and health. But economists typically assume that lifetime utility is temporally additive: the sum across the lifespan of utility in each period (e.g., each year). Thus, we can assume that cohort members have a common *period* utility function, and that the utility of a given LHI history is the sum of its period utility during each period of life (as calculated by the common period utility function, applied to the income and health characteristics during that time slice).

the summation operators, we can see that $W^U(P) = \sum_{i=1}^{N}\sum_{x} \pi_P(x) w_i(x)$, the sum of individual expected well-being, and that $W^{PR}(P) = \sum_{i=1}^{N}\sum_{x} \pi_P(x) g(w_i(x))$, the sum of individual expected transformed well-being. Finally, for a given individual i, her well-being number in an outcome, $w_i(x)$, is determined by her attributes there. Thus the pattern of lotteries over attribute bundles for each person produced by a policy suffices to fix its $W^U(\cdot)$ and $W^{PR}(\cdot)$ values.

III. SWF versus CBA

The keystone of CBA is the monetary equivalent. This can be defined in various ways; the best definition is as follows.[17] An individual's monetary equivalent, for a given policy, is the amount of money, added to her baseline (status quo) income, which makes her indifferent between the baseline and the policy. If we assume a non-satiation condition with respect to income (individuals always prefer more income to less), the monetary equivalent *covaries* with an individual's preferences. Felix's monetary equivalent for a policy is positive if he prefers the policy to baseline, negative if he prefers the baseline to the policy, and zero if he is indifferent. If Felix prefers one policy to a second, his monetary equivalent for the first policy is larger.

CBA's policy evaluation rule is simple: assign each policy an overall number equalling its sum total of monetary equivalents, and rank the policies in the order of these overall numbers.[18]

An individual's monetary equivalent for a given policy *P* depends upon, first, her preferences and, second, the lottery over attribute bundles that she faces as a result of *P*. So a policy can be conceptualised as a series of attribute-bundle lotteries, for each member of the population of interest. In the case of risk regulation, these are lotteries over LHI histories. Further, the CBA analyst need not literally proceed individual by individual; instead, individuals can be placed in cohorts whose members have the same preferences and face the same lotteries. In these respects, CBA is no different from the SWF-based assessment of risk regulation described above in section II.

The difference is in how CBA *quantifies* the value of policies. The utilitarian SWF quantifies a policy's value as the expected sum of individual well-being (or equivalently, the sum of individual expected well-being); a prioritarian SWF quantifies a policy's value as the expected sum of individual transformed well-being (or, equivalently, the sum of individual expected transformed well-being.) By contrast, CBA quantifies policy value as the sum of monetary equivalents.

As we will see in section IV, these differences in the scale used to quantify policy value—monetary equivalent, expected well-being, expected transformed well-being—can yield significant differences in the guidance (the ranking of policies) offered by CBA as compared to the two SWFs.

[17] Adler (n 1) 88–114.

[18] On CBA, see generally Adler (n 1) 88–114; Adler (n 3); Matthew D. Adler and Eric A. Posner, *New Foundations of Cost-Benefit Analysis* (Harvard University Press 2006); Robin Boadway, 'Cost-Benefit Analysis' in Adler and Fleurbaey (n 2) 47; Boadway and Bruce (n 5); Anthony E. Boardman et al., *Cost-Benefit Analysis: Concepts and Practice* (4th edn, Prentice Hall 2011); A. Myrick Freeman, *The Measurement of Environmental and Resource Values: Theory and Methods* (2nd edn, Resources for the Future 2003); Richard E. Just, Darrell L. Hueth, and Andrew Schmitz, *The Welfare Economics of Public Policy: A Practical Approach to Project and Policy Evaluation* (Edward Elgar 2004).

The utilitarian SWF and prioritarian SWFs are the formal expression of major positions within consequentialist ethics: of utilitarianism and prioritarianism, respectively. The CBA rule, summing monetary equivalents, can gain no such direct support from ethical thought. So why believe that this rule is a *justified* method for assessing government policies?

CBA came to the fore at a time in the history of economics, the mid-twentieth century, when many economists were sceptical of interpersonal well-being comparisons.[19] Note that the calculation of monetary equivalents does not presuppose interpersonal comparisons. Assume for the moment that if two individuals, Sam and Sue, have divergent preferences—Sam's ranking of attribute-bundle lotteries is different from Sue's—there is no way to compare their well-being. Even on this assumption, we can calculate Sam's monetary equivalent for any given policy, and we can calculate Sue's monetary equivalent for any given policy. (Doing the first merely requires knowing Sam's preferences; doing the second merely requires knowing Sue's; at no stage do we need to determine whether Sam, with a given bundle or lottery, is better or worse off than Sue, with a given bundle or lottery.) By contrast, the well-being numbers plugged into the SWF (be it utilitarian, prioritarian, or any other plausible SWF) must be interpersonally comparable.

However, ethicists will be dubious about the putative impossibility of interpersonal comparisons. We should distinguish between the propositions (i) that interpersonal comparisons are normative, not purely descriptive; (ii) that interpersonal comparisons are not required for economics as a social science; and (iii) that our best ethical theories should eschew interpersonal comparisons.

Proposition (i) is true. Deciding whether Sam is better off than Sue certainly requires normative judgment. This requires adjudicating between competing normative theories of well-being (preference theories, hedonic theories, objective-good theories). If a preference theory is adopted, it then requires an account of how to make welfare comparisons between individuals with divergent preferences (again, a normative matter).

Proposition (ii) may well also be true. Economics as a social science predicts how markets and other social phenomena will operate in light of individuals advancing their preferences. Interpersonal comparisons are not needed here.

Proposition (iii) is false. Ethical deliberation is shot through with interpersonal well-being comparisons. Let us imagine that Sam is rich, happy, healthy, professionally successful, and surrounded by friends, while Sue is poor, miserable, sick, a professional failure, and friendless. Ethical interlocutors (leaving aside economists

[19] See John. R. Hicks, 'The Foundations of Welfare Economics' (1939) 49.196 The Economic Journal 696; Nicholas Kaldor, 'Welfare Propositions of Economics and Interpersonal Comparisons of Utility' (1939) 49.195 The Economic Journal 549; Harold Hotelling, 'The General Welfare in Relation to Problems of Taxation and of Railway and Utility Rates' (1938) 6.3 Econometrica 242; Lionel Robbins, *An Essay on the Nature and Significance of Economic Science* (first published 1932, 2nd edn, Macmillan 1935).

in the cost-benefit tradition) will generally find absurd the statement that Sam's well-being can't be compared to Sue's; that this comparison is only possible if they have the same preferences; or that interpersonal comparisons are irrelevant to ethics.

A distinct (although related) defence of CBA runs as follows: policy assessment tools that are used *within* government should not involve contestable ethical judgments. It is *legally* problematic to empower bureaucrats to decide the controversial normative questions required by the SWF approach—how to make interpersonal comparisons, which type of SWF to adopt (utilitarian, prioritarian, or other), what degree of priority for the worse off is merited (in the case of a prioritarian SWF), etc.

I assume that the *ultimate* justification for incorporating a policy assessment framework within our legal institutions—for enacting statutes, Presidential directives, or other legal provisions that require officials to use the framework—is an ethical one. If governmental policy-making processes built around CBA, the SWF framework, or some other methodology produce ethically bad results in the long run, why keep these processes in place?

That said, in democratic legal systems there will be legal limits on the extent to which unelected officials possess legal discretion to make controversial ethical judgments. Such limitations are part and parcel of a democracy. Further, if democratic legal systems are ethically *better* legal systems than monarchies, authoritarian regimes, theocracies, and other non-democratic alternatives—if democratic systems tend to produce better outcomes over the long run—then these limitations are themselves ethically attractive.

But none of this yields an argument against the SWF approach, or in favour of CBA. What it shows, rather, is the following: in a democratic legal system where CBA is currently in place, the decision to switch to the SWF framework, and the controversial ethical judgments required to specify the framework, would need to be made by—or at least made in a manner responsive to—elected officials. For example, in the United States, CBA was put in place by a Presidential directive,[20] and its details have been fleshed out in guidance documents issued by an oversight body within the Executive Office of the President.[21] Administrative agencies operating under the current Presidential order *are* legally required to use CBA (not the SWF approach), but there would be nothing legally problematic as a matter of U.S. law—or ethically problematic in light of the value of democratic institutions—for a new

[20] The first Presidential order requiring agencies to use CBA was issued by President Reagan. Exec. Order 12,291, 46 Fed. Reg. 13,193 (17 February 1981). Agencies currently operate under a CBA order issued by President Clinton. Exec. Order No. 12,866, 3 C.F.R. 638 (1994), *reprinted in* 5 U.S.C. § 601 (2012).

[21] That oversight body is OIRA (the Office of Information and Regulatory Affairs). Its head is appointed by the President with Senate confirmation and removable at will by the President. For an example of a major CBA guidance document issued by OIRA, see Office of Management and Budget, Circular No. A-4, *Regulatory Analysis* (2003).

President to repeal the CBA order and require administrative agencies to use the SWF framework instead.

A third defence of CBA has to do with the redistributive potential of the tax system.[22] Assume that a governmental decision maker outside the tax system is choosing between two policies, P^* and P. Policy P^* has a larger sum of monetary equivalents than policy P, and is therefore preferred by CBA, but policy P is favoured by some other methodology (e.g., the SWF framework). Let us call those who prefer policy P^* the 'Reds' and those who prefer policy P the 'Greens'. If policy P^* were chosen, the monetised gain for the Reds would be larger than the monetised loss for the Greens. Thus, policy P^* coupled with a well-designed change to the tax system—taxing the Reds and subsidising the Greens so as to cover the Greens' losses, while still leaving the Reds better off with P^*—would be universally beneficial for Reds and Greens alike.

These observations are sometimes used to argue that non-tax governmental officials (risk regulators, infrastructure planners, etc.) should rely on CBA as their decision procedure, as opposed to any competing procedure—one that could choose P rather P^* in the above paragraph. However, such a defence of CBA overlooks the political constraints that may prevent the tax system from spreading the gains from non-tax policies. It also fails to take sufficient account of the informational asymmetries that may hamper the ability of the tax system to redistribute between those who gain from non-tax policies and those who lose. (For example, in the case of a risk regulation policy choice, the Reds and Greens might be two groups of individuals differentially vulnerable to some health risk in light of difficult-to-ascertain characteristics that aren't feasibly made a determinant of an individual's tax liability, e.g., genetic makeup or health-related behaviours.)

This isn't to say that the SWF framework employed as a methodology to assess risk regulation, or other non-tax policies, should ignore the tax system. Rather, in evaluating non-tax policies, the SWF analyst should consider changes to the tax system that could accompany those policies. Assume that the analyst is advising some non-tax decision maker, who is choosing between P^* and P, and who believes that the legislators in control of the tax system might enact ΔT (a change to the tax code) if P^* were selected. If so, there are three policies to assess, not two: P^*, P, and P^* together with ΔT. It could well be the case that an SWF prefers the second to the first, but the third to the second.

Finally, it should be noted that a modified CBA rule—summing monetary equivalents multiplied by distributional weights—can approximate the SWF

[22] Louis Kaplow, 'The Optimal Supply of Public Goods and the Distortionary Cost of Taxation' (1996) 49.4 National Tax Journal 513; Louis Kaplow, 'On the (Ir)Relevance of Distribution and Labor Supply Distortion to Government Policy' (2004) 18.4 Journal of Economic Perspectives 159; Kaplow (n 15); for a detailed response, see Adler (n 4).

framework.[23] But the weights are specified by choosing an interpersonally comparable well-being measure $w(\cdot)$ and an SWF, which are then (approximately) mimicked by the weights. In this form, CBA is not a competitor to the SWF approach but simply an implementation thereof.

IV. A Simulation Model

This section reports some results from a simulation model (described in detail in Adler 2017)[24] that I constructed to illustrate how the SWF framework can operate as a risk-regulation assessment tool, and how it differs from CBA.

The population is divided into cohorts defined by age and income. In the baseline (status quo), each individual in a given age–income cohort faces a survival curve—her probability of surviving the current year, her probability of surviving the year after that, and so forth.[25] These survival curves are calibrated to U.S. government data about survival probabilities for the entire U.S. population, and then adjusted to take account of the effect of income on survival curves: higher-income groups have more favourable survival curves and, thus, higher life expectancies.

In order to simplify the simulation and facilitate exposition, I assume that the individuals affected by the policy choices at hand fall into five age groups: those currently aged 20, 30, 40, 50, and 60. I assume five different income strata, with income amounts corresponding to the 10th, 30th, 50th, 70th, and 90th percentiles of the U.S. distribution of (after-tax) income. (I refer to these five different strata as 'bottom', 'lower', 'middle', 'higher', and 'top' income, respectively.) This yields twenty-five cohorts, formed by combining the five age groups with the five levels of annual income. I assume an equal number of individuals in each of the twenty-five cohorts.

I assume common preferences, and ignore health differences between the cohorts other than differences in fatality risks. Thus, an LHI history takes the form of a lifespan and an income amount for each year of life. Lifetime utility is assumed to be the sum of annual utility, which in turn is the logarithm of annual income. Note that members of a cohort face a common probability distribution over LHI histories, arising from the common cohort survival curve and common income amounts earned in each year if alive.

I consider policies of the following type. First, a policy may change a cohort's survival probability for the current year. (In the baseline, the cohort's current-year survival probability is p; with the policy, it becomes $p + \Delta p$.) Second, a policy may

[23] Matthew D. Adler, 'Benefit-Cost Analysis and Distributional Weights: An Overview' (2016) 10.2 Review of Environmental Economics and Policy 264; Boadway (n 18).

[24] Adler (n 4).

[25] More precisely, an individual's 'survival probability' is used here to mean a conditional probability: her probability of surviving to the end of the year, conditional on being alive at the beginning.

change a cohort's income for the current year. (In the baseline, the cohort's current-year income is y; with the policy, it becomes $y - \Delta y$.) These changes, together, perturb the cohort's baseline lottery over LHI histories, so that it faces a new lottery.

As already explained, CBA, the utilitarian SWF, and a prioritarian SWF use three distinct metrics for quantifying the social value of an array of individual lotteries over LHI histories: the sum of individuals' monetary equivalents (CBA), the sum of individuals' expected well-being (utilitarian SWF), and the sum of individuals' expected transformed well-being (prioritarian SWF). Let us call these three metrics *CBA value*, *utilitarian value*, and *prioritarian value*. Recall, too, that the well-being number of an LHI history is a *lifetime* number: it is lifetime well-being numbers that are plugged into the SWF (be it utilitarian or prioritarian). So utilitarian value is, more precisely, the sum of individual expected lifetime well-being, and prioritarian value is the sum of individual expected transformed lifetime well-being.

A given policy P, by altering each cohort's current survival probability and/or income, produces a change in social value (CBA value, utilitarian value, or prioritarian value), relative to baseline. The total change in social value is the sum of the changes across the cohorts. Policy P is better than baseline if its total change in social value is positive, and one policy is better than a second if the total change produced by the first is larger than the total change produced by the second.

As one application of this approach, I consider a policy that produces a *uniform* risk reduction: each cohort's current-year survival probability is increased by 1 in 100,000. Whether such a policy will be good, bad, or neutral, as compared to the baseline, will depend upon the associated costs, that is, losses in cohort incomes. Further, how a given *average* loss in incomes (averaged across the twenty-five cohorts) is evaluated may depend upon the *incidence* of that income loss—whether it is spread uniformly (each cohort's income decreases by the same amount), as opposed to the losses varying across the cohorts. I consider three patterns of incidence: uniform incidence, proportional incidence (each cohort loses the same *percentage* of its income, rather than the same absolute amount), and highly progressive incidence (all costs are borne by the top-income cohorts).

Table 8.1 displays the *break-even* average cost, for a uniform 1-in-100,000 risk reduction, as calculated by CBA, the utilitarian SWF, and a prioritarian SWF with a significantly concave transformation function[26]—depending upon the pattern of incidence of income loss (uniform, proportional, highly progressive). 'Break-even' means: a policy P^* producing that average income loss, together with the 1-in-100,000 risk reduction, is equally good as the status quo. If P produces a smaller average income loss, it is better than the status quo; if a larger average income loss, it is worse.

[26] I use a prioritarian SWF with an 'Atkinson' transformation function, $g(w_i) = (1-\gamma)^{-1} w_i^{1-\gamma}$; the parameter γ indicates the degree of concavity of the function. The results reported here set $\gamma = 2$.

Table 8.1 Break-even average cost for a uniform 1-in-100,000 risk reduction

	Utilitarian SWF	Prioritarian SWF	CBA
Uniform Cost Incidence	\$48	\$78	\$91
Proportional Cost Incidence	\$77	\$159	\$91
Highly Progressive Cost Incidence	\$184	\$804	\$91

Note that the two SWFs differ substantially in their policy recommendations, both from each other and from CBA. A policy with a uniform 1-in-100,000 risk reduction *and* uniform income loss (first row) is seen by CBA as a good policy as long as each person's loss is less than \$91; for the utilitarian SWF, the cost needs to be less than \$48; for prioritarianism, it needs to be below \$78. Further, the two SWFs become increasingly willing to impose costs as the incidence pattern shifts from uniform, to proportional, to highly progressive; but CBA's break-even does not change. With proportional cost incidence, the prioritarian SWF is willing to impose average losses larger than CBA's \$91 break-even (up to \$159), while the utilitarian break-even remains lower (\$77). With highly progressive cost incidence, the prioritarian break-even is very high (\$804), and the utilitarian break-even (\$184) now exceeds CBA's, which remains at \$91.

In order to gain a deeper understanding of the differences between the three approaches, it is useful to see how they make across-cohort comparisons with respect to their metrics of social value (CBA value: the sum of individuals' monetary equivalents; utilitarian value: the sum of individual expected lifetime well-being; prioritarian value: the sum of individual expected transformed lifetime well-being). We can ask: if the current survival probability of an individual in cohort C is altered by Δp, how does CBA value/utilitarian value/prioritarian value change, and how does *that* change compare to the change in CBA value/utilitarian value/prioritarian value that occurs with the very same Δp alteration in the current survival probability of an individual in cohort C^*? We can ask a parallel question for income: namely, if the current income of an individual in cohort C is altered by Δy, how does CBA value/utilitarian value/prioritarian value change, and how does *that* change compare to the change in CBA value/utilitarian value/prioritarian value that occurs with the very same Δy alteration in the current income of an individual in cohort C^*?

Tables 8.2 through 8.7 undertake this exercise. The tables immediately below display the change in social value produced by a 1-in-100,000 increase in current survival probability, as calculated using the CBA metric of social value (Table 8.2), the utilitarian metric (Table 8.3), or the prioritarian metric with a significantly concave transformation function (Table 8.4). The results are normalised, so that '1' means the change in social value (as per the corresponding metric) produced by

Table 8.2 CBA value of a 1-in-100,000 increase in survival probability

	Income = bottom	*lower*	*middle*	*higher*	*top*
Age = 20	2.8	6.2	9.9	15.6	44.6
30	2.3	5.2	8.3	13.1	37.8
40	1.8	4.2	6.7	10.7	31.0
50	1.4	3.2	5.2	8.4	24.5
60	1.0	2.3	3.9	6.2	18.4

Table 8.3 Utilitarian value of a 1-in-100,000 increase in survival probability

	Income = bottom	*lower*	*middle*	*higher*	*top*
Age = 20	2.8	3.5	4.0	4.5	5.7
30	2.3	2.9	3.4	3.8	4.8
40	1.8	2.4	2.7	3.1	3.9
50	1.4	1.8	2.1	2.4	3.1
60	1.0	1.3	1.6	1.8	2.3

Table 8.4 Prioritarian value of a 1-in-100,000 increase in survival probability

	Income = bottom	*lower*	*middle*	*higher*	*top*
Age = 20	9.1	7.6	7.0	6.4	5.4
30	5.0	4.2	3.9	3.6	3.0
40	2.9	2.5	2.3	2.1	1.8
50	1.7	1.5	1.4	1.3	1.1
60	1.0	0.9	0.8	0.8	0.7

a 1-in-100,000[27] increase in survival probability for an individual in the sixty-year old, bottom-income cohort.

Table 8.2 should be read as follows. Consider a 1-in-100,000 increase in the current survival probability of someone in the sixty-year-old, bottom-income cohort. With that increase, CBA value changes by a certain amount (let's call it Δv). Now

[27] The relative valuations in these tables would be the same for any small change in the current survival probability of the cohort, not just the specific value of 1-in-100,000. However, so that the values in the income tables below (8.5, 8.6, 8.7) can be interpreted in terms of equivalent survival-probability changes, we need to pick a specific such change.

consider the very same increase in the current survival probability of someone in the sixty-year-old, middle-income cohort. The change in CBA value is 3.9 times larger ($3.9\Delta v$). Consider, instead, a 1-in-100,000 increase in the current survival probability of someone in the fifty-year-old, top-income cohort. The change in CBA value is 24.5 times larger ($24.5\Delta v$).

Table 8.3 should be read the same way, but in terms of utilitarian rather than CBA value. Consider a 1-in-100,000 increase in the current survival probability of someone in the sixty-year-old, bottom-income cohort. With that increase, *utilitarian* value changes by a certain amount (let's call it Δv^*). Now consider the very same increase in the current survival probability of someone in the sixty-year-old, middle-income cohort. The change in *utilitarian* value is 1.6 times larger ($1.6\Delta v^*$). Consider, instead, a 1-in-100,000 increase in the current survival probability of someone in the fifty-year-old, top-income cohort. The change in *utilitarian* value is 3.1 times larger ($3.1\Delta v^*$).

Finally, Table 8.4 should be read in terms of prioritarian value. A 1-in-100,000 increase in the current survival probability of someone in the sixty-year-old, bottom-income cohort produces a certain increase in *prioritarian* value (let's call it Δv^+). The very same increase in the current survival probability of someone in the sixty-year-old, middle-income cohort produces a change in *prioritarian* value that is only 0.8 times as large ($0.8\Delta v^+$). A 1-in-100,000 increase in the survival probability of someone in the fifty-year-old, top-income cohort produces a change in *prioritarian* value that is 1.1 times larger ($1.1\Delta v^+$).

Scanning Tables 8.2, 8.3, and 8.4, it is clear that CBA, the utilitarian SWF, and a prioritarian SWF with a significantly concave transformation function differ substantially in their relative valuations of risk reduction across the twenty-five cohorts. What drives these differences? Let us start with the utilitarian SWF. Within each column (i.e., holding constant income), younger cohorts have larger utilitarian values of risk reduction because they have more years left to live: preventing the current death of a twenty-year-old individual produces a bigger gain in life expectancy, and thus a bigger gain in expected lifetime well-being, than preventing the current death of a sixty-year-old. Across each row (i.e., holding constant age), richer cohorts have larger utilitarian risk-reduction values because the well-being of a year at higher income is larger than that of a year at lower income (after all, income contributes to well-being).

CBA preserves the utilitarian preference for the young. It dramatically increases the utilitarian preference for those at higher incomes; here, it is skewed upwards from utilitarianism by the diminishing marginal utility of income. An individual's monetary equivalent for a risk reduction can be shown to be approximately equal to her change in expected lifetime well-being, that is, her change in utilitarian value, *divided by* her marginal utility of income—this divisor becoming smaller as individuals become richer.

The prioritarian SWF, first, intensifies the utilitarian preference for risk reduction among the young. Younger cohorts are worse off, in terms of lifetime well-being, than older cohorts: they have a greater chance of dying at lower levels of lifetime well-being. But prioritarianism has a preference for the worse off. Thus (holding constant income) the prioritarian value of a given gain in life expectancy is greater if that gain is realised by a younger individual—while the utilitarian values are the same. Second, the prioritarian SWF with a significantly concave transformation function reverses the utilitarian preference for risk reduction among the rich. Holding constant age, a given risk reduction produces more gain in expected lifetime well-being if it befalls a richer person; but that gain is downweighted by prioritarianism, as compared to the same gain for a poorer person.

See Adler (2017)[28] for a fuller explanation of these differences in the relative values of risk reduction as per CBA, the utilitarian SWF, and prioritarian SWFs.

Turn now to the relative valuation of income losses. Tables 8.5 through 8.7 display the change in social value produced by a \$1 increase in current income, as calculated using the CBA metric of social value (Table 8.5), the utilitarian metric (Table 8.6), or the prioritarian metric with a significantly concave transformation function (Table 8.7). The results are normalised, so that '1' means the change in social value (as per the corresponding metric) produced by a 1-in-100,000 increase in survival probability for an individual in the sixty-year-old, bottom-income cohort. This normalisation allows us to commensurate income changes with risk reduction, as well as to see the relative value of income changes (by comparing the pattern within Table 8.5 to that within Table 8.6 and Table 8.7).

Table 8.5 should be read as follows. Consider a 1-in-100,000 increase in the current survival probability of someone in the sixty-year-old, bottom-income cohort. With that increase, CBA value changes by a certain amount (let's call it Δv). Now consider a \$1 increase in the current income of someone in the sixty-year-old, bottom-income cohort. The change in CBA value is $0.12\Delta v$. Consider, next, a \$1 increase in the current income of someone in any other cohort. Because the entry in every cell in Table 8.5 is 0.12, the change in CBA value is, again, $0.12\Delta v$.

Tables 8.6 and 8.7 should be read instead in terms of utilitarian or prioritarian value, respectively, with '1' meaning the change in utilitarian/prioritarian value of a 1-in-100,000 increase in survival probability for someone in the sixty-year-old, bottom-income cohort. For example, note that in Table 8.6 the entry in the cell for a fifty-year-old, lower-income individual is 0.07. This means that if the utilitarian value of a 1-in-100,000 increase in the survival probability of a sixty-year-old, bottom-income individual is Δv^*, the utilitarian value of a \$1 increase in the income of a fifty-year-old, lower-income individual is $0.07\Delta v^*$.

[28] Adler (n 4).

Table 8.5 CBA value of a $1 increase in income

	Income = bottom	*lower*	*middle*	*higher*	*top*
Age = 20	0.12	0.12	0.12	0.12	0.12
30	0.12	0.12	0.12	0.12	0.12
40	0.12	0.12	0.12	0.12	0.12
50	0.12	0.12	0.12	0.12	0.12
60	0.12	0.12	0.12	0.12	0.12

Table 8.6 Utilitarian value of a $1 increase in income

	Income = bottom	*lower*	*middle*	*higher*	*top*
Age = 20	0.12	0.07	0.05	0.03	0.02
30	0.12	0.07	0.05	0.03	0.02
40	0.12	0.07	0.05	0.03	0.02
50	0.12	0.07	0.05	0.03	0.02
60	0.12	0.07	0.05	0.03	0.02

Table 8.7 Prioritarian value of a $1 increase in income

	Income = bottom	*lower*	*middle*	*higher*	*top*
Age = 20	0.13	0.05	0.03	0.02	0.004
30	0.12	0.04	0.02	0.01	0.004
40	0.12	0.04	0.02	0.01	0.004
50	0.11	0.04	0.02	0.01	0.004
60	0.10	0.04	0.02	0.01	0.003

These tables show the change in CBA value/utilitarian value/prioritarian value of a $1 increase in income for each of the twenty-five cohorts, but they can immediately be adapted to show the values of a $1 *loss* in income. Just add a negative sign to the numbers. For example, in Table 8.6 the number in the cell for a forty-year-old, middle-income individual is 0.05. The number in Table 8.3 (the utilitarian risk-reduction table) for a twenty-year-old, lower-income individual is 3.5. With Δv^* denoting the change in utilitarian value of a 1-in-100,000 risk reduction for a sixty-year-old, bottom-income individual, we have that a 1-in-100,000 risk reduction for a twenty-year-old, lower-income individual is $3.5\Delta v^*$. Consider a hypothetical policy that reduces the risk of everyone in the twenty-year-old, lower-income cohort by 1 in 100,000, and does so by imposing costs on everyone in the forty-year-old, middle-income cohort. The change in utilitarian value, for each member of the first cohort, is $3.5\Delta v^*$. If we now impose a $1 cost on each member of the second, the change in utilitarian value is $-0.05\Delta v^*$. Thus the policy is an improvement from baseline as long as the costs on each member of the second cohort are no larger than (3.5/0.05) = $70.

Indeed, the change in social value from baseline of *any* policy can be determined by combining Tables 8.2 and 8.5 (CBA value), Table 8.3 and 8.6 (utilitarian value), or Tables 8.4 and 8.7 (prioritarian value)—by determining the units of risk reduction for each cohort (1 in 100,000 being 1 unit), multiplying by the cohort-specific value for each unit, determining the units of income loss for each cohort ($1 being 1 unit), multiplying by the cohort-specific value for each unit, and adding up across the cohorts. The reader can verify that the numbers in Table 8.1 can be derived in this manner.[29]

What explains the patterns of relative valuation of income change in Tables 8.5, 8.6, and 8.7? The constant pattern in Table 8.5, for CBA, arises because money is CBA's unit of social value. An individual's monetary equivalent, for a $*d* increase in her income, is $*d*; her monetary equivalent, for a $*d* loss, is –$*d*. This is true regardless of the individual's age, income, or other attributes. This constant pattern in turn makes CBA insensitive to the pattern of cost incidence. A given total reduction in population income yields the very same reduction in CBA value, regardless of how the reduction is distributed. For this reason, CBA's break-even value for the policy illustrated in Table 8.1 ($91) is the same regardless of whether the cost incidence is uniform, proportional, or highly progressive.

By contrast, the utilitarian and prioritarian SWFs assign lower values to income gains affecting higher-income individuals; the numbers in Tables 8.6 and 8.7 decline within each row as the cohort's income increases. (For this reason, as shown in Table 8.1, both utilitarianism and prioritarianism are willing to impose greater total losses as the pattern of incidence becomes more progressive.) The utilitarian value of a $1 gain decreases with cohort income because of the declining marginal utility of income. Holding constant age, the change in an individual's expected lifetime well-being that occurs by adding $1 to her income is less if she is high income than middle income, in turn less than if she is low income. The prioritarian value of a $1 gain decreases with cohort income for *two* reasons: because of the declining marginal utility of income *and* because of the lower priority accorded to those who are better off. Thus prioritarian values decrease row-wise in Table 8.7 more rapidly than do the utilitarian values in Table 8.6.

[29] As explained in Adler (n 4) p. 39 n. 86 and p. 75, this methodology for determining a cohort's social value for a policy by adding up its values for the risk-reduction and income-loss components of the policy is an approximation, which is accurate for policies involving small risk and income changes, and becomes less accurate as the magnitude of those changes increases.

V. Conclusion

This chapter has presented a methodology for ethically evaluating governmental policies—the SWF framework—and has shown, specifically, how the framework can operate as a tool for assessing policies that reduce fatality risk. To be sure, the SWF framework is not limited to risk regulation. Rather, this is a *generic* tool, which can be applied to any type of policy choice. Risk regulation was chosen because the SWF methodology is most commonly associated with tax policy—and so a risk-regulation example underscores that the methodology *is* generic. Even more importantly, risk regulation is the dominant application, at least in U.S. governmental practice, of CBA. A risk-regulation example thus serves nicely to illustrate the similarities and differences between SWFs and CBA.

The SWF framework and CBA are similar in being *consequentialist* (policies are assessed in light of their possible outcomes) and, more specifically, *welfarist* (how outcomes compare hinges on individuals' well-being). Further, both methodologies are typically employed in tandem with a preference view of well-being. However, the SWF framework converts each possible outcome into a list ('vector') of interpersonally comparable numbers, representing the well-being levels of the various individuals in the population were that outcome to occur. Outcomes and, ultimately, policies are then ranked via some rule for ranking well-being vectors, such as the utilitarian rule (the sum of well-being) or the prioritarian rule (the sum of well-being 'plugged into' a concave transformation function, thereby giving priority to the worse off). By contrast, CBA eschews interpersonal well-being comparisons and uses *money* as the unit of measurement. Each individual's welfare gain or loss from a policy, relative to baseline, is translated into a monetary equivalent; these monetary equivalents are then added up.

As the chapter illustrates, these structural dissimilarities between the two methodologies with respect to interpersonal comparability and well-being measurement yield significant differences in their guidance regarding the trade off between the welfare benefits (lower fatality risk) and costs (reduced income) of risk-reduction policies. In a nutshell, CBA is biased towards the rich in valuing risk reduction, as compared with the utilitarian SWF, let alone a prioritarian SWF. CBA is also insensitive to the distribution of policy costs. By contrast, both utilitarianism and prioritarianism assign a greater disvalue to an income loss if experienced by a poorer individual. Thus both methodologies (by contrast with CBA) are willing to expend more on risk-reduction policies as policy costs are shifted to those with higher income.

9

Collective Intelligence

Crowd Wisdom versus Herding

Andreas Engert

Abstract: The chapter provides an introduction to the social science of 'collective intelligence', the aggregation of individual judgments for purposes of collective decision making. It starts from the basic logic of the Condorcet jury theorem and summarises the main determinants of the accuracy of collective cognition. The recent research has focused on developing and refining formal aggregation methods beyond majority voting. The chapter presents the main findings on the two general approaches, surveying and prediction markets. It then contrasts these techniques with informal deliberation as a basic and prevalent aggregation mechanism. One conclusion is that while deliberation is prone to herding and can distort collective judgment, it is also more versatile and robust than formal mechanisms.

I. Introduction

Vox populi—when Francis Galton, an English statistician and polymath, published an article under this title in a 1907 issue of *Nature*, he left it to the reader to complete the second half of the famous phrase. Galton was less shy in drawing a bold connection between his finding and the constitutional order of the state, introducing his article with the words: 'In these democratic days, any investigation into the trustworthiness and peculiarities of popular judgments is of interest.'[1] What Galton had to report came not from the lofty spheres of government but from the West of England Fat Stock and Poultry Exhibition at Plymouth. Eight hundred visitors to the show had participated in a competition to submit estimates of the weight that a 'fat ox' would bring to bear after slaughtering and preparation. Tickets were sold at 6 pence, an amount that 'deterred practical joking'. To his pleasant surprise, Galton found that the 'middlemost' estimate was 1,207 pounds (about 547 kilograms), less than 1% off the actual weight of 1,198 pounds (about 543 kilograms).

[1] Francis Galton, 'Vox Populi' (1907) 75 Nature 450, 450.

Andreas Engert, *Collective Intelligence* In: *Theories of Choice.* Edited by: Stefan Grundmann and Philipp Hacker, Oxford University Press (2021). DOI: 10.1093/oso/9780198863175.003.0010

The median estimate, in Galton's view, represents the democratic *vox populi*: it is the only amount that is not 'condemned as too low or too high by a majority of the voters'.[2] Galton considered this result as 'more creditable to the trustworthiness of a democratic judgment than might have been expected'.[3]

The Plymouth judging contest is a foundational tale of a line of research in the social sciences that one can group under the heading 'collective intelligence', or the more catchy 'wisdom of crowds', a phrase that the journalist James Surowiecki coined and popularised in 2004.[4] Galton's short article—less than one page in length—also encapsulates the peculiar mix of ideas that seem to permeate the collective intelligence literature: a great confidence in, and appeal to, the public as arbiter of truth as reflected in the *vox populi, vox dei* formula;[5] more specifically, a belief in public reason that thrives on the independent thinking and free expression of individuals, but then transcends them so that the collective wisdom ultimately surpasses that of any single person or political leader. These views of liberal enlightenment are entwined with formal models from statistics and probability theory, lending them an air of mathematical inevitability[6] but also of marvel and perhaps magical power.[7] Eventually, the formal theories are put to work in ambitious reform proposals for collective decision making in the public and private sphere.[8]

The chapter attempts not to give in to the considerable rhetorical allure, but nonetheless to take advantage of the analytical rigour, theoretical insights, and empirical evidence that the literature offers to the practitioner and researcher, not least the legal scholar. The law has to provide rules under which decisions are made in the various branches and embodiments of government as well as in private organisations. By the binding force of the law, the choices made under these rules can affect many people without their consent. With this power comes the responsibility

[2] Galton (n 1) 450.

[3] Galton (n 1) 451.

[4] James Surowiecki, *The Wisdom of Crowds* (Doubleday 2004). The title mirrors that of Charles Mackay, *Memoirs of Extraordinary Popular Delusions and the Madness of Crowds* (Routledge 1869).

[5] A reference by Machiavelli in the *Discourses on Livy* (1517/1531) resonates strikingly well with the modern notion of collective intelligence: '[A]nd it is not without good reason that it is said, "The voice of the people is the voice of God"; for we see popular opinion prognosticate events in such a wonderful manner that it would almost seem as if the people had some occult virtue, which enables them to foresee the good and the evil.' Niccoló Machiavelli, *The Historical, Political, and Diplomatic Writings*, vol. 2 (Christian Detmold tr, Osgood 1882) 217.

[6] For example, in labelling crowd wisdom a 'truism', John McCoy and Drazen Prelec, *A Statistical Model for Aggregating Judgments by Incorporating Peer Predictions* (Working Paper 2017) 1.

[7] '[O]ccult virtue' in the words of Machiavelli (n 5). The Condorcet jury theorem described in section II.A below provides an example.

[8] Among others Michael Abramowicz, *Predictocracy, Market Mechanisms for Public and Private Decision Making* (Yale University Press 2007); Scott E. Page, *The Difference, How the Power of Diversity Creates Better Groups, Firms, Schools, and Societies* (Princeton University Press 2007); Cass R. Sunstein, *Infotopia, How Many Minds Produce Knowledge* (Oxford University Press 2006); Cass R. Sunstein and Reid Hastie, *Wiser, Getting Beyond Groupthink to Make Groups Smarter* (Harvard Business Review Press 2015).

to foster well-reasoned, rational decision making. Law and legal scholarship, therefore, must take a natural interest in the art and science of collective choice. The chapter seeks to serve this interest by introducing the reader to core findings from research into collective intelligence. Their value is seen not so much in providing a ready blueprint for ground-breaking change but in fostering a better understanding of the workings and weaknesses of institutions—obviously with the hope of improving them.

The research on collective intelligence confines itself to only one aspect of decision making: it studies social cognition; that is, collective judgments on questions that aim at a true or correct answer. This is not to say that the respective questions have an answer that can be determined with certainty, only that they are properly approached as a matter of cognition, not of interests or preferences. Legal judgment is an example. Courts are supposed to decide the case on the merits, not according to judges' whims or preferences. But whether the court has succeeded in determining the actual facts often remains a secret, and a critique of the court's legal argument cannot be proven wrong in any strict sense. Within this broader meaning, any collective choice raises cognitive issues. Another example that will be used in the following is that of a corporation contemplating the acquisition of another firm. To the board of directors, the decision will usually present itself as one in favour or against making an offer at particular terms. One can, however, also frame it as determining a decision threshold; for instance, the maximum price that the corporation should offer in negotiating with the target firm. The optimal reservation price is that which leaves shareholders of the corporation indifferent. The question is one of corporate valuation—an estimate of the expectation value of the stock as a function of the price paid in the acquisition. Such estimates are notoriously uncertain, but they are nonetheless a matter of cognition, not volition.

In addition, the literature on collective intelligence implicitly assumes that preferences in the outcome do not affect decision makers. This is a very unrealistic assumption for collective choice in politics, where the preferences of voters and politicians are likely also to affect and distort their opinions and stated views about the cognitive aspects of a decision. The problem should be less pronounced, and the assumption more defensible, in other areas, such as regulation, law, or business.

The chapter is divided into two main parts. The first introduces key ideas in a form that hopes to be accessible and, more importantly, useful to the legal reader. It concludes with a summary discussion of whether and when collective intelligence is likely to confer advantages over individual judgment (section II). The second part examines the methods of distilling collective intelligence from the separate views of individuals. It starts with the formal techniques that are at the focus of the literature. One approach is surveying—asking group members for standardised responses. Voting is a familiar example (subsection III.A). The second general approach considers 'prediction markets', with betting markets as a long-standing practice (subsection III.B). Finally, opinion aggregation also occurs in the course of ordinary, non-standardised communication among people. Suspected to be a breeding place of animal spirits and 'herding', informal deliberation turns out to have advantages of its own (subsection III.C). Section IV concludes with observations about complementarities between aggregation methods.

II. Statistics of Collective Intelligence

The fundamental claim of collective intelligence is unsurprising. Combining the knowledge of different individuals can lead to better judgment making than that of any single individual. As usual, the squabble lies in the conditions and qualifications as well as ultimately the empirical success of the theory. It is nonetheless worthwhile to start from the most basic idea, the Marquis de Condorcet's jury theorem (subsection II.A). A simple model of individual judgment (subsection II.B) lays the ground for a closer analysis of collective intelligence and its statistical determinants (subsection II.C) before attempting a preliminary conclusion about the benefits of collective judgment (subsection II.D).

A. Condorcet Jury Theorem

The Condorcet jury theorem considers a judgment between two mutually exclusive but jointly exhaustive—binary—alternatives, such as the truth of a statement or the liability of a defendant. Provided that each juror has the same independent probability greater than 0.5 of reaching a correct verdict, the jury theorem implies that the probability of a correct judgment by a majority increases with group size.[9] Table 9.1 demonstrates how larger groups can lever up individual cognitive ability under this simple logic. For advocates of collective intelligence, a tempting reading is that sufficiently large crowds of laypeople (with an error rate of, say, 40%) can trump single experts (e.g., with an error rate of 20%).

The Condorcet argument also extends to continuous judgment. The maximum price a corporation should offer for the acquisition of a target is a judgment on a continuous scale. In the spirit of the jury theorem, all directors on the board are assumed to provide an independent and unbiased guess of the acquirer's optimal reservation price. Harnessing the power of collective intelligence could then mean averaging the individual estimates. The benefit comes from a reduction in

[9] While never stated as an explicit theorem, the result and supporting theory is laid out in Nicolas de Condorcet, *Essai sur l'application de l'analyse à la probabilité des décisions rendues à la pluralité des voix* (1785); see, e.g., ibid. xxiii–xxiv ('si la probabilité de la voix de chaque Votant est plus grande que ½, c'est-à-dire, s'il est plus probable qu'il jugera conformément à la verité, plus le nombre des Votans augmentera, plus la probabilité de la vérité de la décision sera grande: la limite de cette probabilité sera la certitude').

Table 9.1 Probability of correct majority judgment depending on probability of correct judgment by individual juror (row) and number of jurors (column)

	5	11	21	51	101	501	1001
51%	52%	53%	54%	56%	58%	67%	74%
55%	59%	63%	68%	76%	84%	99%	100%
60%	68%	75%	83%	93%	98%	100%	100%
70%	84%	92%	97%	100%	100%	100%	100%
80%	94%	99%	100%	100%	100%	100%	100%
90%	99%	100%	100%	100%	100%	100%	100%

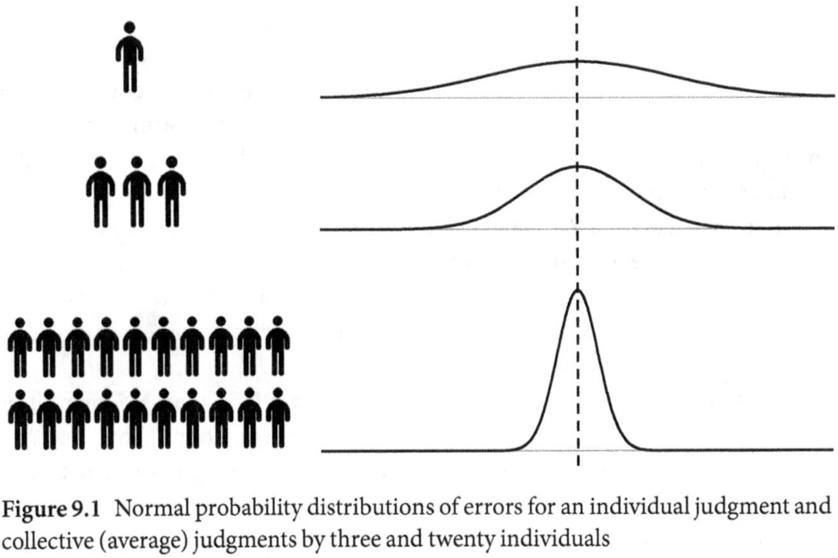

Figure 9.1 Normal probability distributions of errors for an individual judgment and collective (average) judgments by three and twenty individuals

estimation error. If the directors are unbiased, this translates in a narrower confidence interval around the collective estimate. Figure 9.1 demonstrates this effect. It assumes that all individual directors have the same normal distribution of errors.[10] The bell curves can be interpreted roughly as indicating the probability of estimating a value on the horizontal axis when the true value is marked by the vertical line. An individual director's judgment can stray as far away from

[10] Assuming a normal distribution is relatively innocuous in the present context. The central limit theorem ensures that the mean of individual estimates approximates a normal distribution of errors as the number of estimates increases.

the optimal reservation price as the first, wide bell curve implies. Averaging over three directors narrows the distribution notably. With a board composed of twenty directors, the probability of arriving at a collective estimate close to the true value increases considerably.[11]

B. Individual Judgment as Basis

At first, collective intelligence is an application of statistical sampling—learning about the distribution of human judgment in a given population. The judgment of the population, however, is of interest not in its own right but because it promises information about a relevant question, such as the maximum profitable offer price or the liability of a defendant. Collective intelligence thus seeks to capitalise on individual cognition. While being prone to aberrations and distortions, human cognition has the immense advantage of being able to render judgments about all kinds of variables of interest. Statistical models, by contrast, would need repeated observations in homogenous settings to obtain parameter estimates to enable them to produce predictions. In addition, parameter estimation also requires data on actual outcomes of the dependent, predicted variable. Roughly speaking, one needs to feed the model with correct answers before it can predict unknown answers. Yet many settings never reveal a correct answer—for instance, whether the defendant has in fact committed the tort or ought to be held liable as a matter of law. In such cases, people still make choices or provide intuitive guesses while statistical models can at best predict the outcome of fallible human judgment.

Although explicit statistical models cannot replace it, human judgment itself often implicitly consists of statistical prediction or estimation. When asked to adjudicate a case or to assess the value of an acquisition target, jurors will, consciously or unconsciously, evaluate information available to them and draw inferences from it. The information can be diverse, non-standardised, highly specific to a particular issue and situation, soft or hard; it can range from media reports, official documents, websites, statistical data, personal communication in formal or informal settings, rumours and hearsay, to the perceived sentiments of other individuals or a relevant group. It also includes facts, experience, and intuition that bear on the evidentiary weight an individual attaches to any given information and its source. Because evaluators process some—however limited—amount of information their judgment gives at least an indication of the correct answer.

[11] Specifically, the standard error declines compared to a single director's estimate by a factor of $\frac{1}{\sqrt{n}}$ where n is the number of directors.

Asking individuals for their views, therefore, is a versatile way of obtaining at least some insight.

For any but the most straightforward questions, an individual's judgment will not provide a perfectly reliable 'signal' of the 'true state of the world'. The relationship between the individual assessment and the correct answer can itself be expressed as a statistical model. If the task aims at an estimate on a continuous scale, such as the acquirer's optimal reservation price, a model could be captured in the following expression:

$$\text{individual judgment} = \text{true value} + \text{individual bias} + \text{error term}$$

In the model, individual judgment is linked to the correct answer through the first term of the expression. It can deviate from it, possibly by a large amount, because of random noise from mistakes or haphazard choices the individual evaluator makes on the particular occasion. Such randomness is commonly referred to as the 'error term' with an expectation value of zero. The error term creates variation in judgments but does not drive them in a particular direction away from the true value; the evaluator overshoots as much as she undershoots.[12]

At the same time, individuals also have general tendencies to pick a value that is either too high or too low given a particular question.[13] This introduces bias to their judgments. Bias can take a positive or negative value indicating a directional deviation from the true value that persists even when the evaluator forms a new judgment about the same question. Bias can reflect individual characteristics, such as psychological dispositions, reliance on heuristics, or intellectual capability to process certain information. A second source of bias is the information to which an individual is exposed. Education, profession, personal predilections, ideological leanings, media consumption, and social ties all lead to different patterns of available knowledge from both conscious search and incidental discovery. An individual's information set will hardly be representative of the comprehensive knowledge an ideal evaluator would use in answering the question. A marketing expert, financial analyst, labour representative, lawyer, or engineer will rely on different information when called upon to assess the optimal reservation price in a corporate acquisition. As a consequence, their judgments will diverge in predictable ways. Note that individual bias already threatens to vitiate the optimistic outlook of the Condorcet jury theorem: the expectation value of individual predictions in Figure 9.1 equals the true value. The wide spread of the bell curve only represents unbiased random error.

12 The error term is a 'random variable'. It takes a new, random value ('realisation') every time a judgment is made.

13 For a very condensed overview of causes of individual bias, see Clintin P. Davis-Stober et al., 'The Composition of Optimally Wise Crowds' (2015) 12.3 Decision Analysis 130, 131.

C. Statistical Determinants of Collective Intelligence

The goal of utilising collective intelligence is to mitigate the shortcomings of individual judgments—to reduce or eliminate random error and bias. Moving from individual to collective judgment promises progress on both fronts. Perhaps the more fundamental improvement is that individual bias partly cancels out, making collective intelligence less biased than a randomly chosen individual (subsection II.C.1) . In addition, aggregating individual judgments reduces the undirected noise from individual randomness and different individual biases. This lower variance represented the main lesson obtained earlier from the Condorcet jury theorem (subsection II.C.2).

1. Bias

Errors in judgment are deviations from the true value. They can result from persistent deviation (bias) or from random variation (the 'error term' in the expression above). Knowing an evaluator's ability and available information in theory permits an observer to predict a positive or negative, greater or smaller, error in judgment—the individual bias. Unfortunately, such a reliable error forecast is usually not at hand.[14] If it were, the observer and perhaps even the individual herself could correct her bias by simple addition or subtraction. Yet even without knowledge of the sign and extent of individual bias, the use of collective intelligence offers at least a partial repair. For the organiser of collective choice, ignorance of individual biases makes them a random variable of group members. When collective judgment is formed through the averaging of individual judgments, the individual biases add up. As bad as this sounds, it mitigates the bias in collective judgment if individual biases have opposite signs and cancel out. Averaging them reduces collective bias compared to the average individual bias.[15] Fittingly, the idea has been described as 'bracketing' the true value between individual judgments.[16] With much luck, individual biases could reduce to zero so that collective judgment exhibits no bias at all.

The above presentation of the Condorcet jury theorem assumed individual judgments to be unbiased. This could be a shorthand way of saying that in collective

[14] In a specified statistical model of individual judgment, the bias would be a function of observable explanatory variables reflecting the juror's characteristics and information environment. The parameters of the function would have to be estimated based on data from the past on the explanatory variables, judgments, and the true value (!) in the same or sufficiently similar settings.

[15] To be more precise, the absolute value of the average bias is less than the average of absolute biases. With b_i denoting individual bias of individual i in a group of n jurors and equally weighted average, it must be that $\left|\sum_{i=1}^{n} \frac{b_i}{n}\right| < \sum_{i=1}^{n} \left|\frac{b_i}{n}\right|$ if there is any pair of b_i, b_j that have opposite signs.

[16] Richard P. Larrick and Jack B. Soll, 'Intuitions About Combining Opinions: Misappreciation of the Averaging Principle' (2006) 52.1 Management Science 111, 111–12.

cognition, individual biases wash out and can by and large be ignored. But even at the collective level, this seems an extreme and unlikely case. Empirically, whenever the collective judgment of a large group misses the mark by a large margin, this almost certainly reflects aggregate, collective bias; undirected individual errors cannot explain large deviations as they tend to disappear in larger groups.[17] Major errors in collective judgment therefore attest to group bias. The voluminous body of literature in psychology and behavioural economics about biases in individual judgment is, in fact, also a compilation of human errors that fail to average out in large subject pools; it is this property that makes them systematic biases of general interest, rather than just individual gaffes.

We consider only one example, an experiment conducted specifically about collective judgment. Participants were asked to bet on American football games based on 'point spreads'. A point spread is set by bookmakers and added to the score of the home team to designate a game's winner for the purpose of the bet. The aim is to balance the odds of the teams by eliminating the greater probability for the favourite team; historical data suggest that point spreads accomplish this almost perfectly.[18] In the experiment, however, the point spreads were manipulated against the respective favourite teams. Without additional information about the particular games or teams, a rational gambler would have to bet against the favourite. Nonetheless, the majority of participants opted to bet on the favourite in 80–90% of 226 games.[19] A majority vote would have led the group to lose significantly more than half of its bets. The result bodes ill for the Condorcet jury theorem, especially in its original domain of majority voting: the probability of reaching a correct judgment could be below 0.5.[20]

2. Variance

What collective intelligence reliably delivers is a reduction in variance. This concerns the 'error term' in the model of individual judgment, representing random mistakes, arbitrary choices, and whims of the moment. The individual error terms 'drops out' in very large groups and is substantially reduced even in smaller groups because positive and negative deviations cancel each other out. This is precisely the effect showcased in Table 9.1 and Figure 9.1. Pooling evaluators also reduces the variance in bias across group members, compared to picking a single evaluator by chance, and provided that biases are less than perfectly correlated.

[17] This remains the main takeaway from Figure 9.1 and is elaborated further in the following subsection.

[18] For a description and discussion, see Joseph P. Simmons et al., 'Intuitive Biases in Choice versus Estimation: Implications for the Wisdom of Crowds' (2011) 38.1 Journal of Consumer Research 1, 2–3.

[19] The result persisted even when participants were warned of the manipulation. Asking instead for a prediction of the score difference between teams effectively de-biased participants and their collective judgment, Simmons et al. (n 18) 7–12.

[20] Condorcet did anticipate this possibility, especially for large assemblies that, in his view, necessarily had to include less enlightened voters, see Condorcet (n 9) xxiv.

The flip side is that the lower variance also reduces chance corrections of collective bias. Whatever systematic judgment distortion exists will emerge more reliably in the aggregate. Collective intelligence is more persistent also in its mistakes. Because of this, certain decision-making procedures—most prominently the majority principle—can make groups look worse than individuals even if they are in aggregate less biased than the average individual, as one should expect based on the previous analysis. In fact, in the experiment about betting against rigged point spreads, the collective of participants, deciding by the majority rule, performed worse than 93% of its members on an individual basis.[21] Collective intelligence thus seems at a disadvantage to individual judgment. This, however, is an artefact of the majority rule, which translates the group's reduced variance into more consistent implementation of its bias. Based on a continuous measure, the group in the experiment performed better at avoiding the favourites. Knowing the size and direction of the bias, a suitable supermajority requirement could have restored the advantage of collective intelligence.[22]

D. Are Groups Wiser Than Individuals?

The contention of 'wise crowds' raises the question of whether and when groups have an advantage over single evaluators. We leave aside the cost of group judgment; it is most likely to be higher and can only be justified if collective intelligence promises better outcomes. We also assume that individual judgment remains equally accurate—in terms of bias and variance—when it is delivered as sole evaluator compared to as a member of a potentially large group. These aspects are kept for later discussion, as is the possibility of amplified bias from interaction within a group or 'herding'.

With these complications out of the way, one still needs to be explicit about the available knowledge when choosing between collective intelligence and individual judgment. The decision would be trivial and pointless if the social planner already knew the correct answer to the question under consideration. Therefore, one should conceive of her as being susceptible to bias and error as much as any other evaluator. This prevents her from hand-picking a team with zero aggregate bias. But without making her task trivial, the social planner can have—and plausibly has, as other observers may have—some information about the 'general ability' of evaluators, including her own, for particular classes of judgments. In the above expression describing the generation of individual judgment, such (noisy) information could relate to the probability distributions of individual biases, relative to the unknown true value, and of the error terms.

[21] Absent the de-biasing procedure described in n 19, Simmons et al. (n 18) Table 4.

[22] Clintin P. Davis-Stober et al., 'When Is a Crowd Wise?' (2014) 1.2 Decision 79, 94–96.

To illustrate, the social planner may be able to rank potential evaluators by their expertise on the subject matter. If expertise is marked by greater investment in knowledge and frequent validation of past judgments from social feedback and real-world outcomes, one would expect an expert's judgment to reflect more information and different aspects than that of a layperson. Such considerations suggest that expert judgments tend to suffer from less individual bias. Conversely, if non-experts are more prone to using a limited number of cues, this could entail not only greater variance but also higher correlation of individual biases because the available and salient information could come from shared public sources.

Knowledge of differences in cognitive characteristics can guide the choice between collective and individual judgment. If distributions of individual bias and random error among candidates tend to be similar, collective intelligence safely beats a single evaluator— keep in mind that we abstract from decision-making cost, individual effort, and 'herding'. Under these conditions, aggregating the judgments of cognitively similar individuals reduces random variance and has a fair chance of mitigating bias, while never increasing it.

To find advantage in using only a single decision maker, there must be a substantial difference in judgment quality. Even then, the argument is not straightforward. As regards variance, having more evaluators still improves performance provided that one can adjust the weight of individual judgments to differences in variance.[23] Without proper adjustment, however, adding less able evaluators spoils the broth. Expanding the group thus requires knowledge of variances in individual biases and error terms; the social planner would also have to make further adjustments for uncertainty in her own assessment of variances. Further difficulties arise if additional evaluators are susceptible to aggregate bias, as can be suspected in certain instances of lay judgment. While one can try to correct for such systematic bias, this opens up new opportunities for serious mistakes and may not be worth the rather modest gains. Intuitively, one should not meddle with a construction engineer's assessment of the carrying capacity of a building structure based on a population survey. The best response to a cardiac arrest is to call for a doctor, not to conduct a poll among bystanders.[24]

By way of a preliminary conclusion,[25] the collective intelligence of groups has much to commend it. The default advice rarely is to restrict decision making to a single mind. The principal reason to exclude evaluators, perhaps even down to only one person, is the existence of major differences in the quality of individual judgment, specifically in variance and systematic, directional bias, the model example

[23] A higher-variance evaluator optimally receives a lower weight in averaging but should never be completely disregarded.

[24] Albert E. Mannes, Jack B. Soll, and Richard P. Larrick, 'The Wisdom of Select Crowds' (2014) 107.2 Journal of Personality and Social Psychology 276, 278.

[25] Davis-Stober et al. (n 22) provide a more rigorous and comprehensive assessment. See also Mannes et al. (n 24) 278–79 for a discussion of the relevant settings.

being expertise in a field of specialised knowledge or practice. With noticeable differences in evaluator quality, limiting the scope of the group to the more able individuals seems advisable.[26]

III. Generation of Collective Intelligence

Gathering and combining the dispersed knowledge of individuals is not a recent idea; it pertains to human nature as a social animal. What fuels the excitement over collective intelligence are quantitative techniques of extracting or representing the common judgment of a group, starting from the very basic mechanism of majority voting. Besides giving the group's judgment separate expression from that of its members, these formal mechanisms lend themselves to mathematical modelling and empirical evaluation. The resulting framework allows more rigorous analysis and learning about the performance of collective intelligence and about conditions conducive to it. We first consider the more conventional approach of eliciting assessments by asking or 'surveying' individuals (subsection III.A) before turning to the more fanciful contrivance of a prediction market (subsection III.B). These two general types of formal mechanisms are then contrasted with the naturally occurring formation of collective views in informal exchanges or 'deliberation' (subsection III.C).

A. Surveying

Asking participants to answer a question in standardised form and then aggregating the responses is a common technique to arrive at a collective judgment. A prime example is voting in politics, the law, and all kinds of organisations. Voting is set apart, however, because it aims at producing not just a cognitive assessment but a collective choice between alternatives. It often involves divergent preferences and power struggles. Even with uniform preferences, joint decision making through voting is more than just extracting the maximum amount of information from a group. The number of options and the rules to establish a decision—such as majority requirements—reflect considerations about organisational needs, the expected quality of collective judgment, and risk trade-offs. The above example of betting decisions illustrates the difference: the group's informationally superior collective judgment ultimately produced inferior choices under a simple-majority decision rule.[27]

[26] For a simulation of different settings, see Mannes et al. (n 24) 279–84.

[27] For strategic voting in spite of homogenous preferences, see Johanna M. M. Goertz, 'Inefficient Committees: Small Elections with Three Alternatives' (2014) 43.2 Social Choice and Welfare 357, including the short literature overview, ibid. 358–60.

Turning to purely informational surveying, a thriving research branch explores strategies for improving the aggregate estimates of groups. In line with the informal arguments presented above, it has been shown that limiting the group to the most able individuals or giving their assessments greater weight enhances collective judgment.[28] Ability can be measured on a stand-alone basis—having more accuracy individually—or relative to other jurors, either by having less bias or a consistently corrective one.[29] The latter approach overlaps with the notion that the group benefits from using more diverse information.[30] Besides including *individuals* with different cognitive approaches and information backgrounds, researchers have invented algorithms that seek to detect and overweight *judgments* containing novel or divergent information that is under-represented in the group. The common idea behind these algorithms is asking evaluators about not only their own judgment but also the judgment distribution among others. The latter answer reflects what individuals believe to be the group's shared information base, while their own judgment in addition incorporates the respective evaluator's own, private information. Simple averaging underweights private information, which shows only in a single judgment (or few judgments) while there is no a priori reason to assume that it is less relevant than shared information.[31] An improved aggregation rule then strengthens the effect of private information on group judgment.[32]

The accuracy of individual judgments hinges not only on expertise and ability but also on effort. Genuine interest in the question often motivates effort but

[28] Regarding individual differences in ability (outside the group composition literature), a large-scale experiment in forecasting political events over three years showed persistently superior performance of participants with the top 2% record in the respectively previous year, Barbara Mellers et al., 'Identifying and Cultivating Superforecasters as a Method of Improving Probabilistic Predictions' (2015) 10 Perspectives on Psychological Science 267; Barbara Mellers et al., 'Psychological Strategies for Winning a Geopolitical Forecasting Tournament' (2014) 25.5 Psychological Science 1106, 1109, 1111. Note that measuring ability requires information about the correct answer (which in the case of forecasting is provided by future development); for crowd wisdom itself as the target value, see Eyal Baharad et al., 'Beyond Condorcet: Optimal Aggregation Rules Using Voting Records' (2012) 72.1 Theory and Decision 113; for crowd wisdom as indicator of correct answers even when they are in principle observable Ralf H. J. M. Kurvers et al., 'How to Detect High-Performing Individuals and Groups: Decision Similarity Predicts Accuracy' (2019) 5.11 Science Advances eaaw9011.

[29] Evidence for improvements based on stand-alone criteria: Mannes et al. (n 24) 284–86; on contribution to the group: David V. Budescu and Eva Chen, 'Identifying Expertise to Extract the Wisdom of Crowds' (2015) 61.2 Management Science 267, 270–77.

[30] The trade-off between diversity and accuracy is analysed in Davis-Stober et al. (n 13), qualifying the strong emphasis put on diversity by P. J. Lamberson and Scott E. Page, 'Optimal Forecasting Groups' (2012) 58.4 Management Science 805.

[31] See Oliver Kim, Steve C. Lim, and Kenneth W. Shaw, 'The Inefficiency of the Mean Analyst Forecast as a Summary Forecast of Earnings' (2001) 39.2 Journal of Accounting Research 329, 330–33; empirical evidence regarding economic forecasts in Christopher Crowe, *Consensus Forecasts and Inefficient Information Aggregation* (IMF Working Paper 10/178, 2010).

[32] Asa B. Palley and Jack B. Soll, 'Extracting the Wisdom of Crowds When Information is Shared' (2019) 65.5 Management Science 2291 ('pivoting' procedure); Dražen Prelec, H. Sebastian Seung, and John McCoy, 'A Solution to the Single-Question Crowd Wisdom Problem' (2017) 541 Nature 532 ('surprisingly popular' rule for binary choice); McCoy and Prelec (n 6) (providing a generalisation of Prelec et al.).

explicit incentives also matter. Rewards or penalties can attach at the level of the group, such as when committees are held accountable for their decisions. Small and stable groups also are more effective at policing individual shirking. Larger crowds depend more on self-motivated individuals, which can introduce a self-selection bias from participation.[33] Monetary rewards would often be too costly. A different kind of explicit incentives are social 'bragging rights'[34] tied to tournament-style competition over the most accurate judgments.[35] Yet such contests can induce evaluators to report extreme views away from their own best guess to maximise the chance of finishing first.[36]

Incentives—whether they be explicit or implicit—require a measure of success. In many important real-world applications, the correct answer remains subject to debate; think again of the acquirer's optimal reservation price or the judgment rendered by a court. Even without a clear indicator of truth, it is possible, at least theoretically, to provide incentives that induce effort. The key idea is to link rewards or penalties to the reported judgments of others.[37] Implementing such a scheme requires much knowledge about the probability distributions mapping different possible truths to individual judgments.[38] The difficulty explains why the law offers no explicit incentives to judges to promote accurate adjudication.

A final aspect of surveying is the optimal size of the group, about which a lot has already been said. If evaluators differ in ability, expanding the group helps little and could even do harm without proper adjustment of aggregation weights.[39] Effort

[33] A well-known example are online reviews where dissatisfied or moderately satisfied customers tend not to participate, see the overview in Steven Tadelis, 'Reputation and Feedback Systems in Online Platform Markets' (2016) 8 Annual Review of Economics 321, 333–36; for improvements from explicit incentives at a platform for employer reviews, see Ioana Marinescu et al., *Incentives Can Reduce Bias in Online Reviews* (NBER Working Paper 24372, 2018).

[34] Jens Witkowski et al., 'Incentive-Compatible Forecasting Competitions' (2018) 32 AAAI Conference on Artificial Intelligence 1282, 1282.

[35] The top 2% participants in the experiment referred to in note 28 showed far greater effort than other participants; besides explaining their success it also attests to the very lopsided effect of tournament incentives, see Mellers et al., 'Identifying and Cultivating' (n 28) 277; Mellers et al., 'Psychological Strategies' (n 28) 1111.

[36] For a complicated remedy, see Witkowski et al. (n 34). But see also Kenneth C. Lichtendahl Jr, Yael Grushka-Cockayne, and Phillip E. Pfeifer, 'The Wisdom of Competitive Crowds' (2013) 61.6 Operations Research 1383 (discussing the desirable effect that tournament incentives tilt individual judgments away from shared towards private information).

[37] The incentive scheme interprets an evaluator's judgment as a prediction of others' judgments and applies a 'proper scoring rule' that induces truthful reporting of the prediction; see Nolan Miller, Paul Resnick, and Richard Zeckhauser, 'Eliciting Informative Feedback: The Peer-Prediction Method' (2005) 51.9 Management Science 1359, 1360–64; Radu Jurca and Boi Faltings, 'Mechanisms for Making Crowds Truthful' (2009) 34.1 Journal of Artificial Intelligence 209. For a simple explanation of scoring rules, see Abramowicz (n 8) 111–14. On the related notion of evaluating individual ability based on others' behaviour, see the last references in note 28.

[38] Miller et al. (n 37) rightly point out that participants themselves need not possess this information as long as they believe the administrator to apply the scheme properly, ibid. 1363. They argue that Internet rating platforms could have sufficient information, ibid. 1368–69.

[39] For limiting groups to the most able individuals, see again Mannes et al. (n 24). For the gain in accuracy depending on group size, see, e.g., Stefano DellaVigna and Devin Pope, 'Predicting Experimental Results: Who Knows What?' (2018) 126.6 Journal of Political Economy 2410, 2425–26.

motivation and incentives likewise counsel against large groups. Smaller groups also tend to be cheaper to survey and administer. All of these considerations caution against enthusiasm for large crowds as a collective arbiter.

B. Prediction Markets

Asking individuals is straightforward but not particularly inventive. The vision of a collective intelligence might seem to call for something more congenial to spontaneous order than a centrally administered collection and summation of responses. It thus has caught the imagination of many researchers that collective judgment, rather than being established by an intermediating agent, could emerge naturally from the uncoordinated choices of its constituents. Such a procedure in fact exists in the form of 'information' or 'prediction markets'. Hayek is usually cited as the authority for the notion that markets collect dispersed information and incorporate it in a single price.[40] The Hayekian theory, however, related to individual knowledge of needs and resources,[41] that is, to the divergent private values of goods. To become a medium of collective intelligence, the market exchange has to be in goods of a common value reflecting the question of interest. After explaining the design of such markets (subsection III.B.1), their limitations will be considered (subsection III.B.2).

1. Design

To turn market prices into oracles of collective intelligence, the traded good must be imbued with meaning, and that meaning should determine the value of the good for all market participants.[42] The means to this end is a derivative contract or—more simply—a bet: one party promises to pay an amount contingent on an event that the market is meant to predict. A prominent example are bets on the outcome of an election under which the promisor has to pay one euro if a particular candidate wins or loses. In exchange, the promisee pays a contract price for receiving the promise. The good or asset consists of the contractual promise.

Figure 9.2 provides a simplified description how a market in such contracts can aggregate the views of few individual traders. Each of the horizontal lines

[40] Professor Sunstein eloquently characterises prediction markets as 'Hayek's Challenge to Habermas', Cass R. Sunstein, 'Deliberating Groups versus Prediction Markets (or Hayek's Challenge to Habermas)' (2006) 3.3 Episteme 192; see also Sunstein and Hastie (n 8) 181–83; Robert Forsythe et al., 'Anatomy of an Experimental Political Stock Market' (1992) 82.5 American Economic Review 1142, 1143 ('Hayek hypothesis').

[41] The 'particular circumstances of time and place', see Friedrich A. Hayek, 'The Use of Knowledge in Society' (1945) 35.4 American Economic Review 519, 521–22.

[42] That is, the fundamental value of the good—from holding it to maturity—should be the same for all potential owners. In the parlance of bargaining and auction theory, it should be a common, not private value.

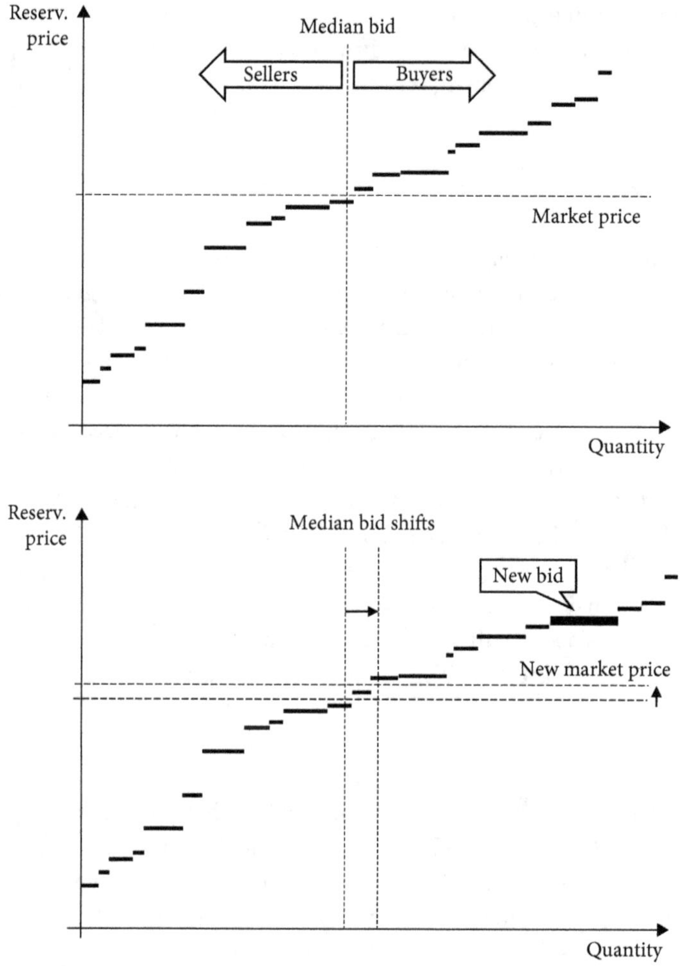

Figure 9.2 Market price depending on buy/sell orders with quantities and truthfully revealed reservation prices (with willingness to pay equal to willingness to accept). Price is set to match as many orders as possible; that is, to clear the market. The graph depicts the price change in response to the arrival of a new order.

represents a trader's order: the length of the lines depicts the quantity of contracts the trader is willing to buy or sell (by taking the position of promisee or promisor), the vertical position shows her reservation price, assumed to be equal for buying or selling. In the example of the one-euro bet on the election of a candidate, a risk-neutral bettor might be willing to pay any amount smaller than her probability estimate times one euro for buying the contract (being the promisee), and take the position of seller (promisor) for any greater amount. For instance, if she tallies the candidate's winning probability at 0.37, she would buy at any price less than 37 cents and sell at any greater price. Competitive bidding—such as through the order book of a stock exchange[43]—should lead the market to 'clear', that is, to realise all trading opportunities from matching orders with different reservation prices. Market clearing results in a price close to the reservation price of the median bid as shown in Figure 9.2.[44]

The lower graph of Figure 9.2 demonstrates how adding an individual judgment—in the form of a new order—affects the market price. The new order shifts the median to the right or left, depending on whether it is above or below the original median bid. The resulting market price reflects the change in the median bid. No central agent attaches weights to individual judgments. In fact, the information contained in the distribution of reservation prices is entirely lost.[45] Order size—the amount a trader is willing to wager—determines how much her judgment counts, not whether it is deemed valuable by a survey organiser. Incentives naturally align as market participants decide how much they invest in the accuracy of their own assessment. As only the more able and diligent traders have positive expected earnings, prediction markets also tend to self-select better evaluators without a need to manage the composition of the group actively.

2. Limitations

The self-governing features of prediction markets have ignited a great deal of excitement. Markets have been hailed as an information panacea for all domains of decision making and credited with staggering forecasting successes.[46] It should be kept in mind, however, that markets are not a divine or natural order that human intervention can only destroy or taint. They are subject to, and are often even the creation of, human design.[47] This is particularly true of prediction markets. With the sole purpose of aggregating the dispersed information or judgments of individuals, prediction markets are up against a fundamental result of economic theory. The 'no-trade theorem' essentially states that market participants are unwilling

[43] For a handy explanation of the operation of order books, see Oxera, 'The design of equity trading markets in Europe' (2019) 19–22 <https://www.oxera.com/wp-content/uploads/2019/03/design-of-equity-trading-markets-1.pdf> accessed 5 October 2020.

[44] The median bid itself can be matched only in part. The market clearing price can be anywhere in the range between the median bid and the next higher or lower reservation price, depending on whether the median trader acts as seller or buyer in the contracts that she can conclude.

[45] The key role of the marginal trader has even been considered the major driver of prediction market accuracy, Forsythe et al. (n 40), 1157–60.

[46] See the call for a regulatory safe harbour from twenty-two leading social scientists in Kenneth J. Arrow et al., 'The Promise of Prediction Markets' (2008) 320.5878 Science 877; Sunstein (n 40) ('In countless domains, their forecasts have proved extremely accurate.'); Robin Hanson, 'Shall We Vote on Values, But Bet on Beliefs?' (2013) 21.2 Journal of Political Philosophy 151, 154 ('While government policy may often suffer info failures, speculative markets show striking info successes.'); Jason Dana et al., 'Are Markets More Accurate Than Polls? The Surprising Informational Value of "Just Asking"' (2019) 14.2 Judgment and Decision Making 135, 135 ('resounding success', 'impressively accurate predictions').

[47] For a more comprehensive summary of the limitations, see Justin Wolfers and Eric Zitzewitz, *Five Open Questions About Prediction Markets* (NBER Working Paper 12060, 2006).

to trade on valuation differences that reflect only private information.[48] The underlying intuition is that rational traders agree on an asset's valuation when they all share the same information.[49] Another trader's willingness to accept (or pay) less (more) than one's own reservation price reveals that the other party has different information and forces a correction of one's own valuation, eliminating the bargaining range. More simply put, without a money inflow from outside, every trader knows the market to be a zero-sum game. Whatever one market participant hopes to gain must come at the expense of another. Trading on valuation differences would be no more than a gamble that risk-averse people usually dislike. It can only arise between parties with inconsistent, self-serving beliefs about their own chances of outsmarting each other.

The emergence of prediction markets becomes even less likely when participation costs are taken into account. These are the costs of entering into transactions but also—more significantly—the effort needed to gather information to avoid losing money against better informed traders. When these effort costs are considered, entering the market becomes a losing proposition. Ironically, while they are supposed to feed on the rational self-interest of traders, many real-world prediction markets depend on non-financial motives such as gambling preferences or a genuine interest in the subject matter (making judgment formation effortless and even a source of utility); examples are betting markets on sports or political events.[50] Information processing can also be a by-product of markets that exist for other purposes. The prime examples are financial markets that offer investment and hedging (insurance) services. Investors and hedgers trade in these markets to match their complementary time and risk preferences—for instance, to invest when others want to liquidate. These complementarities create so many benefits that they can sustain positive expected returns for rational information traders (arbitrageurs, speculators) from exploiting mispricings and thereby enhancing the predictive accuracy of market prices.

Designated prediction markets thus face a similar motivational challenge as do survey techniques. Sustaining them in principle requires an outside subsidy, turning the market into a positive-sum game for traders at the expense of the sponsor.[51] Apart from infusing money, a social planner can try to encourage

[48] Paul Milgrom and Nancy Stokey, 'Information, Trade and Common Knowledge' (1982) 26.1 Journal of Economic Theory 17, 21–24; Jean Tirole, 'On the Possibility of Speculation under Rational Expectations' (1982) 50.5 Econometrica 1163, 1166–68.

[49] More specifically, the theorem assumes traders to have 'common knowledge' of each other's rationality and common Bayesian priors, Milgrom and Stokey (n 48) 19–24.

[50] For betting markets on the outcomes of U.S. presidential elections 1884–1928, see Paul W. Rhode and Koleman S. Strumpf, 'Historical Presidential Betting Markets' (2004) 18.2 Journal of Economic Perspectives 127, 128–29.

[51] Designing a subsidy can be tricky. For instance, simply rewarding trading activity could induce profit-maximising participants to place random orders. An intriguing albeit untested proposal are information-forcing scoring rules (see n 37) directed at the public to induce market activity, see Robin Hanson, 'Combinatorial Information Market Design' (2003) 5.1 Information Systems Frontiers 107.

participation by appealing to curiosity in the question, commitment to a cause or group—that the market is meant to serve—or again to preferences for gambling or competitive contests.[52] Once a sufficient number of traders have been attracted, their behaviour can still fall in line with the logic of self-interested market trading—even if the market uses play money that cannot be exchanged for cash.[53] Market incentives offer distinctive advantages for information aggregation. It was observed earlier that averaging of survey responses should attach greater weight to private information to prevent it from being swamped in the many judgments reflecting only the same widely shared information. Prediction markets provide an inbuilt incentive to behave accordingly. Profits can be made in expectation only based on information that the market price does not already incorporate. Rational traders therefore should act only on information that they believe not to be shared by many others.[54] The very promise of prediction markets rests on this incentive to seek out new information instead of reaffirming the conventional view.

Whether the promise is fulfilled depends on how well individuals ascertain the distribution of information in the market.[55] The available evidence confirms the forecasting faculties[56] of markets but also points to certain persistent biases.[57] In a large-scale experiment involving hundreds of probability estimates for political events, prediction markets turned out to be more accurate than an unweighted average of individual estimates from a survey.[58] However, adjusting weights for

[52] Prediction markets have been used for purposes of public policy, within firms, and for academic research; see, respectively, Robin D. Hanson, 'Designing Real Terrorism Futures' (2006) 128.1–2 Public Choice 257, 258–60; Bo Cowgill and Eric Zitzewitz, 'Corporate Prediction Markets: Evidence from Google, Ford, and Firm X' (2015) 82.4 Review of Economic Studies 1309, 1314–19; Colin F. Camerer et al., 'Evaluating Replicability of Laboratory Experiments in Economics' (2016) 351.6280 Science 1433, 1434–35.

[53] A comparison of two sports betting markets found no significant difference in accuracy between the one operating with real money and the other using play money, Emile Servan-Schreiber et al., 'Prediction Markets: Does Money Matter?' (2004) 14.3 Electronic Markets 243. For the modest incentives in corporate prediction markets, see Cowgill and Zitzewitz (n 52) 1319.

[54] On this anti-herding feature, see Christopher Avery and Peter Zemsky, 'Multidimensional Uncertainty and Herd Behavior in Financial Markets' (1998) 88.4 American Economic Review 724, 725, 728–30.

[55] Avery and Zemsky (n 54) 735–37 offer an explanation of herding in financial markets along these lines.

[56] A well-known success story is elections forecasting where prediction markets tend to perform better than opinion polls, see Forsythe et al. (n 40); Joyce E. Berg, Forrest D. Nelson, and Thomas A. Rietz, 'Prediction Market Accuracy in the Long Run' (2008) 24.2 International Journal of Forecasting 285, 290–98. For corporate prediction markets Cowgill and Zitzewitz (n 52) 1320–32. Further performance results in Justin Wolfers and Eric Zitzewitz, 'Prediction Markets' in Steven N. Durlauf and Lawrence E. Blume (eds.), *New Palgrave Dictionary of Economics* (2nd edn, Palgrave 2008). A classic early reference regarding horse race betting is Stephen Figlewski, 'Subjective Information and Market Efficiency in a Betting Market' (1979) 87.1 Journal of Political Economy 75.

[57] The 'favourite long-shot' bias leads markets to underrate likely winners and to overvalue very low-probability events, see Lionel Page and Robert T. Clemen, 'Do Prediction Markets Produce Well-Calibrated Probability Forecasts?' (2013) 123.568 Economic Journal 491; see also the brief summary of explanations, ibid. 492–94. For over-optimism and other biases in corporate prediction markets, see Cowgill and Zitzewitz (n 52) 1327–32.

[58] Pavel Atanasov et al., 'Distilling the Wisdom of Crowds: Prediction Markets vs. Prediction Polls' (2017) 63.3 Management Science 691, 696–97; Dana et al. (n 46) 138–39.

individual skill and excluding stale forecasts[59] equated performance of the two aggregation methods.[60] Yet again, tweaking the survey predictions requires sufficient data to estimate the parameters of the algorithm[61]—a benefit that the market mechanism provides at no cost.[62]

For all their advantages and allure, prediction markets have one major prerequisite that limits their application: they need something to predict. A derivative contract must relate to a well-defined 'underlying' variable that at some point assumes a verifiable value,[63] such as the outcome of an election, a firm's sales in a given quarter, or the occurrence (or not) of an event within a stipulated timeframe. Many important and much-needed judgments lack such clear validation. The problem surfaced already in connection with possible incentives for survey respondents; sharp incentives for traders are the hallmark of prediction markets. They stand or fall by the prospect of an unequivocal resolution of the question. Where collective intelligence is to pass judgments of a different kind, it cannot be obtained from a market.[64]

C. Deliberation

Formal aggregation procedures are fascinating objects of study and, at least in the form of voting, have broad application and importance for the law. Nonetheless, in the greater scheme of things collective judgment is formed predominantly through non-standardised communication—talking with each other. Like surveys or prediction markets, deliberation among group members leads to an aggregation of views, only that it occurs at the individual level by adjusting individual judgments to what one learns from others. People constantly 'survey' each other. If formal aggregation eventually takes place, it often ingests the results of informal aggregation within individual minds. Yet unavoidable as it is, one may ask whether deliberation helps or hampers collective intelligence, especially when formal aggregation methods could serve as partial substitutes. In fact, the hope that standardised surveys or prediction markets can yield better judgment than conventional discussions accounts for some of the appeal of research in collective intelligence.[65]

[59] The market's prediction was always taken from the most recent price. Excluding older responses from the survey can be seen as a special case of correcting the bias in favour of shared information; see n 31. A third correction consisted of 'extremising' the aggregate estimates. See Atanasov et al. (n 58) 694, 696 for a summary of the algorithm and its justifications.

[60] Atanasov et al. (n 58) 696–97, 702–03; Dana et al. (n 46) 138–39.

[61] Atanasov et al. (n 58) 696–98 (also providing a robustness analysis).

[62] As a final twist of the argument, survey predictions appeared to contain information beyond market prices and to perform better than markets on longer time horizons, Dana et al. (n 46) 139–41.

[63] Wolfers and Zitzewitz (n 47) 9–10 ('contractability').

[64] But see the vision of a 'predictocracy' developed by Abramowicz (n 8) 137 ff where markets are to predict and partially substitute decision makers.

[65] See, e.g., Sunstein (n 40) and the references in n 8.

1. Information suppression ('herding')

Because merging different views can yield a more accurate and reliable judgment, rational individuals should take the opinions of others into account. There is, however, a critical condition: individuals have to act as well-calibrated Bayesian updaters. In incorporating the views of others, they must give adequate weight to the different pieces of information. They should continue to use their own information and, beforehand, produce it through observation and reflection. Sceptics of deliberation question whether this condition is often and sufficiently met. They suspect that individuals are poor aggregators of judgments and dissipate much of the potential of collective intelligence. The conclusion would be to substitute scientifically proven surveying methods or prediction markets as much as possible for unguided deliberation.

Critics of deliberation can point to abundant evidence about people's inclination to neglect their own information and overemphasise the views of others. Common rubrics include 'social influence', 'conformity', or 'herding'. While 'herding' evokes an image of impulsive animal behaviour, it should be repeated that adjusting one's prior assessment to information from others is a tenet of rationality and, after all, the principle behind collective intelligence. People *ought to* 'follow the herd' cognitively if crowd wisdom has greater evidentiary value than the individual's private view. A telling example are experiments from the 1950s where participants succumbed to the consensus of an orchestrated group over the lengths of graphical lines, even though it manifestly contradicted the readily visible evidence.[66] As much as these findings are astonishing, they need not result from erroneous aggregation. If participants did not suspect that other group members had been staged to lie about their perceptions, the very simplicity of the task—comparing the length of lines—provided strong reason to be confident about the independent assessment of *several* others. The unfortunate victims had excellent reason to question their own senses.[67]

The reiterated caveat notwithstanding, judgment aggregation at the individual level is certainly far from optimal. It poses a threat to collective intelligence mostly when it introduces systematic bias in the resulting individual judgments; that is, when all or most group members attribute excessive or too little weight to the same pieces of information. In the model of individual judgment introduced earlier,[68] this adds a uniform bias to the judgments of all group members, preventing

[66] Solomon E. Asch, 'Studies of Independence and Conformity: I. A Minority of One Against a Unanimous Majority' (1956) 70.9 Psychological Monographs 1; Solomon E. Asch, 'Opinions and Social Pressure' (1955) 193.5 Scientific American 31; Morton Deutsch and Harold B. Gerard, 'A Study of Normative and Informational Social Influences upon Individual Judgment' (1955) 51.3 Journal of Abnormal and Social Psychology 51, 629.

[67] In line with this rationalisation, the propensity to yield to the group depended on its size and on the presence of dissenters, Asch 'Opinions' (n 66) 33–35; the experiment by Deutsch and Gerard (n 66) showed that participants gave in even in anonymous settings without social pressure.

[68] Section II.B above.

individual biases from cancelling out. 'Following the herd' by adopting a generally accepted—potentially biased—view can nonetheless be individually rational if the cost of information is taken into account. When several others have endorsed a prevailing judgment, adding another independent evaluation may not be worth the effort individually as even a piece of contradictory evidence would weigh little against the information accumulated in the consensus; collectively, challenging the dominant view could still be worthwhile.[69] In addition, plenty of empirical and theoretical work indicates that people also herd irrationally by using flawed aggregation strategies. For instance, it is both theoretically plausible and supported by experimental evidence that individuals fail to discount properly the weight of identical judgments that reflect the same underlying information.[70] Also credible but less clearly defined is the effect of social norms and 'groupthink' on judgment aggregation at the individual level.[71] A review of the extensive and diverse literature on herding and social influence is beyond the scope of this chapter.[72] Suffice it to say that there is ample evidence for major shortcomings in how individuals factor in the views of others.

[69] The standard references are Sushil Bikhchandani, David Hirshleifer, and Ivo Welch, 'A Theory of Fads, Fashion, Custom, and Cultural Change as Informational Cascades' (1992) 100.5 Journal of Political Economy 992; Abhijit V. Banerjee, 'A Simple Model of Herd Behavior' (1992) 107.3 Quarterly Journal of Economics 797.

[70] See, e.g., Peter M. DeMarzo, Dimitri Vayanos, and Jeffrey Zwiebel, 'Persuasion Bias, Social Influence and Unidimensional Opinions' (2003) 118.3 Quarterly Journal of Economis 909 (theoretical implications of 'persuasion bias' as the failure to adjust to repetitious presentation of the same information); David V. Budescu and Hsiu-Ting Yu, 'Aggregation of Opinions Based on Correlated Cues and Advisors' (2007) 20.2 Journal of Behavioral Decision Making 153, 166–73 (low effect of correlation in the hints of 'advisors' on confidence of 'decision makers' in experiments about a medical diagnostic task); Ilan Yaniv, Shoham Choshen-Hillel, and Maxim Milyavsky, 'Spurious Consensus and Opinion Revision: Why Might People Be More Confident in Their Less Accurate Judgments?' (2009) 35.2 Journal of Experimental Psychology: Learning, Memory, and Cognition 558, 560–61 (lower confidence in aggregated judgment based on *random* sample of 'advisors' as compared to *selective* sample of advisor estimates close to own original judgment); for a review of the 'hidden profile' literature on group deliberation, see Li Lu, Y. Connie Yuan, and Poppy Lauretta McLeod 'Twenty-Five Years of Hidden Profiles in Group Decision Making: A Meta-Analysis' (2012) 16.1 Personality and Social Psychology Review 54; for the general profile of a 'credulous Bayesian', see Edward L. Glaeser and Cass R. Sunstein, 'Extremism and Social Learning' (2009) 1.1 Journal of Legal Analysis 263, 275–300.

[71] The 'groupthink' literature seems not to have coalesced much since the coinage of the term in 1972, see the reviews of James D. Rose, 'Diverse Perspectives on the Groupthink Theory—a Literary Review' (2005) 4.2 Emerging Leadership Journeys 37, 37 ('Groupthink ... ironically is controversial in itself'); Robert S. Baron, 'So Right It's Wrong: Groupthink and the Ubiquitous Nature of Polarized Group Decision Making' (2005) 37.1 Advances in Experimental Social Psychology 219. For an economic model of groupthink driven by anticipatory utility from future prospects (e.g., disutility from bad news about future losses), see Roland Bénabou, 'Groupthink: Collective Delusions in Organizations and Markets' (2013) 80.2 Review of Economic Studies 429. A recent piece of evidence for the cost of dissent in courts is Felipe de Mendonça Lopes, 'Dissent Aversion and Sequential Voting in the Brazilian Supreme Court' (2019) 16.4 Journal of Empirical Legal Studies 933.

[72] For a non-technical exposition, see Sunstein and Hastie (n 8) 21–99; for a survey of herding in financial markets, see David Hirshleifer and Siew Hong Teoh, 'Thought and Behavior Contagion in Capital Markets' in Thorsten Hens and Klaus Reiner Schenk-Hoppé (eds.), *Handbook of Financial Markets: Dynamics and Evolution* (Elsevier 2009) 1.

2. Information discovery

These flaws suggest that free deliberation poses a hazard to collective intelligence. Formal aggregation then presents itself as a superior alternative. Intuitively, it seems clear that ultimately no common judgment can be formed without informal communication. But there is value in explaining why deliberation is more than just a necessary evil and enjoys an additional advantage over aggregation methods that rely on standardised messages, be it survey responses or market orders. This distinctive feature is the lack of pre-imposed structure—the possibility of every participant to refine the space of available signals by specifying the content of her own message. This allows each member of the deliberating group to highlight information complementarities that in a formal aggregation scheme the central designer would have to anticipate.

To elaborate this claim, consider again the examples of adjudicating a case or deciding on the maximum offer price in a corporate acquisition. To rule in favour of the plaintiff, the court has to convince itself that all elements of the claim have been proven. Suppose that in a panel of three judges, two find for the plaintiff and one against her. If the judges disagree on evidence regarding the same element, the majority may well be justified to disregard the opposing vote. If, however, the dissenter has identified a flaw in the plaintiff's argument regarding another element that the other judges have overlooked, learning about the dissenter's reason can be vital to avoid a misjudgment. Simple outcome voting would miss this critical difference. In a similar vein, the reservation price of a corporate acquirer is a function of many variables (say, the expected cash flows of different business divisions of the target, potential cost savings from synergies, legal or reputational risks, the effect of the transaction on the acquirer's cost of capital, etc.). Even if evaluators use the same valuation formula, they will have private information—based on their expertise, research, or random knowledge—on some variables but not on others. Their judgment will reflect updated, posterior estimates for the former and uninformed priors for the latter. Again, information aggregation improves dramatically when evaluators can communicate their information sources and assumptions, instead of averaging only final valuations.

The flexibility of deliberation demonstrates how rigid a structure formal aggregation requires. First, it mechanically limits the effect that any single individual can have on the outcome. Even the clever algorithms for giving greater weight to private information in averaging miss much of what could be distilled from an examination of stated reasons.[73] Similarly in prediction markets, no matter how important a trader's insights, she can invest no more than her capital and what her risk aversion and the market rules permit. In consequence, a group guided by formal aggregation would fatally underweight a single individual's information that the

[73] See n 32 and accompanying text.

building is on fire. Second, formal aggregation is bound by the pre-specified task and the messages made available to individuals. To some extent, the scheme can accommodate information complementarities across evaluators, namely by collecting individual judgments on component variables instead of final outcomes. But this would imply that the sponsor of the survey or prediction market dictates the model structure for making the final judgment—a stark departure from the ideal of tapping the intelligence of the many.

IV. Conclusion

The discussion of freewheeling communication highlights not only the potential 'madness' of crowds[74] but also the comparative weakness of formal aggregation: the amount of structure imposed on the judgment problem and its possibly poor adaptation. In consequence, it would hardly ever be advisable to establish a statutory or regulatory rule prescribing, as a default or mandate, a specific formal aggregation scheme for a class of collective choices. The law does, of course, provide formal rules for making decisions, namely by consent or some variant of majority voting. The rules, however, leave blank the proposal that is to be consented or voted upon. The formal mechanism relies on input from free deliberation that precedes it. The complementarity is mutual: the prospect of a binding decision—including the continuation of the status quo—stimulates the exchange of views during deliberation, as each participant with an interest in the outcome will want to feed her information into the process.

Complementarity between deliberation and formal aggregation can also arise in connection with prediction markets. Because these markets are competitive zero-sum games between the traders, they seem at first not to encourage an exchange of information other than through price. However, once a trader has placed her bet, she should be willing to divulge her information and indeed even try to persuade others of her valuation so as to feed it into the market price and make a profit. A remaining impediment to deliberation arises from the fear that other traders could manipulate the market price by misrepresenting their information. On the flip side, the market creates incentives to uncover new evidence that, after it has been used to take a position, can benefit deliberation.

Overall, it seems a fair assessment that the analysis of collective intelligence so far has failed to deliver a breakthrough technology to revolutionise decision making. The promise of the Condorcet jury theorem dwindles as the underlying assumptions are scrutinised.[75] Prediction markets could hold additional unrealised

74 Mackay (n 4).

75 Condorcet, an aspiring social reformer, cannot be blamed for inspiring excessive optimism, see n 20.

potential but their requirements are demanding and prevent them from becoming a universal cure or improvement for the pitfalls of collective choice. The sober conclusion should not be considered a disappointment. The research on collective intelligence provides valuable insights. Its formalisations and experiments should be conceived less as a practical guidebook to reform than as a disciplined way of studying the relevant trade-offs in shaping collective choice. In this capacity, they contribute to the analysis of legal institutions and eventually to improving them.

PART IV
ORGANISATIONAL CHOICE AND THE LAW

A. FIRMS

10

Decision Theory and Allocating Decision Making in the Firm

Julian Velasco[1]

Abstract: Sometimes it is possible to deal productively with the subject matter of choosing and making decisions without actually settling upon any particular theory of choice. This is the case in the law of business organisations, which does not settle upon a theory of choice because it does not consider itself the ultimate decision maker. Rather, the law develops rules to allocate decision-making authority among the various parties. Utilising only a few basic principles of decision theory, the law of business organisation creates a structure for allocating decision-making responsibility on many different levels. However, it leaves the ultimate decision makers free not only to make substantive decisions for themselves but also to select from among the various theories of choice for doing so.

The topic of this chapter is decision theory and the firm. My area of expertise is the law of business organisation, and Delaware corporate law in particular. I believe that it is possible to deal productively with the subject matter of choosing and making decisions without actually settling upon any particular theory of choice. This is what transpires within the law of business organisation. The law itself need not, and in fact does not, settle upon any particular theory of choice because the law does not consider itself the ultimate decision maker. Rather, it develops rules to allocate decision-making authority among various parties and leaves the ultimate decision makers free to select from among the various theories of choice for themselves. Thus, the law sees its role as offering choices to business people. My contribution, then, is the claim that settling upon a theory of choice is not always necessary. It is through this lens that I will address decision theory and the allocation of decision-making authority in the firm.

Decision theory is the study of making decisions, especially in circumstances involving incomplete information.[2] Decision theory is central to corporate law, but

[1] Associate Professor of Law, Notre Dame Law School. J.D., 1994, Columbia University; B.S., 1991, Georgetown University. I would like to thank Andrew Meerwarth and Nicole A. Paige for their research assistance.

[2] cf. Martin Peterson, *An Introduction to Decision Theory* (2nd edn, Cambridge University Press 2017) 5–8 (distinguishing among risk, ignorance, and uncertainty). See also Andrew S. Gold, 'A

Julian Velasco, *Decision Theory and Allocating Decision Making in the Firm* In: *Theories of Choice*.
Edited by: Stefan Grundmann and Philipp Hacker, Oxford University Press (2021).
DOI: 10.1093/oso/9780198863175.003.0011

not in the most obvious ways. Business itself is all about decision theory. Managers have to make business decisions with incomplete information all the time, and they have developed many tools for doing so. Although one could easily dedicate an entire discussion to decision theory in business, that is not the subject of this chapter.

Instead, I will address decision theory and the law of the firm. For reasons of scope, this chapter will focus mostly on the corporate form, although it will address some other forms of business organisation towards the end. Now, as I have already suggested, corporate law has nothing to do with making actual business decisions. Rather, it is the law concerning who gets to make those business decisions. Thus, corporate law theory could be described as the study of who gets to decide the issue of who gets to decide. So the current discussion is at least one or two levels abstracted from actual business decisions. And yet, corporate law has very many important decisions to make.

As an initial matter, I must set aside one important issue. As I understand it, decision theory is not about setting goals but rather about reaching them. The ultimate goal must be a given.[3] Obviously, one could use decision theory to help decide upon a goal, but that would require a higher-order goal to guide that decision-making process. Now, the goal of corporate law, and business organisation generally, is certainly an open issue in legal scholarship. Nevertheless, I will set the issue aside for three reasons. First, it will make a meaningful discussion considerably easier. After I have considered the matters at hand sufficiently, I can return to explore the ultimate goal. Second, it may not matter to the discussion because there may be a convergence of means despite a divergence of ends.[4] In other words, it is possible—and perhaps even likely—that similar conclusions could be reached about the specifics of corporate law regardless of the goal of the corporation. Finally, it is fair to say, as a purely descriptive matter, that there is a given goal, at least with respect to Delaware corporate law.[5]

Decision Theory Approach to the Business Judgment Rule: Reflection on Disney, Good Faith, and Judicial Uncertainty' (2007) 66 Maryland Law Review 398, 447–52.

[3] cf. Sven Ove Hansson, *Decision Theory: A Brief Introduction* (rev. edn, Royal Institute of Technology 2005) 6–7 ('[D]ecision theory is concerned with goal-directed behaviour in the presence of options… Decision theory does not, according to the received opinion, enter the scene until the ethical or political norms are already fixed.'), http://people.kth.se/~soh/decisiontheory.pdf.

[4] cf. Adrian Vermeule, *Judging Under Uncertainty: An Institutional Theory of Legal Interpretation* (Harvard University Press 2006) 80, 82–83 ('[I]nstitutional considerations may themselves be sufficient to select operating-level rules of interpretation in many domains, because different high-level value theories converge upon similar operating-level prescriptions.').

[5] See Leo E. Strine, Jr., 'The Dangers of Denial: The Need for a Clear-Eyed Understanding of the Power and Accountability Structure Established by the Delaware General Corporation Law' (2015) 50 Wake Forest Law Review 761, 768 ('Despite attempts to muddy the doctrinal waters, a clear-eyed look at the law of corporations in Delaware reveals that, within the limits of their discretion, directors must make stockholder welfare their sole end, and that other interests may be taken into consideration only as a means of promoting stockholder welfare.').

I. Delaware Corporate Law

Delaware law holds that the shareholders are the owners of the corporation, and that they hire management to run the business for them. Thus, the corporation must be run in the interests of the shareholders.[6] Now, because it is a business, there is a strong presumption that the interests of shareholders require wealth maximisation, and that management's discretion is limited to the selection of the means for achieving this end, and not to the determination of another end. This is not the only possible goal for the corporation but it is the legally appropriate one under Delaware corporate law.[7] Because of Delaware's significance to corporate law in the United States, this view provides a reasonable starting point for discussion of decision theory and the firm.

I intend to demonstrate how the allocation of decision-making authority in the law of business organisation, and especially in Delaware corporate law, can be understood through the operation of a few simple decision-making tools, without explicit resort to any theory of choice. I do not mean to suggest that this approach is the only, or even the most appropriate, way to understand corporate law. No doubt, it will amount to an oversimplification. Nevertheless, it is a useful approach, one that should help to elucidate what corporate law is trying to do.

A. Institutional Choice

The first and most fundamental decision-making tool employed by corporate law is institutional choice analysis.[8] Corporate law tries to allocate decision-making responsibilities to the parties that are most competent and best qualified to make such decisions. However, it is important to note that this analysis is not satisfied by one overriding decision as to who should make all business decisions. Rather, it requires a series of decisions about decisions that take place on many different levels.

Consider a basic business decision made in the course of ordinary company business: assume that Public Company makes widgets, but it is considering expanding into gadgets. Who should get to decide whether the company should stick with widgets only or expand into gadgets as well? For present purposes, assume

[6] See *North American Catholic Educational Programming Foundation, Inc v Gheewalla*, 930 A.2d 92, 101 ('Delaware corporate law provides for a separation of control and ownership. The directors of Delaware corporations have "the legal responsibility to manage the business of a corporation for the benefit of its shareholders owners." ') (citations omitted).

[7] See *eBay Domestic Holdings, Inc. v Newark*, 16 A.3d 1, 34 (Del. Ch. 2010) ('Having chosen a for-profit corporate form, the ... directors are bound by the fiduciary duties and standards that accompany that form. Those standards include acting to promote the value of the corporation for the benefit of its stockholders.').

[8] See generally Neil K. Komesar, 'Imperfect Alternatives: Choosing Institutions in Law' in *Economics, and Public Policy* (University of Chicago Press 1994). See also Gold (n 2) 447–52.

widgets and gadgets are substitute goods that compete in the same market. Making the decision would not require a fundamental change in the business but would require deliberate effort. The two most obvious candidates for making this decision are the shareholders, who own the business, and the directors, who run the business.

On the one hand, shareholders have an inherent legitimacy. As the owners of the corporation, they have a strong claim of right to make any and all decisions affecting the corporation. However, shareholders suffer a number of decision-making infirmities. In a public corporation, at least, they are dispersed and suffer from a collective action problem.[9] Nevertheless, shareholders could retain the right to make any decision they want to make, even if they will not care to make most decisions. However, shareholders suffer from other institutional infirmities as well. They are not, as a class, business experts. Thus, they are not reliable decision makers. Moreover, they are not well-informed about the business and its affairs. Thus, they would not be capable of making good decisions. In short, although shareholders may have the moral right to make decisions, they would be unlikely to make consistently good decisions.

Directors do not suffer from such infirmities. They are concentrated rather than dispersed, making collective action easier. They also tend to have more expertise, because of both their education and their experience. Finally, directors have greater access to company-specific information. In short, directors are by nature better decision makers. While they may seem to lack the legitimacy that shareholders enjoy, they in fact have a strong derivative legitimacy because the shareholders elect directors to manage the business on their behalf.

Thus, it is no surprise that corporate law has settled upon a rule that provides that 'the business and affairs of the corporation shall be managed by or under the direction of a Board of Directors',[10] rather than by the shareholders. As will be made clear, this does not settle the matter for all business decisions, but it establishes a strong default rule.

On another level, it must be asked: who got to make that decision? In other words, who gets to decide that the default rule is that the directors get to decide? In the United States, corporate law developed as a matter of state law rather than federal law, so the two obvious candidates are state legislatures and state courts.

On the one hand, legislatures have a strong institutional advantage with a particular type of law: ex ante rules of behaviour.[11] In addition, legislatures have a

[9] See generally Adolf A. Berle, Jr. and Gardiner C. Means, *The Modern Corporation and Private Property* (Transaction Publishers 1932).

[10] Del. Code Ann. tit. 8, § 141(a) (2016).

[11] See Henry M. Hart, Jr. and Albert M. Sacks, *The Legal Process: Basic Problems in the Making and Application of Law* xciii–xciv (William N. Eskridge, Jr. and Philip P. Frickey eds., 1994 Foundatioin Press).

strong claim of legitimacy because they are democratically elected.[12] Where legislatures fall short is their ability to anticipate all possible circumstances; in other words, the rules that they promulgate are inherently incomplete. As a result, statutory law tends to be 'crude' and somewhat arbitrary.[13]

This is where courts have an advantage. In their role of applying and interpreting the law, they can fill in the gaps left by the legislature.[14] Thus, they have a comparative advantage in a different type of law: standards of behaviour applied ex post.[15] Unlike legislatures, courts can consider the facts of each case and develop law that is highly optimised to the particular circumstances.

Business experts insist that wealth creation requires the acceptance of risk. This demands a great deal of flexibility which is incompatible with a highly detailed code of corporate governance. Thus, rather than drafting an extensive body of mandatory law, legislatures have decided to emphasise a different type of law: enabling law—law that empowers corporations to act efficiently.[16] As a result, corporate statutes are intentionally incomplete. However, these statutes are supplemented by the courts, who maintain accountability by applying fiduciary standards of conduct through ex post review of directors' actions.[17] Of course, legislators will enact mandatory rules in other areas of substantive law, including contract law, tort law, labour and employment law, and environmental law, to name just a few examples. However, as to matters of internal corporate governance, legislatures tend to employ a light hand, for the most part delegating the responsibility of policing management to courts of equity. This is an efficient allocation of responsibilities based on institutional competencies.

On yet another level, it could be asked why state law should control matters of corporate governance. Another very real option for doing so is federal law. For the most part, business in the United States operates in the context of a national

[12] See William H. Clune, 'Courts and Legislatures as Arbitrators of Social Change' (1984) 93 Yale Law Journal 763, 763 ('Because the legislature is much better equipped to register popular values than courts, the legislature is presumptively the superior decisionmaker.').

[13] See Richard A. Posner, *Economic Analysis of Law* (9th edn, Wolters Kluwer 2014) 763–64.

[14] See Felix F. Stumpf, *Inherent Powers of the Courts* (National Judiciary College 1994) 37; D. Theodore Rave, 'Institutional Competence in Fiduciary Government, in Research Handbook on Fiduciary Law' in Gold and Smith (eds.), Research Handbook on Fiduciary Law (2018) 418, 421('The potential for ex post judicial review is important because it is difficult to specify and prohibit in advance all of the creative ways in which fiduciaries, with effective power over the practical interests of their beneficiaries, may exploit that power.').

[15] See Hart and Sacks (n 11) xciii–xciv.

[16] See *In re Appraisal of Dell Inc.*, No. CV 9322-VCL, 2015 WL 4313206, at *13 (Del. Ch. July 13, 2015), as revised (30 July 2015) ('[T]he [Delaware General Corporation Law] has not been viewed traditionally as a comprehensive code, but rather as a broadly enabling statute that leaves ample room for private ordering and interpretation.').

[17] See *In re Topps Co.* Shareholders Litig., 924 A.2d 951, 958 (Del. Ch. 2007) ('Delaware's corporate law ... has a broadly enabling statute that gives directors wide leeway to manage the corporation, but subject to fiduciary duty review by a court of equity.'). cf. Leo E. Strine, Jr., 'The Delaware Way: How We Do Corporate Law and Some of the New Challenges We (and Europe) Face' (2005) 30 Delaware Journal of Corporation Law 673, 681 ('Because our statute is an enabling statute, the enforcement of the managers' fiduciary duties is arguably the most important check Delaware imposes on managerial abuse.').

economy. It would seem appropriate to have a national regulator to establish uniform rules. However, having the federal government act as a monopolistic regulator may not be ideal. Permitting corporate law to be decided at the state level allows for legal experimentation and competition among the various states, which can lead to a process of evolution that some have dubbed the 'race to the top'.[18]

For historical and other reasons, corporate law has settled upon the proposition that the states should regulate corporations in the first instance.[19] However, the federal government retains the power to step in, and may choose to do so when national interests are sufficiently at stake. Thus, for example, a demonstrated inability on the part of the states to regulate securities transactions led to the adoption of federal securities law.[20] Originally, federal intervention was limited to the regulation of securities offerings,[21] but it quickly grew to encompass secondary securities transactions,[22] and eventually grew to related matters such as proxy solicitations,[23] tender offers,[24] and even rules of professional conduct for attorneys,[25] as perceived needs arose. It is often said of corporate law that matters of internal corporate governance are regulated by the states, while matters relating to public securities are regulated by the federal government. However, the distinction between the two is arbitrary. It seems fairer to say that corporate law is regulated by the states in the first instance, with the federal government stepping in as necessary.

B. Conflicts of Interest

Thus far, institutional choice has provided a number of broad default rules. A second tool that I will address is conflicts of interest analysis.[26] Corporate law

[18] See generally Ralph K. Winter, Jr., 'State Law, Shareholder Protection, and the Theory of the Corporation' (1977) 6 Journal of Legal Studies 251.

[19] cf. *CTS Corp. v Dynamics Corp. of Am.*, 481 U.S. 69, 91 (1987) ('It . . . is an accepted part of the business landscape in this country for States to create corporations, to prescribe their powers, and to define the rights that are acquired by purchasing their shares.').

[20] cf. Joel Seligman, *The Transformation of Wall Street* (Aspen Publishers 1982) 45–46 ('In the brutal glare that followed the stock market crash [of 1929], it was apparent to virtually all commentators . . . on the subject that the [state] blue sky laws never really had a chance to succeed.').

[21] See Securities Act of 1933, Pub. L. No. 73–22, 48 Stat. 74 (1933) (codified as amended at 15 U.S.C. §§77a–77aa (2012)).

[22] See Securities Exchange Act of 1934, Pub. L. No. 73-291, 48 Stat. 881 (1934) (codified as amended at 15 U.S.C. §§ 78a–78pp (2012 & Supp. V 2017)).

[23] See Exchange Act § 14(a), 15 U.S.C. § 78n (2012); Regulation 14A, 17 C.F.R. §240.14a-1 to §240.14b-2 (2018).

[24] See Williams Act, Pub. L. No. 90-439, 82 Stat. 454 (1968) (codified as amended at 15 U.S.C. §§ 78l, 78m, 78n (2012)); Regulation 14D, 17 C.F.R. §§ 240.14d-1 to 240.14d-103 (2017); Regulation 14F, 17 C.F.R. §§ 240.14e-1 to 240.14e-8, 240.14f-1 (2018).

[25] See Sarbanes–Oxley Act of 2002 § 307, 15 U.S.C. § 7245 (2012); Standards of Professional Conduct for Attorneys Appearing and Practicing Before the Commission in the Representation of an Issuer, 17 C.F.R. Part 205 (2018).

[26] cf. *Guth v Loft*, 5 A.2d 503, 510 (Del. 1939) (discussing 'public policy . . . derived from a profound knowledge of human characteristics and motives . . . that requires an undivided and unselfish loyalty . . . for the purpose of removing all temptation').

starts with the assumption that, as a general matter, the best decision maker can be trusted to make the best decisions in the long run. However, it also recognises that decision makers can be corrupted by conflicts of interest. When they have a competing personal interest in a decision, directors cannot be trusted.[27] This is because they may be tempted to pursue their own interests rather than those of the shareholders. To be fair, they very well may not succumb to the temptation. However, it is impossible to be confident in directors' judgment when they have a conflict of interest.[28]

Yet if directors are conflicted, what can be done? Shareholders still suffer their own institutional infirmities and are not well-suited to making business decisions. Thus, corporate law turns to the courts. Of course, courts are not good business decision makers, either; they are not business experts, and they suffer from various cognitive biases, especially hindsight bias.[29] Nevertheless, courts might be a better choice than either dispersed shareholders or conflicted directors. Recognising their own limitations, courts try not to make actual business decisions. Instead, they rely on their institutional strength: courts are skilled at reviewing the actions of others. Thus, corporate law allows courts to review business decisions made by conflicted directors. If conflicted transactions cannot withstand judicial scrutiny, they will not be permitted to proceed.

A similar conflict of interest analysis can be seen in the choice between state and federal law. As mentioned earlier, corporate law is normally entrusted to the states. However, states are not required to internalise all the costs of their policy decisions. Consider Delaware. It is a small state with relatively few businesses. As the leading state for incorporation, it raises significant revenue through franchise taxes. Now, Delaware would surely like to pass good laws. However, if its laws are too demanding, corporations may decide to look elsewhere for incorporation. In order to attract corporations, Delaware could pass laws that are good for businesses, regardless of the overall effect on society. As a small state, Delaware suffers only a small burden from suboptimal corporate law. Any negative consequences of Delaware corporate law are largely externalised onto larger states, such as California, whose

[27] See William T. Allen, Jack B. Jacobs, and Leo J. Strine, 'Function Over Form: A Reassessment of Standards of Review in Delaware Corporation Law' (2001) 56 Business Law 1287, 1302 ('[A] board that is not conflicted is motivated to achieve the highest transaction price .... Where, however, a majority of a board is conflicted, ... it cannot be presumed that the board will be motivate to achieve the highest transaction price the market will permit.').

[28] cf. *In re Oracle Corp.* Deriv. Litig., 824 A.2d 917, 943 (Del. Ch. 2003) ('Human nature being what it is, it is entirely possible that [a director] would in fact be tougher on [a colleague] than he would on someone with whom he did not have such connections.... [T]hese connections might produce bias in either a tougher or laxer direction.').

[29] cf. *Auerbach v Bennett*, 393 N.E.2d 994, 1000 (N.Y. 1979) ('[T]he business judgment doctrine, at least in part, is grounded in the prudent recognition that courts are ill equipped and infrequently called on to evaluate what are and must be essentially business judgments.'); *Joy v North*, 692 F.2d 880, 886 (2d Cir. 1982) ('[C]ourts recognize that after-the-fact litigation is a most imperfect device to evaluate corporate business decisions.').

businesses are free to incorporate in Delaware. Because of these facts, Delaware may be tempted to pass suboptimal law in order to raise revenue. This has led many to claim that the so-called race to the top may actually be a race to the bottom.[30]

If states cannot be entrusted to make good corporate law, it may be necessary for the federal government to step in with national rules, and from time to time it does so, as with federal securities law. It is worth noting that even the threat of federal intervention can be said to limit Delaware's ability to enact suboptimal law: Delaware must limit the aggressiveness of its competition in the race to the bottom in order to prevent the federal government from passing a national corporate law, which might eliminate Delaware franchise tax revenue altogether.[31] Thus, when states are conflicted, corporate law can turn to the federal government for assistance.

C. Cost-Benefit Analysis

So far, institutional choice has provided a set of default rules, but conflict of interest analysis has required those rules to be altered in certain circumstances. Let us now turn to a third decision tool: cost-benefit analysis. Of course, everything discussed so far could be considered a form of cost-benefit analysis; for example, it would be cost-effective to find the best institution to make decisions, although the costs may outweigh the benefits when that institution is conflicted. However, it is more helpful to discuss costs and benefits at this later stage, after the general rules have been established.[32]

One of the main points to emphasise in a corporate cost-benefit analysis is that shareholder input always involves significant costs. Consider, for example, direct shareholder involvement in corporate governance. It is difficult and costly to get dispersed shareholders to act: solicitations for proxies are time-consuming and expensive. Moreover, a high-quality decision will not be the expected result, given shareholders' lack of expertise and information. Because the costs are high and the benefits are low, shareholder input probably should be sought only infrequently. Shareholder input makes more sense on matters implicating fundamental legitimacy, where shareholders have a specific competence. One example is the election of directors. The benefits of legitimacy on such matters may very well outweigh the

[30] See generally William L. Cary, 'Federalism and Corporate Law: Reflections upon Delaware' (1974) 83 Yale Law Journal 663.

[31] See generally Mark J. Roe, 'Delaware's Politics' (2005) 118 Harvard Law Review 2491.

[32] cf. Baruch Fischoff et al., *Acceptable Risk* (Cambridge University Press 1981) 105 ('Like other formal decision-making tools, cost-benefit analysis may be regarded as either a method or an aid. That is, one can use it to determine which option has the greatest preponderance of benefits over risks, or merely as a guide to be supplemented by other considerations.').

costs. On ordinary business matters, however, the costs of shareholder action are likely to outweigh the benefits.

And yet the calculus may change significantly if shareholders are not as incompetent as they have been described thus far. Increasingly, shares in the United States are held not by individuals but by institutional investors.[33] These institutional shareholders tend to be few in number, have much more business expertise, and are better informed than the average individual shareholder. In many respects, these institutions resemble directors more than they do shareholders. Input from such shareholders might be significantly more cost-effective than that from individual shareholders.[34] Thus, one might expect that institutional shareholders would demand more input in business decisions, whether under existing rules or by demanding new rules. In fact, this has been happening. 'Say on executive pay' is just one example.[35]

On the other hand, there are many different types of institutional investors. Some have interests that might differ significantly from those of other shareholders; in fact, their interests may even conflict with them directly.[36] Although the cost of input from such shareholders may be low, the expected benefit may be low as well. Thus, one could expect some resistance to the wholesale expansion of shareholder rights. This, too, has been happening.[37] Thus, the decision as to exactly how much input into corporate decisions shareholders should have depends upon a careful weighing up of the various costs and benefits.

By now, the overall framework of corporate law can be seen. Legislators focus primarily on enabling law. Most business decisions are allocated to directors. However, shareholders get to elect and remove directors, and directors' actions are subject to judicial review. And yet, on some fundamental matters, authority is shared between shareholders and directors.

I will briefly address this category of business decisions: fundamental matters. Authority is shared, but there are many ways that it can be shared. The cost-benefit analysis may change significantly depending upon which method is selected.

[33] See Matteo Tonello and Stephen Rabimov, 'The 2010 Institutional Investment Report: trends in asset allocation and portfolio composition' (2010) 27, http://www.shareholderforum.com/e-mtg/Library/20101111_ConferenceBoard.pdf, archived at https://perma.cc/YT39-7JKL.

[34] For a classic discussion of the potential of institutional investors, see Bernard S. Black, 'Shareholder Passivity Reexamined' (1990) 89 Michigan Law Review 520, 536–42, and Bernard S. Black, 'Agents Watching Agents: The Promise of Institutional Investor Voice' (1992) 39 UCLA Law Review 811, 823–24.

[35] See Dodd–Frank Wall Street Reform and Consumer Protection Act § 951 (codified at 15 U.S.C. § 77n-1 (2012)).

[36] See, e.g., Henry T. C. Hu and Bernard Black, 'Empty Voting and Hidden (Morphable) Ownership: Taxonomy, Implications, and Reforms' (2006) 61 Business Law 1011 (discussing hedge fund strategies that create 'incentive[s] to vote in ways that reduce the company's share price').

[37] See, e.g., Leo J. Strine, Jr, 'Toward a True Corporate Republic: A Traditionalist Response to Bebchuk's Solution for Improving Corporate America' (2006) 119 Harvard Law Review 1760 (discussing 'traditionalist . . . concern[s] over the potential adverse effects of giving shareholders more influence over corporate governance').

Consider, for example, the rules of the corporate governance game. Corporate law statutes set the default rules for corporate governance, but these rules usually can be altered. The law can provide that any particular change could be made in either the corporate charter (which is the fundamental organisational document) or the bylaws (which are subordinate to the charter). Because of their relative importance, a charter amendment requires the approval of both the directors and the shareholders,[38] while a bylaw amendment generally can be made by either directors or shareholders.[39] The law's decision concerning where to situate a corporate governance rule is an important one, fraught with consequences. To require a change to be made in the charter makes it more difficult to implement. However, if a charter amendment proves to be a mistake, it is also more difficult to undo. To allow a change to be made in the bylaws makes it much easier to implement, but it also makes it easier to undo. This can be of tremendous significance.

A perfect illustration of the point can be seen in the so-called exculpation provision.[40] Simplified, exculpation provisions allow the corporation to eliminate director liability for breach of the duty of care. Because such a decision is of enormous importance, and in order to protect shareholders from unilateral action by self-interested directors, it was decided that exculpation provisions would have to be adopted by charter amendment. Despite the procedural challenge, they were adopted very quickly, almost universally.[41] This appears to have been the correct outcome as there has been no widespread call for repeal. However, if it were ever decided that the policy of exculpation was a mistake, it would be almost impossible to repeal. This is because it would also require a charter amendment. As already mentioned, charter amendments require the consent of directors, and directors could not be expected to approve an increase in their exposure to liability very easily. By comparison, if exculpation policy were legally assigned to the bylaws, it would have been easier to implement, because directors could have adopted such a provision on their own, but also easier to repeal, because shareholders could remove it on their own. Thus, the costs and benefits of each approach must be weighed carefully. Decision theory is important to almost every aspect of corporate law: not only the who, but the what, where, and how, as well.

A different form of shareholder input is litigation; for example, when shareholders sue directors for breach of fiduciary duty. This type of input is also always costly. There are the obvious costs, such as attorney's fees and judicial resources expended, but also other costs, such as the time it takes away from directors, who should be focusing on managing the business, and the increased risk aversion that

[38] See Del. Code Ann. tit. 8, § 242(b) (2016).

[39] See Del. Code Ann. tit. 8, § 109(a) (2016).

[40] See Del. Code Ann. tit. 8, § 102(b)(7) (2016).

[41] See Edward Rock and Michael Wachter, 'Dangerous Liaisons: Corporate Law, Trust Law, and Interdoctrinal Legal Transplants' (2002) 96 Northwestern University Law Review 651, 659–60.

fear of liability would generate among directors. Because judicial review is most likely to entail diminishing returns, the goal should be to find the point at which the costs outweigh the benefits. The general approach of corporate law has been to allow litigation when courts are convinced that it may be necessary, but to shut it down early when it seems to be less promising.

One way to save on litigation costs is to eliminate litigation where possible. Consider a transaction in which one or more directors suffer from a conflict of interests. Judicial review is a possibility. However, it is necessary only to the extent that the conflict persists. If it were possible to eliminate the conflict, then the directors could be permitted to make the decision after all. Corporate law has concluded that there is a way to do that; decision-making authority can be transferred from conflicted directors to unconflicted directors.[42] To the extent that this is effective, confidence in business decisions can be restored and the need for judicial review can be eliminated.

In fact, however, the need for judicial review can only be reduced, not eliminated. There is doubt about whether unconflicted directors are truly independent because of the spectre of structural bias.[43] Structural bias is the theory, based on various notions including the psychological phenomenon of in-group bias, that unconflicted directors will nevertheless be biased in favour of their fellow directors over the interests of the shareholders.[44] Although structural bias theoretically could affect all directors' decisions, the courts seem to believe that the risk is greater in some situations than others. When courts believe that it is a substantial issue—for example, in derivative litigation and takeover situations–they cannot be as deferential as they can when they are convinced that directors are truly independent.[45] Judicial review is more necessary in the former situation than in the latter.

In weighing the costs and benefits of litigation, the concept of error costs must also be considered. What happens if the courts become involved, but they make a mistake? That possibility has to be factored into the analysis. There are two types of errors: false positives, when a problem is found even though none exists, and false negatives, when an existing problem is not found.[46] In the business context, false positives interfere with wealth creation because they limit the freedom of the decision experts without cause, while false negatives allow for shareholder abuse at the

[42] See, e.g., Del. Code Ann. tit. 8, § 141(a)(1) (2016) (approval by disinterested directors).

[43] See generally Julian Velasco, 'Structural Bias and the Need for Substantive Review' (2004) 82 Washington University Law Quarterly 821.

[44] Ibid. 856–65.

[45] See, e.g., *Unocal Corp. v Mesa Petroleum Co.*, 493 A.2d 946 (Del. 1985) (takeover defense); *Zapata Corp. v Maldonado*, 430 A.2d 779 (Del. 1981) (derivative litigation).

[46] See generally Lynn A. Stout, 'Type I Error, Type II Error, and the Private Securities Litigation Reform Act' (1996) 38 Arizona Law Review 711; Kenneth B. Davis, 'Judicial Review of Fiduciary Decisionmaking—Some Theoretical Perspectives' (1986) 80 Northwestern University Law Review 1.

hands of directors. Judicial review must be evaluated in terms of the likelihood and effects of false positives and false negatives.

When it comes to the substantive merits of business decisions, corporate law remains steadfastly agnostic.[47] The law has no way of determining what the 'correct' decision ever is, if indeed there even is such a thing. Because courts lack the competence to find any problems, the risk of false positives in judicial review of substance is great and the risk of false negatives is theoretically non-existent. As a result, courts defer to management to the greatest extent possible. Under the business judgment rule, the substance of a business decision will be upheld if it can be attributed to any rational business purpose.[48] This is the lowest level of scrutiny possible, and can be considered a policy of non-review.[49]

When it comes to the decision-making process, however, the law is slightly more adept. Although the business decision-making process needs to remain flexible, statutory law does provide for some minimal mandatory processes. However, because unconflicted directors are considered trustworthy as a general matter, there is little reason for the courts to interfere. The risk of false positives in judicial review of process is high because it is likely to be tainted by hindsight bias, while the risk of false negatives is low, as long as the directors have followed the minimal statutory requirements. Thus, when shareholders wish to challenge the decision-making process under the duty of care, courts remain deferential. In order to prevail, shareholders must establish that directors were not merely negligent but grossly negligent.[50] Most cases are easily dismissed at the pleading stage, thereby saving on unnecessary litigation costs. The wisdom of this approach is confirmed by the voluntary adoption of exculpation provisions by shareholders: shareholders appear to agree that the remedy of director liability is more harmful than the underlying problem of director breach of the duty of care.

However, the law realises that the cost-benefit analysis changes dramatically with respect to the duty of loyalty. Directors who have conflicts of interests cannot be trusted. In the face of such a conflict, the risk of false positives is slight, because conflicted judgment is inherently tainted, while the risk of false negatives is great, because it is often difficult to detect selfishness. Thus, when shareholders challenge director action for breach of the duty of loyalty, courts are no longer deferential. To

[47] *In re Caremark Int'l, Inc.* Deriv. Litig., 698 A.2d 959, 967 (Del. Ch. 1996) ('[C]ompliance with a director's duty of care can never appropriately be judicially determined by reference to the content of the board decision that leads to a corporate loss … That is, whether a judge or jury considering the matter after the fact, believes a decision substantively wrong, or degrees of wrong extending through 'stupid' to 'egregious' or 'irrational', provides no ground for director liability.').

[48] *Sinclair Oil Corp. v Levien*, 280 A.2d 717, 720 (Del. 1971).

[49] See Lyman Johnson, 'The Modest Business Judgment Rule' (2000) 55 Business Law 625, 632; Stephen M. Bainbridge, 'The Business Judgment Rule as Abstention Doctrine' (2004) 57 Vanderbilt Law Review 83.

[50] See *Aronson v Lewis*, 473 A.2d 805, 812 (Del. 1984).

the contrary, they require conflicted directors to prove that the transaction in question is entirely fair to the corporation and its shareholders.[51] This is considered a very demanding standard of review.[52]

Finally, there are situations that fall somewhere in between those duty of care and loyalty extremes; for example, when structural bias is an issue. In such cases, directors are not quite conflicted in the classical sense, but they are not entirely trustworthy, either.[53] Litigation costs remain high but the potential benefit of judicial review is more than marginal. With respect to this class of case, the risks of neither false negatives nor false positives can be dismissed as insignificant. In many such situations, the courts will employ an intermediate standard of review, such as reasonableness.[54] This allows the court to evaluate whether or not a case is likely to be meritorious.

D. Conclusion

Here is a reasonably nuanced account of Delaware corporate law. It has developed from the goal of maximising shareholder wealth, through an institutional choice analysis that prefers decision making by expert directors, to an understanding of how that principle may have to be limited by conflicts of interest analysis, and finally to a cost-benefit analysis to create more detailed rules about exactly who should get to make each decision and how. In each case, action must be taken with incomplete information. It cannot be known that these decisions are, in fact, the best decisions, but there is a framework for making decisions that seems best suited, in the long run, to lead to the maximisation of shareholder wealth.

Within this framework, directors remain free to make business decisions according to their best judgment. Judicial interference will occur only rarely, when the circumstances make confidence in directors' trustworthiness difficult. Otherwise, directors are not only free to reach almost any conclusion but they are also free to employ whatever decision-making tools and to adopt whatever theories of choice they think are best suited for the creation of wealth for their shareholders.

[51] For a discussion of the entire fairness test, see *Weinberger v UOP, Inc.*, 457 A.2d 701, 711 (Del. 1983) ('The concept of fairness has two basic aspects: fair dealing and fair price.').

[52] See *Kahn v M & F Worldwide Corp.*, 88 A.3d 635, 644 (Del. 2014) ('[E]ntire fairness is the highest standard of review in corporate law.').

[53] cf. *Zapata Corp. v Maldonado*, 402 A.2d 779, 787 (Del. 1981) ('[T]here is a sufficient risk in the realities of the situation ... to justify caution.'); *Unocal Corp. v Mesa Petroleum Co.*, 493 A.2d 946, 954 (Del. 1985) (Acknowledging 'the omnipresent specter that a board may be acting primarily in its own interests, rather than those of the corporation and its shareholders').

[54] See, e.g., *Unocal Corp.*, 493 A.2d at 954 (announcing two-part test invoking reasonableness).

II. Beyond Delaware Corporate Law

I indicated at the beginning of this chapter that I would eventually address the goals of corporate law. Not everyone agrees that the goal should be shareholder wealth maximisation. Many believe that the corporation is not a thing that is owned by shareholders but rather a joint effort by the various factors of production.[55] Even those who do believe that shareholders are owners might nevertheless believe that corporate law should not limit its concern to shareholders but should take others into consideration as well.[56] Views along these lines are even more common in Europe than in the United States. If the goal of corporate law is not a given, as I originally assumed, then everything may need to be re-evaluated. It may very well be the case that the specific rules would not change very much because of a convergence of means despite the divergence of ends. Nevertheless, it would seem appropriate to run through all of the foregoing analyses in order to determine the extent to which the various rules should change. However, this is not what I will do at this point.

A. Deciding on a Goal

Instead, I will consider how decision theory might be used to select a goal for corporate law. The staging point would be to select a higher-order goal to guide our discussion. This is no simple matter, but I will adopt the goal that I believe is least controversial in principle: let us assume that the higher-order goal is the maximisation of societal benefit. What next? It is not entirely clear. While the assumed goal may be uncontroversial, it is also not particularly helpful. One might be tempted to conclude that the goal of corporations should be to benefit everyone, rather than merely shareholders.[57] However, this does not necessarily follow.

It may be that shareholder wealth maximisation would be better for society than any alternative corporate goal. There are many reasons why this might be so. For example, societal welfare maximisation might be too amorphous for directors to implement effectively. After all, they are business experts, not welfare experts.[58] Based on institutional choice analysis, it might be wise to charge people with focusing on their area of expertise. Alternatively, or in addition, it may be that shareholder wealth is a good proxy for societal wealth. This could be because nearly

[55] See., e.g., Margaret M. Blair and Lynn A. Stout, 'A Team Production Theory of Corporate Law' (1999) 85 Virginia Law Review 247.

[56] See, e.g., Edwin Merrick Dodd, Jr., 'For Whom Are Corporate Managers Trustees?' (1932) 45 Harvard Law Review 1145.

[57] See, e.g., Kent Greenfield, 'New Principles for Corporate Law' (2005) 1 Hastings Business Law Journal 87.

[58] See David L. Engel, 'An Approach to Corporate Social Responsibility' (1979) 32 Stanford Law Review 1, 30.

everyone is a shareholder and therefore benefits from the corporation's wealth creation;[59] or it could be because shareholders, as residual risk bearers, have the best incentives to maximise wealth.[60]

In fairness, it is also worth noting that shareholder ownership does not necessarily lead to the goal of shareholder wealth maximisation, either. This is because shareholders also have interests other than wealth creation.[61] While it makes sense that business corporations should focus on wealth creation, it is not necessarily the case that they should focus on wealth *maximisation*. Shareholders want to maximise their overall welfare; they do not necessarily want to maximise their wealth at the expense of their other interests.[62] For example, they might not want to create wealth illegally or immorally, and they might not want to destroy the planet in order to maximise wealth. Thus, it is possible to get to a society-friendly corporate law even with the assumption of shareholder ownership.

My point is not to demonstrate the validity of any of these claims. Rather, it is to point out that if the goal of corporate law is changed, there must be serious analysis in order to arrive at appropriate implementing decisions.

In fact, there seems to be a strong desire for something more other-regarding in at least some corners of the American economy. And this has led to the creation of a new type of business entity—one known as the benefit corporation. The benefit corporation adds to the options available to those who would start a business.

B. Various Forms of Business Organisation

The corporation is only one type of business organisation. It is particularly well-suited to large, public businesses. But there is another type of business that predates the corporation. It is the partnership. A partnership is 'an association of

[59] cf. Adolf A. Berle, Jr., 'For Whom Corporate Managers Are Trustees: A Note' (1932) 45 Harvard Law Review 1365, 1367–68

[60] See Frank H. Easterbrook and Daniel R. Fischel, 'Voting in Corporate Law' (1983) 26 Journal of Law & Economics 395, 403–06.

[61] See Lisa M. Fairfax, 'Making the Corporation Safe for Shareholder Democracy' (2008) 69 Ohio State Law Journal 53, 84–85 ('[O]f course, there exist shareholders who invest with an eye towards advancing social concerns. These so-called "social investors" include faith-based organizations, pension funds, and socially responsible investor funds. Such shareholders clearly have an interest in issues beyond financial matters.'); Lynn Stout, *The Shareholder Value Myth: How Putting Shareholders First Harms Investors, Corporations, and the Public* (Berrett-Koehler Publishers 2012) 97–98 ('There is no reason to think investors are less prosocial than others… [O]ne survey has reported that 97 percent of shareholders agree that corporate managers should take some account of nonshareholders' interests in running firms.').

[62] cf. Daniel J. H. Greenwood, 'Fictional Shareholders: For Whom Are Corporate Managers Trustees, Revisited' (1996) 69 Southern California Law Review 1021 (discussing how the interests of fictional profit-maximising shareholders can vary greatly from those of actual people who own shares).

two or more persons to carry on as co-owners a business for profit'.[63] Unlike a public corporation, where dispersed shareholders are unable to run the business effectively and therefore turn to expert managers, partners generally know each other and work together to run the business. An entirely different set of rules applies in that situation, one in which the owners themselves are the managers.[64] Partnerships tend to raise different issues than corporations, focusing more heavily on issues of agreement than the agency problem. However, the differences between partnerships and corporations are by no means absolute. In fact, large partnerships can resemble corporations, and small corporations can resemble partnerships. Because the law of business organisations tends to utilise enabling law, with default rules that can be changed by the parties, investors can make partnerships legally resemble corporations and corporations legally resemble partnerships, at least to some degree.

In fact, business's demand for flexibility has led to a proliferation of business forms. The most well-known is the limited liability company ('LLC'). The LLC is the culmination of legal flexibility for business organisations. The single most important thing to know about LLCs is that they are almost entirely creatures of contract, such that investors can do almost whatever they want in terms of governance.[65] They can make the business operate as much like a partnership or corporation as they choose, or very different from either.

This raises the question: how should investors decide which form to use for any given business? For the most part, the law has decided to allow the investors to decide for themselves. A small group is free to incorporate, and a larger group is allowed to take the partnership form (at least up to a point), and anyone is free to organise a limited liability company.

With so much flexibility, it might seem that there is nothing left for law to do, and yet that was not the case. Forms continued to proliferate. One reason this was necessary is because all of the forms of business organisation discussed so far seem to assume the goal of wealth maximisation. Even if not strictly required by any of the forms, it was a strong presumption that was virtually impossible to overcome. Some investors wanted a form of business organisation where that presumption would be eliminated from the start. This gave rise to the benefit corporation.[66]

[63] Unif. P'ship Act § 6(1) (Unif. Law Comm'n 1997) [hereinafter UPA]; Rev. Unif. P'ship Act § 101(6) (Unif. Law Comm'n 1997) [hereinafter RUPA].

[64] UPA § 18(e); RUPA § 401(f).

[65] cf. Del. Code Ann. tit. 6, § 18-1101(b) (2016) ('It is the policy of this chapter to give the maximum effect to the principle of freedom of contract and to the enforceability of limited liability company agreements.').

[66] See Frederick H. Alexander, 'The Public Benefit Corporation Guidebook: understanding and optimizing Delaware's benefit corporation governance model', Ch. 2, Part I, at 20–21 (updated 7 October 2017), http://www.mnat.com/epublications/the-public-benefit-corporation-guidebook/.

C. Benefit Corporations

The benefit corporation is a business that is organised with a dual purpose: directors are charged with pursuing not only the interests of shareholders but also one or more societal benefits specified in the charter.[67] Wealth creation remains a goal, but not wealth maximisation; the directors must explicitly seek to balance these competing interests.

The benefit corporation is relatively new. It will be interesting to see how the law will develop and how popular the form will be. One can imagine some benefit corporations being run like non-profit entities, and others being run like an ordinary business corporation. The courts will have to determine what the limits on either end of the spectrum might be. If I might venture a guess, I see the benefit corporation as establishing a 'good citizen corporation': it is still a business corporation seeking wealth for its investors, but its directors are freed from the demands of the wealth maximisation principle in order to allow them to balance the other interests of the shareholders. Under this view, the goal should be understood to be the maximisation of shareholder interests, explicitly acknowledged to include the other specified purpose(s), rather than the maximisation of societal interests, with a slight preference for shareholders.

In any event, it is clear that the law has decided to give shareholders plenty of choices for the organisation of their businesses. And how are shareholders to decide among the various forms for a new business? That is itself a business decision. It is a question that could be resolved with reference to decision theory, provided there is an agreed-upon goal to guide the decision. Decision-making tools do not automatically provide universal answers. They must be applied to the facts and circumstances at hand and require judgment on the part of the decision maker. But the fact that the law leaves it to investors demonstrates that it does not consider itself to be the appropriate decision maker. Investors are free to make their own decisions according to their own preferences and utilising whatever theories of choice they consider appropriate.

III. Conclusion

I began this chapter by suggesting that that it is not always necessary to select a theory of choice; that it is possible to deal productively with the subject matter of choosing and making decisions without actually settling upon any particular theory. My thesis was that the law of business organisations does not settle upon any particular theory of choice because the law does not consider itself the ultimate

[67] See, e.g., Model Benefit Corporation Legislation § 201 (2014), http://benefitcorp.net/sites/default/files/documents/Model_Benefit_Corp_Legislation.pdf.

decision maker. Rather, it develops rules to allocate decision-making authority among various parties. Throughout the chapter, I walked through how the law uses a few basic principles of decision theory to create a structure for allocating decision-making responsibility on many different levels. However, the law leaves the ultimate decision makers free not only to make substantive decisions for themselves, but also to select from among the various theories of choice for doing so.

11

Institutional Investor Voting Behaviour

A Network Theory Perspective

Luca Enriques and Alessandro Romano[1]

Abstract: This chapter shows how network theory can improve our understanding of institutional investors' voting behaviour and, more generally, their role in corporate governance. The standard idea is that institutional investors compete against each other on relative performance and hence might not cast informed votes, due to rational apathy and rational reticence. In other words, institutional investors have incentives to free-ride instead of 'cooperating' and casting informed votes. We show that connections of various kinds among institutional investors, whether from formal networks, geographical proximity, or common ownership, and among institutional investors and other agents, such as proxy advisors, contribute to shaping institutional investors' incentives to vote 'actively'. They also create intricate competition dynamics: competition takes place not only among institutional investors (and their asset managers) but also at the level of their employees and among 'cliques' of institutional investors. Employees, who strive for better jobs, are motivated to obtain more information on portfolio companies than may be strictly justified from their employer institution's perspective, and to circulate it within their network. Cliques of institutional investors compete against each other. Because there are good reasons to believe that cliques of co-operators outperform cliques of non-cooperators, the network-level competition might increase the incentives of institutional investors to collect information. These dynamics can enhance institutional investors' engagement in portfolio companies and also shed light on some current policy issues such as the antitrust effects of common ownership and mandatory disclosures of institutional investors' voting.

[1] We wish to thank Carlo Drago, Ronald Gilson, Martin Gelter, Matteo Godi, Henry Hansmann, Alvin Klevorick, Karina Litvack, John Morley, Roberto Pardolesi, Ed Rock, Roberta Romano, Michael Schouten, Anna Tilba, Luigi Zingales, participants of workshops at the China University of Political Science and Law, the European University Institute, the Laboratoire d'Excellence Régulation Financière, NYU Law School, and the University of Oxford, and especially Ryan Bubb, for helpful comments and discussions. Usual disclaimers apply. A longer version of this article has previously been published in the University of Illinois Law Review (2019) and is reprinted in this volume with its permission.

Luca Enriques and Alessandro Romano, *Institutional Investor Voting Behaviour* In: *Theories of Choice*.
Edited by: Stefan Grundmann and Philipp Hacker, Oxford University Press (2021).
DOI: 10.1093/oso/9780198863175.003.0012

I. Introduction

How can we predict whether singers will be rewarded with a standing ovation at the end of their opera performance? The problem can be framed as a binary choice of the audience members between standing up and applauding and remaining seated. By standing or sitting, members of the audience can send a binary signal (positive or not-so-positive) that reveals members' preferences. According to standard economic theory,[2] to predict whether a standing ovation is triggered one ought to investigate the preferences of the individuals composing the audience and assess the quality of the opera. What is known in the network theory literature as the Standing Ovation Problem suggests that this approach is inadequate. Predicting the behaviour of interconnected agents requires accounting for patterns of connections among them.[3] In other words, the networks linking audience members one to the other and to other agents are key to whether they will stand or sit, a basic intuition that can be extended to analyse a number of social settings.

This chapter is the first legal analysis that builds on this intuition and uses the tools of network theory to explain the incentives and behaviour of one of the key players in today's corporate governance, namely institutional investors (hereinafter also institutions). More specifically, we show that network theory can help us to understand how institutional investors determine whether to vote with or against management.

Pension funds, mutual funds, banks' trust departments, hedge funds, and insurance companies are today the predominant holders of shares in U.S. (and non-U.S.) listed companies.[4] Whether they stay passive or actively use their governance rights to influence portfolio companies' strategies can make an enormous difference to the prospects of capitalism in the United States and elsewhere. This is why legal scholars and financial economists have since long enquired into how such players behave, and can be expected to behave, *qua* shareholders.[5] We argue that

[2] For a clear formulation of this standard view, see, e.g., Geoffrey Brennan and Gordon Tullock, 'An Economic Theory of Military Tactics: Methodological Individualism at War' (1982) 2 Journal of Economic Behavior & Organisation 225, 225 ('Two aspects of economic method are relevant here. The first is the individualistic perspective ... [T]he ultimate unit of analysis is always the individual; more aggregative analysis must be regarded as only provisionally legitimate.'). For a critique, see Alessandro Romano, 'Micro-Meso-Macro Comparative Law: An Essay on the Methodology of Comparative Law' (2016) 17 Chicago Kent Journal of International & Comparative Law 1, 5–7 To be sure, economic theory has long recognised the importance of patterns of interconnections among economic agents and firms. See, e.g., Daron Acemoglu et al., 'Systemic Risk and Stability in Financial Networks' (2015) 105 American Economics Review 564, 564. In rare cases, also legal scholars have attempted to account for patterns of interconnections in their works. See, e.g., Alan Schwartz and Robert E. Scott, 'Third-Party Beneficiaries and Contractual Networks' (2015) 7 Journal of Legal Analysis 325.

[3] For a brief introduction to the Standing Ovation Problem, see John H. Miller and Scott E. Page, 'The Standing Ovation Problem' (2004) 9.5 Complexity 8.

[4] See, e.g., Jan Fichtner et al., 'Hidden Power of the Big Three? Passive Index Funds, Re-Concentration of Corporate Ownership, and New Financial Risk' (2017) 19.2 Business & Politics 298, 298, 302–06.

[5] See section III.

the traditional atomistic focus on the incentives of *individual* institutional investors is inadequate to understand institutional investors' role in corporate governance. Like ties between audience members at the end of an opera, institutions' and their agents' interconnectedness is a key factor in shaping institutions' behaviour vis-à-vis their portfolio companies and, more specifically, their voting decisions.

To give a better sense of how interconnections influence behaviour, let us exploit the standing ovation analogy further.[6] First, consider the case of someone who has never seen an opera before and is in the company of acquaintances that are renowned opera experts. She might decide to stand even if she has not enjoyed the show: if the experts signal their appreciation of the show by standing, it is unlikely that she will remain seated at the risk of revealing her ignorance. That immediately shows that an individual's taste is not the only factor affecting her behaviour: personal ties as well as the tastes of the individuals one is connected to can influence one's decision on whether to stand or to sit. As connections among audience members can determine the outcome, so connections of various kinds among institutional investors can lead to different voting decisions than they would reach independently of others: think of personal links among different institutions' corporate governance teams due to affiliation to the same industry body, social club, and so on.

Second, the decision to stand might be affected by the personal ties that members of the audience have with the artists or the organisers: the fiancé of the soprano is most likely to stand no matter what, in the hope of triggering the standing ovation. Hence, not only ties with other members of the audience are relevant but also connections with other agents. As audience members' connections with artists and organisers can trigger a standing ovation, so institutions' connections and business relationships with portfolio firms, and even the mere prospect thereof, can prompt a pro-management vote.[7]

Third, when deciding whether to stand, one might take information gathered before the opera into account. Reading an article by a worldwide famous critic stating that the opera is a disgrace might induce an agent without strong preferences to sit in order to signal that his tastes are as sophisticated as the critic's. Similar to how critics' reviews can influence audience members, so can proxy advisors and activist hedge funds, in different ways, affect institutions' voting decisions.[8]

Fourth, an individual who does not have a strong opinion about the opera will be more likely to stand if she observes that many people are sending the signal 'stand'. From this perspective, where the individual is sitting becomes important, because

[6] As Miller and Page note, the Standing Ovation Problem is in fact an apt metaphor for situations in which interconnected agents make binary decisions. Miller and Page (n 3) 9.

[7] See, e.g., Rasha Ashraf et al., 'Do Pension-Related Business Ties Influence Mutual Fund Proxy Voting? Evidence from Shareholder Proposals on Executive Compensation' (2012) 47.3 Journal of Financial & Quantitative Analysis 567, 568; Dragana Cvijanović et al., 'Ties That Bind: How Business Connections Affect Mutual Fund Activism' (2016) 71.6 Journal of Finance 2933, 2934.

[8] See note 80–81 and accompanying text.

it determines whose signals she can observe (and who can observe her signal). If she is sitting in the last row, she will be able to observe the signal sent by all the other crowd members, but at the same time hardly anyone will notice her signal. On the other hand, if she is sitting in the first row, all the audience members that are sitting in the rows behind her will observe her signal, whereas she cannot observe the signal of others without turning around to face the rear of the opera house. In a similar fashion, the geographical distribution of institutional investors, whether decentralised or clustered in a given area, can affect their voting behaviour.[9]

Finally, whether a standing ovation is triggered depends on the opera house architecture.[10] For instance, if there are boxes, some members of the audience will be able to observe everyone else's signal while not being as easily observed by those in the stalls. The structure of the opera house can be seen as analogous to the institutional framework: rules that prohibit coordination or make it more expensive will affect the outcome.

The Standing Ovation Problem also sheds light on an important but often overlooked property of social systems, namely that sometimes the tail (of a distribution) can wag the dog.[11] Say, for instance, that the *average* perception of the opera's quality is not high enough to justify a standing ovation. Despite that, a standing ovation can still be triggered, provided that several well-connected members of the audience send a 'stand' signal that is visible by many. In this vein, to increase the likelihood of a standing ovation at the end of the opera, self-confident organisers might assign front row seats to renowned experts who are likely to appreciate the show.

To summarise, we argue that the voting behaviour of institutional investors is affected by their connections with other institutional investors and more generally with the agents that populate their networks (e.g., proxy advisors, portfolio companies' management, etc.). Our approach to institutional investors' role in corporate governance builds upon a rich body of literature as social scientists have long recognised that the actions of agents are shaped by their connections with other agents, by these other agents' connections, and so on.[12] This chapter is grounded on the intuition that this is true also for institutional investors, an intuition that recent empirical studies corroborate.[13] Thus, network theory becomes a natural framework for the study of institutional investors' voting behaviour.

[9] cf. Harrison Hong et al., 'Thy Neighbor's Portfolio: Word-of-Mouth Effects in the Holdings and Trades of Money Managers' (December 2005) 60.6 Journal of Finance 2801, 2802; Veronika K. Pool et al., 'The People in Your Neighborhood: Social Interactions and Mutual Fund Portfolios' (2015) 70 Journal of Finance 2679, 2679. See Section IV.C for a more detailed discussion of the relationship between the geographical location of institutional investors and their voting behaviour.

[10] There are of course many other factors that should be considered, such as theatre lights, but for our purposes, it is superfluous even to mention them.

[11] See Miller and Page (n 3) 9.

[12] See Cvijanović (n 7) 2934; see also Hong et al. (n 9) 2802; Miller (n 3); Pool et al. (n 9) 2679.

[13] See Alan D. Crane et al., 'Institutional Investor Cliques and Governance' (2019) 133.1 Journal of Financial Economics 175; Pool et al. (n 9).

Network theory is a lively area of research that lies at the intersection of many disciplines, including economics, physics, biology, sociology, and computer science. It has helped to shed light on a wide range of very diverse phenomena such as criminal and terrorist organisations,[14] professional communities,[15] predator–prey interactions,[16] and the diffusion of epidemics and sexually transmitted diseases.[17] In the area of corporate governance and financial regulation, network theory has already been used, for example, to understand the diffusion of poison pills[18] and golden parachutes,[19] and to analyse the effects of Security and Exchange Commission ('SEC') sanctions.[20]

Generally, network theory addresses three main questions: what is the architecture of connections among a given set of players? Why has that architecture emerged? What are the effects of the observed pattern of connections?[21] In this chapter, we focus mainly on the last question. More precisely, we show how network theory may help us to understand some of the dynamics that reduce institutional shareholders passivity.

Section II sets the scene by sketching out the function of shareholder voting and how information and coordination costs may be in the way of ensuring that shareholders make the 'right' decisions for the corporation. Next, section III looks into the phenomenon of voting by the predominant users of voting rights in today's corporations, namely institutional investors. We briefly review some widely explored solutions to collective action problems affecting institutions' propensity to cast informed votes.

In section IV, which is the core of the chapter, we use network theory to frame institutional shareholders' voting behaviour in U.S. corporations[22] and to identify

[14] See, e.g., Valdis E. Krebs, 'Mapping Networks of Terrorist Cells' (2002) 24.3 Connections 43 (2002); Matthew J. Salganik and Douglas D. Heckathorn, 'Sampling and Estimation in Hidden Populations Using Respondent-Driven Sampling' (December 2004) 34.1 Sociologial Methodology 193 (studying networks of criminals).

[15] See, e.g., James Coleman et al., 'The Diffusion of an Innovation Among Physicians' (1957) 20.4 Sociometry 253 (studying networks of physicians).

[16] See, e.g., Neo D. Martinez, 'Constant Connectance in Community Food Webs' (1992) 139.6 American Naturalist 1208.

[17] See, e.g., Sunetra Gupta et al., 'Networks of Sexual Contacts: Implications for the Pattern of Spread of HIV' (December 1989) 3.12 AIDS 807; Alden S. Klovdahl et al., 'Social Networks and Infectious Disease: The Colorado Springs Study' (1994) 38 Social Sciences & Medicine 79.

[18] Gerald F. Davis, 'Agents Without Principles? The Spread of the Poison Pill Through the Intercorporate Network' (1991) 36.4 Administrative Science Quarterly 583, 591.

[19] Gerald F. Davis and Henrich R. Greve, 'Corporate Elite Networks and Governance Changes in the 1980s' (1997) 103.1 American Journal of Sociology 1, 1.

[20] Eugene Kang, 'Director Interlocks and Spillover Effects of Reputational Penalties from Financial Reporting Fraud' (2008) 51.3 Academy Management Journal 537, 537.

[21] Sanjeev Goyal, *Connections: An Introduction to the Economics of Networks* (Princeton University Press 2012) 1.

[22] Importantly, the specific analysis presented here (as opposed to the theoretical framework) is not necessarily valid beyond the United States. Just like an ecological network is subject to constraints and laws of interactions, the regulatory framework in which the agents operate shapes the network in which institutional investors are embedded. Thus, different laws and different social norms can produce different network dynamics.

additional ways by which institutions can address collective action problems and resolve the trade-off between minimising the costs of becoming informed and independent decision making. To do this, we highlight the fact that institutional investors are embedded in a network formed by various agents, while also being connected with each other through a complex web of formal, geographical, and co-ownership ties. We also show how these connections affect institutional investors' incentives and ultimately their voting behaviour. Competitive dynamics exist not only among institutional investors but also at a lower level among employees of institutional investors competing for better jobs, and at a higher level among groups, and more precisely cliques,[23] of institutional investors competing to outperform each other. The dynamics at the higher and lower level can enhance (or hinder) the level of institutional investor engagement.[24]

Importantly, as our summary conclusion (section V) reiterates, this is an exploratory study. It remains predominantly positive and descriptive, and we do not strive to understand every nuance of the network in which institutional investors are embedded. This network is immensely complex, populated as it is by a vast array of different actors with different characteristics and incentives. Uncovering all its facets and dynamics would be for a much more ambitious and longer-term research project. Our purpose is more modest: to open a window on a promising way to frame a core corporate governance issue and suggest that scholars and policy makers abandon the atomistic focus on individual institutional investors, to which most of them have been clinging for decades.

II. Setting the Scene: Corporate Governance and Informed Voting

One of the main goals of corporate governance and corporate law is to maximise the benefits of two of a corporation's core features: delegation of management and investor ownership.[25] Delegated management allows for decisions to be taken by specialised agents who may not have the financial means to own the company.[26] Investor (or shareholder) ownership ensures that a relatively homogenous category of stakeholders has ultimate control over the company.[27]

Reaching that goal, in turn, implies minimising the agency costs arising from management delegation as well as the costs of having investors (shareholders)

[23] For a formal definition of cliques see note 107 and accompanying text.

[24] For a discussion of the policy implications of our analysis see Luca Enriques and Alessandro Romano, 'Institutional Investor Voting Behavior: A Network Theory Perspective' (2019) 1 University of Illinois Law Review, 223, 261–67.

[25] See, e.g., John Armour et al., 'Agency Problems and Legal Strategies' in Reinier H. Kraakman et al. (eds.), *The Anatomy of Corporate Law* (3rd edn, Oxford University Press 2017) 29, 29–31.

[26] See, e.g., Robert C. Clark, *Corporate Law* (Little, Brown 1986) 23.

[27]. See, e.g., Henry Hansmann, *The Ownership of Enterprise* 62–63 (Harvard University Press 1996).

exercise their prerogatives as owners.[28] Agency costs arise from directors' and managers' conflicts of interest, misaligned incentives, and biases or incompetence. The costs of shareholder engagement stem from the need to circulate information to shareholders (and therefore the public at large) and to have them process it despite their collective action problems, their necessarily lower degree of company-specific knowledge, and, often, their conflicts of interest.[29] We dub these 'voting costs' because throughout the chapter we focus mainly on shareholder voting as an essential and recurrent form of shareholder engagement.

Shareholder voting is justified for matters that would give rise to higher delegation costs if left to boards or managers. Intuitively, that will be the case for matters in which the interests of managers and shareholders inherently conflict or may lead to shareholder disenfranchisement, such as when it comes to the selection of board members. In addition, there can be matters whose impact on the company's value may be evaluated better by a large number of detached, unbiased shareholders than by managers, who may have more access to hard-to-convey or commercially sensitive private information but who at the same time are more likely to be prone to confirmation bias, hyperopia, and echo-chamber phenomena.[30]

When publicly available information is not skewed or misleading, and shareholders can use it in a decision-making process similar to the one they use to decide whether to invest in a given stock, their collective decision making via voting can lead to better outcomes than a board's decision. That is an application of Condorcet's jury theorem ('CJT'), according to which, so long as each individual in a group has a higher than 50% chance of being right, the probability that a decision taken by a majority of that group is right approaches 1 as the number of group members tends to infinity.[31]

The CJT works on a few assumptions: voters need to be informed, rational (able to reach the logical conclusion on how to vote based on the information they have), and sincere.[32] Moreover, the ability of the group to make the right decision depends on whether its members vote independently one from the other.[33] This

[28] See John Armour et al., 'The Basic Governance Structure: The Interests of Shareholders as a Class' in Kraakman et al. (eds.) (n 25) 49.

[29] Zohar Goshen and Richard Squire, 'A New Theory for Corporate Law and Governance' (2017) 117.3 Colum. L. Rev. 767, 793. Nowadays, the out-of-pocket expenses and the opportunity costs of casting votes at a shareholder meeting have become trivial thanks to the use of information and communication technology. Robert B. Thompson and Paul H. Edelman, 'Corporate Voting' (2009) 62 Vanderbilt Law Review 129, 153.

[30] See, e.g., Thompson and Edelman (n 29) 149–50; see also Luca Enriques et al., 'The Case for an Unbiased Takeover Law (with an Application to the European Union)' (2014) 4.1 Harvard Business Law Review 85, 94.

[31] See, e.g., David Austen-Smith and Jeffrey S. Banks, 'Information Aggregation, Rationality, and the Condorcet Jury Theorem' (1996) 90.1 American Political Science Review 34, 34.

[32] See, e.g., Michael C. Schouten, 'The Mechanisms of Voting Efficiency' (2010) 3 Columbia Business Law Review 763, 773.

[33] Ibid. More precisely, the probability of making the correct choice does not approach one when the group size tends to infinity if the votes are not independent. See Shmuel Nitzan and Jacob Paroush, 'Collective Decision Making and Jury Theorems' in Francesco Parisi (ed.), *Oxford Handbook of Law and Economics*, vol. 1, 494, 503–04 (2017 Oxford University Press).

condition only rarely holds in real life, as in most cases there are pre-voting communications among group members.[34] In itself, this fact alone does not impair the applicability of the CJT because groups outperform individuals even when there is strong dependence among voters.[35] However, it is important at this stage to remark that the effect of this pre-voting information flow is twofold. On the one hand, it increases the competencies of the group members and improves their information set.[36] On the other hand, pre-voting communication decreases the probability that the group comes to the right decision due to psychological factors that reduce the independence of group members' votes.[37]

Intuitively, mechanisms that reduce voting costs are an important component of an effective corporate governance system. Chief among voting costs is the cost of becoming informed, that is, of acquiring, processing, and assessing the implications of relevant information.[38] Such costs are borne by each shareholder, but the benefits of their informed voting accrue to all pro rata. That creates a collective action problem: absent some form of coordination, each shareholder will have an incentive to free-ride on other shareholders' investment in information. And assuming free-riding away for a moment, it is easy to see that, with thousands of shareholders in a listed corporation, if each of them becomes informed independently of others, the multiplication of individual efforts will lead to a waste of resources. In this case as well, the only alternative is some form of coordination.

Yet if shareholders coordinate in the process of gathering and assessing information, the outcome will be a loss in voters' independence. As we have seen, that might reduce the ability of the group to make the right choice.[39] There can thus be a trade-off between the goal of overcoming collective action problems and minimising information gathering and processing costs, on the one hand, and independent decision making on the other: if information is gathered and processed by one on behalf of all, let alone when the decision itself on how to vote is delegated, formally or informally, to one individual or a small group, then information costs are minimised, but the advantage from having a large number of scattered shareholders making the decision may vanish.

[34] See Sven Berg, 'Condorcet's Jury Theorem Revisited' (1993) 9.3 European Journal of Political Economy 437, 445.

[35] Ibid. 438–39. More generally, to iterate, the CJT is subject to a number of caveats. For instance, it is generally postulated that the members of the group have the same competences (i.e., the same probability of being right). If this hypothesis is relaxed, it can happen that the best members of the group outperform the group as a whole, or even that increasing the size of the group reduces accuracy. Nitzan and Paroush (n 33) 496–97. The most relevant point, however, is that the group still outperforms the average member of the group. Note also that even when the competences of group members are heterogeneous, the accuracy of the group tends to one when the size of the group tends to infinity. Ibid. 496.

[36] Nitzan and Paroush (n 33) 503–04.

[37] Ibid. 503.

[38] Thompson and Edelman (n 29) 172.

[39] In fact, even if groups remain superior to individual decision makers when the votes are not independent, positive correlation of the votes does reduce group accuracy. See Berg (n 34) 444.

An additional, often overlooked factor is that the CJT considers the information set of the individuals as exogenous.[40] However, individuals have less incentive to collect information when the size of the group is large.[41] In other words, there is also a trade-off between group size and agents' information:[42] in larger groups it is possible to aggregate information independently collected by more individuals, which increases the likelihood that the group reaches the correct decisions. Other things being equal, though, members of larger groups have less incentive to collect information, thus reducing the likelihood that the group reaches the correct decision. There are therefore complex interactions between information, coordination, and duplication costs, on the one hand, and the number and kind of agents involved in a decision and the amount of information that they produce and process, on the other. These interactions are mediated by pre-voting communications and, clearly, by the channels through which information flows. The rest of this chapter aims to cast new light on how pre-voting communications and the channels through which information can flow affect these trade-offs in the context of shareholder voting. In particular, we focus on the incentives of institutional investors to 'improve' their information set (i.e., to gather information in order to cast an informed vote). By applying network theory to the voting dynamics of institutional investors, we show that the patterns of connections among institutional investors and between institutional investors and other agents populating their network have a significant impact on these trade-offs and ultimately on institutional investors' voting behaviour.

III. Explaining Voting by Institutional Investors: The Atomistic Approach

Corporate voting only makes sense if shareholders can be expected to vote on an informed basis, that is, having gathered the information that is necessary to make a decision about whether approval of a given shareholder meeting proposal will increase the value of the company. If this condition is unfulfilled, there is no reason to expect that the majority of shareholders will get it right any more than if a coin were flipped. Yet it is far from obvious that shareholders in a corporation have sufficient incentives to cast informed votes. In fact, what went on for decades at U.S. companies was that shareholders, whether individuals or institutions, overwhelmingly voted with management or did not bother voting at all.[43] Such 'shareholder passivity'[44] was informed by rational apathy. Becoming informed on how to vote was

[40] Bryan C. McCannon and Paul Walker, 'Endogenous Competence and a Limit to the Condorcet Jury Theorum' (2016) 169.1 Public Choice 1, 1.
[41] Ibid.
[42] Ibid.
[43] See, e.g., Clark (n 26) 94.
[44] Ibid.

(and is) costly; with ownership widely dispersed, the likelihood of one's vote being pivotal was extremely low, and the benefits from successfully casting an informed vote would be shared pro rata with all other shareholders. It was therefore rational to do nothing or, if anything at all was done, to vote with managers.[45]

Formally, rational apathy can be explained as follows: to cast an informed vote, a shareholder *A* holding a fraction of shares w_i in company *i* has to bear a cost c_i to acquire, process, and evaluate all the relevant information. Whoever casts an informed vote does so because she expects thereby to increase the value of the portfolio she holds in that company. Let b_i denote the aggregate expected benefits (the increase in market capitalisation) of an informed vote.[46] If $c_i > w_i b_i$, then *A* will not collect information. Instead, when $c_i < w_i b_i$, then *A* would be inclined to become informed and obtain an expected pay-off of $w_i b_i - c_i > 0$.[47]

With the increased concentration of ownership in the hands of institutional investors that has taken place in the last sixty years,[48] incentives would seem to act against informed voting even more than in the past. That is because institutional investors compete on *relative* performance,[49] in other words on how well they do compared to their competitors: incurring costs to improve performance at a portfolio company will worsen an individual institutional investor's performance compared to others' performance.[50] In our previous illustration, institution *A* might decide not to invest in information even when $c_i < b_i w_i$, so long as its competitors, such as institutional investors *B* and *C*, hold a $c_i < b_i w_i$ comparable (or, for simplicity, the exact same) percentage of shares in company *i*. In fact, *B* and *C*'s pay-off would equal $w_i b_i$. If *A* decides to invest in information, *B* and *C* would gain a competitive advantage over *A*, in the form of a higher return on its investment in *i*, because $c_i > 0$. That is what Gilson and Gordon call rational reticence.[51] Clearly, stakes are not always similar across institutional investors, and when an institutional investor holds a disproportionally large *w* compared to its peers, rational

[45] See, e.g., Edward B. Rock, 'The Logic and (Uncertain) Significance of Institutional Investor Activism' (1991) 79 Georgetown Law Journal 445, 453–57.

[46] Note that a shareholder can expect her vote to increase the value of a company (i.e., $bi > 0$) only when it is pivotal, i.e., when it affects the voting outcome. For instance, assume that *A* is against a given management proposal, but knows for certain that the proposal will be passed despite her opposition. In that case, the benefit of casting an informed vote is 0. The same is true if it is certain that the management proposal will be rejected even without *A*'s opposition. In other words, the lower the likelihood of being pivotal, the lower the incentives to become informed and cast one's vote.

[47] Most recently, see, e.g., Lucian A. Bebchuk et al., 'The Agency Problems of Institutional Investors' (Summer 2017) 31.3 Journal of Economic Perspectives 89, 95–96.

[48] See, e.g., Bebchuk et al. (n 47) 91–93.

[49] See Ronald J. Gilson and Jeffrey N. Gordon, 'The Agency Costs of Agency Capitalism: Activist Investors and the Revaluation of Governance Rights' (2013) 113.4 Columbia Law Review 889–90.

[50] Ibid. 889–95. See also Rock (n 45) 473–75. For the sake of simplicity, we assume here that the institutional investor can charge higher fees such that its clients bear the full amount of c_i.

[51] See Gilson and Gordon (n 49) 867.

reticence is less likely.[52] Despite this, rational reticence remains crucial, especially in light of the unrelenting trend towards passive (indexed) investment.[53] In fact, all passive institutional investors do not overweigh their investment in specific stocks but rather replicate indexes like all their peers and almost exclusively compete on reducing costs.[54]

Despite this gloomy theoretical picture, in the last three decades things seem to have moved away considerably from the rational apathy/reticence model of shareholder passivity. Nowadays, voting turnout at U.S. companies shareholder meetings is high[55] and shareholders are far less inclined to rubber-stamp managers' proposals than in the past.[56]

What happened? Changes in ownership patterns, the emergence of new information intermediaries such as proxy advisors and activist hedge funds, political pressures, and regulatory initiatives have all contributed to the outcome.[57]

Ownership is much more concentrated in the hands of institutions, as opposed to individuals, than in the prototypical Berle and Means corporation.[58] But is a larger average w sufficient to explain the increase in informed voting that we observe? Even ignoring rational reticence for a moment, a higher average w does imply a higher likelihood of being pivotal and a larger benefit for the individual institution, yet most of the benefits accrue to an institutional investor's beneficial owners/clients, not to those, be they its employees or an external asset manager, in charge of making the voting decisions. For instance, in the case of separation between asset owners and managers, only a small fraction of the benefits will go, in the form of higher asset under management-based fees, to the asset managers themselves.[59] In addition, asset managers will also bear any share of the costs that they are unable to transfer on owners or clients in the form of higher fees.[60]

Nevertheless, size alone might still help to explain part of the behaviour of the largest institutional investors, such as BlackRock, Vanguard, American Funds, and State Street, who tend to develop autonomous voting policies and not to follow

[52] See, e.g., Peter Iliev and Michelle Lowry, 'Are Mutual Funds Active Voters?' (2015) 28 Review of Finance Studies 446, 447. See also Bernard S. Black and John C. Coffee Jr, 'Hail Britannia?: Institutional Investor Behavior under Limited Regulation' (June 1994) 92.7 Michigan Law Review 1997, 2048.

[53] See, e.g., Ian R. Appel et al., 'Passive Investors, Not Passive Owners' (2016) 121.1 Journal of Financial Economics 111, 112. There is widespread consensus that the trend towards passive investing is bound to continue. See, e.g., Bebchuk et al. (n 47) 94.

[54] Bebchuk et al. (n 47) 98.

[55] See, e.g., Dragana Cvijanović et al., 'Free-Riders and Underdogs: Participation in Corporate Voting' (2017) 19, https://ssrn.com/abstract=2939744.

[56] See, e.g., Stuart L. Gillan and Laura Starks, 'Corporate Governance Proposals and Shareholder Activism: The Role of Institutional Investors' (2000) 57.2 Journal of Financial Economics 275, 277; Joseph A. McCahery et al., 'Behind the Scenes: The Corporate Governance Preferences of Institutional Investors' (2016) 71.6 Journal of Finance 2905, 2913; Cvijanović et al., (n 55) 20.

[57] Gillan and Starks (n 56) 277–80.

[58] See, e.g., Gilson and Gordon (n 49) 886–88.

[59] cf. Investment Advisers Act of 1940, Ch. 686, 789, 852 § 205(a)(1).

[60] See, e.g., Bebchuk et al. (n 47) 96.

proxy advisors blindly.[61] These institutions are simply too big to be passive:[62] it would be politically unacceptable if their enormous voting power was de facto exercised by an external advisor with no direct or indirect stake in the company. Existing regulations ensure public awareness about such institutions' voting policies by mandating their disclosure.[63]

In addition, information costs have considerably gone down. One of the main factors contributing to the reduction of information cost is the surge of proxy advisory services. The core function of proxy advisors is to offer institutional investors relatively cheap suggestions on how to vote portfolio companies' shares.[64] Mechanically following proxy advisors' voting recommendations has become the voting policy of at least some institutional investors.[65] That allows them to keep the cost of processing the relevant information very low, namely equal to the (contained) fee they pay the proxy advisor.[66]

Proxy advisors simply did not exist until the mid-1980s and they became prominent only one decade later, also following policy measures that came very close to mandating the exercise of voting rights by some categories of institution: that was first the case for pension funds, pursuant to the Department of Labor's Avon Letter, in 1988, and then for mutual funds, following a 2003 SEC rule. The former qualified voting rights as pension plan assets to be voted in accordance with the plan trustee's fiduciary duties.[67] The latter required mutual funds and other investment companies registered under the Investment Company Act to (i) adopt and disclose the policies and procedures that they use to determine how to vote proxies relating to securities held in their portfolios, and (ii) annually disclose voting records.[68]

These requirements, while stopping short of mandating voting, are a powerful nudge in that direction for all institutions to which they apply. Smaller institutions, in order to reduce the costs involved, have a strong incentive to simply follow proxy advisors' recommendations.[69] The SEC rules themselves have pushed in that

[61] See Ryan Bubb and Emiliano Catan, 'The Party Structure of Mutual Funds 3', 14, 23 (2018), https://papers.ssrn.com/sol3/papers.cfm?abstract_id=3124039; Stephen Choi et al., 'Who Calls the Shots? How Mutual Funds Vote on Director Elections' (2013) 3 Harvard Business Law Review 35, 61–63.

[62] For other reasons we do not need to focus on here, they are also too big to be activist. See John D. Morley, 'Too Big to Be Activist' (2018) 92.6 Southern California Law Review 1407.

[63] See note 68.

[64] See Stephen Choi et al., 'The Power of Proxy Advisors: Myth or Reality?' (2010) 59.4 Emory Law Journal 869, 870.

[65] Ibid. 871–72.

[66] Ibid. 884–85.

[67] See U.S. Dep't of Labor, Pension and Welfare Benefit Program, Opinion Letter to Mr. Helmuth Fandl, Chairman of the Retirement Board of Avon Products, Inc., at 3 (23 February 1988).

[68] See Proxy Voting by Investment Advisers, 68 Fed. Reg. 6585 (7 February 2003).

[69] In fact, even relatively large institutions (with assets under management in the hundreds of millions of dollars) do not shy away from declaring that they follow proxy advisors' recommendations as a matter of voting policy, albeit sometimes in limited circumstances. For instance, American Money Management, LLC, an investment company with $239 million of assets under management, declares in its proxy voting policy that it 'has delegated responsibilities for decisions regarding proxy voting for securities held by the Funds to ISS. ISS will vote such proxies in accordance with its proxy policies and

direction in that they specify that a mutual fund manager 'could demonstrate that the vote was not a product of a conflict of interest if it voted client securities, in accordance with a predetermined policy, based upon the recommendations of *an independent third party*',[70] such as a proxy advisor.

Nowadays, virtually all institutional investors buy services from proxy advisors.[71] Many of them just purchase the untailored voting recommendation service, which is based on proxy advisors' own general policies and analyses.[72] Because institutional investors are their patrons, proxy advisors' general policies tend to reflect institutional investors' own widely shared corporate governance preferences, or at least the preferences of the largest and the most strong-minded among them.[73] This is a clear case where the reduction of information costs comes at the price of a loss in voters' independence: all such votes are most likely to be based on the same analysis and cast in the same direction.[74]

To make things slightly less worrying, ISS, the leading proxy advisory firm, develops separate voting policies, which cater to the preferences of different subsets of institutional investors.[75] Hence, they are less likely to provide *all* their clients with exactly the same voting recommendations.

More importantly, not all institutional investors have simply outsourced their voting decisions to proxy advisors. As hinted earlier, many of them, including the largest ones, have devised their own voting policies and set up their own corporate governance departments which make their own final decisions on how to vote on individual resolutions.[76] Yet to lower voting costs, even investors with their own

procedures'. See American Money Management, LLC, Proxy Voting Policies and Procedures (22 March 2018) (on file with the authors); American Money Management, LLC, BrightScope, https://www.brightscope.com/financial-planning/firm/27992/American-Money-Management-LLC/. An example of partial blind reliance on proxy advisors is in the proxy voting policy of Schroders (with US$447 billion assets under management), which declares that 'where a fund has widely diversified holdings that, in aggregate with other funds controlled by Schroders, would only represent a minimal percentage of a company's share capital the interests Schroders control will be voted in accordance with the recommendations of a third party (currently ISS)'. See Annual Results 2017 Date Pack, Schroders (3 January 2018), http://www.schroders.com/en/investor-relations/results-and-reports/results-reports-and-presentations/; see also UK Stewardship Code, Schroders (April 2014), http://www.schroders.com/en/ch/asset-management/fund-centre/esg/uk-stewardship-code/.

70 Proxy Voting by Investment Advisers (n 78) 6588 (emphasis added).

71 See Choi et al. (n 61) 41.

72 See Choi et al. (n 64) 870–71.

73 Ibid. 883.

74 See Schouten (n 32) 828–29.

75 See Choi et al., (n 64) 883. For instance, ISS, in addition to its U.S., European, and International 'Benchmark' policies, has United States Taft–Hartley U.S. Voting Guidelines, Public Fund U.S. Voting Guidelines, Socially Responsible U.S. Voting Guidelines, Faith-Based U.S. Voting Guidelines, and Sustainability U.S. Voting Guidelines. See 2017 Policy Information, Institutional Shareholder Services, https://www.issgovernance.com/policy-gateway/2017-policy-information/.

76 See, e.g., Edward Rock, 'Institutional Investors in Corporate Governance' in Jeffrey N. Gordon and Wolf-Georg Ringe (eds.), *Oxford Handbook of Corporate Law and Governance* (2018 Oxford University Press) 363, 368–71. Truth to tell, some scholars have argued that such governance departments are seriously understaffed. See, e.g., Bebchuk et al. (n 47) 100; Dorothy Shapiro Lund, 'The Case Against Passive Shareholder Voting' (2017) 43.3 Journal of Corporation Law 493, 515–16.

voting policies avail themselves of proxy advisory firms.[77] In this case, the proxy advisor's task is to process company-specific information relating to individual votes in order to find out how an institutional investor client, based on its voting policies, should vote.[78] But, especially for contested votes, such investors' corporate governance departments still evaluate the proxy advisor's recommendation on contentious matters and therefore maintain a certain degree of autonomy in voting decisions.[79]

The empirical evidence on the role of proxy advisors confirms, though, that a significant fraction of the shares held by institutional investors are voted on mechanically, following proxy advisers' advice. ISS alone is able to swing around one-fifth of the votes in the direction of its recommendations,[80] with over one-quarter of all mutual funds indiscriminately voting in line with ISS, according to one study.[81] Yet that influence is likely to be overstated because there is no way of telling whether any of those voting according to ISS recommendations would have voted any differently without it.[82] Proxy advisors are bound to devise voting policies and recommend votes that are in line with the tastes of their clients anyway.[83]

Another source of reduction in information costs comes from hedge fund activism.[84] Activist hedge funds, with their powerful incentive compensation arrangements and heavily overweighted investment in target companies, unearth information that is meant to undermine the incumbent management's record and support an alternative strategy, which they propose to implement, often by submitting a short slate of candidates for the board.[85] Unlike proxy advisors, hedge funds act as partisan information processors, whose credibility is backed by their heavy investment in the target and their track record.[86]

At the core of their campaigns there is usually a strategic decision, such as whether to merge with another company, find a buyer for the company or some of its divisions, or increase leverage.[87] The effects of such changes on a company's share price are bound to be huge, hence leading to institutional investors' attention on the merits of the campaign.[88] Furthermore, the fact itself that an alternative

[77] See ISS, Best Practice Principles for Providers of Shareholder Voting Research & Analysis. ISS Compliance Statement 3 (2017), https://www.issgovernance.com/file/duediligence/best-practices-principles-iss-compliance-statement-april-2017-update.pdf.

[78] See, e.g., Paul H. Edelman et al., 'Shareholder Voting in an Age of Intermediary Capitalism' (2014) 87.6 Southern California Law Review 1359, 1400–01.

[79] See Shapiro Lund (n 76) 516.

[80] See, e.g., Jie Cai et al., 'Electing Directors' (2009) 64 Journal of Finance 2389, 2404.

[81] Iliev and Lowry (n 52) 454.

[82] Choi et al. (n 64) 883–85.

[83] See text preceding n 73.

[84] See Gilson and Gordon (n 49) 896–902.

[85] John C. Coffee Jr and Darius Palia, 'The Wolf at the Door: The Impact of Hedge Fund Activism on Corporate Governance' (2016) 41 Journal of Corporation Law 545, 560.

[86] Ibid. 555.

[87] Ibid. 551.

[88] Gilson and Gordon (n 49) 897 and n. 116.

strategy is on the table makes it possible for institutional investors to reconsider managers' records: without a readily available alternative, a negative vote on the CEO (when it is binding) would be a self-inflicted wound, because it would leave the company without a guide and a strategy until a replacement is found. In other words, hedge funds make alternatives to the status quo viable, thus reducing the cost of a vote against management.

Yet if an institutional investor has reason to doubt that its competitors will similarly engage with the activist hedge fund, rational reticence would be the dominant strategy for the individual institutional investor considering, in isolation from the others, whether to invest in information. While a lot of information may have been unearthed by the activist, the incumbent management will put forward its own views, scenarios, estimates, and facts. Assessing and comparing the two will be costly for the individual institutional investor.[89] Hence, hedge funds alone should not be able to prompt an institution to become informed when rational reticence is at work.

The presence of corporate governance intermediaries such as proxy advisors and hedge funds has reduced the cost of informed voting by institutional investors. At the same time, overweighting and sheer size may explain why institutional investors appear to exercise their voting rights in an informed way. But more is at play to explain why collective action problems do not paralyse institutions.

One possibility is that institutions worry about their clients' perception of their corporate governance record. So long as clients (beneficial owners) have a preference for a proactive stance on the part of their asset managers, the latter will be active, lest they lose clients to the competition. Yet an individual institution's clients, whether retail or institutional themselves, are also rationally apathetic and no less reticent: while collectively, as a class, they would gain from informed voting, they are better off switching to passive institutions and free-riding on active institutions' efforts.[90]

Some of the institutional asset owners that outsource asset management services to investment advisors may well not conform to this description: *union* and *public* pension funds, unlike *corporate* ones, often have strong views about corporate governance issues and may expect their asset managers to vote accordingly.[91] But, again, such clients may find that the best way to combine an independent view of investee companies management's record and strategies with regard to the controlling of costs is for their asset managers to follow (tailored) proxy advisors' recommendations, especially because those pension funds' views on corporate governance issues are likely to be one-size-fits-all. Still, there might be a subset of institutional clients that always prefer informed voting as an expression

[89] cf. Shapiro Lund (n 76) 495.
[90] Bebchuk et al. (n 47) 98.
[91] Ibid. 102.

of responsible investment/ownership and therefore prize truly informed voting in its own right. Pressures from such clients may explain the move away from shareholder passivity by some institutions as a marketing strategy to retain those clients and possibly expand the client base among others with similar views.

In addition to market factors, policy developments have played a role in pushing institutional investors in the direction of active voting. We have seen already that policy makers have nudged some categories of institutions into voting their shares by making voting virtually mandatory.[92] Furthermore, measures have been enacted in the last twenty-five years that have reduced (informed) voting costs and greatly facilitated communications among shareholders.

The expansion of mandatory disclosures has made it less costly for institutional investors, financial analysts, and proxy advisors to have information available that enables them to form an opinion about a company's management and strategy.[93] In addition, the prohibition on selective disclosures[94] has made institutions less dependent on access to managers for material information about portfolio companies.[95]

Finally, while rules still exist that stifle shareholders' coordinated action to affect voting outcomes, such as those providing a broad definition of 'group' for the purposes of ownership disclosure and insider trading rules,[96] simple exchanges of information and contacts among shareholders have ceased to be relevant for the purposes of proxy voting regulations since 1992.[97] Intuitively, the extent to which institutional investors can communicate with each other without triggering costly regulatory burdens is key for their ability to cooperate with other agents in the network.[98]

In this section, we have discussed a number of factors that have arguably contributed to the partial shift from passivity to informed voting by (many) institutional investors and shown how proxy advisors, while contributing to a reduction in the voting costs, also lead to less independent voting. In the next section, after introducing network theory, we show how the network of relationships in which

[92] See notes 67–68 and accompanying text.

[93] See, e.g., Jeffrey N. Gordon, 'The Rise of Independent Directors in the United States, 1950-2005: Of Shareholder Value and Stock Market Prices' (2007) 59 Stanford Law Review 1465, 1548–53.

[94] Regulation Fair Disclosure, 17 C.F.R. §§ 243.100–243.103.

[95] See, e.g., Zohar Goshen and Gideon Parchomovsky, 'The Essential Role of Securities Regulation' (2006) 55.4 Duke Law Journal 711, 746.

[96] Securities Exchange Act of 1934, 17 C.F.R. 240.13d-3; 15 U.S.C. 78m(d)(3) (2012). See, e.g., Coffee and Palia (n 85) 562–63, 568–70 (noticing how the interpretation of the group concept has narrowed throughout the years, but still arguing that a broader interpretation would be more in line with the regulation's legislative intent). McCahery and colleague's survey of asset managers shows that institutions do worry about these constraints. See McCahery et al. (n 56) 2922.

[97] For an overview, see, for example, Coffee and Palia (n 85) 559–61, 568–70.

[98] Section IV discusses how institutional investors can coordinate and how being part of a network can shape their voting strategies.

institutional investors are embedded provides additional mechanisms to address the trade-off between duplication costs avoidance and voting independence.

IV. How Connections Affect Institutional Investor Voting Dynamics

We now investigate how connections among institutional investors influence their incentives to collect information and their voting behaviour. We argue that because (i) institutional investors are embedded in a complex network of connections, and (ii) these connections influence their pay-offs and behaviour, network theory is a natural framework for the study of the behaviour of institutional investors. More precisely, we suggest that network theory can help to explain how cooperative behaviour can emerge among such institutions and be sustained.[99]

Let us define 'cooperation' among institutional investors as casting an informed vote at a portfolio company when they can be expected to be rationally reticent,[100] that is, when investing in information on a portfolio company benefits other institutional investors holding shares in that portfolio company more than the informed institutional investor itself, because competitors do not bear the costs of becoming informed but still reap the benefits of the increased value associated with the informed vote.[101]

A burgeoning literature on social networks shows that cooperative behaviour that benefits others can be sustained even if it harms the cooperator, provided that the population of agents is sufficiently interconnected.[102] Therefore, the level

[99] As previously hinted, our analysis is merely qualitative: we do not attempt to prove, let alone quantify, how (much of) the cooperation we observe is due to institutional investor connections.

[100] Institutional investors can invest resources in many ways to engage with their portfolio companies. As noted by McCahery, Sautner, and Starks, much of the activity takes place behind the scenes. See McCahery et al. (n 56) 2905. In this chapter, however, we focus on voting because, as then Chairwoman of the SEC Mary Shapiro put it, '[t]he proxy is often the principal means for shareholders and public companies to communicate with one another, and for shareholders to weigh in on issues of importance to the corporation'. See Press Release, U.S. Securities and Exchange Commission, SEC Votes to Seek Public Comment on U.S. Proxy System (14 July 2010), https://www.sec.gov/news/press/2010/2010-122.htm.

[101] Cooperation as defined here should not be confused with the kind of coordination underlying the definition of 'group' for securities regulation purposes. According to section 13(d)(3) of the Securities Exchange Act of 1934, '[w]hen two or more persons act as a partnership, limited partnership, syndicate, or other group for the purpose of acquiring, holding, or disposing of securities of an issuer, such syndicate or group shall be deemed a "person."' 15 U.S.C. § 78m(d)(3) (2012). This definition, however vague, presupposes coordinated action with respect to a given issuer. Instead, cooperation as we define it merely implies that one institutional investor collects information despite the free-riding and rational reticence problems. Cooperation might imply that the cooperator shares information with other shareholders. Communication of this kind, in any event, is no longer relevant for the purposes of proxy voting regulations, and is, per se, insufficient to qualify communicating institutions as members of a 'group'. See note 97 and accompanying text; cf. Coffee and Palia (n 85) 569.

[102] See generally Bin Wu et al., 'Evolution of Cooperation on Stochastic Dynamical Networks' (2010) 5 PLoS One 1.

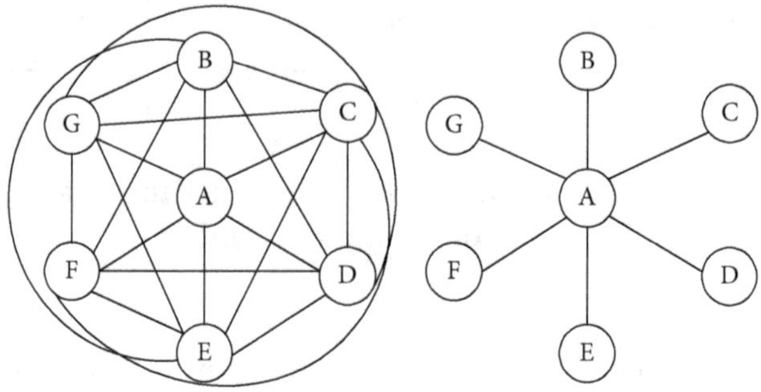

Figure 11.1 Examples of sub-networks. Adapted with permission from University of Illinois Law Review

of free-riding does not depend only on the size of the potential group of cooperators[103] but also on the existing connections among group members. In other words, highly interconnected groups are more likely to display cooperative behaviour. And, given that institutional investors are increasingly interconnected,[104] this insight might help to explain why they are casting informed votes more frequently. In fact, an institutional investor that is gathering information when it should be paralysed by rational reticence is—at first glance—engaging in cooperative behaviour that increases the fitness of its competitors at the cost of its relative performance.[105] In line with the literature on social networks, we argue that connections among institutional investors and between institutional investors and other agents involved in the voting process help to explain this behaviour.

In its bare form, a network can be represented as a series of points connected by lines. In the social sciences literature, the points ('nodes' or 'vertices') represent the *actors*, whereas the lines are called *ties* (or edges). The term 'actor' is used for both individual agents and organisations. Following this terminology, below we refer to institutional investors, hedge funds, proxy advisors, and portfolios firms' management as actors. When a tie connects two actors, we refer to them as 'neighbours'.[106] The largest group of actors each having ties with all other actors is known as a 'clique' (see Figure 11.1, left panel).[107] In our context, institutional investors

[103] See Clark (n 26) 1.

[104] See Jose Azar, A New look at Oligopoly: Implicit Collusion Through Portfolio Diversification 3 (8 November 2011), https://papers.ssrn.com/sol3/papers.cfm?abstract_id=1993364.

[105] The parallel between biology and economic theory has long been recognised. Many biological models use the concept of 'Individual as Maximising Agent' (IMA) that is a close relative of the homo oeconomicus. See, e.g., Stuart A. West et al., 'Sixteen Common Misconceptions About the Evolution of Cooperation in Humans' (2011) 32.4 Evolution & Human Behavior 231, 233.

[106] Note that in network theory the idea of neighbours is not necessarily connected with geographical proximity. For instance, two actors can be connected via the Internet, and hence be considered 'neighbours', even if they are located thousands of kilometres away from each other.

[107] See Robert A. Hanneman and Mark Riddle, 'Introduction to Social Network Methods' (2005) 174, https://faculty.ucr.edu/~hanneman/nettext/Introduction_to_Social_Network_Methods.pdf.

form a clique when they are thus interconnected. When two actors are not directly connected, we refer to them as 'non-neighbours'.

In Figure 11.1 the left panel represents a clique. The right panel does not.

In this chapter, we focus on four kinds of ties: formal networks, geographical proximity, employee connections, and co-ownership. Two institutions are connected via a formal tie if they belong to the same formal network (section IV.B), via a geographical tie if they are located in the same area (section IV.C), and via a co-ownership tie if they both own a stake in the same portfolio company (section IV.E). In addition, institutional investors' employees may have incentives of their own to communicate with other members of the investment community and spread their 'voting ideas' (section IV.D).

A. Inter-Institutional Connections

The literature on social networks offers a comprehensive set of analytical tools to understand the complex dynamics and the constant interplay among the various agents that contribute to shaping the voting strategies of institutional investors. In particular, network theory helps us to shed light on how patterns of connections affect the interplay between group size, free-riding, information and coordination costs, and the amount of information collected by agents before a vote.

Institutional investors can be connected with each other in a number of ways. Here we focus on the four kinds of ties mentioned earlier. We leave aside other ties, such as through proxy advisors, hedge fund activists, and portfolio firms' management. Such actors can all be seen as acting as connections among institutions prior to shareholder meetings.[108] The reason for omitting these ties from our analysis is not that they are less consequential than the ones we focus on, but rather that their role in moulding voting decisions has already been widely analysed in the literature,[109] and while this literature does not rely on network theory, it should already be obvious to the reader that this theory is a useful lens to understand those phenomena.

A standard finding of social network theory is that cooperation is more likely in networks with a high clustering coefficient.[110] The clustering coefficient of a network measures the degree to which the nodes in the network tend to cluster together and can be defined as 'the probability that two neighbours of a given node share also a connection between them'.[111] In our setting, this translates into the idea that cooperative behaviour might be sustained when institutional investors

[108] Technically, they act as 'bridges'. See note 170 and accompanying text.

[109] See, e.g., Bubb and Catan (n 61).

[110] See Salvatore Assenza Jesús Gómez-Gardeñes, and Vito Latora, 'Enhancement of Cooperation in Highly Clustered Scale-free Networks' (2008) 78 Physical Review E 1, 4.

[111] See Assenza et al. (n 110) 1.

are embedded in a highly clustered network. When such a network exists, we can predict a tendency to invest in information rather than to free-ride on other institutional investors.[112] One intuitive reason for this is that the likelihood that one institutional investor's investment in information will be pivotal (i.e., affect the voting outcome) is higher if the investor is part of a network and can use its ties and influence to persuade other nodes to vote in the same direction.

B. Formal Networks

Institutional investors are often connected via formal channels. Associations of institutional investors of various kinds and with different goals are mushrooming in the United States and in the rest of the world.[113] One prominent example is the Council of Institutional Investors ('CII'), which is not only a forum to develop and discuss corporate governance best practices and an effective advocacy group for public and labour pension funds but also a facilitator of interactions among members and asset management industry players.[114] Currently, the CII has more than 120 members with combined assets of over US$3 trillion.[115] A number of empirical studies have analysed whether the action of the CII has an impact on the value of the companies that are in its members' portfolios. Most of these studies concentrate on the effects of the CII 'Focus List' of underperforming companies.[116] The goal of the CII is to get its members to engage in collaborative efforts to induce managers of Focus List firms to improve performance.[117] Two studies out of three conclude that CII's action increases the value of portfolio companies.[118]

Another example is the British Local Authority Pension Fund Forum ('LAPFF'), which claims to be 'one of the leading voices in corporate governance and responsible investment in the UK'.[119] LAPFF routinely engages in proxy voting matters, favouring coordination among its seventy-one members. More specifically, one of its core functions is issuing 'voting alerts' that provide non-binding advice to its

[112] See Crane et al. (n 13) 181–85. See also section IV.B.

[113] See, e.g., Danyelle J. Guyatt, 'Identifying and Mobilising Win-Win Opportunities for Collaboration between Pension Fund Institutions and their Agents' (2012), https://papers.ssrn.com/sol3/papers.cfm?abstract_id=2033516.

[114] Members, Council of Institutional Investors, http://www.cii.org/members.

[115] General Members, Council of Institutional Investors, http://www.cii.org/general_members.

[116] Over the years, (then) giants like IBM, Kodak, and Sears were included in CII's focus list. See Tim C. Opler and Jonathan S. Sokobin, 'Does coordinated institutional activism work? An analysis of the activities of the Council of Institutional Investors 2' (Dice Center for Research in Financial Economics, Working Paper No. 95-5, 1995), https://papers.ssrn.com/sol3/papers.cfm?abstract_id=46880.

[117] Gary L. Caton et al., 'The Effectiveness of Institutional Activism' (2001) 57.4 Financial Analysts Journal 21, 21.

[118] Ibid; Opler and Sobokin (n 116) 2.

[119] See LAPFF History, Local Authority Pension Fund Forum, http://www.lapfforum.org/about-us/history-of-lapff/.

members on how to vote at the annual general meeting of a portfolio company.[120] Two obvious questions are why these institutions are created and why institutional investors are willing to bear a cost to become members. We address these questions in section IV.F.

C. Geographically Linked Networks

Black and Coffee suggest that during the 1990s, British institutional investors might have become more active voters in part to prevent American institutions from determining the outcome of British companies' shareholders meetings.[121] This strategy required cooperation, as otherwise the institutional investors that actively voted would have become less competitive than their domestic competitors that would remain passive.[122] That suggests that institutional investors can also cooperate when they operate in the same geographical area. Cooperation might in fact be easier among geographically proximate institutional investors because information can circulate more easily via informal channels.

Economists have gone beyond anecdotal evidence and produced a number of studies showing that the spatial distribution of institutional investors affects their behaviour.[123] Pool, Stoffman, and Yonker find that when funds are located in the same area, their employees have more frequent occasions of meeting in both formal and informal settings, thus building personal relationships that help information to circulate across institutions.[124] Further, Iliev and Lowry provide additional support for the idea that information travels across geographical ties. They show that funds located in a metropolitan statistical area in which the concentration of funds is high are significantly less likely to be passive voters.[125] This suggests that information on how to vote circulates via geographical networks, inducing institutional investors that are clustered in a given area to become more active voters.

D. Employees' Personal Networks and Career Concerns

Competition does not take place only among individual institutional investors but also among their employees. In a nutshell, at the employer level, the institutional investor compares the expected increase in the value of the holding from casting an

[120] Local Authority Pension Fund Forum, Annual Report 2016 18 (2016), http://www.lapfforum.org/wp-content/uploads/2017s/03/LAPFF-Annual-Report-2016.pdf.

[121] Black and Coffee (n 52) 2040.

[122] Ibid. 2002.

[123] See Hong et al. (n 9) 2801; Pool et al. (n 9) 2679.

[124] See Pool et al. (n 9) 2680.

[125] Iliev and Lowry (n 52) 455.

informed vote with the expected cost of becoming informed. Instead, the employee compares the anticipated effect of her behaviour on her career prospects with the personal cost of becoming informed.[126] Clearly, the reality is much more nuanced than this, and the distinction between employer and employee incentives is less distinct.[127] Introducing an artificial bright-line distinction between employers and employees, however, helps us to emphasise that also in this context the tail may wag the dog. Even in a situation where no institutional investor has incentives to collect information, a vote against management departing from the suggestion of proxy advisors might be cast if an employee of an institutional investor triggers an information cascade.

The argument presented in this section is composed of two separate claims. First, career concerns can shape the behaviour of funds' employees who are in charge of voting shares held by their employer (hereinafter, 'stock voters'). For instance, stock voters might decide to go the extra mile and invest personal resources, such as their free time, to investigate a portfolio company. Second, this information produced at the employee level can circulate within the network and affect the behaviour of other institutional investors. After separately analysing these two claims, we discuss the reliability of information produced at the employee level.

First, while there are no empirical studies that focus explicitly on stock voters, there is significant evidence that career concerns shape the behaviour of actively managed funds' managers (hereinafter 'stock pickers'), and of other actors within institutional investor networks. Chevalier and Ellison focus on the portfolio choices of fund managers and find that the probability of being terminated increases when their returns are lower.[128] Hong, Kubik, and Solomon report similar findings with regards to financial analysts.[129] Moreover, Hong and Kubik find that analysts issuing accurate forecasts are more likely to be promoted or to move to a more prestigious employer than analysts issuing inaccurate forecasts.[130] These results show that stock pickers and financial analysts have incentives to work harder to outperform—or at least not be outperformed by—their peers. Although these findings do not directly relate to stock voters, this evidence still seems a sufficiently solid ground on which to build. Stock voters operate in the same environment as stock pickers and it is safe to assume that they are as interested in their own career as anybody else. It is thus reasonable also to assume that their actions are shaped by

[126] We remark that there is no reason to postulate that the cost-benefit calculus of the employer and of the employee will always point to the same direction.

[127] In fact, some of the arguments and empirical evidence presented in this section overlap with the ones discussed in section IV.C on geographical ties.

[128] Judith Chevalier and Glenn Ellison, 'Career Concerns of Mutual Fund Managers' (1999) 114.2 Quarterly Journal of Economics 389, 391. According to the authors, a manager is 'terminated' if he loses his job and is hired by a smaller fund or abandons fund management.

[129] Harrison Hong et al., 'Security Analysts' Career Concerns and Herding of Earnings Forecasts' (Spring 2000) 31.1 RAND Journal of Economics 121, 123.

[130] Harrison Hong and Jeffrey D. Kubik, 'Analyzing the Analysts: Career Concerns and Biased Forecasts' (February 2003) 58.1 Journal of Finance 313, 315–16.

career concerns. Someone working in the governance department of a fund manager might be interested in moving to a larger asset management company or in moving to a different and higher-paid job within the asset management industry or in other segments of the financial industry. Discussing ideas on how to handle a given controversial issue at an informal meeting appears to offer a good opportunity for an employee to impress potential employers. The possibility of a better career might provide incentives to investigate a portfolio company even when it would not be expected to produce an immediate monetary return for the employee or her employer.[131] Thus, as stated above, stock voters' career concerns might be sufficient to induce them to collect information and communicate it.

We now turn to the second claim and investigate whether information produced by employees is likely to move across the network. An employee cannot hope to derive career benefits from information privately produced unless it shares this information with some potential employers.[132] At the same time, employers might find it cheaper to receive already-processed information, instead of having to collect it.[133]

A last piece of the puzzle would be how information circulates among individuals working in different funds. The literature has found that information can be passed via different kinds of ties. For instance, information can circulate through educational networks[134] and geographical networks of employers[135] or employees.[136]

In sum, competition among stock voters is highly likely to affect their behaviour, giving them incentives to seek information and transmit it to other agents in the network via various forms of connections, such as geographical proximity and educational ties.

An important question is whether the information produced due to competition among employees improves or deteriorates the quality of information that circulates in the network of institutional investors. This chiefly depends on whether (i) employees have incentives to collect and communicate *reliable* information, and (ii) other agents have an incentive to listen and process that information. If an employee discloses unreliable information and other agents, ignoring their own information, follow the employee's lead, the quality of information within the network

131 This might not be true in those cases in which the potential employer can assess whether the behaviour of the stock voter is also in the interest of his current employer. The potential employer might not be interested in hiring someone who is wasting the human resources of his current employer. We remain agnostic on how often the potential employer would be able to assess this.

132 Recall that we are focusing on information on how to vote shares and not on information relative to stock trading.

133 The empirical evidence supporting this claim is inevitably similar to the one discussed in section IV.C on geographical ties.

134 Lauren Cohen et al., 'The Small World of Investing: Board Connections and Mutual Fund Returns' (October 2008) 116.5 Journal of Political Economics 951 (2008).

135 Pool et al. (n 9).

136 Hong et al. (n 9).

is reduced. On the contrary, if the employee truthfully communicates valuable information and the recipients do not endorse it uncritically but rather process and evaluate it independently, then the quality of information within the network is likely to improve.

In order to frame this problem, it is useful to compare the incentives of the employees with those of proxy advisors, another highly relevant source of information. To begin with, individual employees face much more competition in their labour market than ISS and Glass Lewis experience in the proxy advisory services market.[137] At first glance, this seems to suggest that stock voters are more likely than proxy advisors to collect the relevant information rather than adopting one-size-fits-all heuristics.[138] Precisely because stock voters face higher competitive pressures, however, they have stronger incentives to conform to the prior beliefs of their potential employer. For example, if it is known that a potential employer's boss has strong environmental concerns, a stock voter might have more chances of being hired by forcefully criticising an oil company's management for under-investing in alternative sources, irrespective of whether greater investment is now that company's best strategy from a strict shareholder value standpoint. Although proxy advisors similarly have an incentive to cater to the priors of their customers,[139] they might be in a better position to resist this temptation both because they face less competitive pressure and because their client base is wider than the set of potential employers for the stock voter. Therefore, from this perspective, proxy advisors might be a more reliable source of information. In short, it is hard to predict the quality of information produced by the employees, even relative to the information generated by other sources like proxy advisors.

In a similar way, it is hard to make generalised predictions on the behaviour of the recipients of the message. While it might be wise for them to evaluate the information received from employees working for competitors, there are also good reasons to expect the recipients to herd. First, there is ample empirical evidence that stock pickers and financial analysts herd, especially younger ones,[140] and it is hard to see why stock voters might behave differently. Second, there is evidence that stock analysts at heavily diversified firms herd more, because they face

[137] It could be argued that the employees of ISS and Lewis might have similar incentives. For the employee of a proxy advisor, however, it could be more problematic to circulate information for the simple reason that proxy advisors are paid to have and communicate their opinions to others on each and any shareholder meeting resolution. Assume, for instance, that ISS suggested voting 'for' a given proposal, while an ISS employee finds out that voting 'against' would be better from a shareholder perspective. By disclosing this information, the employee would be openly contradicting her employer, something which potential employers, independently of the value of new information, are unlikely to consider positively for recruiting purposes.

[138] For evidence in support of the fact that proxy advisors issue blanket recommendations, see Iliev and Lowry (n 52) 448.

[139] See note 73 and accompanying text.

[140] See Hong et al. (n 129) 123.

a more complex task.[141] In this vein, it is plausible to expect stock voters to sometimes herd, given that they deal with a vast portfolio of firms operating in different sectors.

Regardless of its quality, information spread by institutional investors' employees is an inherent and inevitable characteristic of the network in which institutional investors are embedded. To conclude, an institutional investor's voting decisions can be affected not only by large and visible sources of information such as proxy advisors but also by the behaviour of other institutional investors' employees. Especially when institutional investors have gathered conflicting information, they might decide to ignore it and follow the lead of the employee of another institution. In these cases, the tail will wag the dog and the information produced by an individual based on a private cost-benefit calculus will affect institutional investors' voting behaviour.

E. Intra-Clique Cooperation and Inter-Clique Competition: Co-Ownership Ties

Networks of institutional investors created by co-ownership ties only recently started attracting the attention of economists. Some recent articles focus on co-ownership ties and show that these connections are relevant to understanding institutional investor behaviour. For instance, Bajo, Croci, and Marinelli show that institutional investors that are more connected via co-ownership ties create more value (as measured by Tobin's Q).[142] They argue that occupying a special position in a network can increase the status and the reputation of an agent.[143] In this vein, institutional investors that are central and better connected can be assumed to have a better reputation and can therefore provide a certification of the quality of a company when they acquire its shares.[144]

Crane, Koch, and Michenaud identify roughly twenty cliques of institutional investors[145] and show that members of the same clique tend to use their voice more often and to vote together on proxy items.[146] This finding supports the hypothesis that institutional investors form a highly clustered population and that the presence of cliques of institutional investors connected by co-ownership ties increases the likelihood of cooperation.

141 See Chansog Kim and Christos Pantzalis, 'Global/Industrial Diversification and Analyst Herding' (2003) 59.2 Financial Analysts Journal 69, 69 (2003).

142 See Emanuele Bajo et al., 'Institutional Investor Networks and Firm Value 1' (1 February 2017) (https://papers.ssrn.com/sol3/papers.cfm?abstract_id=2633541).

143 Ibid.

144 Ibid.

145 Crane et al. (n 13), 178–79.

146 Ibid. 177.

The fundamental question then becomes why interconnected competitors should cooperate. One possible explanation is the idea—standard in sociobiology—that cooperators fare worse than defectors within a group, but that groups of cooperators fare better than groups of defectors.[147] To see why this logic would apply to institutional investors' voting, let us return to the example described in section II. Let us now introduce companies *j* and *k*. Let us further assume that *A* and *B* own a fraction $w_{i,A} = w_{i,B}$ of company *i* shares, *A* and *C* own a fraction $w_{j,A} = w_{j,C}$ of company *j* shares, and *B* and *C* own a fraction $w_{k,B} = w_{k,C}$ of company *k* shares. For the sake of simplicity, we consider $w_{i,A} = w_{j,A} = w_{k,B}$.[148] Using network terminology, in this example, *A*, *B*, and *C* form a triangle in which the vertices (the institutional investors) are connected by co-ownership ties.[149] We assume that institutional investors *D*, *E*, and *F* form a similar triangle connected by co-ownership ties in *other* portfolio companies (i.e., they do not own shares in *i*, *j*, and *k*). Further, we assume that *D*, *E*, and *F* do not cooperate, and hence they do not cast an informed vote, which, again by assumption, translates into a pay-off of 0.

C might consider investing c_j to acquire information only if an informed vote can increase the value of *j* by b_j, so that $c_j < w_j b_j$.[150] *C*, however, faces a trade-off. Investing in information would make it more competitive vis-à-vis institutional investors that do not hold shares in *j*(*B*, *D*, *E*, and *F*) by $w_j b_j - c_j > 0$, but less competitive vis-à-vis its neighbour *A* by c_j. Similarly, *B* will investigate company *k* if it might increase its share value by b_k, so that $c_k < w_k b_k$. Also, in this case, *B* might decide not to invest even with $c_k < w_k b_k$, if it considers that becoming less competitive vis-à-vis its neighbour *C* is more relevant than the gains vis-à-vis institutional investors that do not hold shares in *k* (*A*, *D*, *E*, and *F*). If *A*, *B*, and *C* decide not to invest in information, their pay-off will be equal to 0 and therefore they will not outperform *D*, *E*, and *F*.

Let us now assume that *A*, *B*, and *C* acknowledge that they form a triangle and cooperate so that *A* collects information on *i*, *B* collects information on *k*, and *C* gathers information on*j*. *A*'s pay-off would be equal to $w_i b_i + w_j b_j - c_i$, *B*'s pay-off would be $w_i b_i + w_k b_k - c_k$, and *C*'s would equal $w_j b_j + w_k b_k - c_j$. Assuming, for the sake of simplicity, that the costs of collecting information are similar across the three portfolio companies for *A*, *B*, and *C*, then they will increase their performance relative to their non-neighbours without becoming less competitive vis-à-vis their neighbours.

[147] See, e.g., David S. Wilson and Edward O. Wilson, 'Rethinking the Theoretical Foundation of Sociobiology' (2007) 82.4 Quarterly Review of Biology 327, 328.

[148] As noted above, asymmetric stakes might ameliorate the collective action problem. See note 52 and accompanying text.

[149] The number of triangles in a network is a key determinant of its clustering coefficient. See note 111 and accompanying text.

[150] Clearly, *C* applies a similar logic when deciding whether to invest in i, while *A* also considers investing in i, and so on. We present this more stylised version to simplify exposition.

Therefore, under the necessary assumption that informed voting by institutional investors increases value, cliques of cooperators (*A*, *B*, and *C*) will outperform cliques of defectors (*D*, *E*, and *F*). This finding can explain why clique members decide to cooperate and, correspondingly, engage in competition vis-à-vis other cliques.

The idea that costly cooperation among some of the competing firms can make them more competitive vis-à-vis the rest is standard in both the economic and the management literature on research collaboration among firms. For instance, two competing firms sharing technology and know-how become more competitive vis-à-vis all the firms not involved in the exchange.[151] We argue that the same dynamic applies to institutional investors' voting behaviour: the presence of cliques might help to explain why institutional investors sometimes cast informed votes despite rational reticence.[152]

We can draw three inferences from this stylised illustration. First of all, the network structure affects the relationship between group size and free-riding, as discussed in the CJT literature.[153] Remember that in the CJT framework, incentives to free-ride increase with group size.[154] Network theory shows that connections among members can help to overcome free-riding. Thus, apart from group size, the existing patterns of connections among group members influence the levels of cooperation, and ultimately whether institutional investors cast informed votes. Second, 'higher' level competition among cliques of institutional investors defined by co-ownership ties might explain Crane and others' result that clique members tend to use their voice more often.[155] Third, cliques allow for division of labour among institutional investors: each clique member will concentrate its monitoring efforts on a subset of companies in its portfolio. It seems reasonable to hypothesise that each institutional investor will concentrate on companies in which it has a comparative advantage in terms of investigation costs. Notably, leaving aside antitrust concerns, division of labour among a clique's members also improves welfare.[156] In fact, absent cooperation, the sum of the pay-offs of all players is 0 if *A*, *B*, and *C* defect.[157] Instead, if *A*, *B*, and *C* cooperate, the aggregate welfare will be higher.[158]

One could argue, however, that this result only applies to the specific example above, and that it has no general validity. In the example offered we have implicitly assumed that institutional investors can process information received by other

151 See Goyal (n 21) 245–66.
152 See Crane et al. (n 13) 177.
153 McCannon and Walker (n 47).
154 See text accompanying notes 38–44.
155 Crane et al. (n 13) 176–78.
156 Although this is merely our working assumption.
157 Recall that the pay-offs of D, E, and F = 0 in every scenario.
158 In particular, $2w_j b_j + 2w_k b_k + 2w_i b_i - c_i - c_j - c_k > 0$.

clique members without incurring any cost. This assumption is unreasonable, unless one further assumes that clique members blindly follow their clique peers. However, if that is the case, the efficiency of cooperation can be questioned on the basis of the CJT. If institutional investors blindly follow other members of their clique, then cooperation might crowd out information production by institutional investors, or, to put it differently, cooperation would prevent efficient aggregation of private information, leading shareholders to take the wrong decision more frequently. That is unconvincing.

To begin with, although the cost of processing information received by other clique members (define it as $\alpha_i, \alpha_j, \alpha_k$, respectively) is positive, it remains strictly less than the cost of *collecting* and processing it anew.[159] Thus, even relaxing the assumption that processing information is costless, cooperation remains a more efficient alternative to the duplication of costs associated with the scenario in which each institutional investor independently collects information on each portfolio company. Clearly, however, cooperation will not *always* be the best strategy. For instance, when the benefits are lower than the costs, passivity will be preferable.

Let us now turn to the second part of the counterargument, namely that institutional investors might blindly follow other clique members. The problem would be that by crowding out the production of private information, cooperation also entails a cost. More precisely, cooperation of this kind would reduce the likelihood that the shareholder meeting makes the 'right' (i.e., the value-maximising) decision. This cost is borne by the shareholders themselves, and in our example, it would translate into lower b_i, b_j, and . At the same time, compared to the scenario in which each institutional investor must investigate every portfolio company independently, cooperation allows institutional investors to save on information costs. More precisely, the institutional investor C saves $(c_k - \alpha_k) > 0$. Clique members will therefore have to make a choice between the reduced probability of getting the right voting outcome and the potential cost savings. Clique members will only cooperate when the cost savings ensured by cooperation more than compensate for the reduced probability of making the right decision. In other words, institutional investors engage in intra-clique cooperation only when it gives a benefit to clique members vis-à-vis other institutional investors. Thus, clique members would simply have no incentive to engage in cooperation when the reduction in b_i, b_j, and outweighs the cost savings from cooperation.

[159] Gilson and Gordon (n 49). In our framework, $c_i > \alpha_i, c_j > \alpha_j$ and $c_k > \alpha_k$.

F. Can Cooperation Emerge and Be Sustained?

The fact that cooperation might be beneficial for network members does not automatically imply that it will emerge and be sustained. In previous sections, though, we have both seen examples of real-world formal networks and reported empirical evidence of behaviour consistent with intra-network cooperation in the presence of geographical and co-ownership ties. In this section, we provide some intuitions for why such cooperation does emerge and can be sustained.

1. Formal networks

As we noted in section IV.B, cooperation can be mediated and facilitated by formal institutions. Two questions that we left unanswered are, first, why these institutions emerge and, second, why institutional investors are willing to pay fees to become members.[160] Network theory can help us to answer both questions.

We have seen that cooperation can increase the payoffs of the institutional investors that are invested in the same company. However, patterns of cooperative behaviour might collapse due to imperfect monitoring or ineffective sanctions for free-riders. Thus, if the potential gains from cooperating are large enough, the relevant players might decide to invest resources in the creation of a monitoring institution that increases the chances that those patterns of cooperative behaviour are sustained across time.[161] The decision taken in 1985 to create the CII can also be seen as an attempt to introduce such a monitoring institution.[162]

An objection would be that common portfolio investments are not permanent. Although many institutional investors hold shares for a relatively long time,[163] their portfolios are bound to evolve.[164] In this vein, one may wonder why an institutional investor should invest resources in the creation of a monitoring institution together with other investors with which it might not share co-ownership ties in the future. This is a very standard problem in network theory, because networks are often very complex and agents have limited knowledge about the characteristics, or even the identity, of their present and future neighbours.[165]

160 For instance, CII membership fees range between \$3,000 and \$30,000, depending on institutional investor size. See Guyatt (n 125) 94.

161 See Maximilian Mihm et al., What Goes Around Comes Around: A Theory of Indirect Reciprocity in Networks 31 (Center for Analytical Economics, Working Paper No. 09-07, 2009), https://www.econstor.eu/handle/10419/70450. The percentage that they derive is clearly dependent on the characteristics of the model and the effectiveness of the supervising institution. The gist of the argument, however, is that players might be willing to bear a cost in order to ease cooperation.

162 For a brief overview of the history of CII see History, Council of Institutional Investors, http://www.cii.org/cii_history.

163 See note 191 and accompanying text.

164 The same logic applies to other kind of ties, such as geographical and formal ties. In fact, institutional investors might move some of their offices or join (quit) a formal network.

165 cf. Goyal (n 21) 49. Another example are technologies like a phone app or the Internet, as their utility clearly depends on the number of adopters (i.e., agents in the network), yet it is often impossible to know this number in advance.

Institutional investors have at least four reasons to form a monitoring institution despite the imperfect information they hold about the future structure of the network. First, although an institutional investor cannot know which institutional investors it will be connected to in, say, ten years' time, it knows that it will most likely have *some* connections. When an individual decides whether to invest time and resources in learning a language, she does not know with whom (or with how many people) she will speak that language during her life. Yet, in most cases she knows that she will be able to speak the new language with *some* people, and she might even have a rough estimate of their number. This is often sufficient to justify the investment. An institutional investor is in a similar position. It does not know who its neighbours will be, yet it might still have an interest in creating a multilateral platform to communicate with its neighbours because it will most likely have *some* neighbours.[166]

Second, in relative terms the cost that each institutional investor bears to set up a monitoring institution is likely to be miniscule compared to the value of its portfolio. Therefore, if cooperation (i.e., informed voting) increases the value of portfolio assets, however marginally, the benefits derived from cooperation would most likely outweigh the costs borne by each investor in establishing the monitoring institution.[167]

Third, a monitoring institution might have a significant impact on the likelihood of cooperation. Although it is now possible to observe all the votes cast by each mutual fund, this form of ex post monitoring is still imperfect. Cooperation might collapse if institutional investors are not able to identify with sufficient accuracy the instances in which other neighbours cast an informed vote. From this perspective, pre-voting communication might greatly improve the ability of neighbours to detect deviations. By discussing portfolio companies' matters with other network members, it should often be possible to infer whether others have done their 'homework' or rather know nothing about any of their portfolio companies

[166] Organisations like the CII are also established to facilitate lobbying. To some extent, all institutional investors share similar preferences in terms of lobbying, and it is therefore clear why they want to unite forces. To the extent, however, that some of their goals are affected by the composition of their portfolio or their management style (e.g., whether active or passive), their preferences on some issues might be heterogeneous. In the latter case, the analogy with learning a language also works with respect to lobbying: why would any institutional investors create a lobbying association, given that their interests are fluid and depend at least in part on their management styles and the companies that they have in their portfolio at any given moment? The answer is that an institutional investor will most likely share similar goals with some other institutional investors at each point in time. Thus, it might still have an interest in creating a multilateral platform to communicate with other institutional investors.

[167] Given how negligible the fees are, this is most likely to be true even accounting for the fact that the majority of the benefits from an increase in the value of the portfolio do not accrue to the fund manager, but to its clients.

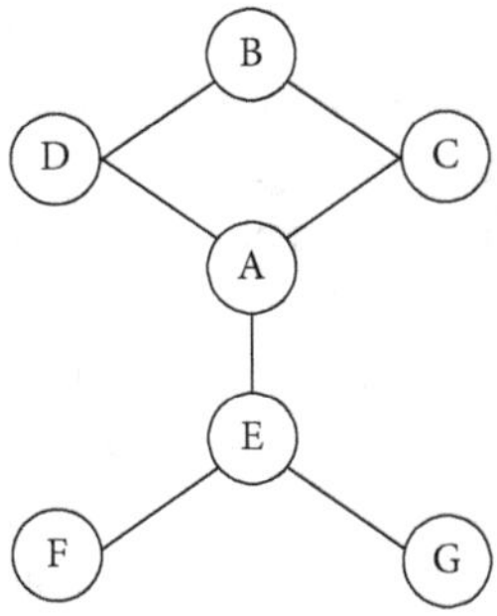

Figure 11.2 Bridge firms A and E connect firms B, C, D to firms F and G. Adapted with permission from University of Illinois Law Review

and merely plan to rubberstamp managers' proposals or blindly follow proxy advisors' recommendations.[168]

Finally, from a purely network perspective, founding or joining the monitoring institution at an early stage can permit the institutional investor to obtain a better position in the network. It is a standard finding of the literature on networks that one actor's pay-off depends on her position within the network.[169] In particular, it has been shown that *ceteris paribus* firms bridging structural holes generally perform better than other firms.[170] A firm bridges structural holes when it connects firms that would otherwise be unconnected. In Figure 11.2, firms *A* and *E* occupy a structural hole, because in their absence firms *B*, *C*, *D*, *F*, and *G* would not be connected.

In our context, an institutional investor *A* joining a formal network would bridge structural holes between its pre-existing neighbours and the institutional investors, like *E*, that are part of the formal network but are not connected to *A*'s neighbours. Institutions bridging structural holes might outperform other institutions for two reasons. First, they have a wider access to information, and therefore potentially to more innovative ideas and know-how.[171] This factor is crucial for mutual fund managers and similar institutional investors.[172] Second, institutions may hesitate to cast a vote against management due to fear of retaliation.[173] An institution that is part of a group that together votes against management faces

168 Notably, a network can sustain cooperation even when there are uncooperative fringes, provided that cooperative players are sufficiently patient and closely connected. See Matthew Haag and Roger Lagunoff, 'Social Norms, Local Interaction, and Neighborhood Planning' (2006) 47.1 International Economics Review 265, 268.

169 Goyal (n 21) 143.

170 See Ronald S. Burt, Structural Holes: The Social Structure of Competition (Harvard University Press 1992) 5.

171 Akbar Zaheer and Geoffrey G. Bell, 'Benefiting from Network Position: Firm Capabilities, Structural Holes, and Performance' (September 2005) 26.9 Strategic Management Journal 809, 811.

172 Ibid.

173 Gerald F. Davis and E. Han Kim, 'Business Ties and Proxy Voting by Mutual Funds' (August 2007) 85.2 Journal of Financial Economics 552, 552.

a lower risk of retaliation from managers.[174] In line with this hypothesis, Matvos and Ostrovsky find evidence of a strong peer effect in fund managers' voting decisions.[175] Funds are more likely to oppose management if their peers are also opposing it.[176] Bridging structural holes allows one to be part of more groups and this, in turn, reduces the risk of retaliation against voting choices.[177]

An obvious corollary is that the level of interconnection of a network is not the only factor that matters; it is also the case that agents' location within the network influences their pay-offs and incentives and therefore affects the overall amount of information that circulates within the network as well as the cost at which it is produced.

2. Information sharing

One might argue that an institutional investor will have insufficient incentive to share valuable information with competitors. In addition, should information be shared, the recipient might decide not to trust it, given that it comes from a competitor. Certainly, an asset manager that has strong reasons to believe that the price of a stock will increase in the coming months might have some incentives to conceal this information from its competitors so as not to improve their performance relative to its own. Similarly, its competitors may question the truthfulness of the voting-related information if she decides to disclose it. The trust problem among asset managers is, however, routinely overcome when they have frequent interactions. In fact, Pool and colleagues show that information travelling through informal personal relationships affect the investment decisions of managers that live in the same area.[178] This result can be obtained only if there is some degree of trust among asset managers living in the same area, even if they work for competing institutional investors.[179] There is no sound theoretical reason to argue that this dynamic applies to stock trading but not to stock voting. If anything, the value of information on voting strategies increases when it spreads, because greater diffusion makes it likelier that a voting majority shares the position of the active institutional

[174] Gregor Matvos and Michael Ostrovsky, 'Heterogeneity and Peer Effects in Mutual Fund Proxy Voting' (2010) 98.1 Journal of Financial Economics, 90, 91–92.

[175] Ibid.

[176] Ibid.

[177] Assume that a first pair of institutional investors, *A* and *B*, are both invested in company *i*, whereas a second pair, *C* and *D*, are both invested in company *j*. Assume further that institutional investor *E* acts as a bridge among these two pairs, having invested in both *i* and *j*. Now, suppose that *A* and *B* want to vote against management at portfolio company *i*, whereas *C* and *D* want to vote against management at portfolio company *j*. As *E* is connected to both pairs (*A*–*B* and *C*–*D*), it will always be part of a coalition of three institutional investors if it decides to vote against management at either *i* or *j*. Instead, *A*, *B*, *C*, and *D* might find themselves in a coalition of two if *E* does not endorse their strategy. As retaliation from management is harder when opposition comes from a larger coalition, bridging structural holes allows more freedom in voting against management.

[178] See Pool et al. (n 9) 2679.

[179] Ibid.

investor. Thus, an institutional investor that has collected information on how to vote on a given company has all the incentives to share it with competitors.

Let us go back to our example in section IV.E[180] and, for simplicity, let us assume that company i issues 100 shares and both A and B (but not C, D, E, and F) hold 30% of them ($w_i = 0.3$). Let us further assume that the cost of acquiring information $c_{i,A} = c_{i,B} = 50$. By investing $c_{i,A}$, A discovers that if the management proposal is rejected, the company's value will increase by 300 ($w_{i,A} b_{i,A} = 90$).[181]

There are three possible scenarios:

1. Firm A does not invest in information. The relative performances of the funds will not change. However, A will forego the possibility to gain 40 vis-à-vis the funds that do not own shares in company i.
2. Firm A invests in information and shares it with firm B. B is persuaded and votes with A. Therefore, the strategy is implemented. In this case, A gains 40 vis-à-vis C, D, E, and F, while B gains 90 and A loses 50 relative to B: A and B reap the same benefits, but only A has borne the costs.
3. Firm A invests in information, does not share it with B, and B votes with management. In this case, assuming that a majority of the other shareholders also vote with management, A's preferred strategy is not implemented. In this scenario, A foregoes the possibility of gaining 40 vis-à-vis C, D, E, and F. In addition, it loses 50 relative to every competitor.

While the choice between (1) and (2) depends on the information ex ante available to A on who its closest competitors are, and on whether A and B are part of a clique that cooperates, it is clear that scenario (2) dominates scenario (3).[182] Thus, once an institutional investor has voting-related information that is likely to improve the performance of a portfolio company, it has very direct and clear incentives to share it with other shareholders.[183]

From this perspective, an institutional investor that obtains information acts as an imperfect surrogate of an activist hedge fund *à la* Gilson and Gordon.[184] According to Gilson and Gordon, hedge funds formulate proposals and present them to institutional investors so that the latter only have to respond to a proposal, instead of having to come up with one themselves. Here, an institutional investor would act as an imperfect surrogate of a hedge fund because it would give

180 See notes 160–164 and accompanying text.

181 For the sake of simplicity, in this example we are assuming that A expects its vote to be pivotal.

182 The only exception would be when the cost of informing B exceeds the weighted benefits of the strategy. Yet, were communication so costly, Hong and colleagues would not have observed the word of mouth effect among stock pickers. Hong et al. (n 9) 2801.

183 We explore elsewhere in this chapter some of the reasons that might prompt the institutional investor to acquire information in the first place, such as informational cascades triggered by employees and inter-clique competition. See sections IV.D and IV.E.

184 Gilson and Gordon (n 49) 896–902.

other institutional investors a recommendation on how to vote, allowing them merely to process the information they receive instead of having to search for it.[185] Clearly, the key word here is 'imperfect. Institutional investors have no interest in embarking on an expensive campaign to persuade other shareholders and, unlike hedge funds, they are generally unwilling to put an alternative strategy on the table. Therefore, their action might not be as strong and as persuasive as that of an activist hedge fund. However, institutional investors investing in voting-related information have the incentive to share it—directly or indirectly—with other institutional shareholders. In turn, that reduces the cost of casting an informed vote for the other institutional shareholders and *ceteris paribus* increases the level of active voting.

Having established that there can be sufficient incentives to circulate information within the network, let us focus on whether intra-clique cooperation specifically is sustainable. Recent works on network theory show that cooperative strategies are sustainable in the presence of highly interconnected networks.[186] In other words, the presence of clusters within the network increases the likelihood of cooperative behaviour. Given that the density of the network of institutional investors is rapidly increasing, that should be the case in our setting too.[187]

In addition, the rate of cooperation significantly increases when the game is repeated,[188] even more so when the game is repeated among experienced players;[189] that is, when players are experienced, the prospect of future rounds of the game has a stronger effect on cooperation rates than with inexperienced players.[190] From this perspective, it must be noted that mutual fund managers and other institutional investors often hold shares in portfolio companies for a relatively long period of time.[191] This gives them the opportunity to repeat the game multiple times while

[185] Ibid.

[186] See Assenza et al. (n 110) 4.

[187] Network density is related to the clustering of a network because it expresses the ratio between the existing ties and all potential ties. For our purpose, it is important to note that the density of the institutional investor network defined in terms of co-ownership ties is growing rapidly. For instance, it has more than tripled between 2000 and 2010. See Azar (n 104) 3. Technically speaking, if institutional investors are large enough to own shares in an extremely high number of firms, one might end up with a single gigantic clique. Realistically, however, a minimum level of co-investment may be needed in order for co-ownership ties to be relevant for coordination purposes. While it cannot be ruled out that there will be ever more concentration within the asset industry market in the future, the multi-decade trend has been the opposite, according to Crane and colleagues, and there are natural limits to aggregate passive investment. See Crane et al. (n 13) 176.

[188] Pedro Dal Bó, 'Cooperation Under the Shadow of the Future: Experimental Evidence from Infinitely Repeated Games' (2005) 95.5 American Economic Review 1591, 1591.

[189] Pedro Dal Bó and Guillaume R. Fréchette, 'On the Determinants of Cooperation in Infinitely Repeated Games: A Survey' (2018) 56.1 Journal of Economics Literature 60, 66–67.

[190] Ibid. 68.

[191] Passive funds are by definition quasi-permanent shareholders. For instance, the CEO of Vanguard once stated that '[o]ur favorite holding period is forever. We're going to hold your stock when you hit your quarterly earnings target. And we'll hold it when you don't. We're going to hold your stock if we like you. And if we don't. We're going to hold your stock when everyone else is piling in. And when everyone else is running for the exits.' F. William McNabb III, 'Getting to Know You: The Case for Significant Shareholder Engagement', Harvard Law School on Corporate Governance and Financial Regulation (24 June 2015), https://corpgov.law.harvard.edu/2015/06/24/

keeping cliques relatively stable. In addition, because most institutional investors hold shares in a very high number of companies, their stock voters can quickly gain a significant experience on how to play the game. As the voting game is repeated a large number of times and played by experienced players, collaboration is likely to emerge.

Consider also that while until 2003 institutional investors could not observe how any other institution voted in each portfolio company, after the SEC required mutual funds to disclose their votes[192] public monitoring of this subset of institutions has become possible. That, in turn, entails a significant increase in the likelihood of cooperation.[193]

Finally, some large institutional investors make their voting intentions available to the public *prior* to shareholders meetings.[194] This can be seen as an attempt to give credibility to their commitments. Casting a different vote after their voting intention has been made public would be most likely to carry a significant reputational hit. Thus, if institutional investors implicitly or explicitly agree to cooperate and gather information, they can then signal that they do not intend to rubber-stamp management's proposals or blindly follow proxy advisors' recommendations by declaring their voting intentions.

V. Conclusion

During recent decades, institutional investors have increasingly become central players in U.S. corporate governance. Key to their influence upon portfolio companies is the exercise of voting rights. Empirical evidence shows that patterns of connections affect institutional investors' behaviour, including in the exercise of voting rights. An atomistic focus is therefore insufficient to understand their governance role fully. This chapter has moved in the direction of shedding light on institutional investor voting behaviour by using network theory, which is *the* methodology to analyse settings in which patterns of connections are relevant. Because ours is an exploratory study, we have stopped short of capturing every nuance and have limited ourselves to the more modest task of uncovering some relevant

getting-to-know-you-the-case-for-significant-shareholder-engagement/. Active mutual funds might have a somewhat shorter time horizon. Large funds, however, tend to be simultaneously connected via many co-ownership ties, thus keeping the core of the cliques relatively stable. For instance, it is implausible to expect Fidelity to suddenly sell all its shares in firms in which also Vanguard is a shareholder.

[192] See note 68 and accompanying text.

[193] Dal Bó and Fréchette (n 189) 63–64.

[194] For example, the California Public Employees' Retirement System (CalPERS) attempts to publish its voting decisions prior to shareholder meetings. See James McRitchie, CalPERS Discloses Proxy Votes in Advance of Meetings, CorpGov.net (22 December 2015), https://www.corpgov.net/2015/12/calpers-discloses-proxy-votes-in-advance-of-meetings/.

insights. In particular, we have shown that competition among nodes in the institutional network takes place at multiple levels (inter-employees, inter-firm, and inter-cliques), and that connections at each of these levels can shape institutional investors' interactions and decisions, including on how to vote.

From within individual institutions, employees compete for better jobs, and by doing so obtain relevant information on portfolio companies and spread it through their network. We have also seen, however, that this information is not necessarily always reliable and can trigger undesirable information cascades.

Institutional investors also compete with each other. The literature has traditionally focused on this level of competition.[195] The key problem is that, even when institutional investors have an incentive to obtain information on their portfolio companies, they might be paralysed by rational apathy and rational reticence. Inter-clique competition might help to explain why the problems of rational reticence and rational apathy are at times overcome. While an individual institution that invests in monitoring (i.e., a cooperator) might become less competitive vis-à-vis institutions that do not (i.e., defectors), a clique of cooperators might outperform a clique of defectors. Therefore, this kind of network dynamic might increase the incentives of institutional investors to cast informed votes in portfolio companies.

To summarise, atomistic explanations of institutional investor voting, which have dominated so far in legal scholarship, do not fully account for the dynamics underlying such key players' behaviour and, more broadly, their corporate governance role. This chapter has illustrated how network theory can help legal scholars as well as policy makers and practitioners to gain a better understanding of how institutional investors decide whether and how to vote.

[195] See Pauline Kennedy et al., 'The Competitive Effects of Common Ownership: Economic Foundations and Empirical Evidence' (2017), https://papers.ssrn.com/sol3/papers.cfm?abstract_id=3008331, 22.

B. INSTITUTIONS, NETWORKS, AND COURTS

12
Conflict of Interest and Decision Making

Geneviève Helleringer[1]

Abstract: This chapter looks at conflicts of interest (COI). It first considers tools of analytic philosophy to highlight the notion of COI, and in particular, the connection between COIs, choice and judgment, emphasising why decision making is a central element in the characterisation of COIs. Drawing on these elements, it is clear that any question of regulation and institutional design requires a sophisticated understanding of the capacity of individuals to recognise and resist bias in themselves and others when making judgments and decisions.

The chapter then studies two specific mechanisms—bounded rationality and cognitive biases—that affect the behaviour of people in COI situations. It starts by analysing how rationalisation can reframe questionable behaviour as appearing acceptable, and how a sense of invulnerability encourages people to downplay the impact of COIs. The chapter then looks at techniques (policies, procedures, incentives, etc.) used to address COI situations in the light of insights from psychological studies. It concludes that both fiduciary duties and procedural requirements reflect an erroneous understanding of psychology and have led institutions and policies to deal ineffectively—if not indeed counterproductively—with the problems caused by COIs.

Finally, the chapter assesses how alternative mechanisms may overcome the highlighted deficiencies. It specifically focuses on the key role that professional norms can play in dealing with unavoidable COIs while preserving trust between the affected parties, and the potential for self-regulation to provide worthwhile tools in combatting the harmful effects of COIs.

***

The issues of greed and corporate ethics are never far from business media headlines. Take—to name just a few recent examples—the media coverage surrounding

[1] Essec Business School / Oxford University, Institute of European and Comparative Law. Large parts of this chapter are based on discussions and work that I did in collaboration with Sunita Sah and Christina Skinner, to whom I am grateful and indebted. All errors remain mine.

Genevieve Helleringer, *Conflict of Interest and Decision Making* In: *Theories of Choice*.
Edited by: Stefan Grundmann and Philipp Hacker, Oxford University Press (2021). © The several contributors.
DOI: 10.1093/oso/9780198863175.003.0013

Goldman Sachs activism defence chief Steven Barg's move to activist investor Elliott;[2] or Vice-President Mike Pence's stay at the Trump International Golf Hotel while on an official visit to Ireland;[3] or credit-rating agency Moody's US$864 million penalty for dishonestly inflating the ratings of its paying customers in the run-up to the 2007 financial crisis.[4]

Despite the best intentions and efforts of policy makers, legislators, boards, and professional consultants, corporate scandals continue to occur. Over and over again, we see benevolent representatives (be they corporate directors, employees, or public officers) and well-meaning advisors (whether accountants, financial advisors, or lawyers) striving to do their best but nonetheless making decisions or taking actions damaging to the entities that rely on them.[5] This reminds us that the ethics of behaviour is not merely a matter of personal moral values,[6] integrity,[7] and moral imagination.[8] Social and financial connections influence behaviour in predictable ways.[9] In particular, as the examples above illustrate, it is not rare for advisors and representatives to face a clash between their professional obligations and their personal interests, and to find themselves in situations generally referred to as 'conflict of interest' ('COI').[10] In concrete terms, they are expected to exercise judgment on behalf of another, because of their position as advisor or representative; however, they also have a special interest that then to interfere

[2] See, e.g., Lindsay Fortado et al., 'Goldman Sachs rivals circle after top banker jumps to Elliott' *Financial Times* (London, 14 August 2019) <https://www.ft.com/content/d0988156-be0b-11e9-b350-db00d509634e>.

[3] See, e.g., Ross Barkan, 'Pence's stay at Trump's Irish hotel shows corruption has become routine' *Guardian* (London, 5 September 2019) < https://www.theguardian.com/commentisfree/2019/sep/05/trump-emoluments-corruption-mike-pence-hotel>.

[4] See, e.g., Aruna Viswanatha and Josh Beckerman, 'Moody's agrees to settle financial crisis-era claims for $864 million' *Wall Street Journal* (New York, 14 January 2017) < https://www.wsj.com/articles/moodys-agrees-to-settle-financial-crisis-era-claims-for-864-million-1484355287>.

[5] Max H. Bazerman and Ann E. Tenbrunsel, *Blind Spots: Why We Fail to Do What's Right and What to Do About It* (Princeton University Press 2011).

[6] That is, an 'enduring belief that a specific mode of conduct or end-state of existence is personally or socially preferable to an opposite or converse mode of conduct or end-state': Milton Rokeach, *The Nature of Human Values* (Free Press 1973).

[7] That is an adherence to a consistent set of moral principles or values, see Ksenia Krylova et al., 'Followers' Moral Judgments and Leaders' Integrity-Based Transgressions: A Synthesis of Literatures' (2017) 28 The Leadership Quarterly 195.

[8] That is 'a sense of the variety of possibilities and moral consequences of their decisions, the ability to imagine a wide range of possible issue, consequences and solutions': Patricia H. Werhane, 'Moral Imagination and the Search for Ethical Decision-Making in Management' (1998) Business Ethics Quarterly 75, 76.

[9] Lee Ross and Richard E. Nisbett, *The Person and the Situation: Perspectives of Social Psychology* (McGraw-Hill 1991).

[10] For examples from business, law, medicine, and public policy, see Don Moore et al. (eds.), *Conflicts of Interest. Challenges and Solutions in Busines, Law, Medicine and Public Policy* (Cambridge University Press 2005).

with the proper exercise of judgment in their relationship with their advisees or representees.[11]

COIs have become a concern in all organisations and in political life. It may therefore come as a surprise that the concept was hardly used until the 1950s,[12] even though some of its core elements were well known—including the idea of imposing special duties on trustees, fiduciaries, judges, and professionals. This belated emergence can partially be explained by the fact that traditional schools of ethical thought were naively inclined merely to instruct the 'conflicted' individual to resist temptation maintain objectivity while carry out their duties. However, experimental psychology has now shown that it is a dead-end, since conflicted individuals can have their judgment compromised even when they try their best to 'correct' for the influence of the conflicting interest. In addition, as the economy has become increasingly interconnected, and as the roles and sizes of governments have grown, opportunities for COI situations have increased.

It is worth stressing that while all professions explicitly make the management of COIs a central feature of their codes of conduct, one does not have to be a member of a profession to have a COI. The law treats many senior managers and 'officers' similarly to how it treats professionals—with very explicit fiduciary obligations to serve others' interests ahead of their own.[13] This development is congruent with widespread and growing pressure from stakeholders on corporations to behave in a responsible manner[14] and on legislators to ensure enhanced disclosure of COIs. By way of illustration, the recent revised EU Shareholders Rights Directive requires heightened transparency in member states for transactions between a director and

[11] For an in-depth analysis of each term of the definition, see Michael Davis, 'Introduction' in Michael Davis and Andrew Stark (eds.), *Conflict of Interest in the Professions* (Oxford University Press 2001) 3–19, at 8.

[12] A lexicological study found no use of the term 'conflict of interest' prior to the 1930s, and prior to the 1950s in court: Neil Luebke, 'Conflict of Interest as a Moral Category' (1987) 6 Business and Professional Ethics Journal 67. Luebke noted that 'conflict of interest' was absent from the 1971 *Oxford English Dictionary* and did not appear in the *Random House Dictionary of the English Language* until 1971, albeit with a definition 'that emphasizes the governmental use of the term to the virtual exclusion of the private sector'. Similarly, among 'standard law dictionaries it does not appear in the exhaustive American and English Encyclopedia of Law of 1887, in John Bouvier's Law Dictionary and Concise Encyclopedia of 1914, or in any edition of Black's Law Dictionary until 1979'.

[13] For example, Section 201 of Title 2 of the Sarbanes–Oxley Act restricts firms in charge of audits from offering other consulting services to the same clients. One part of the firm may indeed have fiduciary obligations to serve the interests of a particular principal (e.g., a client, but also perhaps the public, as in the case of auditors or engineers), but another part of the firm may have an interest in selling services to that client that may not be in its (or the public's) best interests.

[14] See the Business Roundtable Statement on Corporate Purpose rejecting shareholder primacy and embracing stakeholder corporate governance: Kevin J. Wheeler et al., 'Statement on the purpose of a corporation' *Business Roundtable* (19 August 2019) <https://opportunity.businessroundtable.org/

the company (known as self-dealing transactions).[15] Digital technologies, too, contribute to the pressure towards better COIs watch, by creating greater visibility for corporate actions.

More generally, we must be aware that the typical 'look and feel' of a COI may evolve in an environment that is itself evolving ever more quickly. Typically, the widespread introduction of artificial intelligence ('AI') technologies creates unprecedented issues in connection with COIs.[16] For example, AI might legitimately be used by a hospital to improve a person's healthcare. However, the information obtained thereby might also be used to deny the same person health-related insurance.

Another example, in the financial sector, new COIs are on the horizon. As financial institutions become larger and more diversified,[17] decisions must be made about how to allocate investment opportunities between branches and clients. Consider a hypothetical situation: the CEO of Goldman Sachs becomes aware of a unique investment opportunity, one that is 90% likely to generate a handsome (and safe) return. The opportunity could go to Goldman's asset management subsidiary, its retail group, or its wholesale trading arm. How is that decision to be made, and who is to consider the conflicting interests between the retail investment arm and the other parties? The answer is not likely to be dictated by fiduciary duty rules, but it does arguably implicate the best interests of retail investors and whether they are being treated fairly in the mix of the holding company's subsidiaries.

In this chapter, I engage with the question of how institutions (including professions) should be structured so that they and their members can successfully avoid or manage COIs. The core claim is that because COIs harm judgment-making abilities, insights from behavioural sciences need to be harnessed to design policy responses that are behaviourally savvy, and therefore efficient and able to anticipate novel COI challenges on the horizon. The aims of this chapter are twofold, analytical and critical. Section I attempts to conceptualise COIs coherently as a category based on philosophical and behavioural-psychological concepts, and to highlight

wp-content/uploads/2019/09/BRT-Statement-on-the-Purpose-of-a-Corporation-with-Signatures-1.pdf>. See, however, the Council of Institutional Investors' statement that protection of stakeholders other than shareholders should be left to government regulation: Council of Institutional Investors, 'Council of Constitutional Investors responds to Business Roundtable Statement on corporate purpose' <https://www.cii.org/aug19_brt_response>.

[15] Directive (EU) 2017/828 of 17 May 2017 amending Directive 2007/36/EC as regards the encouragement of long-term shareholder engagement.

[16] See Ioannis Ioannou and Sam Baker, 'Thinking ahead: AI and automating corporate ethics' *London Business School* (London, 15 February 2019) <https://www.london.edu/lbsr/thinking-ahead-ai-algorithms-and-automating-corporate-ethics>.

[17] See, e.g., J. Cox, '5 biggest banks now own almost half the industry' *CNBC* (15 April 2015) <https://www.cnbc.com/2015/04/15/5-biggest-banks-now-own-almost-half-the-industry.html>.

the need for more empirical and theoretical work in this regard. Section II, in turn, seeks to analyse the current and potential techniques used to address COIs, with a particular emphasis on the shortcomings of existing formal regulatory mechanisms, and the potential for firm- and industry-led extra-legal mechanisms, such as a firm or industry's culture, to fill the gaps

I. Relevance of Decision-Making to Analyse Conflicts of Interest

Though examples of COI situations easily come to mind, defining them as a category turns out to be rather arduous. Schematically, a COI occurs when an interest interferes with an obligation to act in another person's interest. Scholars have only quite recently attempted to theorise the rough ideas that practitioners have forged in practice through necessity.[18] While the effort remains incomplete, an insightful analysis, inspired by legal ethics scholarship, establishes judgment making and interference with proper judgment and decision making as the central tenets of COIs.

A. Impaired Judgment Making as a Key Feature of Conflict of Interest

1. Defining COI: insights from analytical philosophy

Philosophical debates over the definition of COIs can be traced back to a 1982 article by Michael Davis, entitled 'Conflict of Interest'.[19] Davis worked to reconcile existing legal analyses of COIs with the first previous theoretically significant academic contribution, namely, Joseph Margolis's 'Conflict of Interest and Conflicting Interests'.[20] Building on the foundations of the American Bar Association's understanding of the concept, Davis produced both a full-blown

[18] See, in particular, Joseph Margolis, 'Conflict of Interest and Conflicting Interests' in Tom L. Beauchamp and Norman B. Bowie (eds.), *Ethical Theory and Business* (Prentice Hall 1979) 361; Michael Davis, 'Conflict of Interest' (1982) 1 Business and Professional Ethics Journal 17; William Snead, 'Commentary' (1982) 1 Business and Professional Ethics Journal 29; Neil Luebke, 'Conflict of Interest as a Moral Category' (1987) 6 Business and Professional Ethics Journal 66; Michael Davis, 'Conflict of Interest Revisited' (1993) 4 Business and Professional Ethics Journal 21; Neil Luebke, 'Conflict of Interest: A Response to Michael Davis' (1993) 4 Business and Professional Ethics Journal 47; John Boatright, 'Conflict of Interest: A Response to Michael Davis' (1993) 4 Business and Professional Ethics Journal 43.

[19] Michael Davis, 'Conflict of Interest' (1982) 1 Business and Professional Ethics Journal 17.

[20] Margolis (n 18).

conceptual definition[21] as well as a 'rough formulation' that reads: a person P 'has a conflict of interest if, and only if (1) P is in a relationship with another requiring P to exercise judgment in the other's behalf and (2) P has a (special) interest tending to interfere with the proper exercise of judgment in that relationship'.[22]

The crucial terms in this formulation are 'relationship', 'judgment',[23] 'interest', and 'proper exercise', and there is a broad consensus among theorists on these key features, and on the fact that in COI situations, a representative's judgment and ability to act in the interest of a principal are potentially compromised.

Most disagreements, on the other hand, stem from differences in the ways in which scholars and institutions understand the concept of COI or interpret notions like 'interest' or 'relationship', and to differing degrees of emphasis placed on 'exercising judgment' or 'fulfilling a duty'.[24] As a consequence, discussions remain surrounding the more specific question of what is the most essential element that the COI situation interferes with—the decision-making process, the ability to act in the other's interest, or the ability to carry out one's duty.

When engaging in the legal analysis of COIs and the design of fair behaviour recommendations, there are good reasons to accord special emphasis to the 'judgment impairment' dimension as a particularly important feature of COIs. First, if one reasons *a contrario*, one has to recognise that giving prominence to 'acting in the other's interest' over the decision-making dimension tends to conflate situations of COI and those of the generic 'principal–agent' problem. Although most COIs can be conceived of as involving at least one agent (e.g., the professional or expert in the examples above) and at least one principal (e.g., the client), many

[21] Davis, 'Conflict of Interest' (n 18) 24: '[A] person Pj has a conflict of interest in role R if, and only if:

a. Pj occupies R;
b. R requires exercise of (competent) judgment with regard to certain questions Q;
c. A person's occupying R justifies another person relying on the occupant's judgment being exercised in the other's service with regard to Q;
d. Person P2 is justified in relying on Pj's judgment in R with regard to Q (in part at least) because Pj occupies R; and
e. Pj is (actually, latently, or potentially) subject to influences, loyalties, temptations, or other interests tending to make Pj's (competent) judgment in R with regard to Q less likely to benefit P2 than Pj's occupying R justifies P2 in expecting.'

[22] Michael Davis, 'Introduction' in Michael Davis and Andrew Stark (eds.), *Conflict of Interest in the Professions* (Oxford University Press 2001) 8.

[23] While 'judgment' often includes evaluation and therefore concerns one's opinion about a situation or thing, a 'decision' usually involves the determination to act in one way or another, or not to act at all. See Daniel Kahneman, 'Judgment and Decision Making: A Personal View' (1991) 2 Psychological Science 142. A decision implies therefore some kind of judgment. In the present chapter, we do not need to mark a strict distinction between 'decision' and 'judgment'.

[24] For example, Boatright argues that COIs should be defined not in terms of 'judgment' but more broadly in terms of 'acting' in another's interest: John Boatright, 'Financial Services' in Michael Davis and Andrew Stark (eds.) (n 22) 219. Similarly, Thomas Carson stresses the centrality of 'fulfilling a duty': Thomas Carson, 'Conflict of Interest and Self-Dealing in the Professions: A Review Essay' (2004) 14 Business Ethics Quarterly 165.

principal–agent problems should not be analysed in terms of COI. Take the example of a painter (the agent) hired by an employer (the principal) to do relatively unsupervised work, and who has an interest in shirking by being lazy and doing as little work as he can get away with. There is a conflict between the employer's interest in getting as much work out of the employee as possible, and the employee's interest in not working too hard, but it is not a COI. In the example given, the painter is subject to the will of the employer; as an agent, the painter is under the principal's control (even if monitoring is difficult in practice). In other words, a person has a COI because of the kind of situation he finds himself in, that is, one that requires him to make *a choice between two lines of conduct that are both advisable from the point of view of either of personal interest or consistency with his duties, but which are incompatible with each other* for reasons other than the state of his own desires, motives, etc. This factor distinguishes the conflicted professional from the generic shirking or corrupt agent.[25]

Second, from an analytical perspective, the judgment impairment dimension allows us to recognise that COI situations stem from the mere *existence* of a *moral problem*.[26] Therefore, COI situations can exist even in cases where the professional is morally and psychologically committed to serving his client's interests to the best of his abilities, and not to be influenced by conflicting personal interests. This is so because in this situation, the professional faces the moral problem of having to *exercise judgment* in deciding whether to prioritise the client's interest or his own.[27] In contrast, earlier thinkers like Aristotle and Kant focused the moral analysis of such situations on the 'professional' in question having (or failing to have) the *courage* to do the right and honourable thing and to resist the temptations of corruption. As long as he has remained virtuous and fulfilled his primary duties, nothing morally wrong has happened. There are, however, two problems with this virtue-centric approach. First, it places too much confidence in the ability of conflicted individuals to know if their judgment is being compromised. Second, it does not take into account the fact that the organisation they work for can be harmed merely by the suspicion that the employees are being presented with 'unsupervised' opportunities for corruption.

Because the concept of COI is a construction, there is no independently existing reality against which to test the extent of judgment impairment caused by a COI. Probing the deep meaning of the expression in ordinary language would

[25] An important observation is that an 'agent' is subject to the will of the principal with respect of the agent's conduct of power; fiduciaries act for others but not under their 'control': they are not agents. The relationship between shareholders and directors is not an agency relationship. A board—while obliged to act in the benefit of the firm and, as a consequence, the shareholders—is not subject to the shareholders' control (in the way that corporate officers are subject to the board's control). Like public officials, directors are 'representatives' rather than agents.

[26] What will be morally right or wrong is how one responds to the problem.

[27] The existence of a personal interest opens a possible new course of action that would not have been available otherwise.

likewise not be helpful, as the phrase is of recent use. Nevertheless, COI is now a well-explored concept and the contours of the COI concept outlined above provide a set of specific ethical, legal, economic, and political questions raised by COIs. They also enable us to distinguish COIs from other conflicts, sometimes described as COIs but which are in fact more generic and raise different issues than COIs. An example is the conflict between self-interest and social values: neither self-interest nor social values are identified components of COIs.[28]

2. Further distinctions among conflicts of interest

Although there is substantial agreement that the central case of COI is where an interest conflicts with the exercise of judgment in another's service,[29] it is nevertheless useful to attempt to distinguish between different kinds of conflicts in order to understand why it is morally problematic to be in a COI situation. The categorisation suggested here attempts to single out these various failings, and to distinguish between kinds of conflicts. The categorisation suggested here distinguishes four kinds of COIs based on how they arise: (i) conflicts arising from acts that impair impartiality (e.g., accepting a gift or representing clients with mutually contradictory interests may lead to unreliable professional decisions); (ii) conflicts arising from engagement in direct competition (e.g., an employee of one private endeavour who has an interest in a competing endeavour must decide whether to use, for the latter's benefit, training and competences conferred upon him as employee); (iii) conflicts arising from abuse of position (e.g., characterising a corporate opportunity presupposes a decision as to the company's interest in grabbing that opportunity); and (iv) conflicts arising from the misuse of information (e.g., where a journalist is tempted to delay publishing information that will affect the prices of stocks that he owns personally). The suggested categorisation is based on identifying the specific failings, rather than the legal requirements (duty of loyalty or care) in danger of being breached.

Alternatively, some scholars distinguish between conflicts of *interests* (breach of the duty of loyalty) and conflicts of *duty* (implying a breach of the duty of care, in addition to a breach of the duty of loyalty).[30] On the basis of the definition

[28] Tom Tyler, 'Managing Conflicts of Interest Within Organizations: Does Activating Social Values Change the Impact of Self-Interest on Behavior' in Don A. Moore et al. (eds.), *Conflicts of Interest* (Cambridge University Press 2005) 13.

[29] See, e.g., reluctantly, John Boatright, 'Conflict of Interest: a Response to Michael Davis' (1993) 12 Business and Professional Ethics Journal 43; and, more openly, John Boatright, *Ethics and the Conduct of Business* (7th edn, Pearson 2014) 112.

[30] This distinction is also described as 'out-of-role' (between an individual's professional duties and his private interests) and 'in-role' (involving a tension between two or more different professional duties an individual or firm may have) COIs. 'In-role' conflicts can be subdivided into situations where an agent assumes 'more than one role with respect to any given principal' and those where he assumes the 'same role with respect to many principals': A. Stark, 'Comparing Conflicts' in Davis and Stark (eds.) (n 22) 336. The classic example of the second—'many principals, one role'—type is a lawyer with concurrent adversarial clients. However, it could also include a broker who manages accounts for multiple clients but must choose between them when allocating a security in short supply, or a corporate director

suggested, however, this distinction appears unnecessary:[31] the canonical example of the latter—divided attention between various principles—can be described as an example of direct competition against a given principle. Under these circumstances, when a person is obliged to act in the interest of two different persons or organisations whose interests conflict, the conflict is 'impersonal' rather than 'personal'. It means that organisations experience conflicts that respond to the general definition of COI.

It is, of course, difficult to assess the contribution of such a philosophical definition and to determine whether it helps understand the situation better. In particular, no empirical enquiry is available regarding how closely it coincides with practice in legal ethics across various jurisdictions. No experimental study is available to assess the conceptualisation's utility and reliability (i.e., whether different users are likely to get the same result given the same circumstances), both in itself and by comparison with alternative suggestions. However, the criterion of the reliability of judgment exercised in the service of another person does appear compatible with many circumstances that are recognised in practice as involving a COI.

B. Bounded Rationality and Conflicted Behaviours

Why do COIs cause bad behaviours? According to a frequent metaphor, COI situations tend to sway the compass needle away from north.[32] Because we may not even be aware of this deviation, we may remain convinced that we are behaving ethically while it might be dubious whether in fact we are. Empirical and experimental research[33] have uncovered two mechanisms through which COIs may

dealing with competing interests of minority and majority shareholders. In-role conflicts falling within the first category—'many roles, one principal'—conflicts tend to emerge either (i) because 'the professional simultaneously occupies a judging and an advocating role—an impartial and a partial role —in the work he does for the principal', as when professors grade graduate students, and then agree to write letters of recommendation for them with a hope of landing them jobs; or (ii) because of a 'tension between the professional's diagnostic and service-provision roles, his roles as both a buyer of services for, and a seller of services to, the principal', as when a dentist examines your teeth and then offers to fix the problems she 'discovered'.

[31] The distinction is usually ignored in practice. See, e.g., Rule 1.7(a) of the American Bar Association's Model Rules of Professional Conduct listing under conflicts of interest the case in which a lawyer represents two clients with conflicting interests.

[32] Celia Moore and Francesca Gino, 'Ethically Adrift: How Others Pull Our Moral Compass from True North, and How We Can Fix It' (2013) 33 Research in Organizational Behavior 53–77.

[33] Seminal work on this topic is by Daniel Kahneman and others, investigating cognitive biases (patterned deviations of human cognition from the predictions of rational choice theory) and motivational biases (biases rooted in the tendency for judgment to be affected by the individual's own interests). These biases affect perception and choice in everything from the way individuals evaluate risks and the desirability of particular outcomes to their own understandings of what motivates them to do the things they do. See Daniel Kahneman et al. (eds.), *Judgment Under Uncertainty: Heuristics and Biases* (Cambridge University Press 1982).

influence judgment making unbeknownst of the decision maker. The first consists in humanity' ability to rationalise, while the second relates to cognitive biases that overinflate one's confidence in one's own professionalism.[34]

1. Rationalisation

People usually view themselves as acting ethically and in a competent manner.[35] Having the desire to appear ethical to ourselves and others, we may resist engaging in behaviour that is obviously unethical. Nevertheless, we are also likely to rationalise behaviour that is more self-serving than we would care to admit. In particular, a sense of entitlement tends to unconsciously liberate representatives and advisors to accept gifts from third parties that could be construed as potential bribes.They often rationalise this behaviour by viewing such gifts as a perk of their profession, or as morally acceptable because it is common practice to accept them.

2. Invulnerability

Representatives and advisors, like most individuals, usually consider they are not to be influenced by COIs. They often believe that such conflicts will not affect their ability to make impartial decisions, commonly citing their 'professionalism', as partners from Arthur Andersen and PricewaterhouseCoopers often testified before the US Securities & Exchange Commission.

In reality, however, although professionals may believe that personal interest or a minor gift would not impact their decision making, research on influence and reciprocity demonstrates the contrary.[36] Individuals are unable to remain objective, even when incentivised to be impartial, which suggests an unintentional bias. In addition, they succumb to bias but will deny having done so.[37]

A series of experiments examined how beliefs about one's professionalism contribute to biased judgments in the presence of COIs.[38] Results show that participants report themselves as being less susceptible than the average individual to influence from accepting gifts. Also, the more 'professional' people feel they are—that is, the greater they believe their ability to be in making objective decisions and

[34] Sunita Sah and George Loewenstein, 'Effect of Reminders of Personal Sacrifice and Suggested Rationalizations on Residents' Self-Reported Willingness to Accept Gifts: A Randomized Trial' (2010) 304 Journal of the American Medical Association 1204; Sunita Sah and Richard Larrick, 'The Invulnerability Bias: Self-Perceived Professionalism Predicts Increased Acceptance of, and Influence from, Conflicts of Interest' (2016) Cornell University Working Paper.

[35] Karl Aquino and Americus Reed II, 'The Self-importance of Moral Identity' (2002) 83 Journal of Personality and Social Psychology 1423.

[36] Robert B. Cialdini, *Influence: The Psychology of Persuasion* (HarperBusiness 2006). Sunita Sah and Adriane Fugh-Berman, 'Physicians under The Influence: Social Psychology and Industry Marketing Strategies' (2013) 41 Journal of Law, Medicine & Ethics 665.

[37] Lisa Babcock and George Loewenstein, 'Explaining Bargaining Impasse: The Role of Self-Serving Biases' (1997) 11.1 The Journal of Economic Perspectives 109–26.

[38] Sah and Larrick (n 34).

self-regulating the influence of small gifts—the more likely they are to accept gifts and be influenced by them, while remaining unaware of the influence or their bias.

These results demonstrate that a belief in one's high level of professionalism may actually be associated with unconscious bias. This points to a need not merely to educate decision makers, but also to structure institutions themselves so as to effectively insulate judgments from interests that might otherwise interfere.

II. Ethical Decision-Making in Conflict of Interest Situations

When one analyses the current and potential techniques used to address COIs, shortcomings of existing formal regulatory mechanisms are blatant. However, a case made be argued in favour of firm- and industry-led extra-legal mechanisms such as culture to fill the gaps.

A. The Inadequacy of Existing Policies

Public and private regulation relies on two main types of provisions: standards of conduct, and procedural requirements, which present several shortcomings from a behavioural perspective.

1. Standards of behaviour

In addressing COIs, common law jurisdictions have traditionally relied on fiduciary duties, which provide a standard of behaviour, as well as disgorgement sanctions. Civil law jurisdictions have increasingly adopted a similar approach,[39] especially for conflicts that were traditionally left unsanctioned and therefore less easily incorporated into the existing legal machinery, such as the diversion of corporate opportunities by managers.[40]

Recent research in behavioural ethics suggests that people are more likely to behave unethically if the standards of ethical behaviour are ambiguous.[41] One of the reasons is that under such circumstances, people tend to demonstrate a self-serving bias when interpreting the ethical nature of their own behaviour. The more malleable the standard for unethical behaviour, the more likely it becomes that self-serving bias will push actors into concluding that self-interested behaviour is

[39] See Martin Gelter and Genevieve Helleringer 'Fiduciary Duties in Civil Law Jurisdictions' in Paul Miller and Robert Sitkoff (eds.), *Oxford Handbook on Fiduciary Duties* (Oxford University Press 2019) 583.

[40] See Martin Gelter and Genevieve Helleringer, 'Opportunity Makes the Thief. Corporate Opportunities vs. Private Profits in Comparative Perspective (US, UK, Germany and France)' (2018) 15 Berkeley Journal of Business Law 1 92.

[41] Yuval Feldman, *The Law of Good People* (Cambridge University Press 2018) 185.

not morally problematic. The lack of clear and well-defined borders between COI and non-COI situations strongly suggests that the self-serving bias will cause representatives and advisors to interpret questionable behaviour as falling within the boundaries of what is ethical (or at least not unethical), and thus promote more unethical behaviour as a whole than if the lines of demarcation were clearer ex ante. Disgorgement, therefore, is likely to aggravate rather than improve the behaviour of conflicted people by encouraging them to analyse a decision as a cost-benefit business decision rather than an ethical one.[42]

There is, in addition, the practical problem in that conflicts of divided loyalty may pose an ethics trap by creating a tension between the fiduciary duty of care and the fiduciary duty of loyalty.[43] Take, for example, whistle-blowing, which involves a conflict between two competing duties: the duty to protect the public from serious harm whenever it is in our power, and the duty to be loyal to an organisation of which we form part.

2. Procedural requirements

In civil law jurisdictions, COIs have more often been regulated via procedural requirements, such as disclosure obligations or approval by a designated body. This is an approach that is, in practice, also very prominent in common law countries.[44] At first sight, procedures are rule-based and therefore protected from the risk of rationalisation that corrodes standards. However, a closer look at two common such requirements—fairness opinions and disclosure—shows that they are both flawed.

Fairness opinions typically involve seeking a second opinion as an antidote to potential bias caused by, for example, a primary advisor's COI. For example, a corporate board is able to hire a second advisor to help absolve the first advisor, if the latter is suspected of bias. However, in 2015, social psychologists found strong evidence to suggest that second opinions may not be the panacea they appear to be.[45] This research found that while clients who received a high-quality second opinion made better decisions than clients who did not, a curious thing happened when primary advisors were aware that their clients might seek a second opinion. In such cases, primary advisors adopted a profit-maximising approach and gave even more biased advice than if they were unaware of the possibility of a second opinion being sought.

[42] Ann E. Tenbrunsel and David M. Messick, 'Ethical Fading: The Role of Self-Deception in Unethical Behavior' (2004) 17 Social Justice Research 223; Ann E. Tenbrunsel and David M. Messick, 'Sanctioning Systems, Decision Frames, and Cooperation' (1999) 44 Administrative Science Quarterly 684.

[43] Arthur R. Laby, 'Resolving Conflicts of Duty in Fiduciary Relationships' (2004) 54 American University Law Review 75.

[44] See Genevieve Helleringer and Marco Corradi, 'Board Duty: Duty of Loyalty and Self-Dealing' in Afra Afshari and Martin Gelter (eds.), *Research Handbook on Comparative Corporate Governance* (E Elgar, forthcoming 2020).

[45] Sunita Sah and George Loewenstein 'Conflicted Advice and Second Opinions: Benefits, but Unintended Consequences' (2015) 130 Organizational Behavior and Human Decision Processes 89.

Experimental evidence suggests similar shortcomings regarding disclosure. Disclosure is one of the most common solutions for dealing with COIs across a range of industries and professions. However, a number of unintended consequences of COI disclosures have been documented, including advisors giving even more biased advice with disclosure than without,[46] and advisees reporting increased trust in advisors who disclose bias or conflicts.[47] In addition, advisees who are informed of their advisors' COI sometimes feel increased pressure to comply with their advisor's recommendation despite trusting the advice less than advisees who are not similarly informed.[48]

More generally, procedures known as safe-haven mechanisms tend to offer ways to behave unethically without breaking applicable law. There is indeed a legal trap; not everything that is legal is ethical. For example, under French law, certain self-dealing transactions that are highly suspicious by nature, such as deals between companies that have common directors or managers,[49] are subject to authorisation by the board and approval by the shareholders. Only five years ago, the Commercial Code started to require the board of directors to *justify* its authorisation to proceed with the transaction:[50] until then, the decision had been discretionary, leaving room for group-think effect at the board.[51]

B. Building a Norm-Rich Decision-Making Culture

While designing a clear and compelling normative methodology that would allow corporations and managers to justify the imposition of obligations beyond legal compliance, and to calibrate reasonable trade-offs between claims of competing stakeholders, is crucial, this is beyond the scope of this chapter. However, an important point must be made about one particular deficiency in the legal machinery at play, and how one specific extra-legal mechanism—culture—can fill the gap.[52]

46 Daylian M. Cain et al., 'When Sunlight Fails to Disinfect: Understanding The Perverse Effects of Disclosing Conflicts of Interest' (2011) 37 Journal of Consumer Research 836.

47 Sunita Sah et al., 'Effect of Physician Disclosure of Specialty Bias on Patient Trust and Treatment Choice' (2016) 113 Proceedings of the National Academy of Sciences 7465.

48 Sah and Fugh-Berman (n 37); Sunita Sah et al., 'Insinuation anxiety: fear f signaling distrust after conflict of interest disclosures' (2015) Working Paper <http://media.wix.com/ugd/4aa4b7_ac680ce8d4224a46ab1f8cc54b684ab8.pdf>.

49 Commercial Code Art. L225-38, para. 3.

50 Commercial Code Art. L. 225-38, para. 4.

51 For a more in-depth analysis, see Genevieve Helleringer 'Related-Party Transactions in France. A Critical Assessment' in Lucas Enriques and Tobias Troeger (eds.), *The Law and Finance of Related Party Transactions* (Cambridge University Press forthcoming 2019).

52 These developments are based on Genevieve Helleringer and Christina Parajon Skinner, 'Conflicts of Interest: Comparing Compliance and Culture in the United States and the United Kingdom' in Danny Busch, Guido Ferrarini, and Gerard van Solinge (eds.), *Corporate Governance of Financial Institutions. Law, Conduct and Culture* (Oxford University Press 2019) 489.

1. The role of norms in decision-making

The previous subsection has shown that the usual menu of solutions to the problem of COIs reflects an erroneous understanding of psychology. This ignorance, pervasive among members of the government, industry, and general public has led to institutions and policies that deal ineffectively, and even sometimes counterproductively, with the problems caused by COIs. Because COIs cannot, and perhaps should not,[53] be eliminated, a more realistic objective appears to be to mitigate their harmful consequences. From that perspective, a useful starting point is the empirical observation that people do not always act in ways that are consistent with their own self-interest, and that professional norms are a powerful guide for behaviour.[54] This is explained by the role of context in organisational decision making.[55] Specifically, human action appears 'driven by rules of appropriate or exemplary behaviour, organi[s]ed into institutions. Rules are followed because they are seen as natural, rightful, expected and legitimate'.[56] People take reasoned action by answering (implicitly or explicitly) three questions: (i) Recognition: What kind of situation is this? (ii) Identity: What kind of person am I? (iii) Rules: What does a person such as myself do in a situation like this?[57] Internalised prescriptions, or 'scripts' of what one ought to do, determine the appropriate behaviour. Once ethical motivations are activated, cost-benefit analyses and calculations of self-interest are of little importance in ethical decision making.[58] If an action is viewed as appropriate, right, moral, and just, professionals will simply comply.

Directors as well as lawyers, accountants and, other professional advisors learn norms that define their roles. However, these professional norms are often learned through socialisation practices within the institution in which one works. In some institutions, the primary role may be perceived as: "to make money" for their institutions rather than to serve their representees or advisees.[59] Indeed, bankers and other salespersons may be socialised into a culture in which they can only

[53] For example, self-dealing transactions may be desirable even if the counterparty is conflicted, because the latter is sole able to accurately evaluate the value of the asset without incurring disproportionate costs.

[54] Robert B. Cialdini et al., 'Normative Influences in Organizations' in Leigh L. Thompson et al. (eds.), *Shared Cognition in Organizations: The Management of Knowledge* (Lawrence Erlbaum Associates Publishers 1999) 195.

[55] James G. March, *A Primer on Decision Making: How Decisions Happen* (Free Press 1994).

[56] James G. March and Johan P. Olsen, 'The logic of appropriateness' (2004) Arena Centre for European Studies Working Papers, 2 <http://www.sv.uio.no/arena/english/research/publications/arena-publications/workingpapers/working-papers2004/wp04_9.pdf>.

[57] March (n 56); March and Olsen (n 57).

[58] Tom R. Tyler, 'Managing Conflicts of Interest within Organizations: Does Activating Social Values Change The Impact of Self-Interest on Behavior' in Don A. Moore et al. (eds.), *Conflicts of Interest: Challenges and Solutions in Business, Law, Medicine, and Public Policy* (Cambridge University Press 2005) 13.

[59] Milton Friedman, 'The Social Responsibility of Business is to Increase its Profits' in Walther C. Zimmerli et al. (eds.), *Corporate Ethics and Corporate Governance* (Springer 2007).

succeed by offloading stocks or goods, regardless of their worth or benefit to the client.[60]

Occupations are characterised by commonly perceived standards of ethical behaviour. One study demonstrated that when bankers' professional identity was activated—by reminding them that they were indeed bankers—they were more likely to behave unethically than when their professional identity was not activated.[61] A series of studies, similarly, demonstrated that advisors required to disclose a COI reacted differently depending on the perceived professional norms of the context.[62] When advisors subject to real monetary COIs were informed that they were giving financial advice, the advisors who had to disclose their COI gave more biased advice, and reported that doing so was more appropriate, than those who did not have to disclose their conflict. However, when advisors, subject to the same financial COIs and monetary pay-offs, were informed that they were giving medical advice, the advisors who had to disclose now gave significantly less biased advice, and reported that it was significantly less appropriate to give biased advice, than those advisors who were not required to disclose. The COI disclosure reminded advisors of their professional ethical dilemma and served as a signal that triggered prescribed professional norms—both where these norms dictated self-interested advice and where they dictated that the advisee be put first. Disclosure prompted advisors in the financial context to prioritise their own self-interest, whereas advisors in a medical context prioritised the patient's.

Thus, one way to improve professional advisors' ethical behaviour is to activate feelings of obligation and responsibility towards advisees. In contexts with strong ethical norms, COI disclosure may do so inherently.[63] Where such norms are absent, changing professional norms and the ethical climate from the top down will be necessary.[64] Ways to effect this change may include implementing situational cues to behave ethically, for example with honour codes or repeated reminders,[65] may increase the ethical nature of decisions.

However, ethical codes can only play a limited role on their own, unless accompanied by wider institutional culture change. Thus, in an attempt to 'debias' people, Babcock and Loewenstein educated study participants about

[60] William D. Cohan, 'Wells Fargo scandal may be sign of a poisonous culture' *New York Times* (New York, 17 September 2016) <http://www.nytimes.com/2016/09/17/business/dealbook/wells-fargo-scandal-may-be-sign-of-a-poisonous-culture.html>.

[61] Alain Cohn et al., 'Business Culture and Dishonesty in The Banking Industry' (2014) 516 Nature 86.

[62] Sunita Sah, 'Conflict of Interest Disclosure: Professional Norms and the Appropriateness of Biased Advice' (2016) Cornell University Working Paper.

[63] Ibid.

[64] David M. Mayer et et al., 'How Low Does Ethical Leadership Flow? Test of a Trickle-Down Model' (2009) 108 Organizational Behavior and Human Decision Processes 1.

[65] Nina Mazar et al., 'The Dishonesty of Honest People: A Theory of Self-Concept Maintenance' (2008) 45 Journal of Marketing Research 633.

self-serving biases.[66] While participants' awareness of bias increased, they still believed, often more strongly, that others were susceptible to self-serving biases and that they themselves were not. Even if education or ethics training is incorporated at the start of employment, people often engage in a process called 'ethical fading',[67] a phenomenon whereby difficult moral issues are pushed to the background or removed altogether from a decision-making process, while more straightforward, objective business issues come to the forefront. The fact that Enron had a sixty-four-page 'Code of Ethics' booklet, for instance, serves as a powerful reminder that culture has a stronger impact on moral decision making than formal codes.

2. Promoting ethical decision-making

Concretely, what might organisations do? What follows are two possibilities for implementing a more ethical culture enabling COIs to be identified and managed: conflict modelling, and proxies for personal liability.[68]

a. Conflict modelling

One possible strategy is for organisations to employ more scenario-based exercises in connection with their efforts to improve conduct. Such qualitative, conduct-focused stress testing may involve, for example, the compliance function putting a hypothetical scenario of misconduct to employees, and collecting and modelling their responses. These scenarios could be tailored to COI-type situations, with the idea being to anticipate the types of conflicts that might be coming down the pike. One could readily imagine scenarios crafted around the kinds of conflicts that could emerge in the context of investment allocation decisions, fintech platforms, and the marketing of advisory services, as discussed earlier.

By innovating the method and form of conflicts-oriented stress testing, firms could encourage thinking outside the box, encourage employees to challenge existing ideas (both up and down the firm hierarchy), and generally send a firm-wide message that addressing the risks posed by conflicts is a priority on par with the management of quantitative risks like market and credit risk. To the extent that results of the simulation are voluntarily shared with supervisory authorities, this collaboration may in fact facilitate regulators understanding the

[66] Linda Babcock and George Loewenstein, 'Explaining Bargaining Impasse: The Role of Self-Serving Biases' (1997) 11 Journal of Economic Perspectives 109.

[67] Ann. E. Tenbrunsel and David M. Messick, 'Ethical Fading: The Role of Self-Deception in Unethical Behaviour' (2004) 17 Social Justice Research 223.

[68] These developments are based on Genevieve Helleringer and Christina Parajon Skinner, 'Conflicts of Interest: Comparing Compliance and Culture in the United States and the United Kingdom' in Danny Busch, Guido Ferrarini, and Gerard van Solinge (eds.), *Corporate Governance of Financial Institutions. Law, Conduct and Culture* (Oxford University Press 2019) 489, 511.

most appropriate (and helpful) supervisory role they can play in intervening in firm culture.

b. Proxies for personal liability

As private actors, organisations therefore have considerable latitude to innovate responsibility mechanisms that could become the industry (and even regulatory) gold standard. Responsibility mechanisms might, for instance, be fortified through compensation schemes. Positively, organisations might choose, for example, to calibrate bonuses based on the contribution of an employee who has a role of advisor to the organisation's culture or values (in addition to traditional performance or sales targets). Culture-based compensation awards, however, could also be negative; that is, firms may reduce discretionary compensation awards where the employee is unable to carry forth a burden of showing his contribution to firm culture/values surrounding the ethical treatment of the customers (an even more aggressive approach could be to impute responsibility to managing directors for serious shortcomings in the conduct of associates and analysts).

Organisations could also demonstrate their excellence along a conduct dimension by leading the development of industry standards. While a firm might innovate ways of socialising a more ethical culture among their own employees and directors the firm could then go a step further in pioneering methodologies of propagating those innovations at the industry level. Firms could, for instance, lead their peers by convening forums, working groups, knowledge sharing programmes, or other initiatives for cross-pollinating culture-related ideas.

Doing so would not have to be purely altruistic. On the contrary, taking the initiative to develop industry standards could give a firm the opportunity to set an industry-agreed baseline, possibly, thereby, pre-empting supervisory authorities from establishing more specific (and potentially less appropriate) requirements. Notably, this kind of strategy, where the firm leads the regulator, resonates with various theories of administrative governance, like experimentalism and management-based regulation.

III. Conclusion

COIs increasingly attract attention. However, with much of rule making and guidance-giving centred on fiduciary duty rules, there is some risk that firms, in adhering closely to the regulatory agenda, will fail to respond to the true behavioural traps in decision making that COIs create, and that they will not be able to anticipate the next generation of conflicts on the horizon.

In this context, forward-looking organisations have an opportunity to demonstrate industry leadership in ethical conduct, both to the supervisory authorities and the client. They might do so by pioneering innovative methods for establishing an organisational culture that values conflict-free interactions.

Such efforts, though not mandated by law or regulation, could nonetheless be incentivised by the opportunity to set industry standards and garner conduct-based competitive advantage in a rapidly evolving marketplace.

13
Decision Making in Chains and Networks of Contracts

Stefan Grundmann

Abstract: Networks of contracts serve mainly as a long-term form of organisation, both features being typically combined. This combination—the so-called organisational contract—is seen as a hybrid between market and firm. There are different explanations for its existence and two are particularly prominent. Williamson sees them as a governance device to cope with the problem of uncertainty of future events, namely in situations where one party has invested in a particular relationship more than the other and therefore is 'more dependent' on its continuance. Conversely, Powell sees them as a scenario where neither command nor anonymous exchange dominate, but mutual (often personalised) trust and reciprocity based on strong mutual knowledge of the partners are marked. These two explanations imply how fascinating the organisational contract may be for decision theory and the law. This chapter addresses the phenotype of (long-term) networks of contacts and sees a large variety of them ranging from rather standardised to highly tailor-made arrangements, which implies a heterogeneous basis for decision-making theories and their application. With respect to decision-making theories that are considered in the second section, the chapter takes a broad perspective. While it may be attractive to apply mainly one decision theory to the phenomenon, the chapter asks which decision theories might have particular explanatory value. Thus, a broader survey on a multifaceted compound of theories might be particularly suitable for the heterogeneous aspects of the phenomenon. The chapter also addresses the question of which repercussions the discussed decision theories might have in law.

Stefan Grundmann, *Decision Making in Chains and Networks of Contracts* In: *Theories of Choice*.
Edited by: Stefan Grundmann and Philipp Hacker, Oxford University Press (2021).
DOI: 10.1093/oso/9780198863175.003.0014

I. Phenotypes of Long-term/Network Organisational Contracts

A. Long-term Relationships and Network—A Variety of Arrangements and Core Characteristics

Networks of long duration are not only explained in various ways—for instance, by Williamson on the one hand and Powell on the other. They also exist in quite diverse phenotypes in real life. In all cases, however, the combination of a long duration and of the network character of the organisational basis seem paramount.[1] One point should, however, be clarified from the outset. While, on the one hand, long-term relations without the formation of a network of contracts are possible and even frequent, the opposite does not hold true. There are, of course, long-term loan, agency, and consulting agreements, life-care services, renting of premises, etc.without these contracts being necessarily integrated into a network of contracts arrangement. Conversely, to form a network of contracts—to create a common network goal—makes sense primarily and pays off only when it has an extended duration. Even the most basic form—the arrangement of linked contracts—is characterised by mere exchange contracts ('discrete contracts') on the side of the client only. The opposite is true even for this simple type of linked contracts already on the side of the professional parties involved, such as suppliers of goods/services and professional lenders. On this side, we are confronted with a long-term relationship. Therefore, while the core explanations were historically given earlier for the long-term character (see section II), it is only the network basis that by necessity creates an organisational contract. Both core features are, however, equally interesting from a decision theory perspective, with the difference being that the network feature may not have been the topic of much research from this perspective thus far.

When it is emphasised that long-term/network organisational contracts come in a wide variety, two poles seem to stand out. On the one side, there are standardised networks, used where business processes are repeated and automated, such as for instance in payment systems. On the other, we find completely individualised, tailor-made networks, with high flexibility and informality, often for an intense exchange of information, and particularly well suited to high innovation, like the Silicon Valley network so important for Powell (see below). While these constitute two opposite poles, a large range would seem to lie in between them that reflects a rich and nuanced spectrum of reality. The image is therefore one of a continuum rather than that of two opposite poles and forms. This spectrum is

[1] For a comprehensive survey with social sciences basis, see Stefan Grundmann, Fabrizio Cafaggi, and Giuseppe Vettori (eds.), *The Organizational Contract—From Exchange to Long-Term Network Cooperation in European Contract Law* (Ashgate 2013).

broad even when one does not consider that—beyond the spectrum of long-term networks of contracts—the range of alternatives exists, namely with firm on the one hand and market on the other. When one names at least a few examples it also becomes clear how important the organisational contract is in practice and that it forms the backbone of the modern economy. Despite being rather less well known and researched than the alternatives of market and of firm, it might even be more important or at least older than both, forming the true 'original' phenomenon in business.[2] Indeed, the typical process of shaping and manufacturing products, and often services too, is unthinkable without networks; on the one hand, the upstream network existing in supply chains, on the other, the downstream network of distribution chains. The processes in them may be less mechanical than in a typical payment system yet they are situated on this side of the spectrum, with a relatively high precision and continuity of the characteristics required for performance (high detail of standardisation). One main difference of these chains with payment systems that strongly impacts on the decision-making process would seem to lie in how the requirements of performance are decided. In the case of supply or distribution chains, one party—often the producer, downstream, and also large vending chains, albeit after consultation with the other members of the network—decides on those requirements, while in the case of payment systems, national standard terms and agreements or legislatures play a core role. A similar amount of precision in determining the requirements is not only be found in vertical chains but in horizontal arrangements, namely franchise systems, as well. When one moves to the opposite side of more tailor-made, individualised networks, other networks of exchange relationships than those found, for instance, in Silicon Valley come to mind. Similar, yet often more formalised, are joint ventures for research and development. Here, the borderline with firms is palpable and, in some jurisdictions, such as in German law, it has already been crossed. Research, development, production, distribution, and marketing, uniformity, and the presentation to markets, payment of the product/service, all these would seem impossible without networks of contracts. The overwhelming importance of networks as an organisational form is obvious, yet the amount of formalisation or spontaneity is very different, and hence also problems of decision making largely vary.

Certain core characteristics of the long-term/network organisational contract will be identified here with reference to the two poles referred to earlier. This is done for simplicity's sake but what is explained with regard to the poles applies,

[2] Early for both contentions, see, on the one hand Ian Macneil, 'Relational Contract: What We Do and Do Not Know' (1985) 66 Wisconsin Law Review 483–525, 490: 'Such a discrete economy [consisting of discrete contracts only] would . . . have low *productive* capacity.' See, on the other hand: Walter Powell, 'Neither Market nor Hierarchy—Network Forms of Organization' (1990) 12 Research in Organizational Behaviour 295–336, 296 et seq., 298–301: The market in particular is portrayed as a spin-off of networks, therefore the 'hybrid' (network), historically speaking, rather forming the 'original'.

with modifications, to the variations too. This chapter is not the place to focus on all the characteristics and forms of such networks but it can offer an impression of some of the core characteristics that may more strongly impact on decision making proper.

Three features appear to be of particular importance. First, decision making is highly related to the distribution and use of information. For the standard model of institutional economics, (sufficiently) full information is indispensable for any decision making as a normative prerequisite for the functioning and reliability of the model(s), and even where this assumption is not maintained, as is partly the case in behavioural models, the way information becomes available and is used remains important. Therefore, the theory of decision making under uncertainty is of obvious importance because it deals with settings of incomplete or probabilistic information (see section II.B).

For this reason, second, it is important whether, in the particular arrangement, the exchange of information is an aim in itself and not just an instrument of performance. This is more often the case on one side of the spectrum, that is, in tailor-made individualised networks, namely in exchange arrangements on research and development (such as found in Silicon Valley). Conversely, payment systems are primarily and most directly about transfer of money value, and the transfer of information merely serves this aim and is purely instrumental rather than being the main aim. In this respect, theories on how information is passed on or how it proliferates (including the question of how information then is made use of) would seem to be significant. This relates, for instance, to the theory of information cascades and observational learning (with the wisdom of the crowd), including the question of how eagerly such information is taken up (versus apathy, see section II.C).

Third, the question of how each party can react to what it expects to be the reactions of the other parties is particularly meaningful. This is potentially the domain of game theory, however, in the form of a mutual aspiration theory (Reinhard Selten) rather than in the form of an expectation of fully rational behaviour of the other parties (see section II.D). In this case, however, non-parametric decision making may prove particularly difficult to model. This question is, however, also the domain of a theory that does not see the prime basis for decision making in the expected reactions of other partners but rather in trust concerning a long-term, mutually beneficial outcome of the collaboration more generally (without calculating immediate reciprocity; networks as a 'house of trust', see section II.E). While these three characteristics—with their variations and even divergences in the different types of long-term/network organisational contracts—seem to be particularly important for the question of decision theories and the law, they do not exhaust the potentially important features. They are hence paradigmatic, not comprehensive.

B. Social Sciences Explanations of Long-term/Network Organisational Contracts

When the long-term/network organisational contract is explained nowadays, the articles by Macaulay and Macneil—legal scholars with strong legal sociology backgrounds—are typically seen as the starting point.[3] However, the contributions by Williamson, an institutional economist (for long-term duration and its particular problems and vulnerabilities),[4] and Powell, an economic sociologist (for the network arrangement and its underlying rationale),[5] are genuinely groundbreaking. Williamson argues that the characteristics of *long-term relationships* are often such that the future is unknown and unforeseeable and that it is more costly to try to negotiate all possible future contingencies than leave the decision making to a good ex post governance regime instead. One particular feature in Williamson's theory is that such an arrangement is recommended mainly for one reason. This is the vulnerability that stems from the fact that one party—despite being ignorant of the future—may invest more in this particular relationship (such as into a manufacturing chain for the production of a particular piece, or invests into moving to a certain workplace, etc.) than the other party. Making 'relation-specific investment' renders this party particularly vulnerable (risk of sunk costs in case of opportunistic behaviour of the other side). As such, an investment can, however, be mutually beneficial when the collaboration warrants higher returns, and the 'deadlock' Williamson describes should indeed be broken by installing credible instruments of ex post governance.

Powell, on the other hand, argues for *networks of contracts* as constituting a third organisational design for economic collaboration, different both from markets and from firms and not a hybrid of them both (as was always assumed in conceptualisation of the phenomenon before). What completely distinguishes networks of contracts both from markets and from firms are the highly different party expectations—hence also fields of application—and, as a consequence of this, the completely different decision-making approach by participants in that network. For Powell, decision making in networks is guided by a feeling of generalised trust

[3] See Stewart Macaulay, 'Non-Contractual Relations in Business—A Preliminary Study' (1963) 28 American Sociological Review 55–67; Ian Macneil, 'Relational Contract: What We Do and Do Not Know' (1985) 66 Wisconsin Law Review 483–525 and references in note 2. Moreover discussion in: Stefan Grundmann, 'Betweeen Market and Hierarchy' in Stefan Grundmann, H. Micklitz, and M. Renner (eds.), *New Private Law Theory—A Pluralist Approach* (Cambridge University Press 2020), chapter 17—also for Oliver Williamson, 'Transaction-Cost Economics: The Governance of Contractual Relations' (1979) 22 Journal of Law & Economics 233–61; Oliver Williamson, *The Economic Institutions of Capitalism—Firms, Markets, Relational Contracting* (MacMillan 1985) 15–42; Powell (n 2); and in the text following this footnote.

[4] See Williamson, 'Transaction-Cost Economics' (n 3) and Williamson, *The Economic Institutions of Capitalism* (n 3) particularly at 20–22 and 26 (preference for ex post governance instead of ex ante decision making) and 30–32 (trust relationships as one exception where other mechanisms are at work).

[5] See references in note 2.

in the partners in the network that (on the basis of good mutual knowledge) is bestowed on them without expecting a concrete reward, but rather with trust in a long-term beneficial character of the relationship in the network. While decision making in markets is based on expectations of direct rewards and in firms on the power to instruct within this type of hierarchy, decision making in networks is completely different in this sense. It is seen as decision making between peers (no command power) and with mutual trust and no expectation of immediate and calculable return (reciprocity atmosphere, no 'deal' or market exchange philosophy).

These two approaches by Williamson and Powell—while both are groundbreaking for one of the two key features of long-term *and* network organisational contracts—nevertheless do not have the same pertinence with regard to decision theory. Williamson's theory does not focus on how decisions are made but rather recommends postponing decision making and allocating decision-making power adequately. The only exception would seem to be trust relationships where decision making relying on fair and faithful behaviour of the other party is assumed (because of strong bonds of friendship or family). This case, however, forms a rare exception for Williamson. Therefore, his theory can be seen as elucidating the core features of long-term relations but barely about decision making within them. Conversely, Powell formulates a theory on how and on which basis the partners in networks make their decisions, hence a decision theory, where trust in long-term beneficial effects is the driving force, and substantial irritants are required until this attitude of trust towards the network (or at least one of its partners) is overthrown.

II. Decision Theories Related to Long-term/Network Contracts

Based on this short analysis of the key features, some core characteristics, and the basic rationale for the existence of long-term networks of (organisational) contracts and of their different phenotypes, the next two sections try to enquire into less well-known ground. Current research has yet to focus on the remaining two questions: how decisions are made in networks of contracts of the different kinds named (based on a discussion of the question which theories of decision making explain the decisions typically made) (section II.A-E), and what legal consequences one can derive from such explanations (section III.B).

A. Introduction to Decision Theories for Organisational Contracts—A Pluralist Stance

There can be different expectations with which the question of how decision theories might impact on legal reasoning can be approached. One can wish for the one theory that best explains a phenomenon and gives best guidance for a sound (legal) policy to adopt[6]—an approach adopted in principle by monist approaches such as law and economics.[7] One can also characterise a particular field of law, for instance company law, as an area where legislatures should not decide on the question of which decision theory should be followed, but instead any such choice should be left to the key private law actors. This would imply that even the question regarding whether they behave rationally or not and how information is passed on and used is, at least in principle, irrelevant—better, left to the parties to decide—for and within this legislative choice.[8] The former wish would seem to be not only unrealistic but also normatively problematic (as will be explained later). Similarly, the latter stance can only constitute the result of considerations made and not a starting point in a world where market failure is recognised and where, in a second step, we acknowledge the need for correcting market failure, at least whenever the overall outcome can be enhanced. After having analysed the decision-making processes, the result reached might be that the process is so flawless or vitiated only to such a minor degree that leaving everything to the decision making of the parties constitutes the more advisable solution. As this question is much less well-researched with regard to the long-term/network organisational contract than it is for companies and decision making within them (but also than for markets), it would seem to be appropriate to understand the decision-making processes in our field more intimately in any case and even without such an immediate regulatory perspective.

This approach, however, raises one more question concerning the choice of appropriate method, returning to what has been said about monist approaches. Decision making can of course be analysed from one methodological perspective only—or more accurately, from the perspective of one decision-making theory only. Typically, the advantage of such an approach will be that it is more targeted and thereby will furnish more clear-cut answers as well. This advantage comes, however, at the price of excluding a multitude of approaches that do not seem to be unrelated to the decision-making problem at stake. If in all Western democracies under the rule of law as well as in market economies, the constitutional and democratically posited value basis is pluralistic, and if different disciplines target different values primarily—economics, for instance, targets efficiency and not primarily solidarity (social redistribution) or even human dignity—one conclusion would seem

[6] See in this sense contribution by Sibony in this volume,—however overall critical whether such a choice can ever be made, perhaps even whether it is desirable at all.

[7] On the differentiation of monist and pluralist interdisciplinary approaches to legal scholarship and practice, see Stefan Grundmann, 'Pluralism and Private Law Theory: How From a Pluralist Legal Value Basis Only a Pluralist Law Theory Can Ensue ("Normative Pluralism")' (forthcoming); also for more guidance on the rest of this subsection.

[8] See in this sense, in principle, for decision making in the corporate setting the contribution by Velasco in this volume. More intrigued by questions of whether decision-makers that make use of network effects warrant higher returns and therefore have incentives to make such active decisions in cooperation with others, see the contribution by Enriques and Romano in this volume.

to be obvious.[9] The legal system as a whole—including legal scholarship—cannot dispense of those other decision-making theories developed in other contexts and disciplines at the price of concentrating on one exclusively ('normative superiority' of a pluralist legal theory). This consideration speaks in favour of taking a bird's-eye view here rather than a more targeted 'monist' perspective (even though more focused essays are, of course, helpful). There is one more aspect that prompts us to try to look at and analyse the overall landscape: the multitude rather than the singular approach—an aspect that appears to be particularly strong in the area of long-term/network organisational contracts. It would seem to be the case that in many questions and even, more broadly, fields of law, monist approaches and their results are already well developed. Conversely, however, the overall summary—the interplay, taking stock and weighing, deciding on how to establish hierarchies—of most or of a good deal of the most prominent theories, such as decision theories, has rarely occurred. At least for long-term/network organisational contracts, this is a lacuna that cannot be ignored and that this chapter attempts to map for the first time.

For this purpose, the chapter approaches the question of decision making in chains and networks of contracts in two steps. In this section and as a first step, it sets out those theoretical approaches which seem most promising as explanatory instruments in the sphere of long-term/network contractual networks ('organisational contracts'), followed by the second step, relating such approaches to law (see section III). In this section on decision theories, the chapter identifies four particularly promising approaches. These are theories of decision making under uncertainty (Amos Tversky/Daniel Kahneman; Cass Sunstein/Christine Jolls/Richard Thaler); game theory (namely in the form of repeated games, with a particular emphasis on information problems, Robert Aumann; Reinhard Selten); informational cascades and observational learning (Sushil Bikhchandani/David Hirshleifer/Ivo Welch and colleagues); and networks as the 'house of mutual

[9] See, for instance, on the prevailing view that Western constitutions are based on a concept of pluralist value basis, certainly one where for instance efficiency is not the prevailing one: Stephen Tierney, *Constitutional Law and National Pluralism* (Oxford University Press 2005); Neil Walker, 'The Idea of Constitutional Pluralism' (2002) 65 The Modern Law Review 317–59; Udo Di Fabio, 'Grundrechte als Werteordnung' (2004) 59 Juristenzeitung (JZ) 1–8; Ernst Fraenkel, *Deutschland und die westlichen Demokratien* (6th edn, Kohlhammer 1974) 197 et seq.; also Michal Ovádek, 'Constitutional pluralism between normative theory and empirical fact', VerfBlog (23 October 2018); Art. 2(2) TEU characterises pluralism explicitly as the signature feature of the European Union and the societies and states united in it. For a sociological perception of fundamental rights as guarantees of social differentiation of different areas of and systems in society: Gert Verschraegen, 'Human Rights and Modern Society: A Sociological Analysis from the Perspective of Systems Theory' (2002) 29 Journal of Law and Society 258–81; on the impact of the concept of pluralism in the EU Fundamental Rights Charter on European contract and antidiscrimination law, see Dan Wielsch, 'The Function of Fundamental Rights in EU Private Law—Perspectives for the Common European Sales Law' (2014) 10 European Review of Contract Law 365–89, 370–72. For the consequences specified in the following see Grundmann (n 7); for repercussions on legal methodology see Oliver Lepsius, 'Rechtswissenschaft in der Demokratie' (2013) 52 Der Staat 157–86.

trust/reciprocity' (Walter Powell and colleagues). For these decision theories, the chapter enquires into the question of how fruitfully they can be used in the two main phenotypes named above for (legal) problems arising and for explaining the (legal) decisions made.

One last remark is helpful in viewing the overall picture of 'organised decision making' before entering into the four decision-making theories named above. It is obvious that both markets and firms are researched more broadly than long-term/network organisational contracts. It would seem, however, less acknowledged that the focal points of discussion nowadays—rational choice versus bounded rationality (with different types of biases)—are more directly targeted at markets and even at firms. Even though biases are of course universal and strong in the realm of professional decision making as well,[10] bounded rationality research still maintains its strongest focus on consumers[11] and—similar in this respect—on investors, at least private investors,[12] or even on the heterogeneity of investors as a problem.[13] Conversely, for the peer-to-peer scenario of long-term/network organisational contracts—with a long-term view of overall advantage that is not and need not be exactly calculated—this prominent theme seems to lose much of its

[10] Paul Brest and Linda Hamilton Krieger, *Problem Solving, Decision Making, and Professional Judgment* (Oxford University Press 2010) 300 et seq.; Michael Haigh and John List, 'Do Professional Traders Exhibit Myopic Loss Aversion? An Experimental Analysis' (2005) 60 Journal of Finance 523–34; Mark Fenton-O'Creevy et al., 'Trading on Illusions: Unrealistic Perceptions of Control and Trading Performance' (2003) 76 Journal of Occupational and Organizational Psychology 53–68; Laure Cabantous, 'Ambiguity Aversion in the Field of Insurance: Insurers' Attitude to Imprecise and Conflicting Probability Estimates' (2007) 62 Theory and Decision 219–40; Devin Pope and Maurice Schweitzer, 'Is Tiger Woods Loss Averse? Persistent Bias in The Face of Experience, Competition, and High Stakes' (2011) 101 American Economic Review 129–57; Brad LeVeck et al., 'The Role of Self-Interest in Elite Bargaining' (2014) 111 Proceedings of the National Academy of Sciences 18536–41; Brian Bornstein and A. Christine Emler, 'Rationality in Medical Decision Making: A Review of the Literature on Doctors' Decision-Making Biases' (2001) 7 Journal of Evaluation in Clinical Practice 97–107; Philipp Hacker, *Verhaltensökonomik und Normativität* (Mohr Siebeck 2017) 132–35; in this book, probably most clearly in the contribution by Ahlert and in the contribution by Enrique and Romano.

[11] See, for instance, Richard Thaler, 'Toward a Positive Theory of Consumer Choice' (1980) 1 Journal of Economic Behavior & Organization 39–60; Richard Thaler, 'Mental Accounting and Consumer Choice' (1985) 4 Marketing Science 199–214; Diane DiClemente and Donald Hantula, 'Applied Behavioral Economics and Consumer Choice' (2003) 24 Journal of Economic Psychology 589–602; Gordon Foxall et al., *The Behavioral Economics of Brand Choice* (Palgrave MacMillan 2007); Gordon Foxall, 'Behavioral Economics in Consumer Behavior Analysis' (2017) 40 The Behavioral Analyst 309–13. In this book, this focus is very clear in the contribution by Sibony but implicit probably also in that of Hacker.

[12] On their similarity with consumers in behavioural models of decision making, see Shlomo Benartzi and Richard Thaler, 'How Much Is Investor Autonomy Worth?' (2002) 57 Journal of Finance 1593–616, 1595 et seq.; John Campbell et al., 'Consumer Financial Protection' (2011) 25 Journal of Economic Perspectives 91–114, 105 et seq.; extensively Nick Chater, Steffen Huck, and Roman Inderst, 'Consumer Decision-making in Retail Investment Services: A Behavioural Economics Perspective' Final Report to the European Commission/SANCO (2010).

[13] On this heterogeneity problem (and as well its repercussions on how to conceptualize and potentially influence decision-making processes), see Alan Schwartz, 'Regulating for Rationality' (2015) 67 Stanford Law Review 1373–410; Philipp Hacker, 'The Behavioral Divide' (2015) 11 European Review of Contract Law 299–345, 305 et seqq.; Stefan Grundmann and Philipp Hacker, 'Conflicts of Interest' in Dan Busch and Guido Ferrarini (eds.), *Regulation of the EU Financial Markets* (Oxford University Press 2017) 165–204, at para. 7.23; and also contribution to this volume by Hacker.

sting as well as the dominant position that it holds in current considerations about markets and capital markets (and about professional investors, as in Chapter 11 in this volume). This does not imply that it cannot be helpful in certain other respects, for instance when deciding about which variant of game theory might be particularly elucidating in this scenario (section II. D). Conversely, theories on hierarchical decision making, such as the theory that uncertainty in decision making tends to further a hierarchical command structure to deal with the uncertainty,[14] would also seem to play out less prominently when peer-to-peer is paramount. A significant exception to this statement might be necessary regarding those cases where concrete information is passed on and some members of the network may not have the cognitive means to process it (overly complicated, technical information, see example in section II.C).

B. Decision Making under Uncertainty

While Williamson was the first scholar to conceptualise the vulnerability stemming from the ignorance of the future in the long-term, the underlying problem of uncertainty with respect to how then a decision can be taken has been analysed primarily—and certainly more deeply—along the lines established by Kahneman and Tversky.[15] They first showed that persons, when judging future prospects, typically set a certain expectation level (reference point) below which outcomes are

[14] See, for instance, Sanford Grossman and Oliver Hart, 'The Costs and Benefits of Ownership: A Theory of Vertical and Lateral Integration' (1986) 94 Journal of Political Economy 691–719; Oliver Hart and John Moore, 'Property Rights and the Nature of the Firm' (1990) 98 Journal of Political Economy 1119–58; Oliver Hart, *Firms, Contracts, and Financial Structure* (Oxford University Press 1995); but also for one particularly prominent application, namely in the scenario of take-overs: Sanford Grossman and Oliver Hart, 'One Share/One Vote and the Market for Corporate Control' (1988) 20 Journal of Financial Economics 175–202.

[15] Daniel Kahneman and Amos Tversky, 'Judgment under Uncertainty—Heuristics and Biases' (1974) 185 Science 1124–31; Daniel Kahneman and Amos Tversky, 'Prospect Theory: An Analysis of Decision under Risk' (1979) 47 Econometrica 263–91; the latter, the second most quoted paper in economics during the period 1975–2000 according to David Laibson and Richard Zechhauser, 'Amos Tversky and the Ascent of Behavioral Economics' (1998) 16 Journal of Risk and Uncertainty 7–47, was further refined in Amos Tversky and Daniel Kahneman 'Advances in Prospect Theory: Cumulative Representation of Uncertainty' (1992) 5 Journal of Risk and Uncertainty 297–323, and taken up, for instance, in: Pedro Bordalo, Nicola Gennaioli, and Andrei Shleifer, 'Salience Theory of Choice Under Risk' (2012) 127 Quarterly Journal of Economics 1243–85; Nicholas Barberis and Richard Thaler, 'A Survey of Behavioral Finance' in George Constantinides, Milton Harris, and René Stulz (eds.), *Handbook of the Economics of Finance*, Part 1 B (Elsevier 2003) 1053–128, 1069 et seq.; Matthew Rabin, 'Psychology and Economics' (1998) 36 Journal of Economic Literature 11–46; see also (for risk-taking in traffic circulation): Peter Grossman, Reed Cearley, and Daniel Cole, 'Uncertainty, Insurance and The Learned Hand Formula' (2006) 5 Law, Probability and Risk 1–18; see also contribution by Hacker in this volume. Kahneman and Tversky systematised their research and established a systematic list of biases later on, namely in two papers still strongly related to decision making under uncertainty: Amos Tversky and Daniel Kahneman, 'Extensional versus Intuitive Reasoning—The Conjunction Fallacy in Probability Judgment' (1983) 90 Psychological Review 293–315; Amos Tversky and Daniel Kahneman, 'Rational Choice and the Framing of Decisions' (1986) 59 The Journal of Business 251–78.

seen as losses and above which outcomes are seen as gains. Then, in a second step of evaluation, they typically judge the avoidance of a loss as more important than the acquisition of the same amount of gains ('losses loom larger than gains')—contrary to standard expected utility theory.[16] This approach can be seen as a 'heuristic' that helps decision making in situations of uncertainty with less deep investigation, but the strategy typically falls short of maximising the outcome for the decision maker. Another related aspect can be seen even more clearly as a genuine cognitive bias. This is that in such decision making under uncertainty and with respect to future developments, actors tend to overestimate gains in the immediate future (e.g., consumption) and underrate more distant future gains and especially future risks (such as severe failure to perform resulting in insolvency, so-called present bias).[17]

For long-term relationships, the phenomenon of the ignorance of future developments in the relationship is of obvious importance, as are aspects of decision making under such uncertainty. In long-term/network organisational arrangements, however, not only professional peers and their decision making form the main object of consideration and therefore the problems and the biases described may be of lesser importance.[18] It may also be the case that the main interest of these organisational arrangements is indeed in the overall success of the network and the impact it has on the individual partner and, as both this success and this individual impact depend on so many factors, that a similar mechanism is triggered as with diversification. The loss and problems stemming from uncertainty might to some extent be set off by unexpected additional gains and evened out in an overall perspective (thus being 'diversified' away).[19] Moreover, if peers really only set an aspiration level with which they are happy (better off than without the network), it can probably not be characterised as frustrated expectations if the optimum outcome is not attained.

[16] On this idea, and demonstrating its existence even for small sums, see Matthew Rabin, 'Diminishing Marginal Utility of Wealth Cannot Explain Risk Aversion' in Daniel Kahneman and Amos Tversky (eds.), *Choices, Values, and Frames* (Russell Sage Foundation 2002) 202–08.

[17] See in detail David Laibson, 'Golden Eggs and Hyperbolic Discounting' (1997) 112 Quarterly Journal of Economics 443–78; Jess Benhabib, Alberto Bisin, and Andrew Schotter, 'Present-Bias, Quasi-Hyperbolic Discounting, and Fixed Costs' (2010) 69 Games and Economic Behavior 205–23; Cass Sunstein, 'The Storrs Lectures: Behavioral Economics and Paternalism' (2013) 122 Yale Law Journal 1826–99, 1842–52.

[18] In this sense, for instance Stefano DellaVigna, 'Psychology and Economics: Evidence from the Field' (2009) 42 Journal of Economic Literature 315–72, 361; for a reduction of overconfidence in professional weather forecasters (probably due to immediate 'weather feedback') Sarah Lichtenstein, Baruch Fischhoff, and Lawrence Phillips, 'Calibration of Probabilities: The State of The Art to 1980' in Daniel Kahneman, Paul. Slovic, and Amos Tversky (eds.), *Judgment under Uncertainty: Heuristics and Biases* (Cambridge University Press 1982) 306–34, 330; for the low overconfidence of expert bridge players, see Gideon Keren, 'Facing Uncertainty in The Game of Bridge: A Calibration Study' (1987) 39 Organizational Behavior and Human Decision Processes 98–114; but see also the references in note 10.

[19] A similar idea can be found, for instance, with respect to reducing the impact of biases in investment decisions. See Steven Beach and Clarence Rose, 'Portfolio Rebalancing to Overcome Behavioral Mistakes in Investing' (2009) 1 Journal of Behavioral Studies in Business 1–11, 9: 'Annual portfolio rebalancing appears to help investors achieve investment goals and overcome behavioral mistakes in investing.'

C. Informational Cascades, Wisdom of Collective Learning, or Apathy?

While decision making under uncertainty and the theory pertaining to it can and has of course been applied to multi-party settings,[20] the body of literature on informational cascades and collective learning takes this phenomenon as its very focus of consideration—multi-party settings that are of course related to the second core characteristic of long-term/network organisational contracts, the arrangement within networks. Hence, if decision making under uncertainty theory focuses on the long-term character, information cascades and collective learning theories are more telling for the network character of long-term/network organisational contracts. On the level of a whole political economy, the mechanisms of the proliferation of information are paramount and may even decide on success of the economy.[21] Long-term/network organisational contracts and the problems raised tend to be more granular, more related to individual decision making.

With respect to information cascades, very roughly speaking, the core contribution for our topic would seem to reside in the description of the typical situation where they arise and of the typical behaviour they trigger. The theory applies to situations in which persons make and modify decisions freely, the decision is rather simple (yes/no) and is made sequentially and the decisions made by others can be observed, but not the reasons for which they are made. At the same time—and this is key for the mechanism to be triggered—decision makers observing the others do not have strong personal knowledge on how best to decide. In this case, the first successive decision maker, who observes the first decision made, already tends to stop probing into his preferred solution so strongly and, whenever no rather clear conviction exists, tends to adopt the decision already taken (even though without having witnessed the first decision, she would potentially have made the other one). Moreover, this trend tends to solidify (and opposite decisions to be less likely) the longer the chain of followers becomes—even when all successive decision makers decided again only on the basis of observation and not of their own

[20] See, for instance Peter Jones and Paul Roelofsma, 'The Potential for Social Contextual and Group Biases in Team Decision-Making: Biases, Conditions and Psychological Mechanisms' (2000) 43 Ergonomics 1129–52; Christopher Robert and Peter Carnevale, 'Group Choice in Ultimatum Bargaining' (1997) 72.2 Organizational Behavior and Human Decision Processes 256–79; David Messick, Don Moore, and Max Bazerman, 'Ultimatum Bargaining with a Group: Underestimating the Importance of the Decision Rule' (1997) 69.2 Organizational Behavior and Human Decision Processes 87–101.

[21] Papers already published in the first decades after the Second World War, were ground-breaking, namely Friedrich von Hayek, 'The Use of Knowledge in Society' (1945) 35 American Economic Review 519–30; George Stigler, 'The Economics of Information' (1961) 69 Journal of Political Economy 213–25; context and further developments summarised in Grundmann (n 3) chapter 12. In this book, see contributions by Engel (thick proliferation of knowledge and transparency as ideal basis of market-wide trust); but also contributions by Deakin and Engert (focusing on the aggregation of information).

judgment.[22] On this basis, and even before the global financial crisis, Wagner and colleagues described, for instance, a higher volatility of global financial markets as a paradigmatic case—that is, a case of political economy.[23] In line with information cascades theory, they characterise the overall situation by pointing to the fact that global actors increasingly can no longer judge the reliability and the motives of others. The authors therefore assume a decrease in the possibility to second-guess decisions already made, even to such an extent that even rather implausible decisions are still followed (despite serious doubts held by the decision makers who will make decisions later in the sequence), because a breakthrough of this 'commonly held opinion' would require an increasingly strong and solidly fact-based conviction to the contrary.

Different from herding phenomena in the narrow sense,[24] however, one option of change can indeed be observed (even though not in the global financial crisis), and this option seems to be the more realistic one in cases where greater visibility of the actors and their context occurs, that is, typically the better actors know each other and the smaller the arena is. This is that an actor who has a strong conviction of a better solution than the one commonly held not only chooses this other solution but often has the power to change the decision-making path completely, and for all successive decision makers too. In other words, often this new decision maker convinces more decision makers simply than those who made decisions before her. The explanation here would be that successive decision makers assume that a change in decision making is the expression of very solid knowledge to the contrary.[25]

[22] Ground-breaking as descriptions (also on the following) here, see Sushil Bikhchandani, David Hirshleifer, and Ivo Welch, 'A Theory of Fads, Fashion, Custom, and Cultural Change as Informational Cascades' (1992) 100 Journal of Political Economy 992–1026; Abhijit Banerjee, 'A Simple Model of Herd Behavior' (1992) 107 Quarterly Journal of Economics 797–817; Ivo Welch, 'Sequential Sales, Learning, and Cascades' (1992) 47 Journal of Finance 695–732; Lisa Anderson and Charles Holt, 'Information Cascades in The Laboratory' (1997) 87 American Economic Review 847–62; Sushil Bikhchandani, David Hirshleifer, and Ivo Welch, 'Learning From The Behavior of Others: Conformity, Fads, and Informational Cascades' (1998) 12 Journal of Economic Perspectives 151–70; overview in Markus Brunnermeier, *Asset Pricing under Asymmetric Information* (Oxford University Press 2001) 147 et seq.

[23] Helmut Wagner and Wolfram Berger, 'Globalization, Financial Volatility and Monetary Policy' (2004) 31 Empirica 163–84.

[24] Information cascades and herding are compared, for instance, by Luca Corazzini and Ben Greiner, 'Herding, Social Preferences and (Non-) Conformity' (2007) 97 Economics Letters 74–80, 74 et seq.; Angela Hung and Charles Plott, 'Information Cascades: Replication and an Extension to Majority Rule and Conformity-Rewarding Institutions' (2001) 91 American Economic Review 1508–20, 1508 et seq. While the use of the terminology differs slightly between authors, herding refers to similarities or interdependencies between choices, which may be due to a cascade (see, e.g., Abhijit Banerjee, 'A Simple Model of Herd Behavior' (1992) 107 Quarterly Journal of Economics 797–817, 798), and often has a more negative connotation; cascades, generally, refer to the integration of observational information into the decision-maker's private information, which may be beneficial or detrimental, depending on the quality of the external signal.

[25] See references in note 22 et seq., and more particularly Bikhchandani, Hirshleifer, and Welch (n 22) 994 and 1009; see also, on reversing cascades more generally, In Ho Lee, 'Market Crashes and Informational Avalanches' (1998) 65 Review of Economic Studies 741–59, 746; Jacob Goeree et al., 'Self-correcting Information Cascades' (2007) 74 Review of Economic Studies 733–62.

One final word on apathy, which is discussed much more in the shareholder decision-making world, is due here.[26] Information cascades and observational learning would suggest that in this issue, one can see another comparative advantage of long-term/network organisational contracts over firms (besides those named by Powell). The impediments to make one's own information affect real-world situations are lower, because each actor can decide for herself autonomously, without being dependent on gaining a (majority) consent among the others. This should result in more active information gathering because two typical causes for shareholder apathy are removed (lowered chance to implement the result of information, the need to discount each shareholder's investment in information because he has only a share and thus does not reap 100% of the gains of his decision/intervention). Hence, from an individual decision-maker's perspective, the chances of efficient information gathering and use are considerably enhanced. The additional advantages—now not for the decision maker individually, but for all participants—might even be that the chances that a strongly informed decision then prevails (and is not itself reversed) are increased. As has been stated, such a decision not only deviates from a long row of decisions that have been made beforehand but often completely changes the path of the future decisions made.

D. The Role of Game Theory—Including Repeated Games and Mutual Aspiration Theory

Game theory—in its second branch of repeated games (without definite end) and in its modified variant of Selten's mutual aspiration theory—is at the heart of Ahlert's contribution to this volume[27] and can indeed be used in elucidating long-term/network organisational contracts. In the case of these contracts, this modified form appears as particularly attractive not only because the so-called behavioural turn has also impacted on classical game theory—responding to empirical studies that belie the assumption of fully rational choice in game arrangements.[28] On the

[26] On this phenomenon, see Theodor Baums, 'Germany' in Theodor Baums and Eddy Wymeersch (eds.), *Shareholder Voting Rights and Practices in Europe and the United States* (Kluwer Law International 1999) 109–30, 111 et seq.; Frank Easterbrook and Daniel Fischel, *The Economic Structure of Corporate Law* (2nd edn, Harvard University Press 2005) 66 et seq.; Stefan Grundmann, *European Company Law: Organization, Finance and Capital Markets* (2nd edn, Intersentia 2012) § 3 para. 29 et seq.; and also, contribution to this volume by Velasco.

[27] For an early, ground-breaking paper, see Heinz Sauermann and Reinhard Selten, 'Anspruchsanpassungstheorie der Unternehmung' (1962) 118 Zeitschrift für die Gesamte Staatswissenschaft 557–97; more recently, see Marlies Ahlert and Idiko Lajtos, *60 Years after Nash's Bargaining Solution: Trends in Bargaining Theory* (Working Paper, Martin-Luther-Universität, Jur. und Wirtschaftswiss. Fak. 2011) and the contribution to this volume by Ahlert. The background can be found in Simon's concept of mere 'satisficers' (instead of 'maximisers'), see Herbert Simon, 'A Behavioural Model of Rational Choice' (1955) 69 Quarterly Journal of Economics 99–118, 103–06.

[28] For empirical work belying these forecasts to a considerable extent, see, Richard McKelvey and Thomas Palfrey, 'An Experimental Study of the Centipede Game' (1992) 60 Econometrica 803–36; Rosemarie Nagel and Fang Fang Tang, 'An Experimental Study on the Centipede Game in Normal

side of behavioural assumptions, game theory also has a double problem of cognitive biases, not just a simple one as in most other cases. Indeed, biases can occur both on the side of the decision maker whose ideal decision is sought and modelled in game theory *and* on the side of others whose actions (as forecasted) should be reflected in the ideal decision made, but which, again, can be influenced by biases.[29] For long-term/network organisational contracts, however, the 'behavioural turn' is only one cause for focusing more on mutual aspiration theory and other variants taking biases into account.[30] The other reason is that, as Powell would put it, the strand of willpower might also be different.[31] There might not even be the will to optimise one's position (irrespective of cognitive ability to do so) but rather the desire to reach only a satisfactory level and otherwise put trust in the overall beneficial effect of the network - also with a view to increase trust in the partners (who observe such reduction of selfishness) (see section II.E).

Long-term/network organisational contracts, from a game theoretical perspective, should typically be analysed as repeated games with indefinite end—games different from the others (one-shot games or repeated games with definite ending) in that problems of opportunistic behaviour by others (partners) are seen as being radically reduced because of the mutual possibility of reaction and sanctioning.[32]

Form: An Investigation on Learning' (1998) 42 Journal of Mathematical Psychology 356–84; more broadly Herbert Gintis, *Game Theory Evolving* (2nd edn, Princeton University Press 2009); Colin Camerer, *Behavioral Game Theory: Experiments in Strategic Interaction* (Princeton University Press 2003); for a good survey, see Ahlert and Lajtos (n 27). Carsten Vogt, *Kooperation im Gefangenen-Dilemma durch endogenes Lernen—ein evolutionär spieltheoretischer Ansatz* (VDM Verlag Müller, 2001) reports 21% of cooperation in laboratory cases designed as simple prisoner's dilemma cases—where classical game theory would expect 0%. See also the contribution to this volume by Engel.

[29] In this case, classic game theory struggles with the problem where one party is not behaving rationally, even if the other party is in fact rational (classical game theory depends on computations in light of foreseeable, rational behaviour on the *other* side). The so-called trembling hand problem is groundbreaking in this respect: Reinhard Selten, 'Re-examination of the Perfectness Concept for Equilibrium Points in Extensive Games' (1975) 4 International Journal of Game Theory 22–55 (parties forecast that the other side may commit mistakes when deciding on their 'shot'; i.e. may have a 'trembling hand'). For a good and more recent account of the problem, see Herbert Gintis, *The Bounds of Reason: Game Theory and the Unification of the Behavioral Sciences* (Princeton University Press 2009).

[30] See references cited in notes 27–29 by Gintis and Selten; moreover John Harsanyi, 'Measurement of Social Power, Opportunity Costs, and the Theory of Two-Person Bargaining Games' (1962) 7 Behavioral Science 67–80; John Harsanyi, 'Bargaining in Ignorance of The Opponent's Utility Function' (1962) 6 Journal of Conflict Resolution 29–38.

[31] On bounded willpower, see, e.g., David Laibson, 'Golden Eggs and Hyperbolic Discounting' (1997) 112 Quarterly Journal of Economics 443–78; Richard Thaler, 'Doing Economics without Homo Economicus' in Steven Medema and Warren Samuels (eds.), *Foundations of Research in Economics: How Do Economists Do Economics* (Edward Elgar 1996) 227–37, 232 et seq.; Christine Jolls, Cass Sunstein, and Richard Thaler, 'A Behavioral Approach to Law and Economics' (1998) 50 Stanford Law Review 1471–550, List in Annex 1548–50; on the difference between maximizing and satisficing Herbert Simon, 'Theories of Decision-Making in Economics and Behavioral Science' (1959) 49 American Economic Review 253–83, 262–64; Herbert Simon, 'Theories of Bounded Rationality' in Bart McGuire and Roy Radner (eds.), *Decision and Organization* (North-Holland 1972) 161–76, 168 et seq.

[32] Obvious for one-shot games, but even in repeated games with definite ending, this possibility is seen as being reduced (classic game theory, because of so-called backward induction, would even say reduced to zero). See Robert Aumann, 'Backward Induction and Common Knowledge of Rationality' (1995) 8 Games and Economic Behavior 6–19.

On the other side, game theory is notoriously weak with respect to the impact on third parties—as the core example of the prisoner's dilemma shows[33]—and this forms a serious drawback when networks, especially more informal networks, are considered. Within a legal perspective, establishing the optimum solution would seem less important (as this is an issue that law typically leaves to parties, bestowing party autonomy on them) than guaranteeing the instruments that keep bargaining opportunities intact. Seen in this way, the most important contribution would seem to be one much in line with Williamson's governance concept. Legal analysis should concentrate on instruments where overall outcome in games can be enhanced, namely where regulation sanctions parties who 'defect' (in 'games') (deleterious actions).

E. A House of Mutual Trust and Generous Reciprocity

Powell's seminal article, 'Neither Market nor Hierarchy',[34] contains—albeit in a hidden way—a decision theory as well. In this theory, one can even find a grain of information cascades theory, 'avant la lettre', because Powell seems to insinuate that deviation from the general attitude of trust can be triggered only by serious causes, in other words that deviation from a path once taken requires a strong, triggering momentum. The core structural considerations are, however, rather different in the rest. Most importantly, belief in networks tends to be grounded not in superficial, shallow knowledge but rather in experience that, quite to the contrary, is solid and deep. This explains as well why the forecasts made in both strands of theory lead mostly to different results (see next section).

When Powell describes networks as completely distinct from the market and from the firm, definitely not as a hybrid ('neither fish nor fowl, nor some mongrel hybrid, but a distinctly different form'), the core reason can be summarised as follows. Above all, backed up by his broad, socio-empirical study,[35] Powell sees the

[33] Impacts on third parties are irrelevant 'inside' game theory. This can be inferred from the account of how to solve the prisoner's dilemma (i.e., how to make parties cooperate in not confessing, despite the adverse conditions), for instance D. Ross, 'Game Theory' in *Stanford Encyclopedia of Philosophy* (Center for the Study of Language and Information (CSLI), Stanford University 2010) sub 2.7. It is no concern for Ross that, for justice reasons based on the principle of retribution and on the aim of general deterrence, the legal order would indeed want to prevent cooperation.

[34] See above notes 2 and 3 (on Powell and contextualisation); but also Colin Camerer, *Behavioral Game Theory: Experiments in Strategic Interaction* (Princeton University Press 2003) 2 ('Important steps in the 1960s were the realization that behavior in repeated sequences of one shot games could differ substantially from behavior in one shot games'). Powell owes a lot to Granovetter's idea of 'embeddedness' of economic action in societal norms and contexts. See Marc Granovetter, 'The Impact of Social Structure on Economic Outcomes' (2005) 19 Journal of Economic Perspectives 33–50; Marc Granovetter, 'Economic Action and Social Structure: The Problem of Embeddedness' (1985) 91 American Journal of Sociology 481–510.

[35] Walter Powell, 'Neither Market nor Hierarchy—Network Forms of Organization' (1990) 12 Research in Organizational Behaviour 295–336, 305–22, 299. The ideas reported in the following

arrangement as being—in principle, but not at each moment—'reciprocal', namely with respect to exchange of value and with respect to the flow and distribution of information, and based on individual responsibility of each 'partner' (no pooling of inputs in the arrangements established by the parties). Powell explains in detail why and when networks come into being. This is largely equivalent to the question of what advantages they have over the two alternative forms. His answer—typical for (economic) sociology—is not mono-causal, in the sense of depending, for example, *only* on (transaction) costs. Conversely, Powell interprets the empirical material so as to contradict any claim that parties choose arrangements solely, or even primarily, because of their relative transaction costs advantages.

These are the most striking findings. Networks are much more dependent on reciprocity and continuing mutual trust than either of the alternatives; in markets, an exit is convenient, and in organisations a command structure exists and solves (most) problems.[36] Thus decisions are made in an attitude that puts trusts in long-term beneficial effects and in the partners as long as they are perceived as still being fair. This explains why the market and the firm are institutions with clear legal structures and clear instruments, while networks are more flexible and vaguer (also in the instruments applying to networks). Because of these structural characteristics, the information flow is seen as being of particular relevance, denser than in other relationships, and based on an equal footing of 'peers' (expecting reciprocity and reliability, based, of course, on good experience in dealing with each other).

Networks therefore beat markets where information is complex and individualised, but also prevail over organisations where it is complex, individualised, and rapidly changing, in both cases because the exchange between 'peers' makes a difference. Decision making in trust is the instrument, or the 'price' to be paid. Markets coordinate but (because they only transfer 'signals') are seen as being weak with respect to highly complex, innovative information. Firms are seen as (particularly) strong in mass production, and in repetition of processes, but not for sharp and innovative change. Powell draws on institutional economics as a background, but often refers as well to the insufficient complexity of such approaches. The core contention is that institutional economics relies too heavily on a strict expectation of equivalence in exchange ('*do ut des*'), which he rebuts in favour of an alternative

have certain parallels namely with the corporate reputation thinking. Particularly ground-breaking in this respect is Friedrich von Hayek, *Individualism and Economic Order* (Chicago University Press 1948) 97; for a beautiful conceptualisation and survey, see Lars Klöhn and Ulrich Schmolke, 'Unternehmensreputation (Corporate Reputation)' (2015) 18 Neue Zeitschrift für Gesellschaftsrecht (NZG) 689–97.

[36] Walter Powell 'Neither Market nor Hierarchy—Network Forms of Organization' (1990) 12 Research in Organizational Behaviour 295–336, 296–302, and later—for the destruction of trust as core problem—304 et seq.

model. In line with sociological models, Powell sees how trust reduces complexity (Luhmann).

Therefore, while it is true that there is an expectation of reciprocity which may not be trumped very often, there is no expectation of strict equivalence of exchanges, since such an expectation would destroy the very basis of networks. Powell's model focuses on more accurately explaining why such networks can maintain a balance among equals for a long time, offer good (and better) environments for learning and proliferation of information (as in Silicon Valley), and why they are more prevalent when relationships deal with values which are intangible, not easy to 'grasp', and hard to protect by legal instruments. In this model, transaction cost considerations are marginal; what is immensely more important are strategic considerations for which quantification is simply impossible: 'an exclusive focus on the transaction—rather than the relationship—as the primary unit of analysis is misplaced'.[37] Transfer of know-how, speed of adaptation, and long-term trust are the three core characteristics—this, indeed, constitutes a remarkable analytical framework.

III. Legal Implications of Decision Theories for Long-term/ Network Organisational Contracts?

In a final step, the question has to be approached regarding what consequences can be drawn from such findings for the drafting of long-term/network organisational contracts in chains or for legislation or also development of the law via case law. To this end, this section analyses a certain number of core cases often discussed in law. These range from cases such as the disgorgement of additional gains made within the whole network when chains grow and discounts are therefore received, to those where actions of one member of the network are damaging to the common reputation. Other cases concern the installation of direct revocation or inspection rights in chains and networks and duties to protect and warn members of networks who are not direct contractual partners. In all these cases, the different theoretical approaches unveil different characteristics of each case and speak in favour of different policy approaches to be taken. The link to the decision making is of course typically indirect, in so far as the problems normally arise and the controversial cases take place after the relevant decisions have been made (at the formation of the contract or during the relationship). Thus, the question is rather whether adjudication at this latter moment reflects the expectations in the prior decision-making process. Another important question to consider is how an adjudication or a legal norm will impact on future collaboration and decision making? Thus, while to

[37] Ibid. 323, see mainly 302 et seq., 322 et seq.

some degree indirect, the impact of norms and adjudication is nevertheless on decision making and its consequences.

A. Disgorgement of Windfall Profits?

A case discussed in various jurisdictions is how to distribute windfall profits.[38] The main cases decided on this issue—at least in Germany—deal with franchise agreements,[39] an arrangement that has been located at neither of the two poles (completely mechanic execution networks and highly informal, flexible networks), but at a point along the continuum which lies between them. In payment systems, such windfall profits seem to be impossible. Conversely, in informal, flexible networks for innovation, the idea of an individual responsibility for one's own success prevails. The issue therefore appears to be more relevant for the arrangements within the spectrum than for those at the poles. The typical pattern of facts is as follows. A network—in this case with one dominant partner (the franchisor) who arranges the relationships in a star-like form around him—becomes more successful than assumed or simply grows. Often not only the design but the raw material as well are provided for by the franchisor (joint purchase). In such cases—as in the cases decided at law—the success of the network will lead to an increase in orders via the franchisor who can (and did) profit from the increased demand power for negotiating rebates with the suppliers. The core question raised by such cases then is this: should the prices in the relationship to the franchisees remain unchanged (for performance that has not changed), or should the rebates be disgorged proportionally (and hence the prices in said relationship should reflect the rebates as well)?

[38] See James Brickley and Frederick Dark, 'The Choice of Organizational Form—The Case of Franchising' (1987) 18 Journal of Financial Economics 401–20; Seth Norton, 'Franchising, Brand Name Capital, and The Entrepreneurial Capacity Problem' (1988) 9 Strategic Management Journal 105–14; Antony Dnes, 'The Economic Analysis of Franchising and its Regulation' in Christian Joerges (ed.), *Franchising and the Law—Theoretical and Comparative Approaches in Europe and the United States* (Nomos 1991) 133–42; Hugh Collins, *Regulating Contracts* (Oxford University Press 1999) 253; Christopher Wonnell, 'Unjust Enrichment and Quasi-Contracts' in Boudewijn Bouckaert and Gerrit De Geest (eds.), *Encyclopedia of Law and Economics, Vol. II: Civil Law and Economics* (Elgar 2011) 795, 801.

[39] In favour of duties to disgorge such gains, see German Private Law Supreme Court, *Bundesgerichtshof (BGH)* case KZR 19/02 of 20 May 2003, *Zeitschrift für Wirtschaftsrecht (ZIP)* 2003, 2030–35; at length for instance (for extensive duties to disgorge such gains, in each case): Reinhard Böhner, 'Vom Franchisevertrags- zum Franchisenetzwerkrecht' (2004) 59 Betriebsberater (BB) 119–24; Gunter Teubner, 'Profitsharing als Verbundpflicht? Zur Weiterleitung von Netzvorteilen in Franchise-Systemen' (2004) 168 Zeitschrift für das gesamte Handels- und Wirtschaftsrecht (ZHR) 78–96. Against such duties to disgorge: *Bundesgerichtshof (BGH)* case KZR 11/97 of 2 February 1999, *Neue Juristische Wochenschrift (NJW)* 1999, 2671–77, esp. 2675 et seq. (Sixt) and *Bundesgerichtshof (BGH)* case VIII ZR 59/01 of 17 July 2002, *Neue Juristische Wochenschrift-Rechtsprechungsreport (NJW-RR)* 2002, 1554–56, esp. 1556 (Hertz).

In the cases decided, the increase was unforeseen by all participants when the contracts were formed but known to all at the moment of litigation. Therefore, information cascade and observational learning theories seem not to be of much use. Decision making under uncertainty theory explains that this lack of foresight of rebates, that is additional profits of typically smaller amounts, in a potentially distant future, constitutes a well-known bias. The core question would then be whether correcting of biases in a business-to-business ('B2B') relationship should be undertaken only in extreme cases, when certain thresholds are crossed. Italy, for instance, takes the stance that franchise agreements are similar to consumer relationships, as franchisees are seen as much weaker partners.[40] The German Supreme Court, in principle negated a duty to disgorge such profits, but in the most recent case decided differently, using an argument that, from the outside, might be perceived as a legal sleight of hand. It based its decision on the fact that the boilerplate terms contained the clause 'Apollo supports the partner with respect to the company's performance and system-based operating procedure and relays to the partner, benefits, ideas and improvements to achieving optimum business success'. It argued that this included disgorging these profits, with the consequence that the Apollo franchise agreement was immediately altered so that it no longer contained that clause. What is clear from the judgments (and apparently different primarily in Italy) is that the issue is one that is left to each party in principle (decision of the parties if they wish it to be so). Conversely, in a regulatory perspective, other questions would need to be asked. These include whether regulatory intervention in favour of an allegedly weaker party should be restricted to extreme cases in B2B relationships (not to intervene too much in a competition order), and whether recourse to a rational choice paradigm has not always been used to lower the regulatory burden rather than to raise it. These considerations bring us back to decision theories.

Those decision theories that most directly contribute decisive arguments to the case are the mutual aspiration theory and the vision of networks as a 'house of trust', potentially combined with governance elements. With respect to the mutual aspiration theory, it would seem rather obvious that the 'aspiration' and expectation (also) of the franchisees was to have a solid basis—the actual prices at the beginning—on which to build their business. The argument could then only be that they could have bargained for more had they been more rational. This constitutes the inverse argument to the more common one that would claim that in B2B relationships, guaranteeing a level playing field on which rational partners can make their own decisions is the maximum protection desirable (also for safeguarding a competitive order). Such a level playing of course existed in these cases, because an

[40] See extensive survey and evaluation in Carlotta Rinaldo, 'Beyond Consumer Law—Small Enterprises, Independent Contractors and Other Professional Weak Parties' (2018) 14 European Review of Contract Law 227–50.

increase in business volume for the overall network is a very realistic scenario for any rational player. On the background of these two findings—mutual aspiration is satisfied and it is problematic to extend regulation unless the rationale is made very clear—recourse to the idea of mutual trust as the prime value in networks is still more revealing. The question then is which approach would further mutual trust more? Is it the one of opening new grounds for dispute? Or an approach which would not open up such grounds, beyond those extreme cases that, however, in instances of windfall profits, are difficult to find? Is trust not better served when there is only one precondition—that is, that the mutual expectations are satisfied—but where, on the other hand, individual responsibility remains safeguarded as well? The additional gains are not so clear to attribute. They may also be due to increased networking of the franchisor. Moreover, it would seem rather clear that in the long run, for instance in future negotiation rounds, any such increase would play out in some form. This fits neatly with Powell's idea of a generalised expectation of profiting somehow from an overall beneficial development of the network, even only in so far as its stability is increased. On the basis of theoretical approaches to decision making and their findings, virtually all arguments appear to speak against a strict duty of disgorgement. This is less clear—to add an element of governance in Williamson's line of thinking—if one stated a mere duty to renegotiate in such cases, at least when rebates become more significant.[41] Periodic discussion of the relationship is typically seen as a trust-enhancing instrument.[42] Therefore, discussion of how to deal with rebates achieved—for instance, at a periodical franchise network meeting—might not only be a sound business idea but may be based on a duty in law. The franchisor then can—but also *must*—state her reasons.

B. Protection of Common Value?

It was the most spectacular scandal in the fast-food segment of 2014.[43] The largest franchisee of Burger King in Germany, Yi-Ko, with eighty-nine stores, had been the subject of an enquiry by Team Walraff—an undercover reporter—that showed a massive failure in hygiene and systematic cheating with respect to food standards. As a result, Burger King terminated the contract with Yo-Ko for serious cause.

[41] Under German Law, see Andreas Nelle, *Neuverhandlungspflichten: Neuverhandlungen zur Vertragsanpassung und Vertragsergänzung als Gegenstand von Pflichten und Obliegenheiten* (Beck 1993).

[42] See Bennett Cherry, 'Entrepreneur as Trust-Builder: Interaction Frequency and Relationship Duration as Moderators of The Factors af Perceived Trustworthiness' (2015) 14 International Journal of Business and Globalisation 97–121; cf. also John Rempel, Michael Ross, and John Holmes, 'Trust and Communicated Attributions in Close Relationships' (2001) 81 Journal of Personality and Social Psychology 57–64 (this article is about the content of discussions, not their frequency); Marjorie Jaasma and Randall Koper, 'The Relationship of Student–Faculty out-of-Class Communication to Instructor Immediacy and Trust and to Student Motivation' (1999) 48 Communication Education 41–47.

[43] 'Burger King erwartet längeren Streit mit Yi-Ko', *Die Welt* (23 November 2014).

This is the one case where all jurisdictions would basically converge and grant such a right of termination.[44] In addition, under German law, the majority view is that even the other network partners have a right to force the franchisor to take action when the common value of the brand is affected and they risk serious loss.[45] The Yi-Ko case, however, did not go to court.

The reason for such uniformity can be found in the fact that all decision theories would seem to converge in this case. All the different approaches to decision making see Yi-Ko's behaviour as among the most adverse developments possible. Starting with the theory of decision making under uncertainty, the arena where regulatory intervention is disputed is that of biases influencing the situation. The question then is whether regulation is desirable when uncertainty could have been more correctly assessed but was not because of biases such as the 'present bias'. The assessment perspective is a completely different one concerning information that is structurally unattainable for the party affected, that this party *cannot* retrieve, and even more so when there is a structural information asymmetry, one party knowing while the other party incapable of knowing relevant information (structural *unattainability of information*). All information regulation takes this as the most serious reason for stating disclosure rules—whenever the information is paramount for the relationship (*high relevance of information*).[46] It is beyond doubt that the value of the common brand—the risk of losing clients—is indeed paramount and among the most important assets in business relationships.

Similarly clear is the assessment from a mutual aspiration perspective but also from a trust perspective. Having stability as the key basis of the joint business is clearly among the core aspirations that most business partners have. This includes

[44] For a comparative law survey, see Alberto Venezia (ed.), *Termination of Franchising and Distribution Agreements in EU* (Giuffrè 2018). It is worth mentioning, however, that public/political pressure—Ki-Yo had a workforce of roughly 3,000 employees—finally prompted Burger King to renegotiate and restore the contract with new Ki-Yo management and more far-reaching inspection rights.

[45] See Gunter Teubner, *Netzwerk als Vertragsverbund* (Nomos 2004) 195–97; Oberlandesgericht München (Appellate Court Munich) case 7 U 2604/13 of 14 October 2014, *Betriebsberater* (BB) 60 (2015) 527.

[46] From the host of literature across the fields of law and theory (in consumer law, in capital market law, etc.), see George Akerlof, 'The Market for "Lemons": Quality Uncertainty and the Market Mechanism' (1970) 84 Quarterly Journal of Economics 488–500; Stefan Grundmann, 'Information, Party Autonomy and Economic Agents in European Contract Law' (2002) 39 Common Market Law Review 269–393, 272 et seq.; Oren Bar-Gill and Oliver Board, 'Product-use Information and The Limits of Voluntary Disclosure' (2012) 14 American Law and Economics Review 235–70; Omri Ben-Shahar and Carl Schneider, 'The Failure of Mandated Disclosure' (2011) 159 University of Pennsylvania Law Review 647–749; Stephen Choi and Adam Pritchard, *Securities Regulation* (3rd edn, Thomson Reuters 2012) 22 et seq.; Rüdiger Veil (ed.), *European Capital Markets Law* (Hart Publishing 2013) ch. 4, para. 209-38; Venkat Eleswarapu, Rex Thompson, and Kumar Venkataraman, 'The Impact of Regulation Fair Disclosure: Trading Costs and Information Asymmetry' (2004) 39 Journal of Financial and Quantitative Analysis 209–25, 209 et seq.; Cento Veljanovski, 'Economic Approaches to Regulation' in Robert Baldwin, Martin Cave, and Martin Lodge (eds.), *The Oxford Handbook of Regulation* (Oxford University Press 2010) 17–36, 21; Philipp Hacker, *Verhaltensökonomik und Normativität* (Mohr Siebeck 2017) § 9.

both those businesses already existing when the investment is initially made as well as those businesses still to be created.[47] Thus, the value of the Burger King brand was a core part of what both franchisor and all franchisees, including those outside the Yi-Ko package of eighty-nine stores, wanted. In a mutual trust perspective, where such mutual trust is the essence of peer-to-peer relations, there would seem to be a trade-off occurring. While, on the one hand, no immediate gains can be expected from partners in each exchange between them, long-term reliability is all the more important. In other words, where there are less concrete and calculable instant advantages of each such exchange, the solidity of the long-term relationship is all the more important. Yi-Ko's behaviour was a complete deal breaker in terms of a trust relationship.

Finally, information cascade theory adds an aspect concerning deterrence. As the information cascade—here a potential cascade among clients—may be difficult to interrupt or reverse, and as a particularly clear signal is needed in such a cascade, much would speak in favour of stringent and deterring sanctions. In the case of (the risk of) massive damage to the overall value of the brand combined with an intentional breach of core rules (whose breach foreseeably can trigger such an information avalanche), the most desirable sanction seems to be a right of terminating a contract without further requisites (no requirement of prior disciplinary warning nor notice).

C. The Need of Direct Duties and Claims—namely, Information?

One of the questions in which different jurisdictions diverge more than in others is the question of how to conceive the relationship between members of the network of contracts that are not directly linked by contract. One facet of this question has already been mentioned when, in the Burger King versus Yi-Ko dispute, reference was made to the rule under German law that other franchisees have a right to prompt Burger King to terminate the relationship with Yi-Ko if the latter seriously damaged the common brand (subject to exceptions if there are other, less intrusive but still effective measures of safeguarding the common interest). In that case, those other franchisees would only be able to use their direct contract relationship

[47] For such an impact of the endowment effect on the fixing of mutual aspirations, see, for instance, Daniel Kahneman and Amos Tversky, 'Prospect Theory: An Analysis of Decision under Risk' (1979) 47 Econometrica 263–91, at 286; Maurice Schweitzer, 'Disentangling Status Quo and Omission Effects: An Experimental Analysis' (1994) 58 Organizational Behavior and Human Decision Processes 457–76, 459 (both on the endowment as a reference point for the future evaluation of changes); also Daniel Kahnemann, Jack Knetsch, and Richard Thaler, 'Experimental Tests of the Endowment Effect and the Coase Theorem' (1990) 98 Journal of Political Economy 1325–48; concerning rational expectations as the reference point, see Bottond Kőszegi and Matthew Rabin, 'A Model of Reference-Dependent Preferences' (2006) 121 Quarterly Journal of Economics 1133–65; Devin Pope and Maurice Schweitzer, 'Is Tiger Woods Loss Averse? Persistent Bias in The Face of Experience, Competition, and High Stakes' (2011) 101 American Economic Review 129–57, 155.

with Burger King, however, with indirect effect on Yi-Ko, with whom they did not have contract relationships. The effect on other members of the network of contracts is even more immediate when there are direct claims exercised against them without there being contractual links between claimant and defendant. This is for instance the case if the damaged party can sue a third party that is a member of a network, but not linked to the damaged party by contract directly. One well-known example is the direct claim of a purchaser against a producer (of motor vehicles) when her product is defective but has been sold via a distribution chain with a retail seller (as a direct contractual partner of the purchaser). The buyer may have a claim for losses caused, for instance because she has to rent a substitute car to go for holidays. For reasons of responsibility or of financial status, the producer may be the more attractive defendant. This is one situation where, for instance, French and German law diametrically diverge.[48]

Only one facet of this overall panorama of direct claim questions will be discussed here, that of warning one's partners which is particularly interesting for two reasons. On the one hand, it concerns a case where, in my view, an exception is justified even if more generally one should negate direct claims between partners of the network that are not directly linked by contract. Thus, this constitutes a particularly interesting pattern of cases. On the other hand, this exception can be explained and justified by reference to information cascade theory while this cascade theory has not played such a prominent role in the other case examples. The question has always been disputed as to whether members of a network have to warn those members to whom they are not directly linked by contract in cases where it is obvious that the information is important to all members of that network.[49] Two qualifications should be made. First, such a situation can also involve information that is of particular competitive advantage to the one member (e.g. trade secrets). Second, the same situation can of course also be found in relation to the outside world, to non-members of the network. Despite the difficulties faced in defining what is 'within' the network and 'outside' the network, at least in cases where the information is not of such particular competitive advantage (trade secrets), in my view, the stronger arguments speak in favour of a duty to inform members of the network, even if no contractual link exists to them. It appears as if mutual trust, and

[48] For further references and for the reasons for preferring one approach or the other need not be repeated here, see Stefan Grundmann, 'Contractual Networks in German Private Law' in Fabrizio Cafaggi (ed.), *Contractual Networks, Inter-Firm Cooperation and Economic Growth* (Edgar Elgar 2011) 111–62, 143–51, negating direct claims in this respect). It is, however, worth mentioning that a negative answer in one facet, for instance the motor-vehicle production case, does not necessarily imply a negative answer also in other aspects, as can be seen in the following.

[49] Teubner (n 45) 151 et seq.; Stefan Grundmann, 'Die Dogmatik der Vertragsnetzwerke' (2007) 207 Archiv für die Civilistische Praxis (AcP) 718–67, 757–59; Stefan Grundmann, 'Contractual Networks in German Private Law' in Fabrizio Cafaggi (ed.), *Contractual Networks, Inter-Firm Cooperation and Economic Growth* (Edgar Elgar 2011) 111–62, 151 et seq.; Massimo Bianca, 'Good Faith Related Duties of Disclosure and a View on Franchising' in Grundmann, Cafaggi, and Vettori (eds.) (n 1) 181–96.

even more so, information cascades and observational learning theories made a difference here.

It is exactly in this kind of situation—sharing of non-competitive but important information—that mutual trust can be enhanced. It is in these situations as well that the long-term beneficial, even though not strictly reciprocal, nature of networks can come into play and can therefore also arguably be expected by all partners to be followed. Being 'within' a network makes a difference in so far as trust is positively created, relied upon, and is therefore also worthy of protection. Information cascades add the cornerstone to the argument. They imply that such information is a valuable asset which can justify creating a network. In firms, such information must circulate. In markets, not sharing all information with those that use the anonymous market typically prevails. In networks, this information constitutes a valuable asset because the mechanism of information cascades should typically work more consistently. Members typically will know about other members' actions more easily than they would in firms or in markets; they therefore might follow the cascade also more easily. Hence, not disclosing the information may trigger a downward spiral, while sharing it tends to trigger a positive cascade. When in a society or market economy—as Engel argues in his contribution to this volume—thicker and more broadly spread information creates more general trust, the same is true for networks and with greater intensity. In this scenario, the information that reverses a whole cascade is of particular importance. Unless there is good reason to the contrary (significant competitive advantage), it is exactly in this setting that there are strong arguments to hold that sharing should be the norm. A final twist takes cognitive ability into account. Sharing should only be the norm if the party sharing the information has no reason to suspect that other members will not be able to process the information correctly (as per the heuristics and biases literature). This may be relevant if the information is very technical and complex, but some members of the network are not as sophisticated as the rest and might misunderstand the information or overreact in ways adverse to the entire network.

D. Caveats

The main caveat concerning the preceding discussion is that it concerns only a small sample of cases, some disputed, some undisputed and even solved in the same way across jurisdictions. Even with respect to direct claims (section III.C), there is only one relevant case available, and it has been shown that others would probably have to be solved differently. The core thrust was therefore to show the interplay of theories and their relevance, and in particular also their relative relevance in comparison to each other. Again, the sample would need to be larger in order to reach sound conclusions. It may be particularly striking, however, to see how relatively important the 'house of trust' theory proved to be—a theory grounded in a sociological concept of relations—it turned out to be almost the dominant theory when explaining the cases cited earlier.

IV. Conclusion

Contractual networks of long duration that serve as the organisational basis across a large variety of fields and that also adopt a large variety of forms—ranging from mechanical execution to highly trust-dependent and more informal and innovative networks—are a treasure trove for decision theories. So far, however, decision theories have rarely been applied to them. This chapter tries to fill this gap and 'tests' four decision theories: decision making under uncertainty; mutual aspiration (game) theory; information cascades and observational learning theory; and mutual trust theory. A fifth field of theoretical development, far more prominent than the four others, is looming in the background: this is behavioural law and economics (of which decision making under uncertainty forms one part). Among the core findings, however, the first might be that behavioural law and economics reveals more about market transactions than long-term network relationships. The second core finding combines with this first one. For contractual networks of long duration, the mutual trust theory developed by Powell seems particularly helpful, combined with Selten's mutual aspiration theory as a sub-form of game theory. In some instances, information cascades and observational learning theory explain the fragility of decision making. Overall, preference has been given to an array of theories rather than just one because of normative reasons (the approach seems more suited to reflect what is a clearly pluralistic value basis), but to a large extent as well because this pluralist approach is still so rarely adopted.

14

The Power of Sequence

A Quantum Perspective on Legal Decision Making

Christopher Brett Jaeger and Jennifer S. Trueblood

Abstract: Researchers have documented numerous cognitive biases that are difficult to reconcile with rational choice theory. But is there a more general set of decision-making rules that might account for these cognitive biases and 'rational' decisions alike? Psychologists in search of such rules have developed a theory of quantum decision making. This chapter introduces quantum decision making to a legal audience, explains its intellectual origins, and identifies some contexts in which it provides useful tools for legal theorists. Using the example of a juror evaluating a criminal case, the chapter illustrates how quantum decision making explains and predicts phenomena that are difficult to reconcile with other theories of choice. More generally, quantum decision making highlights the importance of sequence in shaping judgments and decisions—and thus, its importance in law's choice architecture.

Rational choice theory[1] has had tremendous influence on law, but its accuracy in predicting judgments and decisions has long been questioned.[2] A host of puzzling empirical findings—including cognitive biases[3] such as order effects,[4] conjunction

[1] Rational choice theory posits that people make choices that maximise their expected utility. See, e.g., Richard A. Posner, 'Are We One Self or Multiple Selves? Implications for Law and Public Policy' (1997) 3.1 Legal Theory 23, 24. The expected utility of a potential action is equal to the 'probability weighted average of the utilities of outcomes produced by [that] action'. Jerome R. Busemeyer, 'Cognitive Science Contributions to Decision Science' (2015) 135 Cognition 43, 43. Per rational choice theory, 'decision makers act as though they gather the optimal amount of information about decision alternatives, use that information to judge the probabilities of potential outcomes in accordance with the rules of classical (Bayesian) probability theory, and use those probability judgments (in combination with their individual preferences) to select the alternative that offers the greatest expected utility'. Christopher Brett Jaeger and Jennifer S. Trueblood, 'Thinking Quantum: A New Perspective on Decisionmaking in Law' (2019) 46.4 Florida State University Law Review 733, 3..

[2] For an expanded discussion of many of the ideas presented in this chapter, see Jaeger and Trueblood (n 1).

[3] See, e.g., Amos Tversky and Daniel Kahneman, 'Judgment Under Uncertainty: Heuristics and Biases' (1974) 185.4157 Science 1124.

[4] See, e.g., Jennifer S. Trueblood and Jerome R. Busemeyer, 'A Quantum Probability Account of Order Effects in Inference' (2011) 35.8 Cognitive Science 1518; Robin M. Hogarth and Hillel J. Einhorn, 'Order Effects in Updating: The Belief-Adjustment Model' (1992) 24.1 Cognitive Psychology 1.

Christopher Brett Jaeger and Jennifer S. Trueblood, *The Power of Sequence* In: *Theories of Choice*.
Edited by: Stefan Grundmann and Philipp Hacker, Oxford University Press (2021). © The several contributors.
DOI: 10.1093/oso/9780198863175.003.0015

errors,[5] and base rate neglect[6]—demonstrate that human judgment is often inconsistent with the assumptions of rational choice theory. A question that often arises in legal scholarship is: how should law respond to these findings?

Some legal theorists argue that law should account for them—that, in contexts where we know that people are prone to 'irrationality', law should be informed by situation-specific, data-driven models of behaviour rather than rational choice theory. This argument is often associated with the field of 'behavioral law and economics',[7] and it informs 'constructivist' models of adjudication.[8] Other legal theorists argue that, despite a few puzzling findings, rational choice theory remains law's best bet. Although rational choice models may, in certain situations, yield predictions that are systematically wrong, their virtues outweigh this vice. After all, rational choice models have the advantage of parsimony, they can be applied in a wide variety of contexts, and they often yield clear a priori predictions of use to policy makers and scholars. Arguments like these are frequently associated with the field of 'law and economics'[9] and 'rationalist' models of adjudication.[10]

A legal theorist's alternatives have often been framed in this binary manner: on one hand, a potentially limitless set of situation-specific models that accurately reflect behaviour in particular contexts; on the other, a broadly applicable approach that we know, at times, leads to systematically inaccurate results. But are there other options?

In recent years, psychologists have been working to develop theories of choice with the best of both worlds—theories that account for often-observed irrationalities in human judgments but do so using a generally applicable set of decision-making axioms. This work is fuelled by the recognition that, '[a]lthough heuristic concepts (such as representativeness, availability, and anchor adjustment) initially served as a guide to researchers in this area, there is a growing need to move beyond

[5] See, e.g., Amos Tversky and Daniel Kahneman, 'Extensional Versus Intuitive Reasoning: The Conjunction Fallacy in Probability Judgments' (1983) 90.4 Psychological Review 293.

[6] See, e.g., Daniel Kahneman and Amos Tversky, 'On the Psychology of Prediciton' (1973) 80.4 Psychological Review 237.

[7] See, e.g., from the extensive literature, Christine Jolls, Cass R. Sunstein, and Richard Thaler, 'A Behavioral Approach to Law and Economics' (1998) 50.5 Stanford Law Review 1471; Russell B. Korobkin and Thomas S. Ulen, 'Law and Behavioral Science: Removing the Rationality Assumption from Law and Economics' (2000) 88.4 California Law Review 1051; Cass R. Sunstein, *Behavioral Law and Economics* (Cambridge University Press 2000); Philipp Hacker, 'The Behavioral Divide: A Critique of the Differential Implementation of Behavioral Law and Economics in the US and the EU' (2015) 11.4 European Review of Contract Law 299.

[8] For a review of constructivist models of adjudication, see Dan M. Kahan, 'Laws of Cognition and the Cognition of Law' (2015) 135 Cognition 56; see also Jaeger and Trueblood (n 1) 16–18.

[9] See, e.g., from the extensive literature, Richard A. Posner, 'Rational Choice, Behavioral Economics, and the Law' (1998) 50.5 Stanford Law Review 1551; Richard A. Posner, *Economic Analysis of Law* (9th edn, Wolters Kluwer 2014), Thomas S. Ulen, 'Rational Choice Theory in Law and Economics' in Boudewijn Bouckaert and Gerrit De Geest (eds.), *Encyclopedia of Law and Economics* (Edward Elgar 1999) vol. 1, 790.

[10] The rationalist perspective of legal decision making is discussed in Dan Simon, 'A Third View from the Black Box: Cognitive Coherence in Legal Decision Making' (2004) 71.2 University of Chicago Law Review 511.

these intuitions and develop more coherent, comprehensive, and deductive theoretical explanations'.[11] The search for a comprehensive explanation led researchers to develop the theory of quantum decision making.

In this chapter, we introduce quantum decision making to legal readers, discussing the 'what', 'why', 'when', and 'how' of the theory. We frame much of our discussion around the running example of a juror considering the case of a criminal defendant charged with two crimes: robbery and drug trafficking. We focus on this example because, as discussed below, quantum decision making is a particularly good theoretical fit for the type of inferential legal reasoning that jurors (or sometimes judges) engage in when they decide cases.

I. What is Quantum Decision Making?

Quantum decision making is a formal mathematical theory of judgment and decision making. Its foundational premise is that judgments and decisions are influenced by context.[12] Context, as we use the term here, encompasses factors that would be irrelevant to 'rational' decision makers. One especially important contextual factor is *sequence*.[13] Numerous studies in psychology,[14] marketing,[15] polling,[16] and law,[17] among other fields, demonstrate that switching the order in which participants make judgments and decisions affects the outcomes.

Descriptively, the idea that sequence matters is uncontroversial. We expect that most, if not all, choice theorists would agree. But what makes quantum decision making different from other theories of choice is that it aims to account for *how* sequence matters. Quantum decision making provides a formal (i.e., mathematical) way to capture how sequences of information influence final beliefs and decisions.

[11] Jerome R. Busemeyer et al., 'A Quantum Theoretical Explanation for Probability Judgment Errors' (2011) 118.2 Psychological Review 193, 193.

[12] Jennifer S. Trueblood, Emmanuel M. Pothos, and Jerome R. Busemeyer, 'Quantum Probability Theory as a Common Framework for Reasoning and Similarity' (2014) 5 Frontiers in Psychology 322 ('A preference for the unique features of [quantum probability] theory, against [classical probability] theory, can be motivated in situations where there is evidence of context effects, interference effects, and sequence effects.').

[13] Ibid.

[14] For example, Hogarth and Eindhorn (n 4).

[15] For example, Carol W. DeMoranville and Carol C. Beinstock, 'Question Order Effects in Measuring Service Quality' (2003) 20.3 International Journal of Research in Marketing 217.

[16] For example, David W. Moore, 'Measuring New Types of Question-Order Effects: Additive and Subtractive' (2002) 66.1 Public Opinion Quarterly 80.

[17] Jeffrey J. Rachlinksi, Andrew J. Wistrich, and Chris Guthrie, 'Can Judges Make Reliable Numeric Judgments? Distorted Damages and Skewed Sentences' (2015) 90.2 Indiana Law Journal 695; Craig R. M. McKenzie, Susanna M. Lee, and Karen K. Chen, 'When Negative Evidence Increases Confidence: Change in Belief After Hearing Two Sides of a Dispute' (2002) 15.1 Journal of Behavioral Decision Making 1.

Because it is a formal theory, it allows for systematic investigations and rigorous testing.[18]

Quantum decision making can account for the effects of sequence because it makes one fundamentally different assumption from other theories of choice.[19] Other theories, such as rational choice theory, assume that people judge probabilities in accordance with *classical probability theory*.[20] Quantum decision making, by contrast, assumes that people judge probabilities in accordance with *quantum probability theory*.[21]

Quantum probability theory differs from classical probability theory in three critical respects: definiteness, sample spaces, and commutativity. The balance of this section discusses these differences.

Definiteness. Classical probability theory, as it is applied to human judgments, assumes that judgments arise from *definite states*.[22] That is, classical probability theory assumes that people maintain clearly defined mental estimates of the probabilities of events, update those estimates based on information, then 'read out' those existing estimates when necessary for a judgment or decision. For example, after opening statements, a hypothetical juror may think there is a 35% chance the defendant committed the charged robbery, revise that estimate to 65% after strong prosecution evidence, and then revise it down to 5% after some compelling defence witnesses. When asked for her verdict, the juror consults her existing mental probability assessment.[23] If the juror's mental estimate at the end of the trial is 5%, the juror will find the defendant 'not guilty' of robbery.[24]

Quantum probability theory, in contrast, assumes that judgments arise from *indefinite states*.[25] People generally do not clearly define probabilities of events unless prompted. Rather, we tend to remain in states of uncertainty and conflict until we

[18] For an introduction to quantum models, see, e.g., James M. Yearsley and Jerome R. Busemeyer, 'Quantum Cognition and Decision Theories: A Tutorial' (2016) 74 Journal of Mathematical Psychology 99.

[19] Ibid. 99.

[20] See, e.g., Peter D. Bruza, Zheng Wang, and Jerome R. Busemeyer, 'Quantum Cognition: A New Theoretical Approach to Psychology' (2015) 19.7 Trends in Cognitive Science 383; Emmanuel M. Pothos and Jerome R. Busemeyer, 'A Quantum Probability Explanation for Violations of 'Rational' Decision Theory' (2009) 276.1665 Proceedings of the Royal Society B 2171.

[21] See, e.g., Yearsley and Busemeyer (n 18).

[22] Jerome R. Busemeyer and Jennifer S. Trueblood, 'Theoretical and Empirical Reasons for Considering the Application of Quantum Probability Theory' in *Human Cognition in Proceedings of the Quantum Cognition Meets TARK, Workshop* (2011), http://www.ai.rug.nl/conf/quantumTARK/busemeyer.pdf.

[23] Ibid. 1 (under the assumptions of classical probability theory, '[t]he process of [judgment] has no effect on [one's cognitive] state other than to simply record it').

[24] We use a 5% chance that the defendant committed the crime in this example to avoid the potentially thorny issue of where, exactly, a juror might draw the line of certainty 'beyond a reasonable doubt'. For discussion of that issue, see, e.g., Lawrence M. Solan, 'Refocusing the Burden of Proof in Criminal Cases: Some Doubt About Reasonable Doubt' (1999) 78.1 Texas Law Review 105. For our purposes, the key point is that on a classical view, the juror's verdict is driven by her pre-existing, defined probability estimate (compared to whatever threshold).

[25] Bruza, Wang, and Busemeyer (n 20) 384.

have to make a commitment.[26] When we ultimately need to make a judgment, it is '*constructed* based on the interaction of the indefinite state in the decision maker's mind and the question that is posed'.[27] In our example, the hypothetical juror may not form a definite judgment about the defendant's guilt until prompted (e.g., by the need to vote 'guilty' or 'not guilty'). Thus, in a sense, the juror's choice of verdict is reminiscent of Schrödinger's cat; the possibilities of 'guilty' and 'not guilty' are both alive in the juror's mind with some probability, until the juror is asked to render her verdict and then it must be one or the other.[28]

Sample spaces. Classical probability theory not only assumes that people maintain and constantly update mental estimates of event probabilities but also that they consider *all* event probabilities simultaneously within a single, exhaustive mental *sample space*.[29] On this view, a large Venn diagram could capture the probability of any combination of events in a decision-maker's mind. If our juror is asked the joint probability that the defendant is guilty of *both* robbery and drug trafficking, she need only consult this mental Venn diagram and read out the value.

Quantum probability theory, however, does *not* assume one exhaustive sample space.[30] Instead, it allows for multiple sample spaces. This is because cognitive resources are limited; the sample spaces in our minds can only hold so much. Sometimes, we can mentally represent events within the same sample space and consider them simultaneously—such events are said to be '*compatible*'.[31] But more often, we cannot—such events are said to be '*incompatible*'.[32] '[I]ncompatibility is ubiquitous in psychology', particularly for unfamiliar, unrehearsed types of judgments.[33] When events are incompatible, people must evaluate their probabilities one at a time, sequentially.[34] For example, from a quantum perspective, our juror would need to consider the probability that the defendant was guilty of robbery

[26] Ibid.; Busemeyer and Trueblood (n 22) 2 (observing that indefinite states provide 'a better representation of the *conflict, ambiguity, or uncertainty* that people experience at each moment').

[27] Jaeger and Trueblood (n 1).

[28] Pam Frost Gorder, 'You're Not Irrational, You're Just Quantum Probabilistic' *Ohio State News* (Columbus, Ohio 14 September 2015) <https://perma.cc/Y9KC-YQZU> (quoting Professor Zheng Wang: 'it's as if each decision we make is our own unique Schrödinger's cat').

[29] Bruza, Wang, and Busemeyer (n 20) 384.

[30] Busemeyer and Trueblood (n 22) 3 (within a quantum framework, '[i]ncompatible questions cannot be evaluated on the same basis, so that they require setting up different sample spaces').

[31] For example, Yearsley and Busemeyer (n 18).

[32] Ibid. Representations of familiar events are more likely to be compatible. The example used in Jaeger and Trueblood (n 1) is estimating the joint probability that the next vehicle you see will be red and that the next vehicle you see will be a sports utility vehicle ('SUV'). If you are an experienced driver, you might well be able to draw on your experience to make one mental estimate of the proportion of vehicles you see that are red SUVs, rather than separately estimating the proportion of red vehicles and the proportion of vehicles that are SUVs. Representations of less familiar events—such as the probability that the defendant committed robbery and the probability the defendant committed drug trafficking—are more likely to be incompatible, requiring sequential consideration.

[33] Peter D. Bruza, Zheng Wang, and Jerome R. Busemeyer 'Quantum Cognition: A New Theoretical Approach to Psychology' (2015) 20 <https://eprints.qut.edu.au/85145/3/85145.pdf> (unpublished author version).

[34] Yearsley and Busemeyer (n 18); Bruza, Wang, and Busemeyer (n 20).

either *before* considering the probability that the defendant was guilty of drug trafficking, or *after*.

Commutativity. All probability estimates in a classical probability framework are governed by the *commutative property*.[35] The commutative property may be familiar from coursework in mathematics—for addition, x + y = y + x; for multiplication, xy = yx. In the context of probabilities, the commutative property holds that 'any two events can be combined and *the order in which they are combined does not matter:* the probability of the event "X and Y" will always be identical to the probability of the event "Y and X"'.[36] Thus, the classical perspective suggests that, in our example, it is irrelevant whether the juror decides the robbery charge first or the drug trafficking charge first.

Probability estimates in a quantum probability framework are *not* governed by the commutative property.[37] To the contrary, quantum probability assessments tend to be non-commutative. Sequence matters. Considering X might shape subsequent consideration of Y (and vice versa), so the probability of a combined event 'X and Y' may differ from the probability of a combined event 'Y and X'. Indeed, whenever X and Y are *incompatible*, the probability of 'X and Y' and 'Y and X' will necessarily be *unequal*. If our juror considers the robbery charge before the drug trafficking charge, she may make different probability judgments—and reach different verdicts—than she would if she considered the drug trafficking charge before the robbery charge (or than she would if she considered both charges simultaneously, as assumed by classical probability theory).

In sum, quantum decision making differs from other theories of choice in that it is built on a different probability theory. Other theories of choice are built on classical probability theory, while quantum decision making is built on quantum probability theory.[38] Because quantum probability theory entails fundamentally different assumptions about definiteness, sample spaces, and commutativity, models of judgment and decision making grounded in quantum probability theory often yield different predictions than their classically grounded counterparts. And, as an empirical matter, psychologists are finding that these quantum models are often a better match for human judgment and decision making than classical models, accounting for 'rational' decisions as well as numerous heuristics, biases, and other puzzling decision-making phenomena.[39]

[35] Bruza, Wang, and Busemeyer (n 20) 384–85.

[36] Jaeger and Trueblood (n 1) 32.

[37] Zheng Wang et al., 'Context Effects Produced by Question Orders Reveal Quantum Nature of Human Judgments' (2014) 111.26 Proceedings of the National Academy of Sciences 9431; Busemeyer and Trueblood (n 22) 2.

[38] Bruza, Wang, and Busemeyer (n 20).

[39] For a review of findings, see Jaeger and Trueblood (n 1) 43.

II. Why Use Quantum Probability Theory?

The reader may wonder what led researchers to apply quantum probability theory to human judgment and decision making. The word 'quantum' is typically associated with physics; quantum probability theory was developed to describe the behaviour of subatomic particles. What does that have to with human judgment? Although the connection may initially sound strange, there is a compelling analogy between quantum physics and human judgment. Consider the following passage, which lays out key tenets of quantum decision making:

> (a) [J]udgment is not a simple readout from a preexisting or recorded state, but instead it is constructed from the current context and question; from this first point it then follows that (b) making a judgment changes the context which disturbs the cognitive system; and the second point implies that (c) changes in context produced by the first judgment affect the next judgment producing order effects, so that (d) . . . judgments do not obey the commutative rule of classic probability theory.[40]

Now, reread the passage, replacing the word 'judgment' with 'measurement' and the phrase 'cognitive system' with 'physical system'. This exercise reveals that a parallel between the situation physicists faced in the 1920s and the situation psychologists face today.[41] Physicists developed quantum probability theory to account for puzzling, non-commutative findings that they could not square with classical probability theory. Analogously, psychologists are using quantum probability theory to account for puzzling, non-commutative findings in judgment and decision making.

Quantum probability theory is not the first probability theory that social scientists have imported from physics to describe human judgment. Classical probability theory—the foundation of most theories of choice, including rational choice theory—was also imported from physics. It was developed to describe classical Newtonian systems.[42] Thus, it is 'really not so exotic for social scientists to think about quantum systems and their mathematical principles, too'.[43] In fact, social scientists have occasionally called for their fields to incorporate insights from quantum theory since quantum theory was developed.[44]

[40] Trueblood and Busemeyer (n 4) 1519.

[41] Ibid.

[42] Alexander Wendt, *Quantum Mind and Social Science: Unifying Physical and Social Ontology* (Cambridge University Press 2015) 4.

[43] Gorder (n 28) (quoting Professor Wang).

[44] Wendt (n 42) ('This is not the first call for a quantum social science. Already in 1927—just weeks after the Solvay conference marking the culmination of the quantum revolution—the President of the American Political Science Association, William Bennett Munro, challenged social scientists to come to grip with the new physics.'); William Bennett Munro, 'Physics and Politics—An Old Analogy Revised' (1928) 22.1 American Political Science Review 1, 1 ('New truths cannot be quarantined. No branch of

Given that quantum decision making assumes that human judgment is best described by quantum probability theory, one might ask if it also assumes that judgments are produced, *physically*, by quantum processes in the brain. It does not. Researchers in quantum decision making and its parent field, quantum cognition, make no claim about physical processes in the brain. Rather, these researchers use quantum models as algorithms, 'leav[ing] the neural basis for later research.'[45] (This point distinguishes quantum decision making and quantum cognition from the 'quantum brain' research programme.)[46]

III. When Can Quantum Decision Making Most Usefully Inform Law?

It is one thing to assert that law should be informed by theories of choice, but it is another thing to specify which theories of choice should inform which aspects of law. One admirable goal of this volume is that it strives to address the 'selection problem,' connecting particular theories of choice with concrete legal applications. The introductory chapter set forth three criteria to aide regulators and scholars in selecting a theory of choice to apply in a particular legal context: (i) the proximity of conditions of applicability; (ii) the maturity of the theory; and (iii) the theory's ability to generate novel perspectives. Here, we use these criteria to identify areas in which quantum decision making might inform law.

The first criterion concerns how well the conditions for applicability of a theory of choice match the legal context(s) of interest. While the express goal of quantum decision making is to provide a comprehensive account of judgment and decision making, its principles provide more leverage in some contexts than others. The key distinguishing feature of quantum decision making is that it is naturally non-commutative; it assumes that one judgment can, and often will, affect the next.[47] Thus, quantum decision making is particularly useful in situations where people are asked to make multiple judgments or decisions in succession. And its predictions are clearest when the order in which the judgments are made is known or predictable. Law is concerned with many such situations—witnesses identifying

knowledge advances by itself. In its progress it draws others along. By no jugglery of words can we keep Mind and Matter and Motion in watertight compartments.').

[45] Trueblood and Busemeyer (n 4) 1519; see also Andrei Khrennikov et al., 'Quantum Probability in Decision Making From Quantum Information Representation of Neuronal States' (2018) 8.1 Scientific Reports 1, 2 ('As is often the case with cognitive models, in this approach the brain is considered as a black box.').

[46] Yearsley and Busemeyer (n 18) 100–01.

[47] See, e.g., Zheng Wang and Jerome R. Busemeyer, 'A Quantum Question Order Model Supported by Empirical Tests of an A Priori and Precise Prediction' (2013) 5.4 Topics in Cognitive Science 689, 689–90.

suspects from line-ups, voters casting ballots that include multiple issues and races, employees completing benefit election documents, and jurors deciding multiple claims in a suit, to name a few. These are situations where legal thinkers might look to quantum models.

Quantum decision making suggests that the effect of sequence will be most prominent when the decision maker is making a series of unfamiliar, unrehearsed judgments.[48] Thus, the legal situations that most clearly call out for a quantum perspective are those involving people making a series of consequential judgments with which they have little prior experience. Juror judgments may be a particularly good fit here: jurors typically have little experience with law or legal decision making, and often consider multiple claims or charges. (This is why our running example in this chapter is a juror evaluating a two-charge criminal case.)

The second criterion is the maturity of the theory of choice, looking at considerations such as intradisciplinary consensus and empirical track record. Quantum decision making is a relatively young field, but it is mature beyond its years. The most prominent book on this area is perhaps *Quantum Models of Cognition and Decision*, published in 2012.[49] However, scientific papers on quantum decision making began to appear in the mid-1990s.[50] Over the last decade, such papers have regularly been published in top journals in the field of psychology, including *Proceedings of the National Academy of Sciences*,[51] *Proceedings of the Royal Society*,[52] *Psychological Review*,[53] and *Behavioural and Brain Sciences*,[54] among others. Prominent journals such as *Trends in Cognitive Science* and *The Journal of Mathematical Psychology* have published entire special issues on quantum cognition. In addition to gaining traction in the field of psychology, quantum decision making has begun influencing neighbouring disciplines such as economics[55] and

[48] Jennifer S. Trueblood, James M. Yearsley, and Emmanuel M. Pothos, 'A Quantum Probability Framework for Human Probabilistic Inference' (2017) 146.9 Journal of Experimental Psychology: General 1307, 1308 ('It is generally believed that experience with a particular situation, either from previous familiarity or acquired through learning, may allow events to be represented in a compatible way, whereas relatively novel situations are more likely to be represented in an incompatible way.'); see also James M. Yearsley, Jennifer S. Trueblood, and Emmanuel M. Pothos, 'When Are Representations of Causal Events Quantum Versus Classical?' in *Proceedings of the 38th Annual Conference of the Cognitive Science Society* (2016) 2447, <https://perma.cc/6YPW-SRPA>.

[49] Jerome R. Busemeyer and Peter D. Bruza, *Quantum Models of Cognition and Decision* (Cambridge University Press 2012).

[50] E.g., Diedrik Aerts and Sven Aerts, 'Application of Quantum Statistics in Psychological Studies of Decision Processes' (1995) 1.1 Foundations of Science 85.

[51] Wang et al. (n 37); James M. Yearsley and Emmanuel M. Pothos, 'Zeno's Paradox in Decision-making' (2016) 283.1828 Proceedings of the Royal Society B 1.

[52] Pothos and Busemeyer (n 20).

[53] Busemeyer et al. (n 11); Emmanuel M. Pothos, Jerome R. Busemeyer, and Jennifer S. Trueblood, 'A Quantum Geometric Model of Similarity' (2013) 120.3 Psychological Review 679.

[54] Emmanuel M. Pothos and Jerome R. Busemeyer, 'Can Quantum Probability Provide a New Direction for Cognitive Modeling?' (2013) 36.3 Behavioral and Brain Sciences 255 (2013).

[55] See, e.g., Jürgen Eichberger and Hans Jürgen Pirner, 'Decision Theory With a State of Mind Represented by an Element of a Hilbert Space: The Ellsberg Paradox' (2018) 78 Journal of Mathematical Economics 131.

political science.[56] With respect to its empirical track record, quantum models of decision making have accounted for numerous heuristics and biases that appear paradoxical from other theoretical perspectives, including base rate neglect,[57] the anchoring heuristic,[58] subadditivity,[59] and both the conjunction and disjunction fallacies,[60] among others.

The third criterion is the theory's ability to generate novel perspectives. On this score, quantum decision making both explains and predicts phenomena that are difficult to square with other theories of choice. The theory is distinguished by its ability to naturally accommodate order effects in judgment and inferential reasoning. Further, it has predicted, a priori, novel decision-making phenomena, such as the 'quantum Zeno effect'[61] and 'QQ equality',[62] which have been borne out by empirical studies.

Of course, quantum decision making is not without limitations. Often, making clear a priori predictions about particular judgments requires answering preliminary questions: are the relevant judgments compatible or incompatible? If they are incompatible, in what order will they be made? Without clear answers to these questions, 'quantum decision making is arguably vulnerable to some of the same criticism [of being too ad hoc] that has been levied at [behavioural law and economics] and the heuristics and biases research program more generally'.[63] However, in many legal contexts—such as juror judgments in a two-charge criminal case—it is reasonable to expect that the judgments will be incompatible and the order of judgments may be predictable. In such situations, a quantum perspective can yield predictions that differ, meaningfully, from those of other theories of choice.

IV. How Can Quantum Decision Making Inform Law? Examples with Juror Judgments

Above, we have referred to the example of a juror evaluating a criminal case where one defendant faces two charges: robbery and drug trafficking. What might a quantum model of this situation look like? And what would a quantum model

[56] See, e.g., Polina Khrennikova and Emmanual Haven, 'Voters' Preferences in a Quantum Framework' in *The Palgrave Handbook of Quantum Models in Social Science* (Palgrave MacMillan 2017), 141.

[57] Busemeyer et al. (n 11).

[58] Trueblood and Busemeyer (n 4).

[59] Busemeyer et al. (n 11).

[60] Busemeyer et al. (n 11); Jerome R. Busemeyer et al., 'The Conjunction Fallacy, Confirmation, and Quantum Theory: Comment on Tentori, Crupi, and Russo' (2015) 144.1 Journal of Experimental Psychology: General 236.

[61] Yearsley and Pothos (n 51).

[62] Wang and Busemeyer (n 47).

[63] Jaeger and Trueblood (n 1) 64.

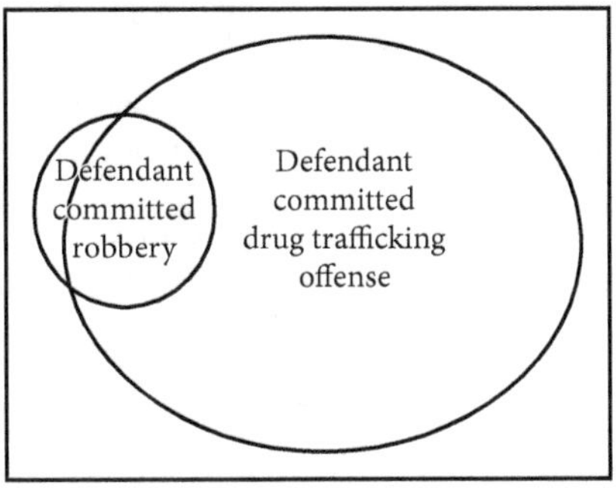

Figure 14.1 The square represents the sample space and the circles represent the event that the defendant committed the charged robbery and the event that the defendant committed the charged drug trafficking offence. The overlap of the two circles represents the joint event in which the defendant committed both the robbery and the drug trafficking offence.

tell us that a classical, rationalist model does not? This section addresses these questions, using a quantum model of the juror's judgments[64] to illustrate how quantum decision making accounts for phenomena like order effects and base rate neglect—phenomena that are difficult to explain from a classical, rationalist perspective. Note that, throughout this section, the focus will be on the *rules* that govern the juror's probabilistic judgments, rather than the specifics of what those judgments are.

To begin, let's discuss the juror's judgments from a classical perspective. We are interested in how the juror views two probabilities: the probability the defendant committed the charged robbery and the probability the defendant committed the charged drug trafficking offence. Under the assumptions of classical probability theory, both of these probability judgments can be represented in one big Venn diagram (i.e., a single sample space).[65] Assume that, based on the evidence thus far, the juror's current judgments are that there is a 0.16 probability that the defendant committed the robbery, a 0.80 probability that the defendant committed the drug offence, and a 0.14 probability that the defendant committed *both* the robbery and the drug offence. These probabilities are represented in the Venn diagram in Figure 14.1. According to classical probability theory, if the juror learns, definitively, that the defendant committed the drug trafficking offence, the juror will update her beliefs about the robbery charge pursuant to a specific rule. This rule is that the probability that the defendant committed the robbery *given that* the defendant committed the drug trafficking offence is equal to the probability of the

[64] The Technical Appendix accompanying Jaeger and Trueblood (n 1) provides a primer on the construction of quantum models.

[65] Bruza, Wang, and Busemeyer (n 20) 384.

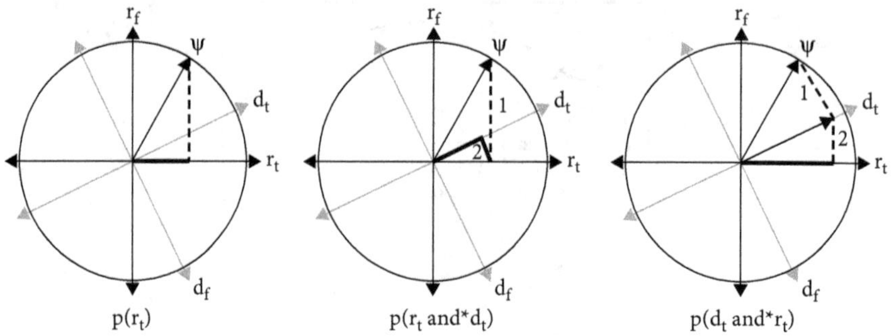

Figure 14.2 The model includes two pairs of basis vectors, one pair for the juror's judgment about the robbery charge (r_f = the defendant did not commit the charged robbery; r_t = the defendant did commit the charged robbery) and one pair for the juror's judgment about the drug trafficking charge (d_f = the defendant did not commit the charged drug trafficking offence; d_t = the defendant did commit the charged drug trafficking offence). By convention, the belief state vector is labelled with the Greek letter psi, ψ. The left panel illustrates a projection for judging the probability that the defendant committed the charged robbery (r_t). The middle panel illustrates the projection sequence for judging the probability that the defendant committed the charged robbery (r_t) followed by judging the probability that the defendant committed the charged drug trafficking offence (d_t). The right panel illustrates the reverse order of judgments.

defendant committing *both* the robbery *and* the drug trafficking offence (the area of the overlap of the two circles in Figure 14.1, which is 0.14) divided by the probability of the defendant committing the drug trafficking offence (again, 0.80). Thus, using the numbers in our example, the juror's updated belief would be that there is a 17.5% chance the defendant committed the robbery (0.14 / 0.80 = 0.175).

If, however, the juror's judgments are made in accordance with quantum probability theory, rather than classical probability theory, a Venn diagram does not (and cannot) capture all the relevant information. A quantum model requires a different approach—we represent the juror's judgments geometrically (see Figure 14.2). The geometric representation consists of a unit circle (a circle with a radius of 1 unit) containing several vectors.[66] Specifically, the unit circle contains one pair of perpendicular vectors (called 'basis vectors') for each relevant, incompatible question the juror considers.[67] In Figure 14.2, one pair of basis vectors (in black) represents the events 'the defendant committed the robbery' and 'the defendant

[66] In geometric terms, a 'vector' is a line with a specified direction (meaning it *starts* at Point A and *ends* at Point B). The *Concise Oxford Dictionary of Mathematics* (5th edn, Oxford University Press 2014), 'Vector'.

[67] Yearsley and Busemeyer (n 18) 100–01.

did not commit the robbery,' and the other pair (in grey) represents the events 'the defendant committed the drug trafficking offence' and 'the defendant did not commit the drug trafficking offence'. Each pair of basis vectors provides a different representation of the overall vector space (i.e., the geometric equivalent of a sample space in classical probability theory). The choice to use two pairs of basis vectors in our model reflects our assumption that the juror's judgments are incompatible—that the juror must evaluate the robbery and drug trafficking charges sequentially, rather than simultaneously. (We posit that incompatibility is a safe default assumption in this context, given both that incompatibility is 'ubiquitous'[68] and that jurors are typically inexperienced with the type of judgments they are being asked to make.)

In addition to the basis vectors, there is one other vector in the unit circle. This vector represents the juror's belief state, and it is called the 'belief state' or 'state vector'. The closer the belief state is to a basis vector, the more probable the juror finds the event represented by that basis vector.[69]

To calculate the precise probability that the juror assigns to any particular event, we 'project' the belief state vector onto the basis vector corresponding to that event.[70] Functionally, this means we draw a line from the end of the belief state vector to the relevant basis vector, such that the line forms a perpendicular intersection with the basis vector (see Figure 14.2—the dotted lines are 'projections').[71] The result, called the 'projected belief state,' is a vector that begins at the centre of the unit circle and ends at the point of the perpendicular intersection (e.g., the thick black line in the left-hand panel of Figure 14.2). The probability that the juror assigns to an event is equal to the length of the projected belief state, squared.[72] In the left-hand panel of Figure 14.2, we project the belief state onto the basis vector representing the event 'the defendant committed the robbery'. The length of the projected belief state is 0.4, and the squared length of the projected belief state is 0.16. This means that, at the moment, the juror's belief state reflects a 16% chance that the defendant committed the robbery, just as in Figure 14.1. If we were to instead project the juror's belief state onto the basis vector corresponding to the event that 'the defendant committed the drug trafficking offence', we would see that it reflects an 80% chance that the defendant committed the drug trafficking offence. Thus, the juror's current belief state in the quantum model reflected in Figure 14.2 is the same as the juror's current belief state reflected in the classical probability model reflected in Figure 14.1.

68 Bruza, Wang, and Busemeyer (n 33).

69 Yearsley and Busemeyer (n 18) 101 ('The second ingredient in any quantum model is the specification of the initial knowledge state of a participant, or group of participants', which is captured in quantum models by the belief state).

70 For example, Busemeyer et al. (n 11) 195.

71 Busemeyer and Bruza (n 49) 15–16, 31–32. 'Projection is akin to shining a light from above and seeing the length of the shadow onto the plane.' Bruza, Wang, and Busemeyer (n 20) 386.

72 Busemeyer and Bruza (n 49) 31; Bruza, Wang, and Busemeyer (n 20) 386.

Why bother using unit circles and basis vectors and a belief state to reflect the same state of affairs captured by the Venn diagram in Figure 14.1? The differences arise when the juror makes a series of judgments. The critical feature of quantum models is that the belief state does not 'reset' after each projection: for models involving multiple judgments, each projection starts where the previous one ended, reflecting the juror's updated belief state (see the middle and right-hand panels of Figure 14.2). In our example, the starting point for calculating the juror's second judgment will be the projected belief state that results from her first judgment. Thus, the order of the judgments *matters*: the probability that the defendant committed the robbery and committed the drug trafficking offence (about 0.10, illustrated by the middle panel of Figure 14.2) is *not equal to* the probability that the defendant committed the drug trafficking offence and committed the robbery (about 0.64, illustrated in the right-hand panel of Figure 14.2). This illustrates how quantum models naturally give rise to order effects. Non-commutativity is a hallmark of quantum decision making.

What happens if, at some point during trial, the juror learns, definitively, that the defendant committed the drug trafficking offence? Assume the defendant gets on the stand and acknowledges as much. To represent a 'given' in a quantum model, we project the belief state onto the given event and then 'normalise' it (i.e., stretch the belief state vector back out to the edge of the unit circle).[73] This reflects that the juror assesses the probability of the given event as 1 (or 100%), and the juror operates from this revised belief state when judging the probability of the next event.[74] This is illustrated in Figure 14.3.

Specifically, Figure 14.3 illustrates a juror's judgment of the probability that the defendant committed the charged robbery *given* that the defendant committed the charged drug trafficking offence. The probability is equal to the length of the thick black line, squared (which equals 0.75). Thus, the juror believes there is a 75% chance the defendant committed the robbery. This updated belief is very different from the updated belief implied by classical probability theory (which was a 17.5% chance the defendant committed the robbery). Critically, in the quantum model, *base rates*—the juror's priors; her baseline assessment of the likelihood the defendant committed the robbery *before* learning the defendant committed the drug trafficking offence—did not factor into the juror's assessment of the robbery charge. Thus, our quantum model captures base rate neglect, one of the puzzling heuristics and biases that is difficult to square with rational choice models—and one cited as a justification for restrictions on character evidence under American evidentiary rules. [75]

[73] Bruza, Wang, and Busemeyer (n 20) 384.
[74] Trueblood and Busemeyer (n 4) 1524.
[75] See, e.g., Korobkin and Ulen (n 7) 1087; Federal Rule of Evidence 404.

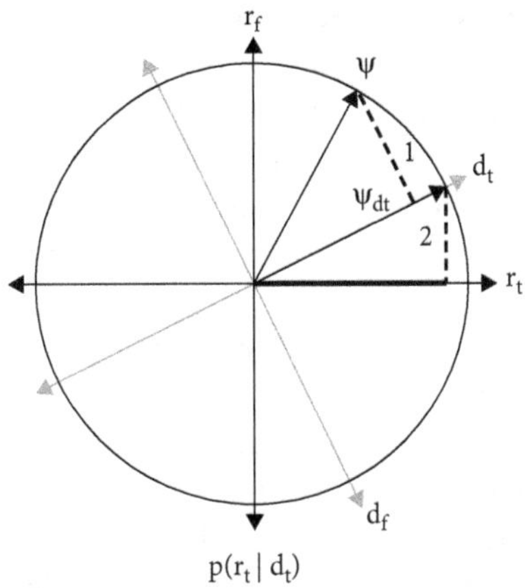

Figure 14.3 Quantum model illustrating base rate neglect in judgement of the probability the defendant committed the charged robbery ($p(r_t)$) when it is a given that the defendant committed the charged drug trafficking offence ($p(d_t) = 1$). The initial belief state is denoted with ψ, and the revised and normalised belief state is denoted with ψ_{dt}.

In addition, the model depicted in Figure 14.3 naturally predicts another frequently observed irrationality called the 'inverse fallacy'—the tendency of people to equate, incorrectly, the conditional probability they are trying to judge with its inverse.[76] Our juror would commit the 'inverse fallacy' if she equated the probability that the defendant committed the robbery given that the defendant committed the drug trafficking offence with the probability that the defendant committed the drug trafficking offence given that the defendant committed the robbery. Performing the relevant projections in the reverse order reveals that this phenomenon arises in the quantum model.[77]

This is just one relatively simple quantum model of juror judgment, but it illustrates how the quantum approach to judgment and decision making uses a different logic than rationalist approaches adopt. In short, quantum models relax some of the assumptions of classical probability theory. Relaxing these assumptions allowed our example model to account for order effects, base rate neglect, and the inverse fallacy.

One question that often arises in connection with heuristics and biases is: what (if anything) can be done to 'debias' people? Quantum decision making suggests

[76] See, e.g., David M. Eddy, 'Probabilistic Reasoning in Clinical Medicine: Problems and Opportunities' in Daniel Kahneman, Paul Slovic, and Amos Tversky (eds.), *Judgments Under Uncertainty: Heuristics and Biases* (Cambridge University Press 1982), 249.

[77] This is only true by necessity in two-judgment models.

that heuristics, biases, and order effects arise from 'incompatible' representations of events.[78] Debiasing, therefore, means fostering compatible representations. Recent studies suggest that people are more likely to use compatible representations as they rehearse or become more familiar with the relevant task.[79] Thus, quantum decision making provides some support for the call to provide jurors with some form of standardised training in logical reasoning.[80] Researchers have also begun drawing connections between the use of compatible representations and measures of cognitive reflection.[81] Future work elaborating on this connection may yield further debiasing prescriptions.

In addition to accounting for phenomena like order effects and base rate neglect, quantum decision making also generates novel, testable predictions about human judgment. One prominent example involves the 'quantum Zeno effect,' demonstrated by Yearsley and Pothos in the context of juror judgment.[82]

In physics, the quantum Zeno effect refers to the principle that repeatedly measuring a particle slows its decay.[83] Analogously, quantum decision making predicts that repeatedly making judgments slows changes in opinions. That is, 'when someone's opinion on a topic is "measured"—when she articulates it or consciously identifies it—it becomes less likely to change, even in the presence of accumulating evidence to the contrary'.[84] Put in terms of a quantum model, the idea is that each time a person makes a judgment, his or her belief state gets 'reset' to reflect it.

Yearsley and Pothos tested this prediction in two experiments, both of which involved the hypothetical murder trial of a defendant named Smith.[85] Participants began by reading some general facts about the case and making a preliminary judgment of Smith's guilt. More than 90% of participants preliminarily judged Smith innocent. Participants then read about twelve pieces of prosecution evidence against Smith, rendering a final judgment of Smith's guilt at the end. Critically, however, some participants made additional judgments about Smith's guilt between the preliminary and final judgments. Of six groups of participants, five were prompted to make intermediate judgments—at intervals of one, two, three, four, or six pieces of prosecution evidence.

The participants judging Smith's case exhibited a quantum Zeno effect—and a dramatic one, at that. Of participants who preliminarily judged Smith innocent,

[78] Bruza, Wang, and Busemeyer (n 20) 392 ('Our view is that incompatibility of events provides an effective solution to bounded resources, which is the reason for bounded rationality.'

[79] Trueblood, Yearsley, and Pothos (n 48); Yearsley, Trueblood, and Pothos (n 48).

[80] See, e.g., Jonathan Koehler, 'Train Our Jurors' in Gerd Gigerenzer and Christoph Engel (eds.), *Heuristics and the Law* (MIT Press 2006), 303.

[81] Yearsley, Trueblood, and Pothos (n 48).

[82] Yearsley and Pothos (n 51).

[83] Ibid. (noting that in physics, 'it can be predicted that a continuously observed unstable particle never decays') (citing Baidyanath Misra and Ennackal C. G. Sudarshan, 'The Zeno's Paradox in Quantum Theory' (1977) 18.4 Journal of Mathematical Physics 756).

[84] Jaeger and Trueblood (n 1) 49.

[85] Yearsley and Pothos (n 51).

those who made twelve intermediate judgments (one after every piece of evidence) found Smith guilty less than 10% of the time. In contrast, participants who made only the preliminary and final judgments (and no intermediate judgments) found Smith guilty close to 50% of the time.[86] This striking difference was not a product of varying the order in which the evidence was presented; rather, it was a product of prompting participants to make conscious intermediate judgments when considering the evidence. The Yearsley and Pothos paper highlights quantum decision-making's potential to generate new, testable predictions about judgment and decision making, including predictions that are relevant in legal decision making.

In this section, we have used the example of juror judgments to demonstrate quantum decision-making's ability to account for puzzling phenomena like order effects and base rate neglect, and also to generate new predictions about cognitive quirks like the quantum Zeno effect. We must note that, in some respects, our discussion of juror judgments is quite simplified. After all, jurors render a verdict as a group; a number of group dynamics exist that might influence our verdict that are not incorporated in the examples we discussed. However, it is typical for jurors to track evidence and form opinions individually during trial,[87] then cast individual votes during deliberations (which, from a quantum perspective, prompts them to construct judgments). Thus, while there is undoubtedly an overlay of social influences in jury deliberations, the inferential processes unfolding at the level of individual jurors largely lend themselves to a quantum approach.[88]

V. Conclusion

In this chapter, we provided an introductory discussion of quantum decision making. In short, quantum decision offers a new, comprehensive set of rules for describing and predicting people's judgments and decisions. We flagged several factors that can help identify legal contexts where quantum decision making may be especially useful to regulators and scholars. We suggest that a quantum perspective is particularly helpful for understanding how people make multiple, unfamiliar judgments in succession. We used one such context, juror judgment, to demonstrate how quantum models work, and specifically, to illustrate how they account for 'irrationalities' that are difficult to reconcile with classical probability theory (and theories of choice built on it). Quantum models highlight the importance of

[86] These figures represent an average across the two experiments.

[87] Indeed, jurors are usually prohibited from discussing the case with each other before deliberations.

[88] Moreover, many verdicts come from an individual decision maker: in bench trials, judges decide both questions of fact and questions of law. Judicial decision making in such cases might also lend itself to quantum modelling. (Although it could be that, due to their expertise in legal decision making, judges' judgments are more likely to be compatible than jurors' judgments; this may be an interesting avenue for future research.)

sequence in judgment and decision making, and therefore the importance of considering sequence in designing law's choice architecture.

We close by stressing that the potential utility of quantum decision making extends well beyond its application to juror judgment. Indeed, the express goal of quantum decision making is to reveal a comprehensive alternative to rational choice theory. Even theories that reject the assumptions of rational choice theory often treat rationality as a benchmark or default. Quantum decision making, however, endeavours to uncover a more comprehensive set of decision-making axioms—one that accounts for rational decisions and 'heuristics and biases' alike.

Index

The manufacturer's authorised representative in the EU for product safety is Oxford University Press España S.A. of el Parque Empresarial San Fernando de Henares, Avenida de Castilla, 2 – 28830 Madrid (www.oup.es/en or product.safety@oup.com). OUP España S.A. also acts as importer into Spain of products made by the manufacturer.

www.ingramcontent.com/pod-product-compliance
Lightning Source LLC
LaVergne TN
LVHW020056220926
848484LV00002BB/598
* 9 7 8 0 1 9 8 8 6 3 1 7 5 *